The WEST *and the* WORLD *Since* 1500

SELECTED READINGS

Arthur Haberman

Professor of History
and Humanities
York University

Adrian Shubert

Professor of History
York University

Educational Consultant

Marc Keirstead
Sacred Heart Catholic School
York Catholic District School Board

gagelearning

© 2004 Gage Learning Corporation
164 Commander Boulevard
Toronto, ON M1S 3C7
www.gagelearning.com

National Library of Canada Cataloguing in Publication

Haberman, Arthur
    The West and the world since 1500 : selected readings / Arthur Haberman,
Adrian Shubert, Marc Keirstead.

Includes index.
ISBN 0-7715-8047-9

    1. History, Modern—Textbooks. 2. Civilization, Western—Textbooks.
I. Shubert, Adrian, 1953- II. Keirstead, Marc III. Title.

D209.H323 2003   909.08   C2003-903028-8

Any Web sites visited through www.gagelearning.com have been checked for
appropriate content. However, these Web sites and any other suggested links
should be periodically checked before the addresses are given to students.
Web addresses change constantly. Teachers should locate the URL through
a search engine, and check the site for appropriate content.

We acknowledge the financial support of the Government of Canada through
the Book Publishing Industry Development Program for our publishing activities.

We acknowledge the Government of Ontario through the Ontario Media
Development Corporation's Ontario Book Initiative.

Project Manager: Nancy Christoffer
Copy Editor: Lara Caplan
Senior Production Co-ordinator: Bev Crann
Permissions Editor: Elizabeth Long
Cover and Page Design: Dave Murphy/ArtPlus Limited
Page Layout: Alicia Countryman/ArtPlus Limited

ISBN 0-7715-8047-9

1 2 3 4 5 FP 08 07 06 05 04

Written, printed, and bound in Canada

Consultants and Reviewers

The author and the publisher wish to thank the consulting scholars and student reviewers for their input — advice, directions, and suggestions — that helped to make this book of readings more accessible to students and useful to teachers. Their contributions in time, effort, and expertise was invaluable.

Consulting Scholars

Vijay Agnew

Professor of Social Science and Director of the Centre for Feminist Research at York University

Amila Buturovic

Associate Professor of Humanities at York University

Paul Lovejoy

Canada Research Professor of African Diaspora History at York University

Bernard Luk

Associate Professor of History at York University

Student Reviewers

— From Sacred Heart Catholic High School

Emily Anderson

Amanda Beattie

Sean Kelly

Dmitri A. Lee

Kristie MacDonald

Caitlin MacKenzie

Kayla Mulroy

Acknowledgments

We are pleased to acknowledge the support of others who helped with this work: Elizabeth Cohen, Margo Gewurtz, Janice Kim, Molly Ladd-Taylor, Bill Larkin, and Steve Wookey. Janice Schoening helped to guide the book through its early stages. Marc Keirstead made many fine suggestions and helped us attain our pedagogical goals. Nancy Christoffer of Gage Learning Corporation was, as always, the model Editor and Project Manager; and Lara Caplan made important contributions as Copy Editor. Our spouses, Jan Rehner and Agueda Shubert, provided extraordinary constancy and support.

Contents

PART V: European Hegemony, 1871–1914 *170*

PART VI: The Weakening of Europe, 1914–1945 *218*

Suggestions for the Effective Use of Primary Sources

Documents are the fragments out of which we reconstruct the past and understand the attitudes, issues, and motivations of historical figures. The set of documents presented in this book tries to give voice to both those in authority and to those who face authority. One of its premises is that the connections between the powerful and the weak, between the wealthy and the poor, between the oppressor and the oppressed, and between the West and the world transform everyone involved. It suggests that a variety of voices and perspectives is important to understand the past, including those traditionally left out of the historical narrative.

Historians use fragments such as these to write history; their interpretations of what happened in the past and why. Whatever the period, place, or issue, the record of the past that survives is always incomplete. The first obligation of the historian is to find as many relevant sources as possible so that the construction and interpretation of the past is based on the fullest evidence. Often, the questions one asks of the past help to guide the process, and the relationship between the past and the present is close and interconnected.

Message to Teachers

This series of primary sources is intended to provide students with the insights, observations, and opinions of a variety of historical figures. One way to introduce students to primary sources is to have them write a response to a significant contemporary event. They could then exchange the work with a partner and analyze it for language, concepts, and opinions. Based on this analysis, they could make some inferences as to the attitudes and insights of the writer. This exercise reinforces the importance of not basing all opinions on one source. Students will require some knowledge of the writer's background and the context of the event if an inference is to be relevant. Students could build on these skills by applying them to a contemporary primary source such as a newspaper account.

The readings in this text are intended to address major issues and philosophies of the World History: The West and the World course. In addition to excerpts from canonical works of Western thought, politics, and literature, the collection presents students with less frequently heard voices: those of people from outside the West as well of those of Westerners from beyond the intellectual, social, and political elites. The questions included at the end of each reading have been developed to assess student comprehension and to challenge students to infer information, make comparisons, or reflect on issues central to the text. Not all questions will be appropriate for all students, and they should be selected accordingly. One aim of these questions is to provide students with personal connections to the events they will study in this fascinating course.

Message to Students

This book of readings is meant to give you first-hand knowledge of a variety of individuals and organizations from both the West and around the world. These primary sources have been selected to give you a broad perspective of the texture of life in a range of societies, as well as to expand on the issues faced by various cultures and civilizations. Especially when read in a systematic manner, they can provide you with many provocative insights.

Before you read a selection, you should attempt to determine what type of document you are about to read. If it is a diary, that could mean that you will be reading information that the author may not have intended others to read. It could be a rich source of information that might not be available in more conventional and public sources; it could also be a source of false information or gossip. It may be written in formal language and intended for a broad audience. You should reflect on the purpose of each document and its intended audience to help you determine how to best interpret the source.

Next you need to identify the author. If the author is known, you can conduct initial research to obtain background information that should aid you in understanding the message of the reading. This will also place the source in its proper historical context, which in turn should help you identify terms, people, and events.

You should also make certain that you have enough information about the period and place of the document to determine its context. Its meaning may have universal themes, but it will have been constructed at a place and time with its own concerns and issues.

Now you can begin to read the selection. It would be helpful to have a dictionary nearby to assist you with any unfamiliar terminology. Some of the readings have long sentences that might be confusing. You should take your time and divide up such sentences into phrases that can be more easily understood. Once you have completed this process, you should be able to determine the message.

To help you assess whether you have a good grasp of the reading, you could summarize the main points and locate specific sentences or phrases that support your interpretation. The questions at the end of the readings can be used as a guide to decipher the thesis of the source. The introductions to the author and the selection, along with the introductions to the individual sections, are meant to provide you with a brief synopsis and set the context for each reading.

These methods should enable you to understand the focus of the selections. However, you should try to go beyond simple comprehension. Try to "read between the lines," to determine what the author is attempting to say. Often there is subtext in a document, a message given indirectly. Sometimes you can learn much by what the author does not say.

We have attempted to provide as much variety as possible within the confines of a single volume. There are documents and statements from the powerful, the marginal, and the outsiders. There is wonder as well as protest: about how the West views the world, about the vast geography and beauty of the planet, about how humans try to understand one another, and about the discovery of the new and a re-evaluation of one's own assumptions on the way we are and the way we ought to be. The human record is rich and diverse, and we hope that this collection both provokes and provides much pleasure.

Bertolt Brecht

Questions from A Worker Who Reads

Who built Thebes of the seven gates?
In the books you will find the name of kings.
Did the kings haul up the lumps of rock?
And Babylon, many times demolished.
Who raised it up so many times? In what houses
Of gold-glittering Lima did the builders live?
Where, the evening that the Wall of China was finished
Did the masons go? Great Rome
Is full of triumphal arches. Who erected them? Over whom
Did the Caesers triumph? Had Byzantium, much praised in song,
Only palaces for its inhabitants? Even in fabled Atlantis
The night the ocean engulfed it
The drowning still bawled for their slaves.

The young Alexander conquered India.
Was he alone?
Caesar beat the Gauls.
Did he not have even a cook with him?
Philip of Spain wept when his armada
Went down. Was he the only one to weep?
Frederick the Second won the Seven Years' War. Who
Else won it?

Every page a victory.
Who cooked the feast for the victors?
Every ten years a great man.
Who paid the bill?

So many reports.
So many questions.

Source: "Fragen eines lesenden Arbeiters," trans. M. Hamburger. From *Bertolt Brecht, Poems 1913–1956*. New York, London: Methuen, 1976.

Modernity and Encounter

CONTENTS

The kingdom of Benin, in West Africa, has a long artistic tradition, especially in the fields of ivory, brass, and terra cotta sculpture. Benin artists used their works to mark important historical events, such as the arrival of the Portuguese. Europeans admired the crafts of the Benin people, and sometimes commissioned works of art from them and other African artists. This sixteenth-century ivory saltcellar exemplifies the striking realism of this artistic genre. It depicts two Portuguese officials, flanked by two assistants. Above them is a Portuguese ship, with a man peering out of the crow's nest. It reminds us that their explorations brought Europeans into contact with a range of highly sophisticated and accomplished peoples, whose influence on European culture was to be felt throughout the modern era.

Women in the Renaissance

Christine de Pisan (c. 1363–c. 1424) was the daughter of Tommaso di Benvenuto da Pizzano, a Venetian who became court astrologer to King Charles V of France when De Pisan was a young girl. In Paris, she received an excellent education, unusual for a female at that time. She married at age fifteen, but her husband died ten years later, and De Pisan then supported herself and her children through her writing. She composed several works on commission, and is probably the first professional writer in the West in modern times. Her *The Book of the City of Ladies* (1405) set out to destroy masculine myths and claim a place for women in society. Modesta dal Pozzo (1555–1592) lived in Venice and published three volumes of poetry in her lifetime. Her poem "Women's Worth" was released by her daughter in 1600. Modesta dal Pozzo (modesty of the well) was also known by the pseudonym Moderata Fonte (calm fountain).

A De Pisan begins *The Book of the City of Ladies* by discussing the purpose of her work. She recounts that "the treatises of all philosophers and poets" claim "that the behavior of women is inclined to and full of every vice."

> Thinking deeply about these matters, I began to examine my character and conduct as a natural woman and, similarly, I considered other women whose company I frequently kept, princesses, great ladies, women of the middle and lower classes, who had graciously told me of their most private and intimate thoughts, hoping that I could judge impartially and in good conscience whether the testimony of so many notable men could be true. To the best of my knowledge, no matter how long I confronted or dissected the problem, I could not see or realize how their claims could be true when compared to the natural behavior and character of women. Yet I still argued vehemently against women, saying that it would be impossible that so many famous men — such solemn scholars, possessed of such deep and great understanding, so clear-sighted in all things, as it seemed — could have spoken falsely on so many occasions that I could hardly find a book on morals where, even before I had read it in its entirety, I did not find several chapters or certain sections attacking women, no matter who the author was. This reason alone, in short, made me conclude that, although my intellect did not perceive my own great faults and, likewise, those of other women because of its simpleness and ignorance, it was however truly fitting that such was the case. And so I relied more on the judgment of others than on what I myself felt and knew. I was so transfixed in this line of thinking for such a long time that it seemed as if I were in a stupor. Like a gushing fountain, a series of authorities, whom I recalled one after

Sources: Christine de Pisan, *The Book of the City of Ladies*, trans. Earl Jeffrey Richards. New York: Persea Books, Inc., 1982, pp. 4–5, 153–155; Modesta dal Pozzo, "Il merito della donne," *From The Defiant Muse: Italian Feminist Poems From the Middle Ages to the Present*, eds. Beverly Allen et. al. New York: The Feminist Press, 1986, p. 23. Translated by Arthur Haberman.

another, came to mind, along with their opinions on this topic. And I finally decided that God formed a vile creature when He made woman, and I wondered how such a worthy artisan could have deigned to make such an abominable work which, from what they say, is the vessel as well as the refuge and abode of every evil and vice. As I was thinking this, a great unhappiness and sadness welled up in my heart, for I detested myself and the entire feminine sex, as though we were monstrosities in nature.

B De Pisan asks an imaginary lady about the role of education for women.

"My lady, I realize that women have accomplished many good things and that even if evil women have done evil, it seems to me, nevertheless, that the benefits accrued and still accruing because of good women — particularly the wise and literary ones and those educated in the natural sciences whom I mentioned above — outweigh the evil. Therefore, I am amazed by the opinion of some men who claim that they do not want their daughters, wives, or kinswomen to be educated because their mores would be ruined as a result."

She responded, "Here you can clearly see that not all opinions of men are based on reason and that these men are wrong. For it must not be presumed that mores necessarily grow worse from knowing the moral sciences, which teach the virtues, indeed, there is not the slightest doubt that moral education amends and ennobles them. How could anyone think or believe that whoever follows good teaching or doctrine is the worse for it? Such an opinion cannot be expressed or maintained. I do not mean that it would be good for a man or a woman to study the art of divination or those fields of learning which are forbidden — for the holy Church did not remove them from common use without good reason — but it should not be believed that women are the worse for knowing what is good.

"Quintus Hortensius, a great rhetorician and consummately skilled orator in Rome, did not share this opinion. He had a daughter, named Hortensia, whom he greatly loved for the subtlety of her wit. He had her learn letters and study the science of rhetoric, which she mastered so thoroughly that she resembled her father Hortensius not only in wit and lively memory but also in her excellent delivery and order of speech — in fact, he surpassed her in nothing. As for the subject discussed above, concerning the good which comes about through women, the benefits realized by this woman and her learning were, among others, exceptionally remarkable. That is, during the time when Rome was governed by three men, this Hortensia began to support the cause of women and to undertake what no man dared to undertake. There was a question whether certain taxes should be levied on women and on their jewelry during a needy period in Rome. This woman's eloquence was so compelling that she was listened to, no less readily than her father would have been, and she won her case.

"Similarly, to speak of more recent times, without searching for examples in ancient history, Giovanni Andrea, a solemn law professor in Bologna not quite sixty years ago, was not of the opinion that it was bad for women to be educated. He had a fair and good daughter, named Novella, who was educated in the law to such an advanced degree that when he was occupied by some task and not at leisure to present his lectures to his students, he would send Novella, his daughter, in his place to lecture to the students from his chair. And to prevent her beauty from distracting the concentration of her audience, she had a little curtain drawn in front of her. In this manner she could on occasion supplement and lighten her father's occupation. He loved her so much that, to commemorate her name, he wrote a book of remarkable lectures on the law which he entitled *Novella super Decretalium*, after his daughter's name.

"Thus, not all men (and especially the wisest) share the opinion that it is bad for women to be educated. But it is very true that many foolish men have claimed this because it displeased them that women knew more than they did. Your father, who was a great scientist and philosopher, did not believe that women were worth less by knowing science; rather, as you know, he took great pleasure from seeing your inclination to learning. The feminine opinion of your mother, however, who wished to keep you busy with spinning and silly girlishness, following the common custom of women, was the major obstacle to your being more involved in the sciences. But just as the proverb already mentioned above says, 'No one can take away what Nature has given,' your mother could not hinder in you the feeling for the sciences which you, through natural inclination, had nevertheless gathered together in little droplets. I am sure that, on account of these things, you do not think you are worth less but rather that you consider it a great treasure for yourself; and you doubtless have reason to."

And I, Christine, replied to all of this, "Indeed, my lady, what you say is as true as the Lord's Prayer."

C In her poem entitled "Women's Worth," Modesta dal Pozzo reflects on similar issues to those raised raised by Christine de Pisan.

> Women in every age were by Nature
> > Gifted with good judgment and pure souls,
> > No less fit to demonstrate with study and care
> > The wisdom and merit of those who are human.
> > And why, if they are similar,
> > If their substance not be different,
> > If they are alike in food and speech,
> > Should they be different in daring and wisdom?
>
> There has always been and continues to be, whenever
> > A woman wishes to put her mind to it,
> > More than one successful woman warrior,
> > Each wresting valour and fame from many men;
> > Also in the arts and in every

Undertaking practiced and spoken of by man,
It is a fact that women have been so fruitful
That they have no reason to envy men.

And, though worthy in itself,
Their number of illustrious ones is not large,
Because to acts heroic and filled with virtue
Their hearts have not been turned.
Gold which remains in the mine
Is no less gold for being buried,
And when it is extracted and well treated,
It is just as beautiful as other gold.

If, when a daughter is born to a father,
She were to be given equal tasks with his son,
In lofty deeds or light she would not be
Inferior or unequal to her brother;
Or if she were put in armed squads
With him, or permitted to learn some liberal art;
But because she is raised to know other matters,
Her education begets little esteem.

1. What impact did the depiction of women in literature have on De Pisan's self-concept?

2. What evidence does De Pisan present to counter the perception of female weaknesses?

3. Why might De Pisan's comments have a greater impact on readers than Dal Pozzo's?

4. How does Dal Pozzo explain the different roles of men and women?

Leonardo Bruni

Leonardo Bruni (c. 1369–1444) was among the first humanists to master classical Latin and Greek. He translated numerous Greek texts, some unknown in the West for many centuries. He was also a civil servant in Florence, acting as the chancellor of the new republic. Bruni came to be seen as a model for the new life of civic humanism introduced in the Renaissance.

In his *On Learning and Literature*, written about 1405, Bruni discusses the importance of classical Latin.

The foundations of all true learning must be laid in the sound and thorough knowledge of Latin: which implies study marked by a broad spirit, accurate scholarship, and careful attention to details. Unless this solid

Source: Franklin Le Van Baumer, ed., *Main Currents of Western Thought*, 4th ed. New Haven: Yale University Press, 1978, pp. 136–138.

basis be secured it is useless to attempt to rear an enduring edifice. Without it the great monuments of literature are unintelligible, and the art of composition impossible. . . . To this end we must be supremely careful in our choice of authors, lest an inartistic and debased style infect our own writing and degrade our taste; which danger is best avoided by bringing a keen, critical sense to bear upon select works, observing the sense of each passage, the structure of the sentence, the force of every word down to the least important particle. In this way our reading reacts directly upon our style. . . .

But the wider question now confronts us, that of the subject matter of our studies, that which I have already called the realities of fact and principle, as distinct from literary form. Here, as before, I am contemplating a student of keen and lofty aspiration to whom nothing that is worthy in any learned discipline is without its interest. But it is necessary to exercise discrimination. In some branches of knowledge I would rather restrain the ardour of the learner, in others, again, encourage it to the uttermost. Thus there are certain subjects in which, whilst a modest proficiency is on all accounts to be desired, a minute knowledge and excessive devotion seem to be a vain display. For instance, subtleties of Arithmetic and Geometry are not worthy to absorb a cultivated mind, and the same must be said of Astrology. . . .

What Disciplines then are properly open to her? In the first place she has before her, as a subject peculiarly her own, the whole field of religion and morals. The literature of the Church will thus claim her earnest study. Such a writer, for instance, as St. Augustine affords her the fullest scope for reverent yet learned inquiry. Her devotional instinct may lead her to value the help and consolation of holy men now living; but in this case let her not for an instant yield to the impulse to look into their writings, which, compared with those of Augustine, are utterly destitute of sound and melodious style, and seem to me to have no attraction whatever.

B Bruni suggests that Christian and classical studies should be combined, that there is no conflict between the two.

Moreover, the cultivated Christian lady has no need in the study of this weighty subject to confine herself to ecclesiastical writers. Morals, indeed, have been treated of by the noblest intellects of Greece and Rome. What they have left to us upon Continence, Temperance, Modesty, Justice, Courage, Greatness of Soul, demands your sincere respect. You must enter into such questions as the sufficiency of Virtue to Happiness; or whether, if Happiness consist in Virtue, it can be destroyed by torture, imprisonment or exile; whether, admitting that these may prevent a man from being happy, they can be further said to make him miserable. Again, does Happiness consist (with Epicurus) in the presence of pleasure and the absence of pain: or (with Xenophon) in the consciousness of uprightness: or (with Aristotle) in the practice of Virtue? These inquiries are, of all others, most worthy to be pursued by men and women alike; they are fit material for formal discussion and for literary exercise. Let religion and morals, therefore, hold the first place in the education of a Christian lady.

C According to Bruni, history, poetry, and philosophy are important, especially as written in the works of antiquity.

But we must not forget that true distinction is to be gained by a wide and varied range of such studies as conduce to the profitable enjoyment of life, in which, however, we must observe due proportion in the attention and time we devote to them.

First amongst such studies I place History: a subject which must not on any account be neglected by one who aspires to true cultivation. For it is our duty to understand the origins of our own history and its development; and the achievements of Peoples and of Kings.

For the careful study of the past enlarges our foresight in contemporary affairs and affords to citizens and to monarchs lessons of incitement or warning in the ordering of public policy. From History, also, we draw our store of examples of moral precepts.

In the monuments of ancient literature which have come down to us History holds a position of great distinction. We specially prize such authors as Livy, Sallust and Curtius; and, perhaps even above these, Julius Caesar; the style of whose Commentaries, so elegant and so limpid, entitles them to our warm admiration. Such writers are fully within the comprehension of a studious lady. For, after all, History is an easy subject: there is nothing in its study subtle or complex. It consists in the narration of the simplest matters of fact which, once grasped, are readily retained in the memory.

The great Orators of antiquity must by all means be included. Nowhere do we find the virtues more warmly extolled, the vices so fiercely decried. From them we may learn, also, how to express consolation, encouragement, dissuasion or advice. . . .

. . . [F]amiliarity with the great poets of antiquity is [also] essential to any claim to true education. For in their writings we find deep speculations upon Nature, and upon the Causes and Origins of things, which must carry weight with us both from their antiquity and from their authorship. Besides these, many important truths upon matters of daily life are suggested or illustrated. All this is expressed with such grace and dignity as demands our admiration. . . .

We know, however, that in certain quarters — where all knowledge and appreciation of Letters is wanting — this whole branch of Literature, marked as it is by something of the Divine, and fit, therefore, for the highest place, is decried as unworthy of study. But when we remember the value of the best poetry, its charm of form and the variety and interest of its subject-matter, when we consider the ease with which from our childhood up it can be committed to memory, when we recall the peculiar affinity of rhythm and metre to our emotions and our intelligence, we must conclude that Nature herself is against such headlong critics. . . . Plato and Aristotle studied the poets, and I decline to admit that in practical wisdom or in moral earnestness they yield to our modern critics. They were not Christians, indeed, but consistency of life and abhorrence of evil existed before Christianity and are independent of it.

1. According to Bruni, what subjects comprise a true education?
2. Why does Bruni downplay mathematics for a woman's education?
3. What qualities should an educated person ideally possess in this time period?
4. What aspects of modern education are reflected in this description?

Giovanni Pico della Mirandola

Though he died young, Giovanni Pico della Mirandola (1463–1494) was among the best-educated and most talented people of the Renaissance. He knew Latin, Greek, Hebrew, and Arabic, as well as the works of the medieval Christian scholars. Della Mirandola wrote the *Oration on the Dignity of Man* to introduce his ideas in a proposed public disputation. The pope, Innocent VIII, suspended the disputation and, later, a papal committee judged some of Della Mirandola's ideas to be heretical. The *Oration on the Dignity of Man* was an important statement about the new humanistic outlook.

 Della Mirandola asserts that human beings are special and are to be admired.

I have read in the records of the Arabians, reverend Fathers, that Abdala the Saracen, when questioned as to what on this stage of the world, as it were, could be seen most worthy of wonder, replied: "There is nothing to be seen more wonderful than man." In agreement with this opinion is the saying of Hermes Trismegistus: "A great miracle, Asclepius, is man." But when I weighed the reason for these maxims, the many grounds for the excellence of human nature reported by many men failed to satisfy me — that man is the intermediary between creatures, the intimate of the gods, the king of the lower beings, by the acuteness of his senses, by the discernment of his reason, and by the light of his intelligence the interpreter of nature, the interval between fixed eternity and fleeting time, and (as the Persians say) the bond, nay, rather, the marriage song of the world, on David's testimony but little lower than the angels. Admittedly great though these reasons be, they are not the principal grounds, that is, those which may rightfully claim for themselves the privilege of the highest admiration. For why should we not admire more the angels themselves and the blessed choirs of heaven? At

Source: Ernst Cassirer et al., eds., *The Renaissance Philosophy of Man*. London: University of Chicago Press, 1948, pp. 223–225.

last it seems to me I have come to understand why man is the most fortunate of creatures and consequently worthy of all admiration and what precisely is that rank which is his lot in the universal chain of Being — a rank to be envied not only by brutes but even by the stars and by minds beyond this world. It is a matter past faith and a wondrous one. Why should it not be? For it is on this very account that man is rightly called and judged a great miracle and a wonderful creature indeed.

B   Humans, he says, have unlimited abilities and potential. They can reach for the divine.

God the Father, the supreme Architect, had already built this cosmic home we behold, the most sacred temple of His godhead, by the laws of His mysterious wisdom. The region above the heavens He had adorned with Intelligences, the heavenly spheres He had quickened with eternal souls, and the excrementary and filthy parts of the lower world He had filled with a multitude of animals of every kind. But, when the work was finished, the Craftsman kept wishing that there were someone to ponder the plan of so great a work, to love its beauty, and to wonder at its vastness. Therefore, when everything was done . . . He finally took thought concerning the creation of man. But there was not among His archetypes that from which He could fashion a new offspring, nor was there in His treasure-houses anything which He might bestow on His new son as an inheritance, nor was there in the seats of all the world a place where the latter might sit to contemplate the universe. All was now complete; all things had been assigned to the highest, the middle, and the lowest orders. But in its final creation it was not the part of the Father's power to fail as though exhausted. . . .

At last the best of artisans ordained that that creature to whom He had been able to give nothing proper to himself should have joint possession of whatever had been peculiar to each of the different kinds of being. He therefore took man as a creature of indeterminate nature and, assigning him a place in the middle of the world, addressed him thus: "Neither a fixed abode nor a form that is thine alone nor any function peculiar to thyself have we given thee, Adam, to the end that according to thy longing and according to thy judgment thou mayest have and possess what abode, what form, and what functions thou thyself shalt desire. The nature of all other beings is limited and constrained within the bounds of laws prescribed by Us. Thou, constrained by no limits, in accordance with thine own free will, in whose hand We have placed thee, shalt ordain for thyself the limits of thy nature. We have set thee at the world's center that thou mayest from thence more easily observe whatever is in the world. We have made thee neither of heaven nor of earth, neither mortal nor immortal, so that with freedom of choice and with honor, as though the maker and molder of thyself, thou mayest fashion thyself in whatever shape thou shalt prefer. Thou shalt have the power to degenerate into the lower forms of life, which are brutish. Thou shalt have the power, out of thy soul's judgment, to be reborn into the higher forms, which are divine."

C Della Mirandola puts forth the modern idea that humans have the ability to shape their own lives.

O supreme generosity of God the Father, O highest and most marvelous felicity of man! To him it is granted to have whatever he chooses, to be whatever he wills. Beasts as soon as they are born (so says Lucilius) bring with them from their mother's womb all they will ever possess. Spiritual beings, either from the beginning or soon thereafter, become what they are to be for ever and ever. On man when he came into life the Father conferred the seeds of all kinds and the germs of every way of life. Whatever seeds each man cultivates will grow to maturity and bear in him their own fruit. If they be vegetative, he will be like a plant. If sensitive, he will become brutish. If rational, he will grow into a heavenly being. If intellectual, he will be an angel and the son of God. And if, happy in the lot of no created thing, he withdraws into the center of his own unity, his spirit, made one with God, in the solitary darkness of God, who is set above all things, shall surpass them all. Who would not admire this our chameleon? Or who could more greatly admire aught else whatever?

1. What qualities does Della Mirandola ascribe to humanity?
2. What aspects of Della Mirandola's writing might be objectionable to the Catholic Church?
3. Compare Della Mirandola's view of humanity with those of Martin Luther (see pages 32–36) and Thomas More (see pages 15–19).

Niccolò Machiavelli

Niccolò Machiavelli (1469–1527) was second chancellor and secretary to the war department of the influential Florentine Republic. He wrote *The Prince* in 1513 after the fall of the Republic, as a reflection on the nature of political power in the new sovereign state. Machiavelli's work is regarded as the first in modern political theory to ask how politics and power actually work. He made wide use of classical history, which he thought served as examples of human behaviour for modern rulers and the state.

A The prince, who is the new type of ruler of the sovereign, autonomous state, is expected to behave differently from the citizen.

It remains now to be seen what style and principles a prince ought to adopt in dealing with his subjects and friends. I know the subject has been treated frequently before, and I fear people will think me rash for trying to do so again, especially since I intend to differ in this discussion from what others have said. But since I intend to write something useful to an understanding reader, it seemed better to go after the real truth of the matter than to repeat what people have imagined. A great many men have imagined states and princedoms such as nobody ever saw or knew in the real world, and there's such a difference between the way we really live and the way we ought to live that the man who neglects the real to study the ideal will learn how to accomplish his ruin, not his salvation. Any man who tries to be good all the time is bound to come to ruin among the great number who are not good. Hence a prince who wants to keep his authority must learn how not to be good, and use that knowledge, or refrain from using it, as necessity requires.

Putting aside, then, all the imaginary things that are said about princes, and getting down to the truth, let me say that whenever men are discussed (and especially princes because they are prominent), there are certain qualities that bring them either praise or blame. Thus some are considered generous, others stingy (I use a Tuscan term, since "greedy" in our speech means a man who wants to take other people's goods; we call a man "stingy" who clings to his own); some are givers, others grabbers; some cruel, others humane; one man is treacherous, another faithful; one is feeble and effeminate, another fierce and spirited; one modest, another proud; one lustful, another chaste; one straightforward, another sly; one harsh, another gentle; one serious, another playful; one religious, another skeptical, and so on. I know everyone will agree that among these many qualities a prince certainly ought to have all those that are considered good. But since it is impossible to have and exercise them all, because the conditions of human life simply do not allow it, a prince must be shrewd enough to avoid the public disgrace of those vices that would lose him his state. If he possibly can, he should also guard against vices that will not lose him his state; but if he cannot prevent them, he should not be too worried about indulging them. And furthermore, he should not be too worried about incurring blame for any vice without which he would find it hard to save his state. For if you look at matters carefully, you will see that something resembling virtue, if you follow it, may be your ruin, while something else resembling vice will lead, if you follow it, to your security and well-being.

Let me begin, then, with the first of the qualities mentioned above, by saying that a reputation for liberality is doubtless very fine; but the generosity that earns you that reputation can do you great harm. For if you exercise your generosity in a really virtuous way, as you should, nobody will know of it, and you cannot escape the odium of the opposite vice. Hence if you wish to be widely known as a generous man, you must seize every opportunity to make a big display of your giving. A prince of this character

Source: Niccolò Machiavelli, *The Prince*, 2nd ed., trans. Robert M. Adams. New York: W. W. Norton & Company, 1992, pp. 42–49.

is bound to use up his entire revenue in works of ostentation. In the end, if he wants to keep a name for generosity, he will have to load his people with exorbitant taxes and squeeze money out of them in every way he can. This is the first step in making him odious to his subjects; for when he is poor, nobody will respect him. Then, when his generosity has angered many and brought rewards to a few, the slightest difficulty will trouble him, and at the first approach of danger, down he goes. If by chance he foresees this, and tries to change his ways, he will immediately be labelled a miser.

Since a prince cannot use this virtue of liberality in such a way as to become known for it unless he harms his own security, he will not mind, if he judges prudently of things, being known as a miser. In due course he will be thought the more liberal man, when people see that his parsimony enables him to live on his income, to defend himself against his enemies, and to undertake major projects without burdening his people with taxes. Thus he will be acting liberally toward all those people from whom he takes nothing (and there are an immense number of them), and in a stingy way toward those people on whom he bestows nothing (and they are very few). . . .

Hence a prince who prefers not to rob his subjects, who wants to be able to defend himself, who wants to avoid poverty and contempt, and who has no desire to become a plunderer, should not mind in the least if people consider him a miser; this is simply one of the vices that enable him to reign. . . . Spending what belongs to other people does no harm to your reputation, rather it enhances it; only spending your own substance harms you. And there is nothing that wears out faster than generosity; even as you practice it, you lose the means of practicing it, and you become either poor and contemptible or (in the course of escaping poverty) rapacious and hateful. The thing above all against which a prince must protect himself is being contemptible and hateful; generosity leads to both. Thus, it is much wiser to put up with the reputation of being a miser, which brings you shame without hate, than to be forced — just because you want to appear generous — into a reputation for rapacity, which brings shame on you and hate along with it.

B In a very famous passage Machiavelli argues that it is better for a prince, as the representative of the state, to be feared than to be loved.

[L]et me say that every prince should prefer to be considered merciful rather than cruel, yet he should be careful not to mismanage this clemency of his. People thought Cesare Borgia was cruel, but that cruelty of his reorganized the Romagna, united it, and established it in peace and loyalty. Anyone who views the matter realistically will see that this prince was much more merciful than the people of Florence, who, to avoid the reputation of cruelty, allowed Pistoia to be destroyed. Thus, no prince should mind being called cruel for what he does to keep his subjects united and loyal; he may make examples of a very few, but he will be more merciful in reality than those who, in their tenderheartedness, allow disorders to occur, with their attendant murders and lootings. Such turbulence brings harm to an entire community, while the executions ordered by a prince affect only one individual at a time. A new prince, above all others, cannot possibly avoid a name for cruelty, since new states are always in danger. . . . Yet a prince should be slow to believe rumors and to commit himself to action on the basis of them. He should not be afraid of his own thoughts; he ought to proceed cautiously, moderating his conduct with prudence and humanity, allowing neither overconfidence to make him careless, nor excess suspicion to make him intolerable.

Here the question arises: is it better to be loved than feared, or vice versa? I don't doubt that every prince would like to be both; but since it is hard to accommodate these qualities, if you have to make a choice, to be feared is much safer than to be loved. For it is a good general rule about men, that they are ungrateful, fickle, liars and deceivers, fearful of danger and greedy for gain. While you serve their welfare, they are all yours, offering their blood, their belongings, their lives, and their children's lives, as we noted above — so long as the danger is remote. But when the danger is close at hand, they turn against you. Then, any prince who has relied on their words and has made no other preparations will come to grief; because friendships that are bought at a price, and not with greatness and nobility of soul, may be paid for but they are not acquired, and they cannot be used in time of need. People are less concerned with offending a man who makes himself loved than one who makes himself feared: the reason is that love is a link of obligation which men, because they are rotten, will break any time they think doing so serves their advantage; but fear involves dread of punishment, from which they can never escape.

Still, a prince should make himself feared in such a way that, even if he gets no love, he gets no hate either; because it is perfectly possible to be feared and not hated, and this will be the result if only the prince will keep his hands off the property of his subjects or citizens, and off their women. When he does have to shed blood, he should be sure to have a strong justification and manifest cause; but above all, he should not confiscate people's property, because men are quicker to forget the death of a father than the loss of a patrimony. . . .

But a prince at the head of his armies and commanding a multitude of soldiers should not care a bit if he is considered cruel; without such a reputation, he could never hold his army together and ready for action. Among the marvelous deeds of Hannibal, this was prime: that, having an immense army, which included men of many different races and nations, and which he led to battle in distant countries, he never allowed them to fight among themselves or to rise against him, whether his fortune was good or bad. . . . The historians who pass snap judgments on these matters admire his accomplishments and at the same time condemn the cruelty which was their main cause. . . .

Returning to the question of being feared or loved, I conclude that since men love at their own inclination but can be made to fear at the inclination of the prince, a shrewd prince will lay his foundations on what is under his own control, not on what is controlled by others. He should simply take pains not to be hated.

C Princes need to understand the distinction between appearance and reality, and the means necessary to advance the interests of the state. They need to have the qualities of both the lion and the fox.

How praiseworthy it is for a prince to keep his word and live with integrity rather than by craftiness, everyone understands; yet we see from recent experience that those princes have accomplished most who paid little heed to keeping their promises, but who knew how to manipulate the minds of men craftily. In the end, they won out over those who tried to act honestly.

You should consider then, that there are two ways of fighting, one with laws and the other with force. The first is properly a human method, the second belongs to beasts. But as the first method does not always suffice, you sometimes have to turn to the second. Thus a prince must know how to make good use of both the beast and man. . . .

Since a prince must know how to use the character of beasts, he should pick for imitation the fox and the lion. As the lion cannot protect himself from traps, and the fox cannot defend himself from wolves, you have to be a fox in order to be wary of traps, and a lion to overawe the wolves. Those who try to live by the lion alone are badly mistaken. Thus a prudent prince cannot and should not keep his word when to do so would go against his interest, or when the reasons that made him pledge it no longer apply. Doubtless if all men were good, this rule would be bad; but since they are a sad lot, and keep no faith with you, you in your turn are under no obligation to keep it with them.

Besides, a prince will never lack for legitimate excuses to explain away his breaches of faith. Modern history will furnish innumerable examples of this behavior, showing how many treaties and promises have been made null and void by the faithlessness of princes, and how the man succeeded best who knew best how to play the fox. But it is necessary in playing this part that you conceal it carefully; you must be a great liar and hypocrite. Men are so simple of mind, and so much dominated by their immediate needs, that a deceitful man will always find plenty who are ready to be deceived. . . .

In actual fact, a prince may not have all the admirable qualities listed above, but it is very necessary that he should seem to have them. Indeed, I will venture to say that when you have them and exercise them all the time, they are harmful to you; when you just seem to have them, they are useful. It is good to appear merciful, truthful, humane, sincere, and religious; it is good to be so in reality. But you must keep your mind so disposed that, in case of need, you can turn to the exact contrary. This has to be understood: a prince, and especially a new prince, cannot possibly exercise all those virtues for which men are called "good." To preserve the state, he often has to do things against his word, against charity, against humanity, against religion. Thus he has to have a mind ready to shift as the winds of fortune and the varying circumstances of life may dictate. And as I said above, he should not depart from the good if he can hold to it, but he should be ready to enter on evil if he has to.

Hence a prince should take great care never to drop a word that does not seem imbued with the five good qualities noted above; to anyone who sees or hears him, he should appear all compassion, all honor, all humanity, all integrity, all religion. Nothing is more necessary than to seem to have this last virtue. Men in general judge more by the sense of sight than by the sense of touch, because everyone can see but only a few can test by feeling. Everyone sees what you seem to be, few know what you really are; and those few do not dare take a stand against the general opinion, supported by the majesty of the government. In the actions of all men, and especially of princes who are not subject to a court of appeal, we must always look to the end. Let a prince, therefore, win victories and uphold his state; his methods will always be considered worthy, and everyone will praise them, because the masses are always impressed by the superficial appearance of things, and by the outcome of an enterprise. And the world consists of nothing but the masses; the few have no influence when the many feel secure.

1. What is Machiavelli's opinion of human nature?

2. What are the qualities of a successful leader?

3. Can Machiavelli's prince be both politically astute and morally bankrupt? Explain.

4. Are Machiavelli's descriptions of leadership still relevant for contemporary leaders? Defend your position.

Thomas More

Thomas More (1478–1535) was a scholar, lawyer, civil servant, and the author of numerous works. He also served as Lord Chancellor to King Henry VIII of England. In short, he was a model of the new Renaissance man. More wrote *Utopia* in 1516 to challenge the existing political and social system in England, and to suggest a new model of social organization. His beliefs were deeply influenced by the Christian Humanism of northern Europe.

Raphael Hythloday, the wise traveller in Utopia who recounts his own experiences, argues that the economic conditions of England are very unfair and social misery leads people to behave badly.

"'This enclosing has had the effect of raising the price of grain in many places. In addition, the price of raw wool has risen so much that poor people who used to make cloth are no longer able to buy it, and so great numbers are forced from work to idleness. . . . But even if the number of sheep should increase greatly, their price will not fall a penny. The reason is that the wool trade, though it can't be called a monopoly because it isn't in the hands of one single person, is concentrated in few hands (an oligopoly, you might say) and these so rich, that the owners are never pressed to sell until they have a mind to, and that is only when they can get their price.

"'For the same reason other kinds of livestock also are priced exorbitantly, and this is all the easier because, with so many cottages being pulled down, and farming in a state of decay, there are not enough people to look after the breeding of cattle. These rich men will not breed calves as they do lambs, but buy them lean and cheap, fatten them in their own pastures, and then sell them at a high price. I don't think the full impact of this bad system has yet been felt. . . . So your island [England], which seemed especially fortunate in this matter, will be ruined by the crass avarice of a few. For the high price of grain causes rich men to dismiss as many retainers as they can from their households; and what, I ask, can these men do, but rob or beg? And a man of courage is more likely to steal than to cringe.

"'To make this hideous poverty worse, it exists side by side with wanton luxury. Not only the servants of noblemen, but tradespeople, farmers, and people of every social rank are given to ostentatious dress and gluttonous greed. Look at the eating houses, the bawdy houses, and those other places just as bad, the taverns, wine-shops, and alehouses. Look at all the crooked games of chance like dice, cards, backgammon, tennis, bowling, and quoits, in which money slips away so fast. Don't all these lead their habitués straight to robbery? Banish these blights, make those who have ruined farms and villages restore them, or rent them to someone who will rebuild. Restrict the right of the rich to buy up anything and everything, and then to exercise a kind of monopoly. Let fewer people be brought up in idleness. Let agriculture be restored and the wool manufacture revived, so there will be useful work for the whole crowd of those now idle — whether those whom poverty has already made into thieves, or those whom vagabondage and habits of lazy service are converting, just as surely, into the robbers of the future.

"'If you do not find a cure for these evils, it is futile to boast of your severity in punishing theft. Your policy may look superficially like justice, but in reality it is neither just nor practical. If you allow young folk to be abominably brought up and their characters corrupted, little by little, from childhood; and if then you punish them as grownups for committing crime to which their early training has inclined them, what else is this, I ask, but first making them thieves and then punishing them for it?'"

Source: Thomas More, *Utopia*, 2nd ed., ed. and trans. Robert M. Adams. New York: W. W. Norton & Company, 1992, pp. 13–14, 28–29, 50–52.

B For Raphael it is the Utopians who have the solution.

"But as a matter of fact, my dear More, to tell you what I really think, as long as you have private property, and as long as cash money is the measure of all things, it is really not possible for a nation to be governed justly or happily. For justice cannot exist where all the best things in life are held by the worst citizens; nor can anyone be happy where property is limited to a few, since those few are always uneasy and the many are utterly wretched.

"So I reflect on the wonderfully wise and sacred institutions of the Utopians who are so well governed with so few laws. Among them virtue has its reward, yet everything is shared equally, and all men live in plenty. I contrast them with the many other nations which are constantly passing new ordinances and yet can never order their affairs satisfactorily. . . . When I consider all these things, I become more sympathetic to Plato and do not wonder that he declined to make laws for any people who refused to share their goods equally. Wisest of men, he easily perceived that the one and only road to the welfare of all lies through the absolute equality of goods. I doubt whether such equality can ever be achieved where property belongs to individual men. However abundant goods may be, when every man tries to get as much as he can for his own exclusive use, a handful of men end up sharing the whole thing, and the rest are left in poverty. The result generally is two sorts of people whose fortunes ought to be interchanged: the rich are rapacious, wicked, and useless, while the poor are unassuming, modest men who work hard, more for the benefit of the public than of themselves.

"Thus I am wholly convinced that unless private property is entirely done away with, there can be no fair or just distribution of goods, nor can mankind be happily governed. As long as private property remains, by far the largest and the best part of mankind will be oppressed by a heavy and inescapable burden of cares and anxieties. This load, I admit, may be lightened a little bit under the present system, but I maintain it cannot be entirely removed. . . ."

"But I don't see it that way," I replied. "It seems to me that men cannot possibly live well where all things are in common. How can there be plenty of commodities where every man stops working? The hope of gain will not spur him on; he will rely on others, and become lazy. If a man is driven by want of something to produce it, and yet cannot legally protect what he has gained, what can follow but continual bloodshed and turmoil, especially when respect for magistrates and their authority has been lost? I for one cannot conceive of authority existing among men who are equal to one another in every respect."

"I'm not surprised," said Raphael, "that you think of it in this way, since you have no idea, or only a false idea, of such a state. But you should have been with me in Utopia, and seen with your own eyes their manners and customs as I did — for I lived there more than five years, and

would never have left, if it had not been to make that new world known
to others. If you had seen them, you would frankly confess that you had
never seen a people so well governed as they are."

C The values of the Utopians, which More supports, are those of the new Christian
Humanism.

In matters of moral philosophy, they carry on much the same arguments
as we do. They inquire into the nature of the good, distinguishing goods
of the body from goods of the mind and external gifts. They ask whether
the name of "good" may be applied to all three, or applies simply to goods
of the mind. They discuss virtue and pleasure, but their chief concern is
human happiness, and whether it consists of one thing or many. They seem
overly inclined to the view of those who think that all or most human
happiness consists of pleasure. . . .

Their religious principles are of this nature: that the soul of man is
immortal, and by God's goodness it is born for happiness; that after this
life, rewards are appointed for our virtues and good deeds, punishments
for our sins. Though these are indeed religious beliefs, they think that
reason leads men to believe and accept them. And they add unhesitat-
ingly that if these beliefs were rejected, no man would be so stupid as not
to realize that he should seek pleasure regardless of right and wrong. . . .

In fact, the Utopians believe that happiness is found, not in every
kind of pleasure, but only in good and honest pleasure. Virtue itself, they
say, draws our nature to this kind of pleasure, as to the supreme good.
There is an opposed school which declares that virtue is itself happiness.

They define virtue as living according to nature; and God, they say,
created us to that end. When a man obeys the dictates of reason in choosing
one thing and avoiding another, he is following nature. Now the first
rule of reason is to love and venerate the Divine Majesty to whom men
owe their own existence and every happiness of which they are capable.
The second rule of nature is to lead a life as free of anxiety and as full of
joy as possible, and to help all one's fellow men toward that end. . . . It is
especially praiseworthy, they tell us, when we provide for our fellow-crea-
ture's comfort and welfare. Nothing is more humane (and humanity is
the virtue most proper to human beings) than to relieve the misery of
others, assuage their griefs, and by removing all sadness from their life,
to restore them to enjoyment, that is, pleasure. . . . But if such a life is
good, and if we are supposed, indeed obliged, to help others to it, why
shouldn't we first of all seek it for ourselves, to whom we owe no less
charity than to anyone else? When nature prompts us to be kind to our
neighbors, she does not mean that we should be cruel and merciless to
ourselves. Thus they say that nature herself prescribes for us a joyous life,
in other words, pleasure, as the goal of our actions; and living according
to her prescriptions is to be defined as virtue. And as nature bids men to

make one another's lives merrier, to the extent that they can, so she warns us constantly not to seek our own advantages so avidly that we cause misfortune to our fellows. And the reason for this is an excellent one; for no man is placed so highly above the rest, that he is nature's sole concern; she cherishes alike all those living beings to whom she has granted the same form.

Consequently, the Utopians maintain that men should not only abide by their private agreements, but also obey all those public laws which control the distribution of vital goods, such as are the very substance of pleasure. Any such laws, provided they have been properly promulgated by a good king, or ratified by a people free of force and fraud, should be observed; and as long as they are observed, any man is free to pursue his own interests as prudence prompts him. If, in addition to his own interests, he concerns himself with the public interest, that is an act of piety; but if, to secure his own pleasure, he deprives others of theirs, that is injustice. . . .

By pleasure they understand every state or movement of body or mind in which man naturally finds delight. They are right in considering man's appetites natural. By simply following his senses and his right reason a man may discover what is pleasant by nature — it is a delight that does not injure others, that does not preclude a greater pleasure, and that is not followed by pain.

1. What criticisms does More level against the agricultural structure in England?

2. How does More view the Utopian plan of sharing in relation to human nature?

3. In what ways does More see religion as both liberating and restrictive?

4. Why would a prominent member of the British government advocate a limit on private property?

Christopher Columbus

The first voyage of Christopher Columbus (1451–1506) in 1492 is regarded as the starting point of the series of contacts between the West and the world in the modern era that profoundly changed world history. Backed financially by Queen Isabella of Castile (1474–1504), Columbus sought a western route to India in the quest for spices and other wealth. He landed in the Caribbean, thinking he was close to China.

 About five months after his contact with the peoples of the Caribbean, Columbus composed a formal letter, one of the most widely distributed documents of the time.

A Letter addressed to the noble Lord Raphael Sánchez, Treasurer to their most invincible Majesties, Ferdinand and Isabella, King and Queen of Spain, by Christopher Columbus, to whom our age is greatly indebted, treating of the islands

of India recently discovered beyond the Ganges, to explore which he had been sent eight months before under the auspices and at the expense of their said Majesties.

Knowing that it will afford you pleasure to learn that I have brought my undertaking to a successful termination, I have decided upon writing you this letter to acquaint you with all the events which have occurred in my voyage, and the discoveries which have resulted from it. Thirty-three days after my departure from Cádiz I reached the Indian sea, where I discovered many islands, thickly peopled, of which I took possession without resistance in the name of our most illustrious Monarch, by public proclamation and with unfurled banners. To the first of these islands, which is called by the Indians Guanahani, I gave the name of the blessed Saviour (San Salvador), relying upon whose protection I had reached this as well as the other islands; to each of these I also gave a name. In the mean time I had learned from some Indians whom I had seized, that that country was certainly an island: and therefore I sailed towards the east, coasting to the distance of three hundred and twenty-two miles, which brought us to the extremity of it; from this point I saw lying eastwards another island, fifty-four miles distant from Juana, to which I gave the name of Española: I went thither, and steered my course eastward as I had done at Juana, even to the distance of five hundred and sixty-four miles [907.5 km] along the north coast. This said island of Juana is exceedingly fertile, as indeed are all the others; it is surrounded with many bays, spacious, very secure, and surpassing any that I have ever seen; numerous large and healthful rivers intersect it, and it also contains many very lofty mountains. All these islands are very beautiful, and distinguished by a diversity of scenery; they are filled with a great variety of trees of immense height, and which I believe to retain their foliage in all seasons; for when I saw them they were as verdant and luxuriant as they usually are in Spain in the month of May — some of them were blossoming, some bearing fruit, and all flourishing in the greatest perfection, according to their respective stages of growth, and the nature and quality of each: yet the islands are not so thickly wooded as to be impassable. The nightingale and various birds were singing in countless numbers, and that in November, the month in which I arrived there. There are besides in the same island of Juana seven or eight kinds of palm trees, which, like all the other trees, herbs, and fruits, considerably surpass ours in height and beauty. The pines also are very handsome, and there are very extensive fields and meadows, a variety of birds, different kinds of honey, and many sorts of metals, but no iron. In that island also which I have before said we named Española, there are mountains of very great size and beauty, vast plains, groves, and very fruitful fields, admirably adapted for tillage, pasture, and habitation.

Source: Christopher Columbus, *Letters*, ed. and trans. R. H. Major. London: The Hakluyt Society, 1843, pp. 35–43.

B Columbus describes the inhabitants of the islands.

The inhabitants of both sexes in this island, and in all the others which I have seen, or of which I have received information, go always naked as they were born, with the exception of some of the women, who use the covering of a leaf, or small bough, or an apron of cotton which they prepare for that purpose. None of them are possessed of any iron, neither have they weapons, being unacquainted with, and indeed incompetent to use them, not from any deformity of body (for they are well-formed), but because they are timid and full of fear.

They carry however in lieu of arms, canes dried in the sun, on the ends of which they fix heads of dried wood sharpened to a point, and even these they dare not use habitually; for it has often occurred when I have sent two or three of my men to any of the villages to speak with the natives, that they have come out in a disorderly troop, and have fled in such haste at the approach of our men, that the fathers forsook their children and the children their fathers. This timidity did not arise from any loss or injury that they had received from us; for, on the contrary, I gave to all I approached whatever articles I had about me, such as cloth and many other things, taking nothing of theirs in return: but they are naturally timid and fearful. As soon however as they see that they are safe, and have laid aside all fear, they are very simple and honest, and exceedingly liberal with all they have; none of them refusing any thing he may possess when he is asked for it, but on the contrary inviting us to ask them. They exhibit great love towards all others in preference to themselves: they also give objects of great value for trifles, and content themselves with very little or nothing in return.

I however forbade that these trifles and articles of no value (such as pieces of dishes, plates, and glass, keys, and leather straps) should be given to them, although if they could obtain them, they imagined themselves to be possessed of the most beautiful trinkets in the world. It even happened that a sailor received for a leather strap as much gold as was worth three golden nobles, and for things of more trifling value offered by our men, especially newly coined blancas, or any gold coins, the Indians would give whatever the seller required; as, for instance, an ounce and a half or two ounces of gold [42 or 56 g], or thirty or forty pounds of cotton [13 or 18 kg], with which commodity they were already acquainted. Thus they bartered, like idiots, cotton and gold for fragments of bows, glasses, bottles, and jars; which I forbade as being unjust, and myself gave them many beautiful and acceptable articles which I had brought with me, taking nothing from them in return; I did this in order that I might the more easily conciliate them, that they might be led to become Christians, and be inclined to entertain a regard for the King and Queen, our Princes and all Spaniards, and that I might induce them to take an interest in seeking out, and collecting, and delivering to us such things as they possessed in abundance, but which we greatly needed.

They practise no kind of idolatry, but have a firm belief that all strength and power, and indeed all good things, are in heaven, and that I had descended from thence with these ships and sailors, and under this impression was I received after they had thrown aside their fears. Nor are they slow or stupid, but of very clear understanding; and those men who have crossed to the neighbouring islands give an admirable description of everything they observed; but they never saw any people clothed, nor any ships like ours.

In all these islands there is no difference of physiognomy, of manners, or of language, but they all clearly understand each other, a circumstance very propitious for the realization of what I conceive to be the principal wish of our most serene King, namely, the conversion of these people to the holy faith of Christ, to which indeed, as far as I can judge, they are very favourable and well-disposed. There was one large town in Española of which especially I took possession, situated in a remarkably favourable spot, and in every way convenient for the purposes of gain and commerce. To this town I gave the name of Navidad del Señor, and ordered a fortress to be built there, which must by this time be completed, in which I left as many men as I thought necessary, with all sorts of arms, and enough provisions for more than a year. I also left them one caravel, and skilful workmen both in ship-building and other arts, and engaged the favor and friendship of the King of the island in their behalf, to a degree that would not be believed, for these people are so amiable and friendly that even the King took a pride in calling me his brother. But supposing their feelings should become changed, and they should wish to injure those who have remained in the fortress, they could not do so, for they have no arms, they go naked, and are moreover too cowardly; so that those who hold the said fortress, can easily keep the whole island in check, without any pressing danger to themselves, provided they do not transgress the directions and regulations which I have given them.

As far as I have learned, every man throughout these islands is united to but one wife, with the exception of the kings and princes, who are allowed to have twenty: the women seem to work more than the men. I could not clearly understand whether the people possess any private property, for I observed that one man had the charge of distributing various things to the rest, but especially meat and provisions and the like. I did not find, as some of us had expected, any cannibals amongst them, but on the contrary men of great deference and kindness. Neither are they black, like the Ethiopians: their hair is smooth and straight: for they do not dwell where the rays of the sun strike most vividly, and the sun has intense power there, the distance from the equinoctial line being, it appears, but six-and-twenty degrees. On the tops of the mountains the cold is very great, but the effect of this upon the Indians is lessened by their being accustomed to the climate, and by their frequently indulging in the use of very hot meats and drinks.

C Columbus ends with a summary of his purpose.

Finally, to compress into few words the entire summary of my voyage and speedy return, and of the advantages derivable therefrom, I promise, that with a little assistance afforded me by our most invincible sovereigns, I will procure them as much gold as they need, as great a quantity of spices, of cotton, and of mastic (which is only found in Chios), and as many men for the service of the navy as their Majesties may require. I promise also rhubarb and other sorts of drugs, which I am persuaded the men whom I have left in the aforesaid fortress have found already and will continue to find; for I myself have tarried no where longer than I was compelled to do by the winds, except in the city of Navidad, while I provided for the building of the fortress, and took the necessary precautions for the perfect security of the men I left there. Although all I have related may appear to be wonderful and unheard of, yet the results of my voyage would have been more astonishing if I had had at my disposal such ships as I required.

But these great and marvellous results are not to be attributed to any merit of mine, but to the holy Christian faith, and to the piety and religion of our Sovereigns; for that which the unaided intellect of man could not compass, the spirit of God has granted to human exertions, for God is wont to hear the prayers of his servants who love his precepts even to the performance of apparent impossibilities. Thus it has happened to me in the present instance, who have accomplished a task to which the powers of mortal men had never hitherto attained; for if there have been those who have anywhere written or spoken of these islands, they have done so with doubts and conjectures, and no one has ever asserted that he has seen them, on which account their writings have been looked upon as little else than fables. Therefore let the king and queen, our princes and their most happy kingdoms, and all the other provinces of Christendom, render thanks to our Lord and Savior Jesus Christ, who has granted us so great a victory and such prosperity. Let processions be made, and sacred feasts be held, and the temples be adorned with festive boughs. Let Christ rejoice on earth, as he rejoices in heaven in the prospect of the salvation of the souls of so many nations hitherto lost. Let us also rejoice, as well on account of the exaltation of our faith, as on account of the increase of our temporal prosperity, of which not only Spain, but all Christendom will be partakers.

Such are the events which I have briefly described. Farewell.
Lisbon, the 14th of March.

CHRISTOPHER COLUMBUS
Admiral of the Fleet of the Ocean

1. What impression does Columbus present in his letter of 1493?

2. What is Columbus' attitude toward the inhabitants of the lands he has explored?

3. How does Columbus try to reconcile his actions as a Christian missionary and exploiter of the inhabitants?

Vasco da Gama

Vasco da Gama (c. 1460–1524) opened the sea route to India in 1497 and 1498. By sailing around the Cape of Good Hope to Calcutta, he and his crew became the first Europeans to travel by sea to the Indian subcontinent. Although Da Gama encountered some difficulties on his first voyage, Portugal followed with other expeditions, with fleets that could wage war as well as trade, and they founded a prosperous trading empire.

 Da Gama arrives at Calicut, his destination, in May 1498, to find a very different civilization.

On . . . May 22 these same boats came again alongside, when the captain-major sent one of the convicts to Calicut, and those with whom he went took him to two Moors from Tunis, who could speak Castilian and Genoese. The first greeting that he received was in these words: "May the Devil take thee! What brought you hither?" They asked what he sought so far away from home, and he told them that we came in search of Christians and of spices. They said: "Why does not the King of Castile, the King of France, or the Signoria of Venice send thither?" He said that the King of Portugal would not consent to their doing so, and they said he did the right thing. After this conversation they took him to their lodgings and gave him wheaten bread and honey. When he had eaten he returned to the ships, accompanied by one of the Moors, who was no sooner on board, than he said these words: "A lucky venture, a lucky venture! Plenty of rubies, plenty of emeralds! You owe great thanks to God, for having brought you to a country holding such riches!" We were greatly astonished to hear his talk, for we never expected to hear our language spoken so far away from Portugal.

The city of Calicut is inhabited by Christians. [The first voyagers to India mistook the Hindus for Christians.] They are of tawny complexion. Some of them have big beards and long hair, whilst others clip their hair short or shave the head, merely allowing a tuft to remain on the crown as a sign that they are Christians. They also wear moustaches. They pierce the ears and wear much gold in them. They go naked down to the waist, covering their lower extremities with very fine cotton stuffs. But it is only the most respectable who do this, for the others manage as best they are able. The women of this country, as a rule, are ugly and of small stature. They wear many jewels of gold round the neck, numerous bracelets on their arms, and rings set with precious stones on their toes. All these people are well-disposed and apparently of mild temper. At first sight they seem covetous and ignorant. . . .

When we were at anchor, a message arrived informing the captain-major that the king was already in the city. At the same time the king sent a bale, with

Source: Vasco da Gama, "Vasco da Gama: Round Africa to India, 1497–1498 CE." www.fordham.edu/halsall/mod/1497degama.html (Jan. 4, 2003)

other men of distinction, to Pandarani, to conduct the captain-major to where the king awaited him. This bale is like an alcaide [commander of a fortress], and is always attended by two hundred men armed with swords and bucklers. . . .

On the following morning, which was Monday, May 28th, the captain-major set out to speak to the king, and took with him thirteen men. On landing, the captain-major was received by the alcaide, with whom were many men, armed and unarmed. The reception was friendly, as if the people were pleased to see us, though at first appearances looked threatening, for they carried naked swords in their hands. . . .

When we disembarked, the captain-major once more entered his palanquin. The road was crowded with a countless multitude anxious to see us. Even the women came out of their houses with children in their arms and followed us. When we arrived (at Calicut) they took us to a large church, and this is what we saw: The body of the church is as large as a monastery, all built of hewn stone and covered with tiles. At the main entrance rises a pillar of bronze as high as a mast, on the top of which was perched a bird, apparently a cock. In addition to this, there was another pillar as high as a man, and very stout. In the center of the body of the church rose a chapel, all built of hewn stone, with a bronze door sufficiently wide for a man to pass, and stone steps leading up to it. Within this sanctuary stood a small image which they said represented Our Lady. Along the walls, by the main entrance, hung seven small bells. In this church the captain-major said his prayers, and we with him.

We did not go within the chapel, for it is the custom that only certain servants of the church, called quafees, should enter. . . .

After we had left that place, and had arrived at the entrance to the city (of Calicut) we were shown another church, where we saw things like those described above. Here the crowd grew so dense that progress along the street became next to impossible, and for this reason they put the captain-major into a house, and us with him. The king sent a brother of the bale, who was a lord of this country, to accompany the captain-major, and he was attended by men beating drums, blowing arafils and bagpipes, and firing off matchlocks. In conducting the captain-major they showed us much respect, more than is shown in Spain to a king. The number of people was countless, for in addition to those who surrounded us, and among whom there were two thousand armed men, they crowded the roofs and houses. . . .

May 28. The king was in a small court, reclining upon a couch covered with a cloth of green velvet, above which was a good mattress, and upon this again a sheet of cotton stuff, very white and fine, more so than any linen. The cushions were after the same fashion. . . . On the right side of the king stood a basin of gold, so large that a man might just encircle it with his arms: this contained the herbs. There were likewise many silver jugs. The canopy above the couch was all gilt. . . .

[T]he captain-major told him he was the ambassador of a King of Portugal, who was Lord of many countries and the possessor of great wealth of every description, exceeding that of any king of these parts; that for a period of sixty years his ancestors had annually sent out vessels to make discoveries in the direction of India, as they knew that there were Christian kings there like themselves. This, he said, was the reason which induced them to order this country to be discovered, not because they sought for gold or silver, for of this they had such abundance that they needed not what was to be found in this country. He further stated that the captains sent out traveled for a year or two, until their provisions were exhausted, and then returned to Portugal, without having succeeded in making the desired discovery. There reigned a king now whose name was Dom Manuel, who had ordered him to build three vessels, of which he had been appointed captain-major, and who had ordered him not to return to Portugal until he should have discovered this King of the Christians, on pain of having his head cut off. That two letters had been intrusted to him to be presented in case he succeeded in discovering him, and that he would do so on the ensuing day; and, finally, he had been instructed to say by word of mouth that he [the King of Portugal] desired to be his friend and brother.

In reply to this the king said that he was welcome; that, on his part, he held him as a friend and brother, and would send ambassadors with him to Portugal. This latter had been asked as a favor, the captain-major pretending that he would not dare to present himself before his king and master unless he was able to present, at the same time, some men of this country. These and many other things passed between the two in this chamber, and as it was already late in the night, the king asked the captain-major with whom he desired to lodge, with Christians or with Moors? And the captain-major replied, neither with Christians nor with Moors, and begged as a favor that he be given a lodging by himself. The king said he would order it thus, upon which the captain-major took leave of the king and came to where the men were, that is, to a veranda lit up by a huge candlestick. By that time four hours of the night had already gone.

B The captain-major has a meeting with the king, which brings fear to the Europeans.

May 30. On Wednesday morning the Moors returned, and took the captain-major to the palace. The palace was crowded with armed men. Our captain-major was kept waiting with his conductors for fully four long hours, outside a door, which was only opened when the king sent word to admit him, attended by two men only, whom he might select. . . .

The king . . . asked what it was he had come to discover: stones or men? If he came to discover men, as he said, why had he brought nothing? Moreover, he had been told that he carried with him the golden image of a Santa Maria. The captain-major said that the Santa Maria was not of gold, and that even if she were he would not part with her, as she had guided him across the ocean, and would guide him back to his own country. . . .

The king then asked what kind of merchandise was to be found in his country. The captain-major said there was much corn, cloth, iron, bronze, and many other things. The king asked whether he had any merchandise with him. The captain-major replied that he had a little of each sort, as samples, and that if permitted to return to the ships he would order it to be landed, and that meantime four or five men would remain at the lodgings assigned them. The king said no! He might take all his people with him, securely moor his ships, land his merchandise, and sell it to the best advantage. . . .

When they returned [June 1] the captain-major again asked for boats to take him to his ships. They then began to whisper among themselves, and said that we should have them if we would order our vessels to come nearer the shore. . . .

We passed all that day most anxiously. At night more people surrounded us than ever before, and we were no longer allowed to walk in the compound, within which we were, but confined within a small tiled court, with a multitude of people around us. We quite expected that on the following day we should be separated, or that some harm would befall us, for we noticed that our jailers were much annoyed with us. . . .

On the following day, Saturday, June 2, in the morning, these gentlemen [i.e., the bale and others] came back, and this time they wore better faces. They told the captain-major that as he had informed the king that he intended to land his merchandise, he should now give orders to have this done, as it was the custom of the country that every ship on its arrival should at once land the merchandise it brought, as also the crews, and that the vendors should not return on board until the whole of it had been sold. The captain-major consented, and said he would write to his brother to see to its being done. They said this was well, and that immediately after the arrival of the merchandise he would be permitted to return to his ship. The captain-major at once wrote to his brother to send him certain things, and he did so at once. On their receipt the captain was allowed to go on board, two men remaining behind with the things that had been landed. At this there was great rejoicing, thanks being rendered to God for having extricated us from the hands of people who had no more sense than beasts, for we knew well that once the captain-major was on board those who had been landed would have nothing to fear. When the captain-major reached his ship he ordered that no more merchandise should be sent.

1. What impressions does Da Gama have of the inhabitants he met?

2. What evidence of European arrogance and superiority can be found in this document?

3. Why might the inhabitants of Calicut be suspicious of Da Gama and his men?

4. How does Columbus' description of the inhabitants (see pages 19–23) compare to Da Gama's?

Álvar Núñez Cabeza de Vaca

Álvar Núñez Cabeza de Vaca (c. 1490–c.1560) was a Spanish soldier and explorer who was part of the 1527 expedition to establish a colony in Florida. Following a shipwreck, he began an eight-year odyssey that took him from Texas to the Pacific coast of Mexico. During this time he was, among other things, a slave, a merchant, and a healer. Shortly after reaching Mexico, Cabeza de Vaca composed an account of his journey, which has become a classic of European literature of exploration.

A Cabeza de Vaca describes his first encounter with the indigenous people.

Upon seeing the disaster we had suffered, our misery and distress, the Indians sat down with us and all began to weep out of compassion for our misfortune, and for more than half an hour they wept so loud and so sincerely that it could be heard far away.

Verily, to see beings so devoid of reason, untutored, so like unto brutes, yet so deeply moved by pity for us, it increased my feelings and those of others in my company for our own misfortune. When the lament was over, I spoke to the Christians and asked them if they would like me to beg the Indians to take us to their homes. Some of the men, who had been to New Spain, answered that it would be unwise, as, once at their abode, they might sacrifice us to their idols.

Still, seeing there was no remedy and that in any other way death was surer and nearer, I did not mind what they said, but begged the Indians to take us to their dwellings, at which they showed great pleasure, telling us to tarry yet a little, but that they would do what we wished. Soon thirty of them loaded themselves with firewood and went to their lodges, which were far away, while we stayed with the others until it was almost dark. Then they took hold of us and carried us along hurriedly to where they lived.

Against the cold, and lest on the way some one of us might faint or die, they had provided four or five big fires on the road, at each one of which they warmed us. As soon as they saw we had regained a little warmth and strength they would carry us to the next fire with such haste that our feet barely touched the ground.

So we got to their dwellings, where we saw they had built a hut for us with many fires in it. About one hour after our arrival they began to dance and to make a great celebration (which lasted the whole night), although there was neither pleasure, feast nor sleep in it for us, since we expected to be sacrificed. In the morning they again gave us fish and roots, and treated us so well that we became reassured, losing somewhat our apprehension of being butchered. . . .

Source: Álvar Núñez Cabeza de Vaca, *The Journey of Álvar Núñez Cabeza de Vaca*, ed. A. F. Bandelier. New York: AMS Press, 1973, pp. 59–61, 68–71, 121–123, 163, 159–160, 170–172.

On the island I have spoken of they wanted to make medicine men of us without any examination or asking for our diplomas, because they cure diseases by breathing on the sick, and with that breath and their hands they drive the ailment away. So they summoned us to do the same in order to be at least of some use. We laughed, taking it for a jest, and said that we did not understand how to cure.

Thereupon they withheld our food to compel us to do what they wanted. Seeing our obstinacy, an Indian told me that I did not know what I said by claiming that what he knew was useless, because stones and things growing out in the field have their virtues, and he, with a heated stone, placing it on the stomach, could cure and take away pain, so that we, who were wiser men, surely had greater power and virtue.

At last we found ourselves in such stress as to have to do it, without risking any punishment. Their manner of curing is as follows: When one is ill they call in a medicine man, and after they are well again not only do they give him all they have, but even things they strive to obtain from their relatives. All the medicine man does is to make a few cuts where the pain is located and then suck the skin around the incisions. They cauterize with fire, thinking it very effective, and I found it to be so by my own experience. Then they breathe on the spot where the pain is and believe that with this the disease goes away.

The way we treated the sick was to make over them the sign of the cross while breathing on them, recite a Pater noster and Ave Maria, and pray to God, Our Lord, as best we could to give them good health and inspire them to do us some favors. Thanks to His will and the mercy He had upon us, all those for whom we prayed, as soon as we crossed them, told the others that they were cured and felt well again. For this they gave us good cheer, and would rather be without food themselves so as to give it to us, and they gave us hides and other small things. So great was the lack of food then that I often remained without eating anything whatsoever for three days, and they were in the same plight, so that it seemed to me impossible for life to last, although I afterwards suffered still greater privations and much more distress, as I shall tell further on.

B Cabeza de Vaca admires the warrior qualities of the Indians.

Those Indians are the readiest people with their weapons of all I have seen in the world, for when they suspect the approach of an enemy they lie awake all night with their bows within reach and a dozen of arrows, and before one goes to sleep he tries his bow, and should the string not be to his liking he arranges it until it suits him. Often they crawl out of their dwellings so as not to be seen and look and spy in every direction after danger, and if they detect anything, in less than no time are they all out in the field with their bows and arrows. Thus they remain until day-break, running hither and thither whenever they see danger or suspect their enemies might approach. When day comes they unstring their bows until they go hunting.

The strings of their bows are made of deer sinews. They fight in a crouching posture, and while shooting at each other talk and dart from one side to the other to dodge the arrows of the foe. In this way they receive little damage from our crossbows and muskets. On the contrary, the Indians laugh at those weapons, because they are not dangerous to them on the plains over which they roam. They are only good in narrows and in swamps.

Horses are what the Indians dread most, and by means of which they will be overcome.

Whoever has to fight Indians must take great care not to let them think he is disheartened or that he covets what they own; in war they must be treated very harshly, for should they notice either fear or greed, they are the people who know how to abide their time for revenge and to take courage from the fears of their enemy. After spending all their arrows, they part, going each their own way, and without attempting pursuit, although one side might have more men than the other; such is their custom.

Many times they are shot through and through with arrows, but do not die from the wounds as long as the bowels or heart are not touched; on the contrary, they recover quickly. Their eyesight, hearing and senses in general are better, I believe, than those of any other men upon earth. They can stand, and have to stand, much hunger, thirst and cold, being more accustomed and used to it than others. This I wished to state here, since, besides that all men are curious to know the habits and devices of others, such as might come in contact with those people should be informed of their customs and deeds, which will be of no small profit to them. . . .

We travelled over a great part of the country, and found it all deserted, as the people had fled to the mountains, leaving houses and fields out of fear of the Christians. This filled our hearts with sorrow, seeing the land so fertile and beautiful, so full of water and streams, but abandoned and the places burned down, and the people, so thin and wan, fleeing and hiding; and as they did not raise any crops their destitution had become so great that they ate tree-bark and roots. Of this distress we had our share all the way along, because they could provide little for us in their indigence, and it looked as if they were going to die. They brought us blankets, which they had been concealing from the Christians, and gave them to us, and told us how the Christians had penetrated into the country before, and had destroyed and burnt the villages, taking with them half of the men and all the women and children, and how those who could escaped by flight. . . .

We told them, by signs which they understood, that in Heaven there was a man called God, by us, who had created Heaven and earth, and whom we worshipped as our Lord; that we did as he ordered us to do, all good things coming from his hand, and that if they were to do the same they would become very happy; and so well were they inclined that, had there been a language in which we could have made ourselves perfectly understood, we would have left them all Christians. All this we gave them to understand as clearly as possible, and since then, when the sun rose, with great shouting they would lift their clasped hands to Heaven and then pass them all over their body. The same they did at sunset. They are well conditioned people, apt to follow any line which is well traced for them.

C Cabeza de Vaca finds a Christian European force and discusses how the indigenous people responded to them.

When they arrived at where I was [Diego De] Alcaraz [the commander of a Christian force which was on horseback] begged me to send for the people of the villages along the banks of the river, who were hiding in the timber, and he also requested me to order them to fetch supplies. There was no occasion for the latter, as the Indians always took good care to bring us whatever they could; nevertheless, we sent our messengers at once to call them, and six hundred persons came with all the maize they had, in pots closed with clay, which they had buried for concealment. They also brought nearly everything else they possessed, but we only took of the food, giving the rest to the Christians for distribution among themselves.

Thereupon we had many and bitter quarrels with the Christians, for they wanted to make slaves of our Indians, and we grew so angry at it that at our departure we forgot to take along many bows, pouches and arrows, also the five emeralds, and so they were left and lost to us. We gave the Christians a great many cow-skin robes, and other objects, and had much trouble in persuading the Indians to return home and plant their crops in peace. They insisted upon accompanying us until, according to their custom, we should be in the custody of other Indians, because otherwise they were afraid to die; besides, as long as we were with them, they had no fear of the Christians and of their lances. At all this the Christians were greatly vexed, and told their own interpreter to say to the Indians how we were of their own race, but had gone astray for a long while, and were people of no luck and little heart, whereas they were the lords of the land; whom they should obey and serve.

The Indians gave all that talk of theirs little attention. They parleyed among themselves, saying that the Christians lied, for we had come from sunrise, while the others came from where the sun sets; that we cured the sick, while the others killed those who were healthy; that we went naked and shoeless, whereas the others wore clothes and went on horseback and with lances. Also, that we asked for nothing, but gave away all we were presented with, meanwhile the others seemed to have no other aim than to steal what they could, and never gave anything to anybody. In short, they recalled all our deeds, and praised them highly, contrasting them with the conduct of the others.

1. How do Cabeza de Vaca's impressions of the inhabitants compare to those of Da Gama and Columbus (see pages 24–27 and 19–23)?

2. What qualities does Cabeza de Vaca admire in the inhabitants he encounters?

3. How does Cabeza de Vaca's relationship with the inhabitants differ from that of the Christian community he encounters?

Martin Luther

Martin Luther (1483–1546) was the central figure in bringing about the Reformation. He first sought to reform the institution of the Catholic Church, and then broke with it on matters of dogma. Luther's ideas and acts had social and political implications as well. In attacking papal governance, he challenged tradition and sought to change the daily lives of Christian people.

 Luther believed in salvation by faith, and here he challenges the importance of works in attaining grace. He recounts his inner struggle and dialogue:

> *The full disclosure [passages composed in 1545 and 1532]:* I greatly longed to understand Paul's Epistle to the Romans and nothing stood in the way but that one expression, "the justice of God," because I took it to mean that justice whereby God is just and deals justly in punishing the unjust. My situation was that, although an impeccable monk, I stood before God as a sinner troubled in conscience, and I had no confidence that my merit would assuage him. Therefore I did not love a just and angry God, but rather hated and murmured against Him. Yet I clung to the dear Paul and had a great yearning to know what he meant.
>
> Night and day I pondered until I saw the connection between the justice of God and the statement that "the just shall live by his faith." Then I grasped that the justice of God is that righteousness by which through grace and sheer mercy God justifies us through faith. Thereupon I felt myself to be reborn and to have gone through open doors into paradise. The whole of Scripture took on a new meaning, and whereas before the "justice of God" had filled me with hate, now it became to be inexpressibly sweet in greater love. This passage of Paul became to me a gate to heaven. . . .
>
> If you have a true faith that Christ is your Saviour, then at once you have a gracious God, for faith leads you in and opens up God's heart and

Sources: Roland H. Bainton, *The Age of the Reformation.* Princeton, N. J.: D. Van Nostrand Company, 1956, pp. 97–98; Eric Cochrane and Julius Kirshner, eds., *Readings in Western Civilization: Volume 5, The Renaissance.* Chicago: The University of Chicago Press, 1986, pp. 335–338, 343, 344, 345–346.

will, that you should see pure grace and overflowing love. This it is to behold God in faith that you should look upon His fatherly, friendly heart, in which there is no anger nor ungraciousness. He who sees God as angry does not see Him rightly but looks only on a curtain, as if a dark cloud had been drawn across his face.

B The Reformation contributed to the justification of many rural uprisings on the part of German peasants who sought political reform. In 1525, peasant rebels drew up the *Twelve Articles*, asking for their rights, using Luther's new theology in support of their claims.

The First Article

First, we humbly ask and request — in accordance with our unanimous will and desire — that in the future the entire community have the power and authority to choose and appoint a pastor. We also desire the power to depose him, should he conduct himself improperly. The pastor whom we thus choose for ourselves shall preach the holy Gospel to us clearly and purely. . . .

The Second Article

Second, since the tithe is prescribed in the Old Testament, although it is fulfilled in the New, we are willing to pay the just tithe of grain, but it must be done in a proper way. Since men ought to give it to God and distribute it to those who are his, it belongs to the pastor who clearly proclaims the word of God, and we desire that in the future this tithe be gathered and received by our church provost, appointed by the community. . . .

The Third Article

Third, it has been the custom for men to hold us as their own property. . . . It is not our intention to be entirely free. God does not teach us that we should desire no rulers. We are to live according to the commandments, not the free self-will of the flesh; but we are to love God, recognize him in our neighbor as our Lord, and do all (as we gladly would do) that God has commanded in the Lord's Supper; therefore, we ought to live according to his commandment. This commandment does not teach us to disobey our rulers; rather to humble ourselves, not before the rulers only, but before everyone. . . .

The Fourth Article

Fourth, it has been the custom that no poor man has been allowed to catch game, wild fowl, or freshwater fish, which seems to us altogether improper and unbrotherly, selfish, and not according to the word of God. In some places the rulers keep the game to our vexation and great loss . . . .

The Fifth Article

Fifth, we also have a grievance about wood cutting, for our lords have appropriated all the forests solely to themselves, and when the poor man needs any wood, he must buy it at a double price. . . .

The Sixth Article

Sixth, we are grievously oppressed by the free labor which we are required to provide for our lords. The amount of labor required increases from day to day and [the variety of services required] increases from day to day. We ask that an appropriate investigation be made of this matter and that the burdens laid upon us not be too heavy. We ask that we be dealt with graciously, just as our ancestors were, who provided these services according to the word of God.

The Seventh Article

Seventh, in the future we will not allow ourselves to be further oppressed by the lords. Rather, a man shall possess his holding according to the terms on which it has been granted, that is, according to the agreement between the lord and the peasants. . . .

The Eighth Article

We are greatly aggrieved because many of us have holdings that do not produce enough to enable us to pay the rents due on them. As a result, the peasants bear the loss and are ruined. We ask that the lords have honorable men inspect the said holdings, and fix a fair rent, so that the peasant shall not labor for nothing; for every laborer is worthy of his hire.

The Ninth Article

We are aggrieved by the great wrong of continually making new laws. Punishment is inflicted on us, not according to the facts in the case, but at times by great ill-will, at times by great partiality. . . .

The Tenth Article

We are aggrieved because some have expropriated meadows from the common fields which once belonged to a community. We would take these back again into the hands of our communities, unless they have been honestly purchased. . . .

The Eleventh Article

We would have the custom called death tax entirely abolished. We will not tolerate it or allow widows and orphans to be so shamefully robbed by those who ought to guard and protect them, as now happens in many places and under many forms, contrary to God and honor. . . .

The Twelfth Article

Twelfth, it is our conclusion and final opinio[...]
articles set forth here is not in agreement wi[...]
we think this is not the case), and this disa[...]
the basis of Scripture, we shall withdraw such [...]
is explained to us on the basis of Scripture.

[handwritten note: had + wanted to retain support from Secular German Princes ↓]

C Luther did not support the peasants in their insurgency. He believed that they should continue to obey secular authority in their quest for divine salvation. He writes:

In the first place, dear brethren, you bear the name of God and call your-selves a "Christian association" or union, and you allege that you want to live and act according to divine law. Now you know that the name, word, and titles of God are not to be assumed idly or in vain, as he says in the second commandment, "Thou shalt not take the name of the Lord your God in vain," and adds, "for the Lord will not hold him guiltless who takes his name in vain" [Deut. 5:11]. . . .

Second, it is easy to prove that you are taking God's name in vain and putting it to shame; nor is there any doubt that you will, in the end, encounter all misfortune, unless God is not true. For here is God's word, spoken through the mouth of Christ, "All who take the sword will perish by the sword" [Matt. 26:52]. That means nothing else than that no one, by his own violence, shall arrogate authority to himself; but as Paul says, "Let every person be subject to the governing authorities with fear and reverence" [Rom. 13:1].

How can you get around these passages and laws of God when you boast that you are acting according to divine law, and yet take the sword in your own hands, and revolt against "the governing authorities that are instituted by God?" Do you think that Paul's judgment in Romans 13 [:2] will not strike you, "He who resists the authorities will incur judgment"? You take God's name in vain when you p[...]
right, and under the pretense of his name w[...]
Be careful, dear sirs. It will not turn out tha[...]

[handwritten note: ie you have no rights give the gov all power (Leviathan)]

Third, you say that the rulers are wicked [...]
not allow us to have the Gospel; they oppr[...]
dens they lay on our property, and they are [...]
I answer: The fact that the rulers are wicked and unjust does not excuse disorder and rebellion, for the punishing of wickedness is not the respon-sibility of everyone, but of the worldly rulers who bear the sword. Thus Paul says in Romans 13 [:4] and Peter, in I Peter 3 [2:14], that the rulers are instituted by God for the punishment of the wicked. . . .

I make you the judges and leave it to you to decide who is the worse robber, the man who takes a large part of another's goods, but leaves him something, or the man who takes everything that he has, and takes his life besides. The rulers unjustly take your property; that is the one side.

On the other hand, you take from them their authority, in which their whole property and life and being consist. Therefore you are far greater robbers than they, and you intend to do worse things than they have done. "Indeed not," you say, "we are going to leave them enough to live on." If anyone wants to believe that, let him! I do not believe it. Anyone who dares to go so far as to use force to take away authority, which is the main thing, will not stop at that, but will take the other, smaller thing that depends upon it. The wolf that eats a whole sheep will also eat its ear. And even if you permitted them to keep their life and some property, nevertheless, you would take the best thing they have, namely, their authority, and make yourselves lords over them. That would be too great a robbery and wrong. God will declare you to be the greatest robbers.

Can you not think it through, dear friends? If your enterprise were right, then any man might become judge over another. Then authority, government, law, and order would disappear from the world; there would be nothing but murder and bloodshed. . . . What do you expect God and the world to think when you pass judgment and avenge yourselves on those who have injured you and even upon your rulers, whom God has appointed?

Now in all this I have been speaking of the common, divine, and natural law which even the heathen, Turks, and Jews have to keep if there is to be any peace or order in the world. Even though you were to keep this whole law, you would do no better and no more than the heathen and the Turks do. For no one is a Christian merely because he does not undertake to function as his own judge and avenger but leaves this to the authorities and the rulers. You would eventually have to do this whether you wanted to or not. But because you are acting against this law, you see plainly that you are worse than heathen or Turks, to say nothing of the fact that you are not Christians. What do you think that Christ will say about this? You bear his name, and call yourselves a "Christian association," and yet you are so far from being Christian, and your actions and lives are so horribly contrary to his law, that you are not worthy to be called even heathen or Turks. You are much worse than these, because you rage and struggle against the divine and natural law, which all the heathen keep.

1. What is Luther's interpretation of Paul's epistle that included the dogma that by faith alone one could find eternal salvation? How did Luther's interpretation of Paul's epistle contradict Church teaching?

2. Based on the grievances presented, describe the relationship between the peasants and their lords.

3. How do the peasants employ Christianity as a support for their grievances? How does Luther use biblical references to refute the peasant grievances?

4. How can Luther acknowledge the unjust actions of some lords and still condemn the peasants?

The Scientific Revolution

One of the most important intellectual transformations in the modern era came from what has been called the Scientific Revolution, a series of breakthroughs in our understanding and interpretation of the heavens and the earth. Two major figures were the Italian Galileo Galilei (1564–1642) and the Englishman Isaac Newton (1642–1727). Through his use of the telescope Galileo discovered many things about the heavens, and he also made important contributions to the development of laws for bodies in motion. Sir Isaac Newton was the most important scientist of the period, the thinker who was seen to have given final proof of an orderly universe governed by laws that were unchangeable. This mechanical model came to be accepted as the basis of the new scientific method.

A In 1615 Galileo, who came from Florence in the province of Tuscany, wrote a defence of his work to Christina, the Grand Duchess of the province. The *Letter to the Grand Duchess Christina* opens with the problem of scientific truth and the challenge of theologians.

> Some years ago, as Your Serene Highness well knows, I discovered in the heavens many things that had not been seen before our own age. The novelty of these things, as well as some consequences which followed from them in contradiction to the physical notions commonly held among academic philosophers, stirred up against me no small number of professors — as if I had placed these things in the sky with my own hands in order to upset nature and overturn the sciences. They seemed to forget that the increase of known truths stimulates the investigation, establishment, and growth of the arts; not their diminution or destruction.
>
> Showing a greater fondness for their own opinions than for truth, they sought to deny and disprove the new things which, if they had cared to look for themselves, their own senses would have demonstrated to them. To this end they hurled various charges and published numerous writings filled with vain arguments, and they made the grave mistake of sprinkling these with passages taken from places in the Bible which they had failed to understand properly, and which were ill suited to their purposes.

B The conflict he had with Catholic theologians continued, as the Church denounced the new system being worked out by him and others as an error. Here, Galileo defends the new method of scientific inquiry.

> I think that in discussions of physical problems we ought to begin not from the authority of scriptural passages, but from sense-experiences and

Sources: *Discoveries and Opinions of Galileo*, trans. Stillman Drake. Garden City, New York: Doubleday and Company, Inc., 1957, pp. 175, 182–183; *Sir Isaac Newton's Mathematical Principles of Natural Philosophy and his System of the World*, Vol. II, trans. Andrew Motte, revised by Florian Cajori. Berkeley: University of California Press, 1966, pp. 544–546.

necessary demonstrations; for the holy Bible and the phenomena of nature proceed alike from the divine Word, the former as the dictate of the Holy Ghost and the latter as the observant executrix of God's commands. It is necessary for the Bible, in order to be accommodated to the understanding of every man, to speak many things which appear to differ from the absolute truth so far as the bare meaning of the words is concerned. But Nature, on the other hand, is inexorable and immutable; she never transgresses the laws imposed upon her, or cares a whit whether her abstruse reasons and methods of operation are understandable to men. For that reason it appears that nothing physical which sense-experience sets before our eyes, or which necessary demonstrations prove to us, ought to be called in question (much less condemned) upon the testimony of biblical passages which may have some different meaning beneath their words. For the Bible is not chained in every expression to conditions as strict as those which govern all physical effects; nor is God any less excellently revealed in Nature's actions than in the sacred statements of the Bible. . . .

From this I do not mean to infer that we need not have an extraordinary esteem for the passages of holy Scripture. On the contrary, having arrived at any certainties in physics, we ought to utilize these as the most appropriate aids in the true exposition of the Bible and in the investigation of those meanings which are necessarily contained therein, for these must be concordant with demonstrated truths. . . .

But I do not feel obliged to believe that that same God who has endowed us with senses, reason, and intellect has intended to forgo their use and by some other means to give us knowledge which we can attain by them. He would not require us to deny sense and reason in physical matters which are set before our eyes and minds by direct experience or necessary demonstrations. This must be especially true in those sciences of which but the faintest trace (and that consisting of conclusions) is to be found in the Bible.

C Newton, at the close of his *The Mathematical Principles of Natural Philosophy* (1687), reflects on the broader implications of the new science and the mechanical model.

This most beautiful system of the sun, planets, and comets, could only proceed from the counsel and dominion of an intelligent and powerful Being. And if the fixed stars are the centres of other like systems, these, being formed by the like wise counsel, must be all subject to the dominion of One . . . .

The Being governs all things, not as the soul of the world, but as Lord over all; and on account of his dominion he is wont to be called *Lord God* . . . or *Universal Ruler* . . . . The word God usually signifies *Lord*: but every lord is not a God. It is the dominion of a spiritual being which constitutes a God: a true, supreme, or imaginary dominion makes a true, supreme, or imaginary God. And from his true dominion it follows that the true God is a living, intelligent, and powerful Being; and, from his other perfections, that he is supreme, or most perfect. He is eternal and infinite, omnipotent and omniscient; that is, his duration reaches from eternity to eternity; his presence from infinity to infinity; he governs all things, and knows all things that are or can be done. He is not eternity and infinity, but eternal and infinite; he is not duration or space, but he endures and is present. He endures forever, and is everywhere present; and, by existing always and everywhere, he constitutes duration and space. . . . God is the same God, always and everywhere. . . . As a blind man has no idea of colors, so have we no idea of the manner by which the all-wise God perceives and understands all things. He is utterly void of all body and bodily figure, and can therefore neither be seen, nor heard, nor touched; nor ought he to be worshipped under the representation of any corporeal thing. We have ideas of his attributes, but what the real substance of anything is we know not. . . . We know him only by his most wise and excellent contrivances of things, and final causes; we admire him for his perfections; but we reverence and adore him on account of his dominion: for we adore him as his servants; and a god without dominion, providence, and final causes, is nothing else but Fate and Nature.

1. What type of opposition did Galileo face with his scientific pronouncements?
2. How does Galileo attempt to reconcile his science with the scriptural teachings of the Church?
3. Why did the Church find it difficult to accept Galileo's science that was based on observation and logic?
4. Describe Newton's vision of the nature of God.

René Descartes

The *Discourse on Method* (1637) by René Descartes (1596–1650) has had enormous influence on the development of rationalism, deduction, and modern science. Descartes was a mathematician, and he stressed the importance of using the mathematical method to obtain precise and verifiable knowledge. Emphasizing the centrality of the mind in defining human nature, Descartes' work lent authority to those who were investigating nature as an orderly system that could be understood by human beings.

 The *Discourse on Method* is a kind of intellectual autobiography, in which Descartes tells the reader how he arrived at his methodology. He discusses his early education and why he determined to seek a new method of obtaining knowledge.

When I was younger, I had studied a little logic in philosophy, and geometrical analysis and algebra in mathematics, three arts or sciences

Source: René Descartes, *Discourse on Method and the Meditations*, trans. F. E. Sutcliffe. Harmondsworth: Penguin Books, 1968, pp. 40–41, 53–56.

which would appear apt to contribute something towards my plan. But on examining them, I saw that, regarding logic, its syllogisms and most of its other precepts serve more to explain to others what one already knows, or even . . . to speak without judgement of those things one does not know, than to learn anything new. And although logic indeed contains many very true and sound precepts, there are, at the same time, so many others mixed up with them, which are either harmful or superfluous, that it is almost as difficult to separate them as to extract a Diana or a Minerva from a block of unprepared marble. Then, as for the geometrical analysis of the ancients and the algebra of the moderns, besides the fact that they extend only to very abstract matters which seem to be of no practical use, the former is always so tied to the inspection of figures that it cannot exercise the understanding without greatly tiring the imagination, while, in the latter, one is so subjected to certain rules and numbers that it has become a confused and obscure art which oppresses the mind instead of being a science which cultivates it. This was why I thought I must seek some other method which, while continuing the advantages of these three, was free from their defects. And as a multiplicity of laws often furnishes excuses for vice, so that a State is much better ordered when, having only very few laws, they are very strictly observed, so, instead of this great number of precepts of which logic is composed, I believed I would have sufficient in the four following rules, so long as I took a firm and constant resolve never once to fail to observe them.

The first was never to accept anything as true that I did not know to be evidently so: that is to say, carefully to avoid precipitancy and prejudice, and to include in my judgements nothing more than what presented itself so clearly and so distinctly to my mind that I might have no occasion to place it in doubt.

The second, to divide each of the difficulties that I was examining into as many parts as might be possible and necessary in order best to solve it.

The third, to conduct my thoughts in an orderly way, beginning with the simplest objects and the easiest to know, in order to climb gradually, as by degrees, as far as the knowledge of the most complex, and even supposing some order among those objects which do not precede each other naturally.

And the last, everywhere to make such complete enumerations and such general reviews that I would be sure to have omitted nothing.

These long chains of reasoning, quite simple and easy, which geometers are accustomed to using to teach their most difficult demonstrations, had given me cause to imagine that everything which can be encompassed by man's knowledge is linked in the same way, and that, provided only that one abstains from accepting any for true which is not true, and that one always keeps the right order for one thing to be deduced from that which precedes it, there can be nothing so distant that one does not reach it eventually, or so hidden that one cannot discover it. . . .

[W]hat satisfied me the most about this method was that, through it, I was assured of using my reason in everything, if not perfectly, at least to the best of my ability. Moreover, I felt that, in practising it, my mind was accustoming itself little by little to conceive its objects more clearly and distinctly, and not having subjected it to any particular matter, I promised myself that I would apply it just as usefully to the difficulties of the other sciences as I had to those of algebra.

B The mind/body distinction is an important one for Descartes. In his *Discourse on Method* he arrives at his famous definition of being: "I think, therefore I am."

I do not know if I ought to tell you about the first meditations I pursued there, for they are so abstract and unusual that they will probably not be to the taste of everyone; and yet, so that one may judge if the foundations I have laid are firm enough, I find myself to some extent forced to speak of them. I had long ago noticed that, in matters relating to conduct, one needs sometimes to follow, just as if they are absolutely indubitable, opinions one knows to be very unsure, as has been said above; but as I wanted to concentrate solely on the search for truth, I thought I ought to do just the opposite, and reject as being absolutely false everything in which I could suppose the slightest reason for doubt, in order to see if there did not remain after that anything in my belief which was entirely indubitable. So, because our senses sometimes play us false, I decided to suppose that there was nothing at all which was such as they cause us to imagine it; and because there are men who make mistakes in reasoning, even with the simplest geometrical matters, and make paralogisms [illogical reasoning], judging that I was as liable to error as anyone else, I rejected as being false all the reasonings I had hitherto accepted as proofs. And finally, considering that all the same thoughts that we had when we are awake can also come to us when we are asleep, without any one of them then being true, I resolved to pretend that nothing which had ever entered my mind was any more true than the illusions of my dreams. But immediately afterwards I became aware that, while I decided thus to think that everything was false, it followed necessarily that I who thought thus must be something; and observing that this truth: *I think, therefore I am*, was so certain and so evident that all the most extravagant suppositions of the sceptics were not capable of shaking it, I judged that I could accept it without scruple as the first principle of the philosophy I was seeking.

Then, examining attentively what I was, and seeing that I could pretend that I had no body and that there was no world or place that I was in, but that I could not, for all that, pretend that I did not exist, and that, on the contrary, from the very fact that I thought of doubting the truth of other things, it followed very evidently and very certainly that I existed; while, on the other hand, if I had only ceased to think, although all the rest of what I had ever imagined had been true, I would have had no reason to believe that I existed; I thereby concluded that I was a substance, of which the whole essence or nature consists in thinking, and which, in order to exist, needs no place and depends on no material thing; so that this 'I', that is to say, the mind, by which I am what I am, is entirely distinct from the body, and even that it is easier to know than the body, and moreover, that even if the body were not, it would not cease to be all that it is.

After this, I considered in general what is needed for a proposition to be true and certain; for, since I had just found one which I knew to be so, I thought that I ought also to know what this certainty consisted of. And having noticed that there is nothing at all in this, *I think, therefore I am*, which assures me that I am speaking the truth, except that I see very clearly that in order to think one must exist, I judged that I could take it to be a general rule that the things we conceive very clearly and very distinctly are all true, but that there is nevertheless some difficulty in being able to recognize for certain which are the things we see distinctly.

C God is conceived by Descartes as a "perfect Being." Descartes uses concepts of nature and mathematics to discuss his idea of a deity.

Following this, reflecting on the fact that I had doubts, and that consequently my being was not completely perfect, for I saw clearly that it was a greater perfection to know than to doubt, I decided to inquire whence I had learned to think of some thing more perfect than myself; and I clearly recognized that this must have been from some nature which was in fact more perfect. As for the notions I had of several other things outside myself, such as the sky, the earth, light, heat and a thousand others, I had not the same concern to know their source, because, seeing nothing in them which seemed to make them superior to myself, I could believe that, if they were true, they were dependencies of my nature, in as much as it had some perfection; and, if they were not, that I held them from nothing, that is to say that they were in me because of an imperfection of my nature. But I could not make the same judgement concerning the idea of a being more perfect than myself; for to hold it from nothing was something manifestly impossible; and because it is no less contradictory that the more perfect should proceed from and depend on the less perfect, than it is that something should emerge out of nothing, I could not hold it from myself; with the result that it remained that it must have been put into me by a being whose nature was truly more perfect than mine and which even had in itself all the perfections of which I could have any idea, that is to say, in a single word, which was God. . . . So I saw that doubt, inconstancy, sadness and similar things could not be in him, seeing that I myself would have been very pleased to be free from them. Then, further, I had ideas of many sensible and bodily things; for even supposing that I was dreaming, and that everything I saw or imagined was false, I could not, nevertheless, deny that the ideas were really in my thoughts. But, because I had already recognized in myself very clearly that intelligent nature is distinct from the corporeal, considering that all composition is evidence of dependency, and that dependency is manifestly a defect, I thence judged that it could not be a perfection in God to be composed of these two natures, and that, consequently, he was not so composed; but that, if there were any bodies in the world or any intelligences or other natures which were not wholly perfect, their existence must depend on his power, in such a way that they could not subsist without him for a single instant.

1. List and explain, in your own words, Descartes' four rules of problem solving.
2. How does Descartes employ his rules to conclude that thought equates existence?
3. How does Descartes use logic to prove the existence of God?
4. What reaction might the Catholic Church have had to Descartes' proof of the existence of God?

Thomas Hobbes

Thomas Hobbes (1588–1679) wrote *Leviathan* (1651) while England was in the midst of its civil wars. He was a rationalist and attempted to use the new methods of scientific inquiry in his work on politics, power, and human nature. Hobbes believed human beings were organisms in motion and that they needed to be restrained by authority from pursuing selfish ends. He rejected arguments that placed secular power under theological authority. His rationalism had great influence on subsequent writing about the state and political authority.

 Early in the work Hobbes speculates on human nature.

What is here meant by manners. By MANNERS I mean not here decency of behavior — as how one should salute another, or how a man should wash his mouth or pick his teeth before company, and such other points of the *small morals* — but those qualities of mankind that concern their living together in peace and unity....

A restless desire of power in all men. [I]n the first place, I put for a general inclination of all mankind a perpetual and restless desire of power after power that ceases only in death. And the cause of this is not always that a man hopes for a more intensive delight than he has already attained to, or that he cannot be content with a moderate power,

Source: Thomas Hobbes, *Leviathan*, ed. Herbert Schneider. Indianapolis: The Bobbs-Merrill Company, 1958, pp. 86–87, 106–109, 139, 142–143.

but because he cannot assure the power and means to live well which he has present without the acquisition of more. And from hence it is that kings, whose power is greatest, turn their endeavors to the assuring it at home by laws or abroad by wars; and when that is done, there succeeds a new desire — in some, of fame from new conquest; in others, of ease and sensual pleasure; in others, of admiration or being flattered for excellence in some art or other ability of the mind.

B The need for an authority to keep the peace is one of Hobbes' key ideas.

Again, men have no pleasure, but on the contrary a great deal of grief, in keeping company where there is no power able to overawe them all. For every man looks that his companion should value him at the same rate he sets upon himself; and upon all signs of contempt or undervaluing naturally endeavors, as far as he dares (which among them that have no common power to keep them in quiet is far enough to make them destroy each other), to extort a greater value from his contemners by damage and from others by the example. . . .

Out of civil states, there Hereby it is manifest that, during the time men live
is always war of every without a common power to keep them all in awe, they
one against every one. are in that condition which is called war, and such a war as is of every man against every man. . . .

The incommodities Whatsoever, therefore, is consequent to a time of war
of such a war. where every man is enemy to every man, the same is consequent to the time wherein men live without other security than what their own strength and their own invention shall furnish them withal. In such condition there is no place for industry, because the fruit thereof is uncertain: and consequently no culture of the earth; no navigation nor use of the commodities that may be imported by sea; no commodious building; no instruments of moving and removing such things as require much force; no knowledge of the face of the earth; no account of time; no arts; no letters; no society; and, which is worst of all, continual fear and danger of violent death; and the life of man solitary, poor, nasty, brutish, and short. . . .

In such a war To this war of every man against every man, this also
nothing is unjust. is consequent: that nothing can be unjust. The notions of right and wrong, justice and injustice, have there no place. Where there is no common power, there is no law; where no law, no injustice. . . .

The passions that The passions that incline men to peace are fear of death,
incline men to peace. desire of such things as are necessary to commodious living, and a hope by their industry to obtain them. And reason suggests convenient articles of peace, upon which men may be drawn to agreement. These articles are they which otherwise are called the Laws of Nature.

C According to Hobbes, authority is given power in order for a commonwealth to exist and prosper. The people derive rights from the sovereign.

The end of commonwealth, particular security. The final cause, end, or design of men, who naturally love liberty and dominion over others, in the introduction of that restraint upon themselves in which we see them live in commonwealths is the foresight of their own preservation, and of a more contented life thereby — that is to say, of getting themselves out from that miserable condition of war which is necessarily consequent, as has been shown to the natural passions of men when there is no visible power to keep them in awe and tie them by fear of punishment to the performance of their covenants and observation of those laws of nature set down in the fourteenth and fifteenth chapters.

Which is not to be had from the law of nature. For the laws of nature — as *justice, equity, modesty, mercy,* and, in sum, *doing to others as we would be done to* — of themselves, without the terror of some power to cause them to be observed, are contrary to our natural passions, that carry us to partiality, pride, revenge, and the like. And covenants without the sword are but words, and of no strength to secure a man at all. Therefore, notwithstanding the laws of nature (which everyone has then kept when he has the will to keep them, when he can do it safely), if there be no power erected, or not great enough for our security, every man will — and may lawfully — rely on his own strength and art for caution against all other men. . . .

The generation of a commonwealth. The only way to erect such a common power as may be able to defend them from the invasion of foreigners and the injuries of one another, and thereby to secure them in such sort as that by their own industry and by the fruits of the earth they may nourish themselves and live contentedly, is to confer all their power and strength upon one man, or upon one assembly of men that may reduce all their wills, by plurality of voices, unto one will; which is as much as to say, to appoint one man or assembly of men to bear their person. . . . [E]very man should say to every man, *I authorize and give up my right of governing myself to this man, or to this assembly of men, on this condition, that you give up your right to him and authorize all his actions in like manner.* This done, the multitude so united in one person is called a COMMONWEALTH, in Latin CIVITAS. This is the generation of that great LEVIATHAN (or rather, to speak more reverently, of that *mortal god*) to which we owe, under the *immortal God,* our peace and defense. For by this authority, given him by every particular man in the commonwealth, he has the use of so much power and strength conferred on him that, by terror thereof, he is enabled to form the wills of them all to peace at home and mutual aid against their enemies abroad.

The definition of a commonwealth. And in him consists the essence of the commonwealth, which to define it, is *one person, of whose acts a great multitude, by mutual covenants one with another, have made themselves every one the author, to the end he may use the strength and means of them all as he shall think expedient for their peace and common defense.*

Sovereign and subject, what. And he that carries this person is called SOVEREIGN and said to have *sovereign power*; and everyone besides, his SUBJECT.

The attaining to this sovereign power is by two ways. One, by natural force, as when a man makes his children to submit themselves and their children to his government, as being able to destroy them if they refuse, or by war subdues his enemies to his will, giving them their lives on that condition. The other is when men agree among themselves to submit to some man or assembly of men voluntarily, on confidence to be protected by him against all others. This latter may be called a political commonwealth, or commonwealth by *institution*, and the former a commonwealth by *acquisition*.

1. Why does Hobbes believe "manners" and desire for power result in selfishness and potential violence?
2. According to Hobbes, what causes war?
3. Besides maintaining peace, what other functions does authority fulfil?
4. How does Hobbes' commonwealth deter the subjects from rebelling against the sovereign?

John Locke

The philosopher who placed rights at the centre of his political theory was John Locke (1632–1704), whose *Two Treatises of Government* (1690) challenged authority as it had been formulated by Thomas Hobbes. Locke was writing at the time of the Glorious Revolution (1688), and he wished to find the proper limits of authority. He believed in a bilateral contract between the people and the government, and in a human nature that was characterized by tolerance and reason. Locke's ideas about natural rights and social contract had wide influence in constitutional thought and helped to form the basis of modern liberalism.

 Locke, like Hobbes, discusses the human condition in a "state of nature," a time when there was no government.

To understand Political Power right, and derive it from its Original, we must consider what State all Men are naturally in, and that is, a *State of perfect Freedom* to order their Actions, and dispose of their Possessions, and Persons as they think fit, within the bounds of the Law of Nature, without asking leave, or depending upon the Will of any other Man.

Source: John Locke, *Two Treatises of Government*. New York: New American Library, 1960, pp. 309, 311–312, 374–377, 416, 448,

A *State* also of *Equality*, wherein all the Power and Jurisdiction is reciprocal, no one having more than another: there being nothing more evident, than that Creatures of the same species and rank promiscuously born to all the same advantages of Nature, and the use of the same faculties, should also be equal one amongst another without Subordination or Subjection, unless the Lord and Master of them all, should by any manifest Declaration of his Will set one above another, and confer on him by an evident and clear appointment on undoubted Right to Dominion and Sovereignty. . . .

But though this be a *State of Liberty*, yet it is *not* a *State of Licence*, though Man in that State have an uncontrollable Liberty, to dispose of his Person or Possessions, yet he has not Liberty to destroy himself, or so much as any Creature in his Possession, but where some nobler use, than its bare Preservation calls for it. The *State of Nature* has a Law of Nature to govern it, which obliges every one; And Reason, which is that Law, teaches all Mankind, who will but consult it, that being all equal and independent, no one ought to harm another in his Life, Health, Liberty, or Possessions. . . .

And that all Men may be restrained from invading others' Rights, and from doing hurt to one another, and the Law of Nature be observed, which willeth the Peace and *Preservation of all Mankind*, the *Execution* of the Law of Nature is in that State, put into every Man's hands, whereby every one has a right to punish the transgressors of that Law to such a Degree, as may hinder its Violation. For the *Law of Nature* would, as all other Laws that concern Men in this World, be in vain, if there were no body that in the State of Nature, had a *Power to Execute* that Law, and thereby preserve the innocent and restrain offenders.

B   Individuals form a community, according to Locke, for their mutual benefit.

Men being, as has been said, by Nature, all free, equal and independent, no one can be put out of this Estate, and subjected to the Political Power of another, without his own *Consent*. The only way whereby any one devests himself of his Natural Liberty, and *puts on the bonds of Civil Society* is by agreeing with other Men to joyn and unite into a Community, for their comfortable, safe, and peaceable living one amongst another, in a secure Enjoyment of their Properties, and a greater Security against any that are not of it. . . . When any number of Men have so *consented to make one Community* or Government, they are thereby presently incorporated, and make *one Body Politick*, wherein the *Majority* have a Right to act and conclude the rest. . . .

. . . And therefore we see that in Assemblies impowered to act by positive Laws where no number is set by that positive Law which impowers them, the *act of the Majority* passes for the act of the whole, and of course determines, as having by the Law of Nature and Reason, the power of the whole.

And thus every Man, by consenting with others to make one Body Politick under one Government, puts himself under an Obligation to every one of that Society, to submit to the determination of the *majority*, and to be concluded by it; or else this *original Compact*, whereby he with others incorporates into *one Society*, would signifie nothing, and be no Compact, if he be left free, and under no other ties, than he was in before in the State of Nature. . . .

Whosoever therefore out of a state of Nature unite into a *Community*, must be understood to give up all the power, necessary to the ends for which they unite into Society, to the *majority* of the Community, unless they expressly agreed in any number greater than the majority. And this is done by barely agreeing to *unite into one Political Society,* which is *all the Compact that* is, or needs be, between the Individuals, that enter into, or make up a *Commonwealth.* And thus that, which begins and actually *constitutes any Political Society,* is nothing but the consent of any number of Freemen capable of a majority to unite and incorporate into such a Society. And this is that, and that only, which did, or could give *beginning* to any *lawful Government* in the World.

C The people have a contract with a sovereign. If the sovereign breaks the arrangement, the right of resistance may be used.

As Usurpation is the exercise of Power, which another hath a Right to; so *Tyranny* is *the exercise of Power beyond Right*, which no Body can have a Right to. And this is making use of the Power any one has in his hands; not for the good of those, who are under it, but for his own private separate Advantage. When the Governour, however intituled, makes not the Law, but his Will, the Rule; and his Commands and Actions are not directed to the preservation of the Properties of his People, but the satisfaction of his own Ambition, Revenge, Covetousness, or any other irregular Passion. . . .

Where-ever Law ends Tyranny begins, if the Law be transgressed to another's harm. And whosoever in Authority exceeds the Power given him by the Law, and makes use of the Force he has under his Command, to compass that upon the Subject, which the Law allows not, ceases in that to be a Magistrate, and acting without Authority, may be opposed, as any other Man, who by force invades the Right of another.

1. Describe Locke's position on the rights of man in the state of nature.

2. How does Locke distinguish between a state of liberty and a state of licence?

3. Why does humanity form a community with a government?

4. Compare Locke's description of the relationship between the governed and the governor to Hobbes' view of the subject and sovereign (see pages 43–46).

The World and the West in the Early Modern Era

CONTENTS

This miniature of the Virgin Mary was created by the Hindu artist Manohar (fl. 1580–c. 1620) who worked at the courts of the Mughal emperors Akbar (1556–1605) and Jahangir (1605–1628). The establishment of Jesuit missions in India in the 1570s led these rulers to become interested in Western religious art. The works they commissioned synthesized Catholic themes with local artistic traditions, such as Muslim miniatures and Hindu sculptures. This interest reflected the Mughal tolerance of all faiths and an open-mindedness in religious questions largely alien to Westerners at this time. For their part, the missionaries commissioned local artists to create illustrations for religious texts produced in Persian, and in order to better reach the people they were trying to convert, the missionaries permitted the artists to present Christian themes in local artistic idioms.

Mahommah Gardo Baquaqua

Mahommah Gardo Baquaqua was born to a family of Muslim merchants in Djougou (in the modern Republic of Benin) between 1824 and 1831. He was enslaved in 1845 and sent to Brazil. Baquaqua was first purchased by a baker, and then sold to a ship's captain. When the ship sailed to New York City in 1847, he escaped. His life in freedom took him to Haiti, McGrawville (upstate New York), and then to Chatham (Canada), where he wrote his autobiography. Shortly after the book was published, he went to England; he was living there in 1857 when he disappeared from the historical record. Baquaqua's autobiography is particularly important because it is one of the few narratives written by former slaves who were born in Africa. It is also the only one among ex-slave narratives in the United States written by a person who was not born there.

A Baquaqua writes about being sold and of his resistance to the condition of slavery.

These slaves never knew they were to be sent away, until they were placed on board the ship. I remained in this slave market but a day or two, before I was again sold to a slave dealer in the city, who again sold me to a man in the country, who was a baker, and resided not a great distance from Pernambuco.

When a slaver comes in, the news spreads like wild-fire, and down come all those that are interested in the arrival of the vessel with its cargo of living merchandize, who select from the stock those most suited to their different purposes, and purchase the slaves precisely in the same way that oxen or horses would be purchased in a market; but if there are not the kind of slaves in the one cargo, suited to the wants and wishes of the slave buyers, an order is given to the Captain for the particular sorts required, which are furnished to order the next time the ship comes into port. Great numbers make quite a business of this buying and selling human flesh, and do nothing else for a living, depending entirely upon this kind of traffic.

I had contrived whilst on my passage in the slave ship, to gather up a little knowledge of the Portuguese language, from the men before spoken of, and as my master was a Portuguese I could comprehend what he wanted very well, and gave him to understand that I would do all he needed as well as I was able, upon which he appeared quite satisfied.

His family consisted of himself, wife, two children and a woman who was related to them. He had four other slaves as well as myself. He was a Roman Catholic, and had family worship regularly twice a day, which was something after the following: He had a large clock standing in the entry

Source: Mahommah Gardo Baquaqua, *An Interesting Narrative.* Detroit: Pomeroy, 1854, pp. 44–48, 58–60, 64. Also available as Robin Law and Paul E. Lovejoy, eds., *The Biography of Mahommah Gardo Baquaqua: His Passage from Slavery to Freedom in Africa and America.* Princeton, N. J.: Markus Wiener Publishers, 2001.

of the house in which were some images made of clay, which were used in worship. We all had to kneel before them, the family in front, and the slaves behind. We were taught to chant some words which we did not know the meaning of. We also had to make the sign of the cross several times. Whilst worshipping, my master held a whip in his hand, and those who showed signs of inattention or drowsiness, were immediately brought to consciousness by a smart application of the whip. This mostly fell to the lot of the female slave, who would often fall asleep in spite of the images, crossings, and other like pieces of amusement.

I was soon placed at hard labor, such as none but slaves and horses are put to. At the time of this man's purchasing me, he was building a house, and had to fetch building stone from across the river, a considerable distance, and I was compelled to carry them that were so heavy it took three men to raise them upon my head, which burden I was obliged to bear for a quarter of a mile at least, down to where the boat lay. Sometimes the stone would press so hard upon my head that I was obliged to throw it down upon the ground, and then my master would be very angry indeed, and would say the cassoori [dog] had thrown down the stone, when I thought in my heart that he was the worst dog; but it was only a thought, as I dared not give utterance in words.

I soon improved in my knowledge of the Portuguese language whilst here, and was able very shortly to count a hundred. I was then sent out to sell bread for my master, first going round through the town, and then out into the country, and in the evening, after coming home again, sold in the market till nine at night. Being pretty honest and persevering, I generally sold out, but sometimes was not quite so successful, and then the lash was my portion. . . .

Things went on worse and worse, and I was very anxious to change masters, so I tried running away, but was soon caught, tied and carried back. I next tried what it would do for me by being unfaithful and indolent; so one day when I was sent out to sell bread as usual, I only sold a small quantity, and the money I took and spent for whiskey, which I drank pretty freely, and went home well drunk, when my master went to count the days taking in my basket and discovering the state of things, I was beaten very severely. I told him he must not whip me any more, and got quite angry, for the thought came into my head that I would kill him, and afterwards destroy myself. I at last made up my mind to drown myself; I would rather die than live to be a slave. I then ran down to the river and threw myself in, but being seen by some persons who were in a boat, I was rescued from drowning. The tide was low at the time, or their efforts would most likely have been unavailing, and notwithstanding my predetermination, I thanked God that my life had been preserved, and that so wicked a deed had not been consummated. It led me seriously to reflect that "God moves in a mysterious way," and that all his acts are acts of kindness and mercy.

I was then but a poor heathen, almost as ignorant as a Hottentot, and had not learned the true God, nor any of his divine commandments. Yet ignorant and slave as I was, slavery I loathed, principally as I suppose, because I was its victim. After this sad attempt upon my life, I was taken to my master's house, who tied my hands behind me, and placed my feet together and whipped me most unmercifully, and beat me about the head and face with a heavy stick, then shook me by the neck, and struck my head against the door posts, which cut and bruised me about the temples, the scars from which savage treatment are visible at this time, and will remain so as long as I live.

After all this cruelty he took me to the city, and sold me to a dealer, where he had taken me once before . . . .

The man to whom I was again sold was very cruel indeed. He bought two females at the time he bought me; one of them was a beautiful girl, and he treated her with shocking barbarity.

After a few weeks he shipped me off to Rio Janeiro, where I remained two weeks previous to being again sold. There was a colored man there who wanted to buy me, but for some reason or other he did not complete the purchase. I merely mention this fact to illustrate that slaveholding is generated in power, and any one having the means of buying his fellow creature with the paltry dross, can become a slave owner, no matter his color, his creed or country, and that the colored man would as soon enslave his fellow man as the white man, had he the power.

I was at length sold to a Captain of a vessel who was what may be termed "a hard case." He invited me to go and see his Senora. I made my best bow to her, and was soon installed into my new office, that of scouring the brass work about the ship, cleaning the knives and forks, and doing other little matters necessary to be done about the cabin. I did not at first like my situation; but as I got acquainted with the crew and the rest of the slaves, I got along pretty well. In a short time I was promoted to the office of under-steward. The steward provided for the table, and I carried the provisions to the cook and waited at table; being pretty smart, they gave me plenty to do. A short time after, the captain and steward disagreed, and he gave up his stewardship, when the keys of his office were entrusted to me. I did all in my power to please my master, the captain, and he in return placed confidence in me.

B In Brazil, Baquaqua hopes to sail to New York, and to obtain his freedom.

When the cargo was landed, an English merchant having a quantity of coffee for shipment to New York, my master was engaged for the purpose, and it was arranged, after some time that I should accompany him, together with several others to serve on ship board.

We all had learned, that at New York there was no slavery; that it was a free country and that if we at once got there we had nothing to dread from our cruel slave masters, and we were all most anxious to get there.

Previous to the time of the ship's sailing, we were informed that we were going to a land of freedom. I said then you will never see me any more after I once get there. I was overjoyed at the idea of going to a free country, and a ray of hope dawned upon me, that the day was not far distant when I should be a free man. Indeed I felt myself already *free*! How beautifully the sun shone on that eventful morning, the morning of our departure for that land of freedom we had heard so much about.

C In Haiti, Baquaqua enters the service of Rev. William L. Judd.

I remained with him upwards of two years, and a better man or christian than Mr. Judd, in my opinion, cannot be found. He treated me with every kindness; color to him being no cause of ill treatment. Neither shall I ever forget the kindness of his good lady; she behaved to me all the time of my servitude even as a christian should behave. I loved her for her goodness, although at all times I did not behave even to them as they deserved. I must confess, I sometimes treated them rather badly. I had not much gratitude then. I would often get very drunk and be abusive to them, but they over-looked my bad behavior always, and when Mrs. Judd would try to coax me to go home and behave myself, I would fight her and tell her I would not.

After my conversion to christianity I gave up drinking and all other kinds of vices. At the end of that time a stir was made in Hayti to enrol the militia; and being opposed to the spirit of war as well as was my master and mistress, it was agreed that I should leave Hayti on that account, and they provided for me a passage on board a vessel bound to New York, in order to educate me preparatory to going to my own people in Africa, to preach the Gospel of glad tidings of great joy to the ignorant and benighted of my fellow country-men who are now believers in the false prophet Mahomed.

D Baquaqua leaves McGrawville after a short stay and goes to Canada.

After this I returned to McGrawville for a short time, when, having a desire to see the manners and customs of the people living under the Government of Queen Victoria, of whom I had heard so much, induced me to go to Canada, where I remained a short time, and being so well pleased with the reception I there met with, I at once determined to become a subject of her Majesty, for which purpose I attended at the proper office, gave the oath of allegiance, and procured my papers of naturalization without any difficulty.

I was kindly treated by all classes wherever I went, and must say in my heart I never expected to receive in a nation so distant from my native home, so much kindness, attention and humanity. I am thankful to God that I enjoy the blessings of liberty, in peace and tranquility, and that I am now in a land where "none dare make me afraid," where every man can or may "sit down under his own vine, and under his own fig tree" where every man acting as a man, no matter what his color, is regarded as a brother, and where all are equally free to do and to say.

1. What contradiction is presented in the description of the slaves attending a religious ceremony while the master carries a whip?

2. In what ways did slaves rebel against their masters?

3. What part of this narrative indicates that Baquaqua was being assimilated?

4. What impact did slavery have on owners as well as slaves?

Spain and its Empire

The idea that the King of Spain and his justice were accessible to all was one of the key elements that held together the vast Spanish empire in the Americas. The Aboriginal peoples who were subjects of that empire quickly learned how to function in the Spanish legal system; they were certainly not hesitant to appeal to the distant monarch to protect them from abuses committed by local Spaniards.

 Some town leaders, one of whom was a son of Montezuma, petition King Philip II for protection. Among the measures they request is that Bartolomé de las Casas be appointed their defender.

> To His Majesty [Don Philip, king of Spain], from the lords and principals [leaders] of the peoples of New Spain, May 11, 1556. . . .
> Our very High and very Powerful King and Lord:
> The lords and principals of the peoples of this New Spain, of Mexico and its surroundings, subjects and servants of Your Majesty, we kiss the royal feet of Your Majesty and with dutiful humility and respect we implore You and state that, given that we are in such great need of the protection and aid of Your Majesty, both for ourselves and for those whom we have in our charge, due to the many wrongs and damages that we receive from the Spaniards, because they are amongst us, and we amongst them, and because for the remedy of our necessities we are very much in need of a person who would be our defender, who would reside continuously in that royal court, to whom we could go with [our necessities], and give Your Majesty notice and true accounts of all of them, because we cannot, given the long distance there is from here to there, nor can we manifest them in writing, because they are so many and so great that it would be a great bother to Your Majesty, thus we ask and humbly beseech Your Majesty to appoint to us the bishop of Chiapas Don Fray Bartolomé de las Casas to take this charge of being our defender and that Your Majesty order him

Source: Miguel León-Portilla, ed., *The Broken Spears: The Aztec Account of the Conquest of Mexico.* Boston: Beacon Press Books, 1992, pp. 152–158.

to accept; and if by chance said bishop were unable because of his death or sickness, we beseech Your Majesty in such a case to appoint to us one of the principal persons of your royal court of good will and very Christian to whom we can appeal with the things that would come up, because so many of them are of such a type that they require solely your royal presence, and from it only, after God, do we expect the remedy, because otherwise we will suffer daily so many needs and we are so aggrieved that soon we will be ended, since every day we are more consumed and finished, because they expel us from our lands and deprive us of our goods, beyond the many other labors and personal tributes that daily are increased for us.

B Four years later, the Council of Huejotzingo writes to King Philip complaining of how their town's tribute had been assessed. The Council's letter begins by recounting how the town had supported the Spaniards against the Aztecs and how they had readily adopted Christianity.

Our Lord sovereign, you the king don Felipe. . . .

[B]efore anyone told us of or made us acquainted with your fame and your story, . . . and before we were told or taught the glory and name of our Lord God, . . . when your servants the Spaniards reached us and your captain general don Hernando Cortés arrived, . . . our Lord God the ruler of heaven and possessor of earth . . . enlightened us so that we took you as our king to belong to you and become your people and your subjects; not a single town surpassed us here in New Spain in that first and earliest we threw ourselves toward you, we gave ourselves to you, and furthermore no one intimidated us, no one forced us into it, but truly God caused us to deserve that voluntarily we adhered to you so that we gladly received the newly arrived Spaniards who reached us here in New Spain. . . . We received them very gladly, we embraced them, we saluted them with many tears, though we were not acquainted with them, and our fathers and grandfathers also did not know them; but by the mercy of our Lord God we truly came to know them. Since they are our neighbors, therefore we loved them; nowhere did we attack them. Truly we fed them and served them; some arrived sick, so that we carried them in our arms and on our backs, and we served them in many other ways which we are not able to say here. Although the people who are called and named Tlaxcalans indeed helped, yet we strongly pressed them to give aid, and we admonished them not to make war; but though we so admonished them, they made war and fought for fifteen days. But we, when a Spaniard was afflicted, without fail at once we managed to reach him. . . . We do not lie in this, for all the conquerors know it well, those who have died and some now living.

And when they began their conquest and war-making, then also we prepared ourselves well to aid them, for out came all of our war gear, our arms and provisions and all our equipment, and we not merely named someone, we went in person, we who rule, and we brought all our nobles and all of our vassals to aid the Spaniards. We helped not only in warfare, but we also gave them everything they needed; we fed and clothed them, and we would carry in our arms and on our backs those whom they wounded in war or who were very ill, and we did all the tasks in preparing for war. . . .

Our lord sovereign, we also say and declare before you that your fathers the twelve sons of St. Francis reached us, whom the very high priestly ruler the Holy Father sent and whom you sent, both taking pity on us so that they came to teach us the gospel, to teach us the holy Catholic faith and belief, to make us acquainted with the single deity God our Lord, and likewise God favored us and enlightened us, us of Huejotzingo, who dwell in your city, so that we gladly received them. When they entered the city of Huejotzingo, of our own free will we honored them and showed them esteem. When they embraced us so that we would abandon the wicked belief in many gods, we forthwith voluntarily left it; likewise they did us the good deed [of telling us] to destroy and burn the stones and wood that we worshiped as gods, and we did it; very willingly we destroyed, demolished, and burned the temples. Also when they gave us the holy gospel, the holy Catholic faith, with very good will and desire we received and grasped it; no one frightened us into it, no one forced us, but very willingly we seized it, and they gave us all the sacraments. Quietly and peacefully we arranged and ordered it among ourselves; no one, neither nobleman nor commoner, was ever tortured or burned for this, as was done on every hand here in New Spain. [The people of] many towns were forced and tortured, were hanged or burned, because they did not want to leave idolatry, and unwillingly they received the gospel and faith.

C After a lengthy prologue, the Council sets out its grievance.

Therefore now, in and through God, may you hear these our words, . . . so that you will exercise on us your rulership to console us and aid us in [this trouble] with which daily we weep and are sad. We are afflicted and sore pressed, and your town and city of Huejotzingo is as if it is about to disappear and be destroyed. Here is what is being done to us: now your stewards the royal officials and the prosecuting attorney Dr. Maldonado are assessing us a very great tribute to belong to you. The tribute we are to give is 14,800 pesos in money, and also all the bushels of maize.

Our lord sovereign, never has such happened to us in all the time since your servants and vassals the Spaniards came to us, for your servant don Hernando Cortés, late captain general, the Marqués del Valle, in all the time he lived here with us, always greatly cherished us and kept us happy; he never disturbed nor agitated us. Although we gave him tribute, he assigned it to us only with moderation; even though we gave him gold, it was only very little; no matter how much, no matter in what way, or if not very pure, he just received it gladly. He never reprimanded us or afflicted us, because it was evident to him and he understood well how very greatly we served and aided him. Also he told us many times that he would speak in our favor before you, that he would help us and inform you of all the ways in which we have aided and served you. . . . But perhaps before you he forgot us. How then shall we speak? We did not reach you, we were not given audience before you. Who then will speak for us? Unfortunate are we. Therefore now we place ourselves before you, our sovereign lord. . . .

> Your poor vassals who bow down humbly to you from afar,
> Don Leonardo Ramírez, governor. Don Mateo de la Corona, alcalde. . . .

Toribio de San [Cristó]bal Motolinía.

1. Why would the petitioners nominate a bishop as their protector?
2. How does this account compare to the actual events of the Spanish conquest?
3. How does this selection show the close ties that existed between the Spanish Crown and the Catholic Church?

Diego de Vargas

The northernmost point of the Spanish empire in the Americas was the province of New Mexico. In 1690, the Pueblo Indians rebelled and forced the Spaniards to flee. This was the only time that Native Americans succeeded in forcing Europeans to totally withdraw. Even in this case, success was only temporary; in 1692 a Spanish force commanded by Diego de Vargas (1643–1704) reclaimed the territory. De Vargas described the reconquest in his journals.

 On September 13, 1692, the Spaniards approach Santa Fe, the capital of New Mexico.

> Once they were all together, I told them that my order was that, after entering the plaza of the villa in sight of and near the fortress of the apostate, rebel, treacherous traitors, and their pueblo, the whole camp was to say five times, "Praise be the blessed sacrament of the altar." No one was to begin the battle, neither the men-at-arms nor the Indian allies, who are to be told this by the interpreters, although most of them and their captains speak and understand our language. The signal I would give to all to begin the battle and start the war with all force and courage was for me to unsheathe the sword I carried.
>
> Having given the order, I continued the march, going in close formation. After a short distance, I found myself in the villa's milpas [planted field], which surround its plaza, and we gave praise to the Lord. Having done so,

Source: Diego de Vargas, *By Force of Arms: The Journals of don Diego de Vargas, New Mexico, 1691–93.* Albuquerque: University of New Mexico Press, 1992, pp. 388–402.

the people of the villa immediately came out onto the ramparts of the fortress, occupying them from end to end with all sorts of people, men, women, boys and girls, and children. As dawn was breaking, their forms could be distinguished and "Praise be the holy sacrament" was repeated to them. The interpreters . . . spoke to them in their languages, Tewa and Tano, which are one and the same.

They replied that they believed we were not Spaniards, but Pecos and Apache liars. . . .

After sunrise, I approached about twenty paces closer with the interpreter, my secretary of government and war, and the captain of the presidio, telling them that I had come, sent from Spain by his majesty, the king, our lord, to pardon them and so that they might again be Christians, as they had been, and the devil would not lead them astray. This was so they might be assured of my truthfulness, given that they knew the Virgin, our Lady, whose image was on the standard, as witness to the truth I was telling them so that they might believe and be assured of my good intentions. I ordered the royal alferez [standard bearer] to show them the image of the Virgin, as I myself took it in my hand, showing it and saying to them that they had but to look at her and recognize her to be our Lady the Queen and the Blessed Virgin and that on the other side of the royal standard were the arms of the king, our lord, so that they might know he sent me. . . .

So that they might believe that peace was sure and I would pardon them in the name of his majesty, the king, our lord, I would offer as a witness the image of the Blessed Virgin on the royal standard, which I again showed them, taking it anew in my hand. Bracing myself in the stirrups, I effectively made the gestures necessary because of their disbelief. Taking the rosary from my pocket, I showed them a holy cross of Jerusalem I had placed on it, telling them that I took as my witnesses the holy cross and the Virgin, our most holy Lady, whose image I carried on the royal standard they were looking at. I would pardon them in his majesty's name, and they should believe me and come down and shake hands with me. I also brought the three fathers so that they might absolve them of the great sin they had committed of having left our holy faith.

B Despite De Vargas' assurances, the Pueblos refused to submit. Only after he cut off the water supply to the fortress and laid siege to it, did the Pueblos surrender. On September 14, De Vargas formally took possession of New Mexico once again.

Today, Sunday, 14 of the present month of the current year, the Day of the Exaltation of the Holy Cross, I, the governor and captain general, spent the night with the vigilance required and the men-at-arms on guard duty. They told me that many people had come and gone from the fortress all night long and it would be risky to enter in my finery, as I had dressed, without weapons. Nevertheless, I told them I was going to be present at the absolution the reverend missionary fathers were going to grant the rebel, apostate Indians and that no one should fire without my order. They should remain on horseback in the plaza of the villa with only the leaders, their captain, and the citizens entering with me and the missionary fathers.

In this manner, I left, marching from the plaza de armas toward the fortress. When the alferez arrived with the royal standard, I ordered him to enter with me, the fathers, and the men-at-arms indicated. Once inside, I found a cross slightly shorter than a man's height set up on the patio. Within view of the Indians, I knelt on one knee and kissed the cross. . . .

Once all the people had come down and assembled, I told them through the interpreters that they could be calm, now that they knew my good intentions, and content that they would be pardoned and reduced to our holy faith and the king, our lord (may God keep him). They were his vassals, and in his royal name, I was returning to revalidate and reclaim his possession not only of this kingdom, provinces, and all the land, but also of them. This was because he was their lord and rightful king, and no other, and they should consider themselves fortunate to be his vassals and have such a king, lord, and sovereign monarch.

I also ordered the alferez to raise the royal standard three times, while I, the governor and captain general, told and ordered them to repeat three times, "Long live the king, our lord (may God keep him), Carlos II, king of all the Spains, all this New World, and the kingdom and provinces of New Mexico," which they said three times. "These are his kingdom and provinces and his vassals, newly reduced and conquered." They responded three times, "May he live for many years and reign happily." Having done so, with great rejoicing and showing their happiness, they threw their hats in the air, and the religious, the reverend missionary fathers, knelt and offered a prayer of thanksgiving.

All the populace was in front of the holy cross to hear the Te Deum. The holy water having already been prepared, they then absolved them of their apostasy. This was preceded by a sermon the reverend father, fray Francisco Corvera, gave through an interpreter. After he granted absolution, which the Indians received kneeling with their hands together, some of them sang and repeated the alabado. When the ceremony was over, I embraced each of them again, shook their hands, and was greatly pleased by hearing them repeat the alabado to the women and children.

. . . So that what has been referred to — the possession, the absolution and the rest — may be of record, I signed it with those who knew how and my secretary of government and war.

1. How does De Vargas attempt to solve the confrontation peacefully?

2. What leadership qualities does De Vargas demonstrate?

3. Considering that De Vargas was sent to reconquer New Mexico, what details appear to be lacking from his account of the events?

St. Francis Xavier

St. Francis Xavier (1506–1552) was born in Spain, and along with St. Ignatius Loyola (1491–1556), he founded the Society of Jesus. Immediately after its creation, St. Francis went to Asia as a missionary. He arrived in Goa in 1542 and spent the remaining ten years of his life in Asia. He was canonized in 1622. His letters are an important source for seeing early European reactions to the people and societies of the region. Following are excerpts from his "Letter from Japan, to the Society of Jesus in Europe" (1552).

A St. Francis Xavier begins this letter with a general description of the Japanese people and their religion.

> May the grace and charity of our Lord Jesus Christ be ever with us! Amen.
>
> Japan is a very large empire entirely composed of islands. One language is spoken throughout, not very difficult to learn. This country was discovered by the Portuguese eight or nine years ago. The Japanese are very ambitious of honours and distinctions, and think themselves superior to all nations in military glory and valour. They prize and honour all that has to do with war, and all such things, and there is nothing of which they are so proud as of weapons adorned with gold and silver. They always wear swords and daggers both in and out of the house, and when they go to sleep they hang them at the bed's head. In short, they value arms more than any people I have ever seen. . . . They are very polite to each other, but not to foreigners, whom they utterly despise. They spend their means on arms, bodily adornment, and on a number of attendants, and do not in the least care to save money. They are, in short, a very warlike people, and engaged in continual wars among themselves; the most powerful in arms bearing the most extensive sway. They have all one sovereign, although for one hundred and fifty years past the princes have ceased to obey him, and this is the cause of their perpetual feuds.
>
> In these countries there is a great number, both of men and of women, who profess a religious rule of life; they are called bonzes and bonzesses. There are two sorts of bonzes — the one wear a grey dress, the others a black one. There is great rivalry between them, the grey monks being set against the black monks, and accusing them of ignorance and bad morals. . . .
>
> On certain days the bonzes preach publicly. The sum of all their discourses is that none of the people will be condemned to hell, whatever may be the number of their past and present crimes, for the founders of their sects will take them out of the midst of those flames, if perchance they are condemned to them, especially if the bonzes who have made satisfaction for them constitute themselves their intercessors. And indeed

Source: Henry James Coleridge, ed., *The Life and Letters of St. Francis Xavier*, 2nd ed., 2 Vols., Vol. II. London: Burns & Oates, 1890, pp. 331–350.

the bonzes boast greatly to the people of their own holiness, on the ground of their obedience to the five laws. At the same time, they also say that the poor who are unable to show kindness to the bonzes have no hope of escaping hell. And they say women are as badly off if they neglect the five precepts. For they say that each woman, on account of her monthly courses, is covered with more sins than all men put together, and that thus so foul a creature can hardly be saved. They go on to say that there is some hope even for women of escaping from the prison of hell, if they give a great deal more than the men to the bonzes. . . .

The Japanese doctrines teach absolutely nothing concerning the creation of the world, of the sun, the moon, the stars, the heavens, the earth, sea, and the rest, and do not believe that they have any origin but themselves. The people were greatly astonished on hearing it said that there is one sole Author and common Father of souls, by whom they were created. This astonishment was caused by the fact that in their religious traditions there is nowhere any mention of a Creator of the universe. If there existed one single First Cause of all things, surely, they said, the Chinese, from whom they derive their religion, must have known it. For the Japanese give the Chinese the pre-eminence in wisdom and prudence in everything relating either to religion or to political government. They asked us a multitude of questions concerning this First Cause of all things; whether He were good or bad, whether the same First Cause were the origin of good and of evil.

B St. Francis Xavier then describes some of the aspects of Christianity that most puzzled the Japanese.

They were quite unable to digest the idea that men could be cast into hell without any hope of deliverance. They said, therefore, that their doctrines rested, more than ours, on clemency and mercy. In the end, by God's favour, we succeeded in solving all their questions, so as to leave no doubt remaining in their minds. The Japanese are led by reason in everything more than any other people, and in general they are all so insatiable of information and so importunate in their questions that there is no end either to their arguments with us, or to their talking over our answers among themselves. They did not know that the world is round, they knew nothing of the course of the sun and stars, so that when they asked us and we explained to them these and other like things, such as the causes of comets, of the lightning and of rain, they listened to us most eagerly, and appeared delighted to hear us, regarding us with profound respect as extremely learned persons. This idea of our great knowledge opened the way to us for sowing the seed of religion in their minds. . . .

One of the things that most of all pains and torments these Japanese is, that we teach them that the prison of hell is irrevocably shut, so that there is no egress therefrom. For they grieve over the fate of their departed children, of their parents and relatives, and they often show their grief by their tears. So they ask us if there is any hope, any way to free them by prayer from that eternal misery, and I am obliged to answer that there is absolutely none. Their grief at this affects and torments them wonderfully; they almost pine away with sorrow. But there is this good thing about their trouble — it makes one hope that they will all be the more laborious for their own salvation, lest they like their forefathers, should be condemned to everlasting punishment. They often ask if God cannot take their fathers out of hell, and why their punishment must never have an end. We gave them a satisfactory answer, but they did not cease to grieve over the misfortune of their relatives; and I can hardly restrain my tears sometimes at seeing men so dear to my heart suffer such intense pain about a thing which is already done with and can never be undone.

 St. Francis Xavier includes a brief mention of China, which he hoped to visit but never reached.

Opposite to Japan lies China, an immense empire, enjoying profound peace, and which, as the Portuguese merchants tell us, is superior to all Christian states in the practice of justice and equity. The Chinese whom I have seen in Japan and elsewhere, and whom I got to know, are white in colour, like the Japanese, are acute, and eager to learn. In intellect they are superior even to the Japanese. Their country abounds in plenty of all things, and very many cities of great extent cover its surface. The cities are very populous; the houses ornamented with stone roofings, and very elegant. All reports say that the empire is rich in every sort of produce, but especially in silk. I find, from the Chinese themselves, that amongst them may be found many people of many different nations and religions, and, as far as I could gather from what they said, I suspect that among them are Jews and Mahometans.

Nothing leads me to suppose that there are Christians there. I hope to go there during this year, 1552, and penetrate even to the Emperor himself. China is that sort of kingdom, that if the seed of the Gospel is once sown, it may be propagated far and wide. And moreover, if the Chinese accept the Christian faith, the Japanese would give up the doctrines which the Chinese have taught them. . . . I am beginning to have great hopes that God will soon provide free entrance to China, not only to our Society, but to religions of all Orders, that a large field may be laid open to pious and holy men of all sorts, in which there may be great room for devotion and zeal, in recalling men who are now lost to the way of truth and salvation.

1. How does St. Francis Xavier describe Japanese society regarding politics and religion?

2. Compare his concept of hell to the Japanese perspective.

3. What does St. Francis Xavier admire in the Japanese?

4. Why does he not condemn the Japanese and Chinese for not being Christian?

Matteo Ricci

Matteo Ricci (1552–1610) joined the Society of Jesus, known as the Jesuits, in Italy. He arrived in China in 1582, and spent the following eighteen years learning Chinese language and customs and studying Confucian philosophy. He was the first educated European to have lived for a long time in East Asia and he acquired a deep knowledge of East Asian society. His *Journals*, diaries written in Italian and Latin, were first published in Europe shortly after his death. Ricci also wrote numerous books in Chinese about Western civilization and Christianity.

A Ricci describes the abundance and beauty of China.

> Due to the great extent of this country north and south as well as east and west, it can be safely asserted that nowhere else in the world is found such a variety of plant and animal life within the confines of a single kingdom. The wide range of climatic conditions in China gives rise to a great diversity of vegetable products, some of which are most readily grown in tropical countries, others in arctic, and others again in the temperate zones. The Chinese themselves, in their geographies, give us detailed accounts of the fertility of the various provinces and of the variety of their products. It hardly falls within the scope of my present treatise to enter into a comprehensive discussion of these matters. Generally speaking, it may be said with truth that all of these writers are correct when they say that everything which the people need for their well-being and sustenance, whether it be for food or clothing or even delicacies and superfluities, is abundantly produced within the borders of the kingdom and not imported from foreign climes. I would even venture to say that practically everything which is grown in Europe is likewise found in China. If not, then what is missing here is abundantly supplied by various other products unknown to Europeans. To begin with, the soil of China supplies its people with every species of grain — barley, millet, winter wheat, and similar grains. . . .
>
> Much the same can be said of the variety and quality of table vegetables and the cultivation of garden herbs, all of which the Chinese use in far greater quantities than is common among the people of Europe. In fact, there are many among the common folk who live entirely upon a vegetable diet through the whole course of their lives, either because they are forced to do so by reason of poverty or because they embrace this course of life for some religious motive. The profusion of flowering plants really leaves nothing to be desired, as the Chinese have many species unknown to us which make a deep appeal to the aesthetic sense and show forth the lavish bounty of the Creator.

Source: Matteo Ricci, *China in the Sixteenth Century: The Journals of Matteo Ricci: 1583–1610*, trans. Louis Gallagher. New York: Random House, 1953, pp. 10–11, 20–21, 25, 54–55, 98, 96–97.

B Printing, Ricci realizes, was present in China long before it was "invented" in the West.

> The art of printing was practiced in China at a date somewhat earlier than that assigned to the beginning of printing in Europe, which was about 1405. It is quite certain that the Chinese knew the art of printing at least five centuries ago, and some of them assert that printing was known to their people before the beginning of the Christian era, about 50 B.C. Their method of printing differs widely from that employed in Europe, and our method would be quite impracticable for them because of the exceedingly large number of Chinese characters and symbols. At present they cut their characters in a reverse position and in a simplified form, on a comparatively small tablet made for the most part from the wood of the pear tree or the apple tree, although at times the wood of the jujube tree is also used for this purpose.
>
> Their method of making printed books is quite ingenious. The text is written in ink, with a brush made of very fine hair, on a sheet of paper which is inverted and pasted on a wooden tablet. When the paper has become thoroughly dry, its surface is scraped off quickly and with great skill, until nothing but a fine tissue bearing the characters remains on the wooden tablet. Then, with a steel graver, the workman cuts away the surface following the outlines of the characters until these alone stand out in low relief. From such a block a skilled printer can make copies with incredible speed, turning out as many as fifteen hundred copies in a single day. Chinese printers are so skilled in engraving these blocks, that no more time is consumed in making one of them than would be required by one of our printers in setting up a form of type and making the necessary corrections.

C According to Ricci, China and the West have much in common.

> In the practice of the arts and the crafts we have mentioned, the Chinese are certainly different from all other people, but for the most part their practice of the other arts and sciences is quite the same as our own, despite the great distance that separates them from our civilization. In fact, the similarity of customs is rather remarkable when we consider their methods of eating and sitting and sleeping, in which they alone of all nations outside of Europe are quite in accord with the West. Their use of tables, chairs, and beds is wholly unknown to any of the peoples of the states that border on China, all of whom place straw mats on the ground or floor and use them in place of chair, bed, or table. This difference of custom is quite remarkable, and I am somewhat at a loss to explain it . . . . One may gather from what has been said that there are numerous points of advantageous contact between ourselves and the Chinese people.

D Ricci notes significant differences as well. He has great respect for Chinese culture and for Confucianism.

Before closing this chapter on Chinese public administration, it would seem to be quite worth while recording a few more things in which this people differ from Europeans. To begin with, it seems to be quite remarkable when we stop to consider it, that in a kingdom of almost limitless expanse and innumerable population, and abounding in copious supplies of every description, though they have a well-equipped army and navy that could easily conquer the neighboring nations, neither the King nor his people ever think of waging a war of aggression. They are quite content with what they have and are not ambitious of conquest. In this respect they are much different from the people of Europe, who are frequently discontent with their own governments and covetous of what others enjoy. While the nations of the West seem to be entirely consumed with the idea of supreme domination, they cannot even preserve what their ancestors have bequeathed them, as the Chinese have done through a period of some thousands of years. . . .

Another remarkable fact and quite worthy of note as marking a difference from the West, is that the entire kingdom is administered by the Order of the Learned, commonly known as The Philosophers. The responsibility for orderly management of the entire realm is wholly and completely committed to their charge and care. The army, both officers and soldiers, hold them in high respect and show them the promptest obedience and deference, and not infrequently the military are disciplined by them as a schoolboy might be punished by his master. Policies of war are formulated and military questions are decided by the Philosophers only, and their advice and counsel has more weight with the King than that of the military leaders. . . .

. . . The Literati deny that they belong to a sect and claim that their class or society is rather an academy instituted for the proper government and general good of the kingdom. One might say in truth that the teachings of this academy, save in some few instances, are so far from being contrary to Christian principles, that such an institution could derive great benefit from Christianity and might be developed and perfected by it. . . .

The Temple of Confucius is really the cathedral of the upper lettered and exclusive class of the Literati. The law demands that a temple be built to the Prince of Chinese Philosophers in every city, and in that particular part of the city which has been described as the center of learning. These temples are sumptuously built and adjoining them is the palace of the magistrate who presides over those who have acquired their first literary degree. In the most conspicuous place in the temple there will be a statue of Confucius, or if not a statue, a plaque with his name carved in large letters of gold. Near to this are placed the statues of certain of his disciples whom the Chinese revere as saints, but of an inferior order. . . .

The ultimate purpose and the general intention of this sect, the Literati, is public peace and order in the kingdom. They likewise look toward the economic security of the family and the virtuous training of the individual. The precepts they formulate are certainly directive to such ends and quite in conformity with the light of conscience and with Christian truth. They make capital of five different combinations, making up the entire gamut of human relations; namely, the relations of father and son, husband and wife, master and servants, older and younger brothers, and finally, of companions and equals. According to their belief, they alone know how to respect these relationships, which are supposed to be wholly unknown to foreigners, or if known, wholly neglected. Celibacy is not approved of and polygamy is permitted. Their writings explain at length the second precept of charity: "Do not do unto others what you would not wish others to do unto you." It really is remarkable how highly they esteem the respect and obedience of children toward parents, the fidelity of servants to a master, and devotion of the young to their elders.

1. What observations demonstrate Ricci's admiration of the Chinese?

2. What advantages does Ricci think would occur in Europe through contact with China?

3. How might Ricci's observations confirm the Chinese belief that they were the most civilized nation on earth?

The Closure of Japan

Japanese rulers were much more concerned about the presence of Europeans than were the rulers of China. The Japanese sought to limit European presence as much as possible. The early success of Catholic missionaries only heightened these concerns. The Shogun Ieyasu issued the following two decrees, which effectively closed Japan to Westerners, in 1635 and 1639. This closure would last until 1854, and was ended only under the threat of force.

 The "Closed Country Edict of 1635" was directed to the two commissioners of the port city of Nagasaki, one of the centres of Japanese Christianity.

Closed Country Edict of 1635

1. Japanese ships are strictly forbidden to leave for foreign countries.

2. No Japanese is permitted to go abroad. If there is anyone who attempts to do so secretly, he must be executed. The ship so involved must be impounded and its owner arrested, and the matter must be reported to the higher authority.

Source: David John Lu, ed. and trans., *Sources of Japanese History,* vol. I. New York: McGraw-Hill, 1974, pp. 207–209.

3. If any Japanese returns from overseas after residing there, he must be put to death.

4. If there is any place where the teachings of padres is practiced, the two of you must order a thorough investigation.

5. Any informer revealing the whereabouts of the followers of padres must be rewarded accordingly. If anyone reveals the whereabouts of a high ranking padre, he must be given one hundred pieces of silver. For those of lower ranks, depending on the deed, the reward must be set accordingly.

6. If a foreign ship has an objection (to the measures adopted) and it becomes necessary to report the matter to Edo, you may ask the Omura domain to provide ships to guard the foreign ship. . . .

7. If there are any Southern Barbarians who propagate the teachings of padres, or otherwise commit crimes, they may be incarcerated in the prison. . . .

8. All incoming ships must be carefully searched for the followers of padres.

9. No single trading city shall be permitted to purchase all the merchandise brought by foreign ships.

10. Samurai are not permitted to purchase any goods originating from foreign ships directly from Chinese merchants in Nagasaki.

11. After a list of merchandise brought by foreign ships is sent to Edo, as before you may order that commercial dealings may take place without waiting for a reply from Edo.

12. After settling the price, all white yarns brought by foreign ships shall be allocated to the five trading cities and other quarters as stipulated.

14. The date of departure homeward of foreign ships shall not be later than the twentieth day of the ninth month. Any ships arriving in Japan later than usual shall depart within fifty days of their arrival. As to the departure of Chinese ships, you may use your discretion to order their departure after the departure of the Portuguese *galeota* [fleet].

15. The goods brought by foreign ships which remained unsold may not be deposited or accepted for deposit.

16. The arrival in Nagasaki of representatives of the five trading cities shall not be later than the fifth day of the seventh month. Anyone arriving later than that date shall lose the quota assigned to his city.

17. Ships arriving in Hirado must sell their raw silk at the price set in Nagasaki, and are not permitted to engage in business transactions until after the price is established in Nagasaki.

   You are hereby required to act in accordance with the provisions set above. It is so ordered.

B The edict on the "Exclusion of the Portuguese" of 1639 is about the activities of the Portuguese in support of the spread of Catholicism.

Exclusion of the Portuguese, 1639

1. The matter relating to the proscription of Christianity is known (to the Portuguese). However, heretofore they have secretly transported those who are going to propagate that religion.

2. If those who believe in that religion band together in an attempt to do evil things, they must be subjected to punishment.

3. While those who believe in the preaching of padres are in hiding, there are incidents in which that country (Portugal) has sent gifts to them for their sustenance.

In view of the above, hereafter entry by the Portuguese *galeota* is forbidden. If they insist on coming (to Japan), the ships must be destroyed and anyone aboard those ships must be beheaded. We have received the above order and are thus transmitting it to you accordingly.

The above concerns our disposition with regard to the *galeota*.

Memorandum

With regard to those who believe in Christianity, you are aware that there is a proscription, and thus knowing, you are not permitted to let padres and those who believe in their preaching to come aboard your ships. If there is any violation, all of you who are aboard will be considered culpable. If there is anyone who hides the fact that he is a Christian and boards your ship, you may report it to us. A substantial reward will be given to you for this information.

This memorandum is to be given to those who come on Chinese ships. (A similar note to the Dutch ships.)

1. What foreign activities does the Edict of 1635 prohibit?
2. How does this Edict attempt to control trade between Japan and other states?
3. What aspects of Christian teachings may have been seen as a threat to Japanese authorities?

Chrestien LeClerq and the Mi'Kmaq

Chrestien LeClerq (1641–1700) was a French Recollet (a Catholic missionary order) who spent the period between 1675 and 1687 among the Mi'Kmaq of the Gaspésie region of New France. His book, *New Relation of Gaspesia, with the Customs and Religion of the Gaspesian Indians*, which was published in Paris in 1691, is a central source for our knowledge about the Mi'Kmaq during the first years of their encounter with the French.

A LeClerq relates how one Mi'Kmaq saw the new arrivals.

I am greatly astonished that the French have so little cleverness, as they seem to exhibit in the matter of which thou hast just told me on their behalf, in the effort to persuade us to convert our poles, our barks, and our wigwams into those houses of stone and of wood which are tall and lofty, according to their account, as these trees. Very well! But why now, . . . do men of five to six feet in height need houses which are sixty to eighty? For, in fact, as thou knowest very well thyself, Patriarch — do we not find in our own all the conveniences and the advantages that you have with yours, such as reposing, drinking, sleeping, eating, and amusing ourselves with our friends when we wish? This is not all, . . . my brother, hast thou as much ingenuity and cleverness as the Indians, who carry their houses and their wigwams with them so that they may lodge wheresoever they please, independently of any seignior whatsoever? Thou art not as bold nor as stout as we, because when thou goest on a voyage thou canst not carry upon thy shoulders thy buildings and thy edifices. Therefore it is necessary that thou preparest as many lodgings as thou makest changes of residence, or else thou lodgest in a hired house which does not belong to thee. As for us, we find ourselves secure from all these inconveniences, and we can always say, more truly than thou, that we are at home everywhere, because we set up our wigwams with ease wheresoever we go, and without asking permission of anybody. Thou reproachest us, very inappropriately, that our country is a little hell in contrast with France, which thou comparest to a terrestrial paradise, inasmuch as it yields thee, so thou sayest, every kind of provision in abundance. Thou sayest of us also that we are the most miserable and most unhappy of all men, living without religion, without manners, without honour, without social order, and, in a word, without any rules, like the beasts in our woods and our forests, lacking bread, wine, and a thousand other comforts which thou hast in superfluity in Europe. Well, my brother, if thou dost not yet know the real feelings which our Indians have towards thy country and towards all thy nation, it is proper that I inform thee at once.

B The Mi'Kmaq believes that his people are far happier than the French.

I beg thee now to believe that, all miserable as we seem in thine eyes, we consider ourselves nevertheless much happier than thou in this, that we are very content with the little that we have; and believe also once for all, I pray, that thou deceivest thyself greatly if thou thinkest to persuade us that thy country is better than ours. For if France, as thou sayest, is a little terrestrial paradise, art thou sensible to leave it? And why abandon wives, children, relatives, and friends? Why risk thy life and thy property every year, and why venture thyself with such risk, in any season whatsoever,

Source: C. G. Calloway, ed., *The World Turned Upside Down.* New York: St. Martin's Press, 1994, pp. 50–52.

to the storms and tempests of the sea in order to come to a strange and barbarous country which thou considerest the poorest and least fortunate of the world? Besides, since we are wholly convinced of the contrary, we scarcely take the trouble to go to France, because we fear, with good reason, lest we find little satisfaction there, seeing, in our own experience, that those who are natives thereof leave it every year in order to enrich themselves on our shores. We believe, further, that you are also incomparably poorer than we, and that you are only simple journeymen, valets, servants, and slaves, all masters and grand captains though you may appear, seeing that you glory in our old rags and in our miserable suits of beaver which can no longer be of use to us, and that you find among us, in the fishery for cod which you make in these parts, the wherewithal to comfort your misery and the poverty which oppresses you. As to us, we find all our riches and all our conveniences among ourselves, without trouble and without exposing our lives to the dangers in which you find yourselves constantly through your long voyages. And, whilst feeling compassion for you in the sweetness of our repose, we wonder at the anxieties and cares which you give yourselves night and day in order to load your ship. We see also that all your people live, as a rule, only upon cod which you catch among us. It is everlastingly nothing but cod — cod in the morning, cod at midday, cod at evening, and always cod, until things come to such a pass that if you wish some good morsels, it is at our expense; and you are obliged to have recourse to the Indians, whom you despise so much, and to beg them to go a-hunting that you may be regaled. Now tell me this one little thing, if thou hast any sense: Which of these two is the wisest and happiest — he who labours without ceasing and only obtains, and that with great trouble, enough to live on, or he who rests in comfort and finds all that he needs in the pleasure of hunting and fishing? It is true, . . . that we have not always had the use of bread and of wine which your France produces; but, in fact, before the arrival of the French in these parts, did not the Gaspesians live much longer than now? And if we have not any longer among us any of those old men of a hundred and thirty to forty years, it is only because we are gradually adopting your manner of living, for experience is making it very plain that those of us live longest who, despising your bread, your wine, and your brandy, are content with their natural food of beaver, of moose, of waterfowl, and fish, in accord with the custom of our ancestors and of all the Gaspesian nation. Learn now, my brother, once for all, because I must open to thee my heart: there is no Indian who does not consider himself infinitely more happy and more powerful than the French.

1. Which observations made by the Mi'Kmaq question the French thoughts of superiority?

2. Why does the Mi'Kmaq feel he has more reason to be happy than the French?

3. Considering the living conditions in seventeenth-century France, how accurate are the Mi'Kmaq's observations of French life?

Peter the Great

Czar Peter the Great (1689–1725) was the first ruler of Russia to feel the need to undertake a comprehensive program of "Westernization." The stimulus, as it would be in other places later on, was the belief that the adoption of Western techniques and customs would help overcome his country's military inferiority. The following are only a handful of over three hundred decrees made by Peter that touched virtually all aspects of Russian life.

A Peter decrees that Russians should dress in the Western style.

Decree on Western Dress (1701)

Western dress shall be worn by all the boyars, members of our councils and of our court . . . gentry of Moscow, secretaries . . . provincial gentry, gosti [Russian merchants who often served the Czar and the state], government officials, strel'tsy [members of the imperial guard in Moscow], members of the guilds purveying for our household, citizens of Moscow of all ranks, and residents of provincial cities . . . excepting the clergy and peasant tillers of the soil. The upper dress shall be of French or Saxon cut, and the lower dress . . . — (including) waistcoat, trousers, boots, shoes, and hats — shall be of the German type. They shall also ride German saddles. Likewise the womenfolk of all ranks, including the priests', deacons', and church attendants' wives, the wives of the dragoons, the soldiers, and the strel'tsy, and their children, shall wear Western dresses, hats, jackets, and underwear — undervests and petticoats — and shoes. From now on no one of the above-mentioned is to wear Russian dress or Circassian coats, sheepskin coats, or Russian peasant coats, trousers, boots, and shoes. It is also forbidden to ride Russian saddles, and the craftsmen shall not manufacture them or sell them at the marketplaces.

B Peter's most famous decree was on shaving. Here, he challenges traditional religious dress as well as social customs.

Decree on Shaving (1705)

A decree to be published in Moscow and in all the provincial cities: Henceforth, in accordance with this, His Majesty's decree, all court attendants . . . provincial service men, government officials of all ranks, military men, all the gosti, members of the wholesale merchants' guild, and members of the guilds purveying for our household must shave their beards and moustaches. But, if it happens that some of them do not wish to shave their beards and moustaches, let a yearly tax be collected from such persons; from court attendants . . . provincial service men, military men, and government

Source: Kevin Reilly, *Readings in World Civilizations,* Vol. II. New York: St. Martin's Press, 1992, pp. 79–81.

officials of all ranks — 60 rubles per person; from the gosti and members of the wholesale merchants' guild of the first class — 100 rubles per person; from members of the wholesale merchants' guild of the middle and the lower class (and) . . . from (other) merchants and townsfolk — 60 rubles per person; . . . from townsfolk (of the lower rank), boyars' servants, stage-coachmen, waggoners, church attendants (with the exception of priests and deacons), and from Moscow residents of all ranks — 30 rubles per person. Special badges shall be issued to them from the Administrator of Land Affairs of Public Order . . . which they must wear. . . . As for the peas-ants, let a toll of two half-copecks per beard be collected at the town gates each time they enter or leave a town; and do not let the peasants pass the town gates, into or out of town, without paying this toll.

C Peter himself had studied shipbuilding abroad, and he had great respect for Western science, mathematics, and technology.

Decree on Compulsory Education of the Russian Nobility (1714)

Send to every administrative district some persons from mathematical schools to teach the children of the nobility — except those of freeholders and government clerks — mathematics and geometry; as a penalty for evasion establish a rule that no one will be allowed to marry unless he learns these subjects. Inform all prelates to issue no marriage certificates to those who are ordered to go to schools. . . .

The Great Sovereign has decreed; in all administrative districts children between the ages of ten and fifteen of the nobility, of government clerks, and of lesser officials, except those of freeholders, must be taught math-ematics and some geometry. . . . No fees should be collected from students. When they have mastered the material, they should then be given certifi-cates written in their own handwriting. When the students are released they ought to pay one ruble each for their training. Without these certificates they should not be allowed to marry nor receive marriage certificates.

An Instruction to Russian Students Abroad Studying Navigation (1714)

1. Learn how to draw plans and charts and how to use the compass and other naval indicators.
2. Learn how to navigate a vessel in battle as well as in a simple maneuver, and learn how to use all appropriate tools and instruments; namely, sails, ropes, and oars, and the like matters, on row boats and other vessels.
3. Discover as much as possible how to put ships to sea during a naval battle. Those who cannot succeed in this effort must diligently ascertain what action should be taken by the vessels that do and those that do not put to sea during such a situation (naval battle). Obtain from foreign

naval officers written statements, bearing their signatures and seals, of how adequately you are prepared for naval duties.

4. If, upon his return, anyone wishes to receive from the Tsar greater favors for himself, he should learn, in addition to the above enumerated instructions, how to construct those vessels abroad which he would like to demonstrate his skills.

1. What Western values does Peter feel are important for Russians to adopt?

2. What evidence exists that not all nobles shared Peter's vision?

3. What weaknesses in Russia's military and social organization is Peter trying to address?

Ogier Ghislen de Busbecq

Ogier Ghislen de Busbecq (1522–1592), scholar and diplomat, was born in Flanders and entered the service of the Hapsburg king, Ferdinand, in 1552. He was soon appointed ambassador to the Ottoman Empire. When he arrived in Istanbul in January 1555, De Busbecq found out that the Ottoman Sultan was wintering with his army at Amasya in Anatolia. He served as an ambassador of Ferdinand (who meanwhile became the Holy Roman Emperor) in Istanbul until 1562. De Busbecq's account of his embassy, written in Latin and organized in the form of four letters to a friend, was first published in 1588 and soon became a primary sourcebook on the Ottomans. It was published in twenty editions in seven languages throughout Europe over the next century.

 De Busbecq's description of the Ottoman military camp at Amasya contains a blunt criticism of European aristocracy, which was extremely radical for his time.

> The Sultan's head-quarters were crowded by numerous attendants, including many high officials. All the cavalry of the guard were there . . . . In all that great assembly no single man owed his dignity to anything but his personal merits and bravery; no one is distinguished from the rest by his birth, and honour is paid to each man according to the nature of the duty and offices which he discharges. Thus there is no struggle for precedence, every man having his place assigned to him in virtue of the function which he performs. The Sultan himself assigns to all their duties and offices, and in doing so pays no attention to wealth or the empty claims of rank, and takes no account of any influence or popularity which a candidate may possess; he only considers merit and scrutinizes the character, natural ability, and disposition of each. Thus each man is rewarded according to his deserts, and offices are filled by men capable of performing them. In Turkey every

Source: Ogier Ghislen de Busbecq, *Turkish Letters*, trans. Edward Forster. London: Sickle Moon Books, 2001, pp. 39–41, 76–77.

man has it in his power to make what he will of the position into which he is born and of his fortune in life. Those who hold the highest posts under the Sultan are very often the sons of shepherds and herdsmen, and, so far from being ashamed of their birth, they make it a subject of boasting, and the less they owe to their forefathers and to the accident of birth, the greater is the pride which they feel. They do not consider that good qualities can be conferred by birth or handed down by inheritance, but regard them partly as the gift of heaven and partly as the product of good training and constant toil and zeal. Just as they consider that an aptitude for the arts, such as music or mathematics or geometry, is not transmitted to a son and heir, so they hold that character is not hereditary, and that a son does not necessarily resemble his father, but his qualities are divinely infused into his bodily frame. Thus, among the Turks, dignities, offices, and administrative posts are the rewards of ability and merit; those who are dishonest, lazy, and slothful never attain to distinction, but remain in obscurity and contempt. This is why the Turks succeed in all that they attempt and are a dominating race and daily extend the bounds of their rule. Our method is very different; there is no room for merit, but everything depends on birth; considerations of which alone open the way to high official position. On this subject I shall perhaps say more in another place, and you must regard these remarks as intended for your ears only.

Now come with me and cast your eye over the immense crowd of turbaned heads, wrapped in countless folds of the whitest silk, and bright raiment of every kind and hue, and everywhere the brilliance of gold, silver, purple, silk, and satin. A detailed description would be a lengthy task, and no mere words could give an adequate idea of the novelty of the sight. A more beautiful spectacle was never presented to my gaze. Yet amid all this luxury there was a great simplicity and economy. The dress of all has the same form whatever the wearer's rank; and no edgings or useless trimmings are sewn on, as is the custom with us, costing a large sum of money and worn out in three days. Their most beautiful garments of silk or satin, even if they are embroidered, as they usually are, cost only a ducat to make.

The Turks were quite as much astonished at our manner of dress as we at theirs. They wear long robes which reach almost to their ankles, and are not only more imposing but seem to add to the stature; our dress, on the other hand, is so short and tight that it discloses the forms of the body, which would be better hidden, and is thus anything but becoming, and besides, for some reason or other, it takes away from a man's height and gives him a stunted appearance.

What struck me as particularly praiseworthy in that great multitude was the silence and good discipline. There were none of the cries and murmurs which usually proceed from a motley concourse, and there was no crowding. Each man kept his appointed place in the quietest manner possible. The officers, namely, generals, colonels, captains, and lieutenants — to all of whom the Turks themselves give the title of Aga — were seated; the common soldiers stood up. The most remarkable body of men were several thousand Janissaries, who stood in a long line apart from the rest and so motionless that, as they were at some distance from me, I was for a while doubtful whether they were living men or statues, until, being advised to follow the usual custom of saluting them, I saw them all bow their heads in answer to my salutation. On our departure from that part of the field, we saw another very pleasing sight, namely, the Sultan's bodyguard returning home mounted on horses, which were not only very fine and tall but splendidly groomed and caparisoned.

B De Busbecq also admires the Turkish soldiers, and writes a warning to Europe. At the time, the Ottoman Empire was at its height, ruling from the outskirts of Vienna to the horn of Africa.

All this will show you with what patience, sobriety, and economy the Turks struggle against the difficulties which beset them, and wait for better times. How different are our soldiers, who on campaign despise ordinary food and expect dainty dishes . . . and elaborate meals. If these are not supplied, they mutiny and cause their own ruin; and even if they are supplied, they ruin themselves just the same. For each man is his own worst enemy and has no more deadly foe than his own intemperance, which kills him if the enemy is slow to do so. I tremble when I think of what the future must bring when I compare the Turkish system with our own; one army must prevail and the other be destroyed, for certainly both cannot remain unscathed. On their side are the resources of a mighty empire, strength unimpaired, experience and practice in fighting, a veteran soldiery, habituation to victory, endurance of toil, unity, order, discipline, frugality, and watchfulness. On our side is public poverty, private luxury, impaired strength, broken spirit, lack of endurance and training; the soldiers are insubordinate, the officers avaricious; there is contempt for discipline; licence, recklessness, drunkenness, and debauchery are rife; and, worst of all, the enemy is accustomed to victory, and we to defeat. Can we doubt what the result will be? Persia alone interposes in our favour; for the enemy, as he hastens to attack must keep an eye on this menace in his rear. But Persia is only delaying our fate; it cannot save us. When the Turks have settled with Persia, they will fly at our throats supported by the might of the whole East; how unprepared we are I dare not say!

1. How is the Sultan's appointment of officials different from that of European monarchs?

2. What warning does De Busbecq give to European powers regarding the Turkish military?

3. How does De Busbecq's description of the Turkish headquarters compare to Spain, the major European power at the time?

Lady Mary Wortley Montagu

Lady Mary Wortley Montagu (1689–1762) was the daughter of a rich and powerful English aristocrat. She was well educated, an independent thinker, and was instrumental in introducing inoculation against smallpox into Britain. Critical of the arranged marriages so typical of her class, in which the dowry was more important than the woman, she eloped with the man who became her husband. In the 1730s, she wrote articles on women's issues, one of them entitled "Feminism." Montagu's *Turkish Embassy Letters* date from the period her husband served as British ambassador to the Ottoman court. Her criticism of the social customs of the English elite made her unusually receptive to the very different customs of the Ottoman world.

 Many of Montagu's observations deal with the situation of elite Ottoman women. For a Westerner she was a privileged observer, as she could go where no Western man had ever been. The following excerpt describes a visit to a Turkish bath.

> In one of these covered waggons, I went to the bagnio about ten o'clock. It was already full of women. It is built of stone in the shape of a dome, with no windows but in the roof, which gives light enough. There was [sic] five of these domes joined together, the outmost being less than the rest and serving only as a hall, where the portress stood at the door. Ladies of quality generally give this woman the value of a crown or ten shillings and I did not forget that ceremony. The next room is a very large one paved with marble, and all round it raised two sofas of marble one above another. There were four fountains of cold water in this room, falling first into marble basins, and then running on the floor in little channels made for that purpose, which carried the streams into the next room, something less than this, with the same sort of marble sofas, but so hot with steams of sulphur proceeding from the baths joining to it, 'twas impossible to stay there with one's clothes on. The two other domes were the hot baths, one of which had cocks of cold water turning into it to temper it to what degree of warmth the bathers have a mind to.
>
> I was in my travelling habit, which is a riding dress, and certainly appeared very extraordinary to them. Yet there was not one of them that showed the least surprise or impertinent curiosity, but received me with all the obliging civility possible. I know no European court where the ladies would have behaved themselves in so polite a manner to a stranger. I believe, in the whole, there were two hundred women, and yet none of those disdainful smiles or satirical whispers that never fail in our assemblies when anybody appears that is not dressed exactly in fashion. They repeated over and over to me; 'Güzelle, pek güzelle', which is nothing but 'charming, very charming'. The first sofas were covered with cushions and rich carpets, on

Source: Lady Mary Wortley Montagu, *Turkish Embassy Letters*. London: William Pickering, 1993, pp. 58–60, 90–91, 108, 130, 92–93, 142.

which sat the ladies, and on the second their slaves behind them, but without any distinction of rank by their dress, all being in the state of nature, that is, in plain English, stark naked, without any beauty or defect concealed. Yet there was not the least wanton smile or immodest gesture amongst them. They walked and moved with the same majestic grace which Milton describes of our general mother. There were many amongst them as exactly proportioned as ever any goddess was drawn by the pencil of Guido or Titian, and most of their skins shiningly white, only adorned by their beautiful hair divided into many tresses, hanging on their shoulders, braided either with pearl or ribbon, perfectly representing the figures of the Graces. . . .

. . . [S]o many fine women naked, in different postures, some in conversation, some working, others drinking coffee or sherbet, and many negligently lying on their cushions while their slaves (generally pretty girls of seventeen or eighteen) were employed in braiding their hair in several pretty manners. In short, 'tis the women's coffee house, where all the news of the town is told, scandal invented etc. They generally take this diversion once a week, and stay there at least four or five hours, without getting cold by immediate coming out of the hot bath into the cool room, which was very surprising to me. The lady that seemed the most considerable amongst them entreated me to sit by her and would fain have undressed me for the bath. I excused myself with some difficulty, they being however all so earnest in persuading me, I was at last forced to open my shirt, and show them my stays, which satisfied them very well, for I saw they believed I was so locked up in that machine, that it was not in my own power to open it, which contrivance they attributed to my husband.

B In a number of other areas, Montagu provides a much more positive assessment of the Ottomans than was usual for Westerners: music, law, and slaves.

Music

She made them a sign to play and dance. Four of them immediately begun to play some soft airs on instruments, between a lute and a guitar, which they accompanied with their voices, while the others danced by turns. This dance was very different from what I had seen before. Nothing could be more artful or more proper to raise certain ideas; the tunes so soft, the motions so languishing, accompanied with pauses and dying eyes, half falling back and then recovering themselves in so artful a manner that I am very positive the coldest and most rigid prude upon earth could not have looked upon them without thinking of something not to be spoke of. I suppose you may have read that the Turks have no music but what is shocking to the ears, but this account is from those who never heard any but what is played in the streets, and is just as reasonable as if a foreigner should take his ideas of English music from the bladder and string or the marrow-bones and cleavers.

Law

I am also charmed with many points of the Turkish law, to our shame be it spoken, better designed and better executed than ours, particularly the punishment of convicted liars (triumphant criminals in our country, God knows). They are burnt in the forehead with a hot iron, being proved the authors of any notorious falsehood. How many white foreheads should we see disfigured? How many fine gentlemen would be forced to wear their wigs as low as their eyebrows were this law in practice with us?

Slaves

The markets are most of them handsome squares, and admirably well provided, perhaps better than in any other part of the world. I know you'll expect I should say something particular of that of the slaves, and you will imagine me half a Turk when I don't speak of it with the same horror other Christians have done before me, but I cannot forbear applauding the humanity of the Turks to those creatures. They are never ill used and their slavery is in my opinion no worse than servitude all over the world. 'Tis true they have no wages, but they give them yearly clothes to a higher value than our salaries to any ordinary servant.

C She also notes the prominent place of Jews in Ottoman society.

17 May 1718

I observed most of the rich tradesmen were Jews. That people are in incredible power in this country. They have many privileges above the natural Turks themselves and have formed a very considerable commonwealth here, being judged by their own laws and have drawn the whole trade of the empire into their hands . . . . Every pasha has his Jew who is his homme d'affaires. He is let into all his secrets and does all his business. No bargain is made, no bribe received, no merchandise disposed of but what passes through their hands. They are the physicians, the stewards and the interpreters of all the great men. You may judge how advantageous this is to a people who never fail to make use of the smallest advantages. They have found the secret of making themselves so necessary they are certain of the protection of the court whatever ministry is in power. Even the English, French and Italian merchants, who are sensible in their artifices are however forced to trust their affairs to their negotiation, nothing of trade being managed without them and the meanest amongst them is too important to be disobliged since the whole body take care of his interests with as much vigour as they would those of the most considerable of their members. They are many of them vastly rich but take care to make little public show of it, though they live in their houses in the utmost luxury and magnificence.

D As she is about to leave Constantinople, Montagu provides her overall assessment of the Ottoman approach to life.

19 May 1718

Thus you see, sir, these people are not so unpolished as we represent them. 'Tis true their magnificence is of a different taste from ours, and perhaps of a better. I am almost of opinion they have a right notion of life; while they consume it in music, gardens, wine and delicate eating, while we are tormenting our brains with some scheme of politics or studying some science to which we can never attain, or if we do, cannot persuade people to set that value upon it we do ourselves. 'Tis certain what we feel and see is properly (if anything is properly) our own, but the good of fame, the folly of praise, hardly purchased, and when obtained, poor recompense for loss of time and health! We die, or grow old and decrepit before we can reap the fruit of our labours. Considering what short lived, weak animals men are, is there any study so beneficial as the study of present pleasure? . . . I allow you to laugh at me for the sensual declaration that I had rather be a rich effendi with all his ignorance than Sir Isaac Newton with all his knowledge. I am, sir, etc.

1. Why does Montagu not criticize the lack of inhibitions displayed in the Turkish baths?
2. What aspects of European life does Montagu indirectly criticize in her observations?
3. How does the treatment of Jews in the Islamic Ottoman Empire compare to their treatment in Christian Europe?
4. How might European readers respond to Montagu's observations?

The Yoruba Kingdom of Oyo, Nigeria

Oyo was an important kingdom located in the southwest of contemporary Nigeria. Although few Europeans actually visited Oyo until the 1820s, it had long been involved in trade with Europe, especially the trade in slaves. This crucial trade connection meant that Europeans were interested in what happened in Oyo. However, their sources of information were second-hand, limited to what they could learn from other Africans, who lived on or near the coast where the Europeans' trading factories were located. Europeans, especially English and French, reported on political developments in the region with a degree of attention that matched that of diplomats posted to other European countries.

 The Chevalier des Marchais commands a ship belonging to the French Compagnie des Indes which visits the slave trade port of Ouidah in the 1720s.

I now speak for those who have never traded at Juda [Ouidah] so that they will learn how to know the selection that must be made of the Blacks because there are good and bad among them according to the different countries they are from, for you must not believe that all the slaves are from Juda or Ardre. Here are the names of the countries which furnish them and the quality of the slaves and their marks. . . .

Nago. Those of this nation have the same qualities as those from Ardre [viz. good, docile, and hard-working], they are recognised by long lines which they have on their forehead in the shape of animals. . . .

Ayois. Those of this nation are warriors, hardy and very daring, they are bad for work, they are recognised by lines crossing their cheeks which begin in a point from the eyes and finish at the ears, these marks make them frightful, a single one of these people in a cargo is enough to cause a revolt in it. The Blacks of every other nation are afraid of them.

Trade is the sole pleasure of the Blacks of Juda . . . .

B Brazil was the destination for many of the enslaved Africans from the region. In 1730, the Viceroy of Brazil reported on conditions on the Slave Coast.

[29 April 1730] The Mina Coast situation is still the same. As long as King Daome exists these disorders will continue. He has entered into negotiations with Ayo, the only one he fears and who attacked him on the side of Ajuda. If they make peace there will be no hope of seeing a remedy to the harm done, because he stops the passage of slaves and robs the Negroes who go into the interior to buy them. . . .

[30 July 1730] The trade continues in the same state of decline, for reasons which had already been stated. Daome has closed the roads through which the slaves come down, but as he has suffered great losses from the King of Ayo, who waged war on him in favour of Ajuda, he has tried through the intermediary of our director, to persuade the Ayo to withdraw from his country, promising him good friendliness. If this happens, an end would be put to the disorders of these Negroes, and the trade would continue with better luck.

C Captain John Adams (d. 1866) published his book on West Africa, *Remarks on the Country Extending from Cape Palmas to the River Congo*, in 1823.

Lagos only rose into importance as a place of trade, when the European war and the revolution in France prevented the slave-ships belonging to France carrying on their usual trade at Ardrah; and the latter place derived its consequence from the king of Dahomy monopolizing the trade in slaves in his own dominions, which proving extremely injurious to the interests of both the white and black traders, drove them to the expedient of seeking another market. Ardrah became the refuge of the Wydah [Ouidah] traders . . . .

Source: Robin Law, ed., *Contemporary Source Material for the History of the Old Oyo Empire, 1627–1824.* Toronto: Harriet Tubman Resource Centre on the African Diaspora, 2002, pp. 12–13, 23, 61–62. www.yorku.ca/nhp/shadd/law/index.asp

The negroes obtained . . . at Ardrah were natives belonging to Hio, Housa, Dahomy, Mahee, and Ardrah. . . .

I have little doubt that the Niger might be visited by way of Ardrah and Hio, with less personal risk to the traveller, from the natives, than by any other route we are at present acquainted with. Horses are to be obtained at Ardrah, and also natives who understand both the Hio and French languages.

Many of the slaves of the Housa nation, with whom I have conversed, both at Ardrah and Lagos, and also on board of vessels slaving there, have invariably stated, that they travelled on foot from their own country through that of Hio. . . .

Slaves of the Housa nation are brought to Ardrah by the Hio traders, and then sold, either to European or black traders, belonging to Lagos and Badagry. . . .

Cowries. Are shells brought to Europe from the Maldive islands in the East Indies, and are always in great demand at Wydah [Ouidah], Ardrah, and Lagos, at which places they are not only the medium of exchange, but from whence they are also sent to Dahomy, Hio, Housa, Jaboo, and into the very heart of North Africa, where it is known that they are the circulating currency.

1. How does Des Marchais' description dehumanize the African slaves he observes?

2. What result did the war have on the Dahomets?

3. Describe the impact the Europeans had on the various African tribes they encountered.

4. Compare the tone of these narratives to that of Baquaqua (see pages 50–54).

Mary Jemison

Mary Jemison (1743–1833) was born on the ship on which her parents were migrating from Ireland to British North America, and she grew up on a farm in Pennsylvania. At age fifteen, Jemison was taken captive by Shawnee who raided the farm. She was adopted by a Seneca family and married a Seneca, with whom she had a number of children. Known by her Seneca name of Dehgewanus, she lived the rest of her life as a Native American. When she was eighty, she was interviewed by Dr. James Seaver and this led to the publication of the popular *A Narrative of the Life of Mrs. Mary Jemison* (1824).

 Jemison describes her arrival among the Senecas.

At night we arrived at a small Seneca Indian town, at the mouth of a small river, that was called by the Indians, in the Seneca language, She-nan-jee,

Source: James E. Seaver, ed., *A Narrative of the Life of Mrs. Mary Jemison.* Norman: University of Oklahoma Press, 1992, pp. 73–77.

where the two Squaws to whom I belonged resided. There we landed, and the Indians went on; which was the last I ever saw of them.

Having made fast to the shore, the Squaws left me in the canoe while they went to their wigwam or house in the town, and returned with a suit of Indian clothing, all new, and very clean and nice. My clothes, though whole and good when I was taken, were now torn in pieces, so that I was almost naked. They first undressed me and threw my rags into the river; then washed me clean and dressed me in the new suit they had just brought, in complete Indian style; and then led me home and seated me in the center of their wigwam.

I had been in that situation but a few minutes, before all the Squaws in the town came in to see me. I was soon surrounded by them, and they immediately set up a most dismal howling, crying bitterly, and wringing their hands in all the agonies of grief for a deceased relative.

Their tears flowed freely, and they exhibited all the signs of real mourning. At the commencement of this scene, one of their number began, in a voice somewhat between speaking and singing, to recite some words to the following purport, and continued the recitation till the ceremony was ended; the company at the same time varying the appearance of their countenances, gestures and tone of voice, so as to correspond with the sentiments expressed by their leader:

"Oh our brother! Alas! He is dead — he has gone; he will never return! Friendless he died on the field of the slain, where his bones are yet lying unburied! Oh, who will not mourn his sad fate? No tears dropped around him; oh, no! No tears of his sisters were there! He fell in his prime, when his arm was most needed to keep us from danger! Alas! he has gone! and left us in sorrow, his loss to bewail: Oh where is his spirit? His spirit went naked, and hungry it wanders, and thirsty and wounded it groans to return! Oh helpless and wretched, our brother has gone! No blanket nor food to nourish and warm him; nor candles to light him, nor weapons of war: — Oh, none of those comforts had he! But well we remember his deeds! — The deer he could take on the chase! The panther shrunk back at the sight of his strength! His enemies fell at his feet! He was brave and courageous in war! As the fawn he was harmless: his friendship was ardent: his temper was gentle: his pity was great! Oh! our friend, our companion is dead! Our brother, our brother, alas! he is gone! But why do we grieve for his loss? In the strength of a warrior, undaunted he left us, to fight by the side of the Chiefs! His war-whoop was shrill! His rifle well aimed laid his enemies low: his tomahawk drank of their blood: and his knife flayed their scalps while yet covered with gore! And why do we mourn? Though he fell on the field of the slain, with glory he fell, and his spirit went up to the land of his fathers in war! Then why do we mourn? With transports of joy they received him, and fed him, and clothed him, and welcomed him there! Oh friends, he is happy; then dry up your tears! His spirit has seen our distress, and sent us a helper whom with pleasure we greet. Dickewamis has come: then let us receive her with joy! She is handsome and pleasant! Oh! she is our sister, and gladly we welcome her here. In the place of our brother she stands in our tribe. With care we will guard her from trouble; and may she be happy till her spirit shall leave us."

In the course of that ceremony, from mourning they became serene — joy sparkled in their countenances, and they seemed to rejoice over me as over a long lost child. I was made welcome amongst them as a sister to the two Squaws before mentioned, and was called Dickewamis; which being interpreted, signifies a pretty girl, a handsome girl, or a pleasant, good thing. That is the name by which I have ever since been called by the Indians.

I afterwards learned that the ceremony I at that time passed through, was that of adoption. The two squaws had lost a brother in Washington's war, sometime in the year before, and in consequence of his death went up to Fort Pitt, on the day on which I arrived there, in order to receive a prisoner or an enemy's scalp, to supply their loss.

It is a custom of the Indians, when one of their number is slain or taken prisoner in battle, to give to the nearest relative to the dead or absent, a prisoner, if they have chanced to take one, and if not, to give him the scalp of an enemy. On the return of the Indians from conquest, which is always announced by peculiar shoutings, demonstrations of joy, and the exhibition of some trophy of victory, the mourners come forward and make their claims. If they receive a prisoner, it is at their option either to satiate their vengeance by taking his life in the most cruel manner they can conceive of; or, to receive and adopt him into the family, in the place of him whom they have lost. All the prisoners that are taken in battle and carried to the encampment or town by the Indians, are given to the bereaved families, till their number is made good. And unless the mourners have but just received the news of their bereavement, and are under the operation of a paroxysm of grief, anger and revenge; or, unless the prisoner is very old, sickly, or homely, they generally save him, and treat him kindly. But if their mental wound is fresh, their loss so great that they deem it irreparable, or if their prisoner or prisoners do not meet their approbation, no torture, let it be ever so cruel, seems sufficient to make them satisfaction. It is family, and not national, sacrifices amongst the Indians, that has given them an indelible stamp as barbarians, and identified their character with the idea which is generally formed of unfeeling ferocity, and the most abandoned cruelty.

It was my happy lot to be accepted for adoption; and at the time of the ceremony I was received by the two squaws, to supply the place of their brother in the family; and I was ever considered and treated by them as a real sister, the same as though I had been born of their mother.

During my adoption, I sat motionless, nearly terrified to death at the appearance and actions of the company, expecting every moment to feel their vengeance, and suffer death on the spot. I was, however, happily disappointed, when at the close of the ceremony the company retired, and my sisters went about employing every means for my consolation and comfort.

B   Now settled, Jemison begins to integrate into the Seneca community, but has concerns about her own identity.

> Being now settled and provided with a home, I was employed in nursing the children, and doing light work about the house. Occasionally I was sent out with the Indian hunters, when they went but a short distance, to help them carry their game. My situation was easy; I had no particular hardships to endure. But still, the recollection of my parents, my brothers and sisters, my home, and my own captivity, destroyed my happiness, and made me constantly solitary, lonesome and gloomy.
>
> My sisters would not allow me to speak English in their hearing; but remembering the charge that my dear mother gave me at the time I left her, whenever I chanced to be alone I made a business of repeating my prayer, catechism, or something I had learned in order that I might not forget my own language. By practising in that way I retained it till I came to Genesee flats, where I soon became acquainted with English people with whom I have been almost daily in the habit of conversing.
>
> My sisters were diligent in teaching me their language; and to their great satisfaction I soon learned so that I could understand it readily, and speak it fluently. I was very fortunate in falling into their hands; for they were kind good natured women; peaceable and mild in their dispositions; temperate and decent in their habits, and very tender and gentle towards me. I have great reason to respect them, though they have been dead a great number of years.
>
> The town where they lived was pleasantly situated on the Ohio, at the mouth of the Shenanjee: the land produced good corn; the woods furnished a plenty of game, and the waters abounded with fish. Another river emptied itself into the Ohio, directly opposite the mouth of the Shenanjee. We spent the summer at that place, where we planted, hoed, and harvested a large crop of corn, of an excellent quality.

C   Jemison is soon at home among the Senecas, and finds them to be kind and peaceful.

> I had then been with the Indians four summers and four winters, and had become so far accustomed to their mode of living, habits and dispositions, that my anxiety to get away, to be set at liberty, and leave them, had almost subsided. With them was my home; my family was there, and there I had many friends to whom I was warmly attached in consideration of the favors, affection and friendship with which they had uniformly treated me, from the time of my adoption. Our labor was not severe; and that of one year was exactly similar, in almost every respect, to that of the others, without that endless variety that is to be observed in the common labor of the white people. Notwithstanding the Indian women have all the fuel and bread to procure, and the cooking to perform, their task is probably not harder than that of white women, who have those articles

provided for them; and their cares certainly are not half as numerous, nor as great. In the summer season, we planted, tended and harvested our corn, and generally had all our children with us; but had no master to oversee or drive us, so that we could work as leisurely as we pleased. We had no ploughs on the Ohio; but performed the whole process of planting and hoeing with a small tool that resembled, in some respects, a hoe with a very short handle.

Our cooking consisted in pounding our corn into samp [a coarse mush] or hommany [hulled and dried kernels of corn], boiling the hommany, making now and then a cake and baking it in the ashes, and in boiling or roasting our venison. As our cooking and eating utensils consisted of a hommany block and pestle, a small kettle, a knife or two, and a few vessels of bark or wood, it required but little time to keep them in order for use.

Spinning, weaving, sewing, stocking knitting, and the like, are arts which have never been practised in the Indian tribes generally. After the revolutionary war, I learned to sew, so that I could make my own clothing after a poor fashion; but the other domestic arts I have been wholly ignorant of the application of, since my captivity. In the season of hunting, it was our business, in addition to our cooking, to bring home the game that was taken by the Indians, dress it, and carefully preserve the eatable meat, and prepare or dress the skins. Our clothing was fastened together with strings of deer skin, and tied on with the same.

In that manner we lived, without any of those jealousies, quarrels, and revengeful battles between families and individuals, which have been common in the Indian tribes since the introduction of ardent spirits amongst them.

The use of ardent spirits amongst the Indians, and the attempts which have been made to civilize and christianize them by the white people, has constantly made them worse and worse; increased their vices, and robbed them of many of their virtues; and will ultimately produce their extermination. I have seen, in a number of instances, the effects of education upon some of our Indians, who were taken when young, from their families, and placed at school before they had had an opportunity to contract many Indian habits, and there kept till they arrived to manhood; but I have never seen one of those but what was an Indian in every respect after he returned. Indians must and will be Indians, in spite of all the means that can be used for their cultivation in the sciences and arts.

One thing only marred my happiness, while I lived with them on the Ohio; and that was the recollection that I had once had tender parents, and a home that I loved. Aside from that consideration, or, if I had been taken in infancy, I should have been contented in my situation. Notwithstanding all that has been said against the Indians, in consequence of their cruelties to their enemies — cruelties that I have witnessed, and had abundant proof of — it is a fact that they are naturally kind, tender and peaceable towards their friends, and strictly honest; and that those cruelties have been practised, only upon their enemies, according to their idea of justice.

1. How does Jemison's description of the Seneca people both reinforce and challenge some of the stereotypes prevalent at the time?

2. White society often attempted to convert Native peoples to Christianity. What impact did this have on the Seneca?

3. Are Jemison's observations of Seneca resistance to white culture relevant today?

Adam Smith

Adam Smith's *An Inquiry into the Nature and Causes of the Wealth of Nations* was the most influential work on economics of the Enlightenment. Still viewed as an apostle of economic liberalism, the Scotsman Smith (1723–1790) challenged many of the assumptions of the prevailing mercantilist theories. He recognized that a new economic structure was coming into being in the late eighteenth century and he believed there was a science of wealth, similar to that of the physical world. The economic sphere, Smith believed, had a natural order, and great progress could be achieved by permitting individuals to pursue their own vision of their economic well-being. He claimed the public good would be enhanced through the workings of individual self-interest.

  In his work, Smith discusses the development of Europe's colonies in the Americas and the relative virtues of the different economic policies applied by European countries.

> The establishment of the European colonies in America and the West Indies arose from no necessity: and though the utility which has resulted from them has been very great, it is not altogether so clear and evident. It was not understood at their first establishment, and was not the motive either of that establishment or of the discoveries which gave occasion to it; and the nature, extent, and limits of that utility are not, perhaps, well understood at this day. . . .
>
> The progress of all the European colonies in wealth, population, and improvement, has accordingly been very great. . . . But there are no colonies of which the progress has been more rapid than that of the English in North America. Plenty of good land, and liberty to manage their own affairs their own way, seem to be the two great causes of the prosperity of all new colonies. . . .

Source: Adam Smith, *An Inquiry into the Nature and Causes of the Wealth of Nations*, vol. 2. London: J. M. Dent, 1910, pp. 56, 65, 69, 73–74, 78, 82, 84–85, 87–88, 121–122.

Every European nation has endeavoured more or less to monopolize to itself the commerce of its colonies, and, upon that account, has prohibited the ships of foreign nations from trading to them, and has prohibited them from importing European goods from any foreign nation. But the manner in which this monopoly has been exercised in different nations has been very different.

Some nations have given up the whole commerce of their colonies to an exclusive company, of whom the colonists were obliged to buy all such European goods as they wanted, and to whom they were obliged to sell the whole of their own surplus produce. It was the interest of the company, therefore, not only to sell the former as dear, and to buy the latter as cheap as possible, but to buy no more of the latter, even at this low price than what they could dispose of for a very high price in Europe. It was their interest, not only to degrade in all cases the value of the surplus produce of the colony, but in many cases to discourage and keep down the natural increase of its quantity. Of all the expedients that can well be contrived to stunt the natural growth of a new colony, that of an exclusive company is undoubtedly the most effectual. This, however, has been the policy of Holland, though their company, in the course of the present century, has given up in many respects the exertion of their exclusive privilege. . . . It has occasionally been the policy of France, and of late, since 1755, after it had been abandoned by all other nations on account of its absurdity, it has become the policy of Portugal with regard at least to two of the principal provinces of Brazil. . . . Such exclusive companies, therefore, are nuisances in every respect; always more or less inconvenient to the countries in which they are established, and destructive to those which have the misfortune to fall under their government. . . .

Other nations, without establishing an exclusive company, have confined the whole commerce of their colonies to a particular port of the mother country, from whence no ship was allowed to sail, but either in a fleet and at a particular season, or, if single, in consequence of a particular licence, which in most cases was very well paid for. This policy opened, indeed, the trade of the colonies to all the natives of the mother country, provided they traded from the proper port, at the proper season, and in the proper vessels. . . . [T]he trade which was carried on in this manner would necessarily be conducted very nearly upon the same principles as that of an exclusive company. The profit of those merchants would be almost equally exorbitant and oppressive. The colonies would be ill supplied, and would be obliged both to buy very dear, and to sell very cheap. This, however, till within these few years, had always been the policy of Spain.

Other nations leave the trade of their colonies free to all their subjects who may carry it on from all the different ports of the mother country, and who have occasion for no other licence than the common despatches of the custom-house. In this case the number and dispersed situation of the different traders renders it impossible for them to enter into any general combination, and their competition is sufficient to hinder them from making very exorbitant profits. Under so liberal a policy the colonies are enabled both to sell their own produce and to buy the goods of Europe at a reasonable price. But since the dissolution of the Plymouth company, when our colonies were but in their infancy, this has always been the policy of England. . . .

The most perfect freedom of trade is permitted between the British colonies of America and the West Indies, both in the enumerated and in the non-enumerated commodities. Those colonies are now become so populous and thriving that each of them finds in some of the others a great and extensive market for every part of its produce. All of them taken together, they make a great internal market for the produce of one another. . . .

But though the policy of Great Britain with regard to the trade of her colonies has been dictated by the same mercantile spirit as that of other nations, it has, however, upon the whole, been less illiberal and oppressive than that of any of them.

B Smith finds the English colonies superior in other respects as well.

In every thing, except their foreign trade, the liberty of the English colonists to manage their own affairs their own way is complete. It is in every respect equal to that of their fellow-citizens at home, and is secured in the same manner, by an assembly of the representatives of the people, who claim the sole right of imposing taxes for the support of the colony government. . . .

The absolute governments of Spain, Portugal, and France, on the contrary, take place in their colonies; and the discretionary powers which such governments commonly delegate to all their inferior officers are, on account of the great distance, naturally exercised there with more than ordinary violence.

C In the case of sugar colonies, however, Smith notes that the English approach was not the best.

[I]n the good management of their slaves the French planters, I think it is generally allowed, are superior to the English. The law, so far as it gives some weak protection to the slave against the violence of his master, is likely to be better executed in a colony where the government is in a great measure arbitrary than in one where it is altogether free. In every country where the unfortunate law of slavery is established, the magistrate, when he protects the slave, intermeddles in some measure in the management of the private property of the master; and, in a free country, where the master is perhaps either a member of the colony assembly, or an elector of such a member, he dare not do this but with the greatest caution and circumspection. The respect which he is obliged to pay to the master renders it more difficult for him to protect the slave. But in a country where the government is in a great measure arbitrary, where it is usual for the magistrate to intermeddle even in the management of the private property of individuals, and to send them, perhaps, a *lettre de cachet* if they do not manage it according to his liking, it is much easier for him to give some protection to the slave; and common humanity naturally disposes him to do so. The protection of the magistrate renders the slave less contemptible in the eyes of his master, who is thereby induced to consider him with more regard, and to treat him with more gentleness. Gentle usage renders the slave not only more faithful, but more intelligent, and therefore, upon a double account, more useful. He approaches more to the condition of a free servant, and may possess some degree of integrity and attachment to his master's interest, virtues which frequently belong to free servants, but which never can belong to a slave who is treated as slaves commonly are in countries where the master is perfectly free and secure.

That the condition of a slave is better under an arbitrary than under a free government is, I believe, supported by the history of all ages and nations.

D Smith discusses whether Europe derived benefits from its American colonies.

The general advantages which Europe, considered as one great country, has derived from the discovery and colonization of America, consist, first, in the increase of its enjoyments; and, secondly, in the augmentation of its industry.

The surplus produce of America, imported into Europe, furnishes the inhabitants of this great continent with a variety of commodities which they could not otherwise have possessed, some for conveniency and use, some for pleasure, and some for ornament, and thereby contributes to increase their enjoyments. . . .

The discovery of America, and that of a passage to the East Indies by the Cape of Good Hope, are the two greatest and most important events recorded in the history of mankind. Their consequences have already been very great: but, in the short period of between two and three centuries which has elapsed since these discoveries were made, it is impossible that the whole extent of their consequences can have been seen. . . .

In the mean time, one of the principal effects of those discoveries has been to raise the mercantile system to a degree of splendour and glory which it could never otherwise have attained to. It is the object of that system to enrich a great nation rather by trade and manufactures than by the improvement and cultivation of land, rather by the industry of the towns than by that of the country. But, in consequence of those discoveries, the commercial towns of Europe, instead of being the manufacturers and carriers for but a very small part of the world (that part of Europe which is washed by the Atlantic ocean, and the countries which lie round the Baltic and Mediterranean seas), have now become the manufacturers for the numerous and thriving cultivators of America, and the carriers, and in some respects the manufacturers too, for almost all the different nations of Asia, Africa, and America. Two new worlds have been opened to their industry, each of them much greater and more extensive than the old one, and the market of one of them growing still greater and greater every day. . . .

We must carefully distinguish between the effects of the colony trade and those of the monopoly of that trade. The former are always and necessarily beneficial; the latter always and necessarily hurtful.

1. Why does Smith believe that the English colonies in North America have been the most progressive?
2. How does Smith's criticism of various economic policies indirectly promote his philosophy of free trade?
3. Reviewing the readings, do you think Smith would support the American Revolution? Compare the economic complaints of the colonists with Smith's pronouncements on economic policy.
4. Does Smith advocate better treatment for slaves from a moral or economic perspective?
5. According to Smith, is colonization only truly beneficial for the colonizing power?

Enlightenment and Revolution, 1680–1840

On October 5, 1789, ten thousand people, mostly women, angered at the price of bread, marched in protest to the palace of King Louis XVI at Versailles, the site of the government of France for over a century. The next day the crowd forced the king and his court to move to Paris, thereby symbolically shifting the centre of France from the grandeur and luxury of Versailles to its largest city and the traditional capital. Protest and rebellion became part of the reality of the West in the late eighteenth century, as groups left out of the development of modernity sought social and political change. Privilege was challenged and the ideas of political rights and legal equality were powerful forces for change.

Jean-Jacques Rousseau

Jean-Jacques Rousseau (1712–1778), one of the most controversial figures of the Enlightenment, challenged many assumptions of mainstream eighteenth-century thought. He believed human beings were good in a state of nature, and that in civilization there is the basis of corruption. Rousseau put emphasis on the importance of sentiment as well as reason, and stressed emotional and intuitive elements in assessing human nature. Rousseau's *Social Contract* (1762) recognized many of the difficulties in thinking about freedom and authority, as he tried to reconcile the need for individual expression with the well-being of community life.

A Rousseau opens his work with a critique of society and a discussion of its foundations.

Man was born free, and everywhere he is in chains. Many a one believes himself the master of others, and yet he is a greater slave than they. How has this change come about? I do not know. What can render it legitimate? I believe that I can settle this question.

If I considered only force and the results that proceed from it, I should say that so long as a people is compelled to obey and does obey, it does well; but that, so soon as it can shake off the yoke and does shake it off, it does better; for, if men recover their freedom by virtue of the same right by which it was taken away, either they are justified in resuming it, or there was no justification for depriving them of it. But the social order is a sacred right which serves as a foundation for all others. This right, however, does not come from nature. It is therefore based on conventions. The question is to know what these conventions are. Before coming to that, I must establish what I have just laid down.

B Freedom for Rousseau is one of the conditions of our being human.

The earliest of all societies, and the only natural one, is the family; yet children remain attached to their father only so long as they have need of him for their own preservation. As soon as this need ceases, the natural bond is dissolved. The children being freed from the obedience which they owed to their father, and the father from the cares which he owed to his children, become equally independent. If they remain united, it is no longer naturally but voluntarily; and the family itself is kept together only by convention.

This common liberty is a consequence of man's nature. His first law is to attend to his own preservation, his first cares are those which he owes to himself; and as soon as he comes to years of discretion, being sole judge of the means adapted for his own preservation, he becomes his own master. . . .

Source: Jean-Jacques Rousseau, *The Social Contract [and] Discourse on the Origin of Inequality*, ed. Lester G. Crocker. New York: Washington Square Press, 1967, pp. 7–8, 10, 11–13, 17–22.

The strongest man is never strong enough to be always master, unless he transforms his power into right, and obedience into duty. Hence the right of the strongest — a right apparently assumed in irony, and really established in principle. But will this phrase never be explained to us? Force is a physical power; I do not see what morality can result from its effects. To yield to force is an act of necessity, not of will; it is at most an act of prudence. . . .

Let us agree, then, that might does not make right, and that we are bound to obey none but lawful authorities. . . .

Since no man has any natural authority over his fellow men, and since force is not the source of right, conventions remain as the basis of all lawful authority among men. . . .

To say that a man gives himself for nothing is to say what is absurd and inconceivable; such an act is illegitimate and invalid, for the simple reason that he who performs it is not in his right mind. To say the same thing of a whole nation is to suppose a nation of fools; and madness does not confer rights. . . .

To renounce one's liberty is to renounce one's quality as a man, the rights and also the duties of humanity. For him who renounces everything there is no possible compensation. Such a renunciation is incompatible with man's nature, for to take away all freedom from his will is to take away all morality from his actions. In short, a convention which stipulates absolute authority on the one side and unlimited obedience on the other is vain and contradictory. Is it not clear that we are under no obligations whatsoever towards a man from whom we have a right to demand everything? And does not this single condition, without equivalent, without exchange, involve the nullity of the act? For what right would my slave have against me, since all that he has belongs to me? His rights being mine, this right of me against myself is a meaningless phrase.

C The state has its origins in the social contract.

I assume that men have reached a point at which the obstacles that endanger their preservation in the state of nature overcome by their resistance the forces which each individual can exert with a view to maintaining himself in that state. Then this primitive condition can no longer subsist, and the human race would perish unless it changed its mode of existence.

Now, as men cannot create any new forces, but only combine and direct those that exist, they have no other means of self-preservation than to form by aggregation a sum of forces which may overcome the resistance, to put them in action by a single motive power, and to make them work in concert.

This sum of forces can be produced only by the combination of many; but the strength and freedom of each man being the chief instruments of his preservation, how can he pledge them without injuring himself, and without neglecting the cares which he owes to himself? This difficulty, applied to my subject, may be expressed in these terms: —

"To find a form of association which may defend and protect with the whole force of the community the person and property of every associate, and by means of which each, coalescing with all, may nevertheless obey only himself, and remain as free as before." Such is the fundamental problem of which the social contract furnishes the solution.

The clauses of this contract are so determined by the nature of the act that the slightest modification would render them vain and ineffectual; so that, although they have never perhaps been formally enunciated, they are everywhere the same, everywhere tacitly admitted and recognized, until, the social pact being violated, each man regains his original rights and recovers his natural liberty, while losing the conventional liberty for which he renounced it.

These clauses, rightly understood, are reducible to one only, viz., the total alienation to the whole community of each associate with all his rights; for, in the first place, since each gives himself up entirely, the conditions are equal for all; and, the conditions being equal for all, no one has any interest in making them burdensome to others.

Further, the alienation being made without reserve, the union is as perfect as it can be, and an individual associate can no longer claim anything; for, if any rights were left to individuals, since there would be no common superior who could judge between them and the public, each, being on some point his own judge, would soon claim to be so on all; the state of nature would still subsist, and the association would necessarily become tyrannical or useless.

In short, each giving himself to all, gives himself to nobody; and as there is not one associate over whom we do not acquire the same rights which we concede to him over ourselves, we gain the equivalent of all that we lose, and more power to preserve what we have.

If, then, we set aside what is not of the essence of the social contract, we shall find that it is reducible to the following terms: "Each of us puts in common his person and his whole power under the supreme direction of the general will; and in return we receive every member as an indivisible part of the whole."

D The nature of sovereign authority is one of Rousseau's most controversial concepts, one debated ever since by social and political philosophers in an attempt to grasp and solve the problems raised when considering differences between individual desires and community needs.

We see from this formula that the act of association contains a reciprocal engagement between the public and individuals, and that every individual, contracting so to speak with himself, is engaged in a double relation, viz., as a member of the sovereign towards individuals, and as a member of the State towards the sovereign. . . .

But the body politic or sovereign, deriving its existence only from the sanctity of the contract, can never bind itself, even to others, in anything that derogates from the original act, such as alienation of some portion of itself, or submission to another sovereign. To violate the act by which it exists would be to annihilate itself; and what is nothing produces nothing.

So soon as the multitude is thus united in one body, it is impossible to injure one of the members without attacking the body, still less to injure the body without the members feeling the effects. Thus duty and interest alike oblige the two contracting parties to give mutual assistance; and the men themselves should seek to combine in this twofold relationship all the advantages which are attendant on it.

Now, the sovereign, being formed only of the individuals that compose it, neither has nor can have any interest contrary to theirs; consequently the sovereign power needs no guarantee towards its subjects, because it is impossible that the body should wish to injure all its members; and we shall see hereafter that it can injure no one as an individual. The sovereign, for the simple reason that it is so, is always everything that it ought to be.

But this is not the case as regards the relation of subjects to the sovereign, which, notwithstanding the common interest, would have no security for the performance of their engagements unless it found means to ensure their fidelity.

Indeed, every individual may, as a man, have a particular will contrary to, or divergent from, the general will which he has as a citizen; his private interest may prompt him quite differently from the common interest; his absolute and naturally independent existence may make him regard what he owes to the common cause as a gratuitous contribution, the loss of which will be less harmful to others than the payment of it will be burdensome to him; and, regarding the moral person that constitutes the State as an imaginary being because it is not a man, he would be willing to enjoy the rights of a citizen without being willing to fulfil the duties of a subject. The progress of such injustice would bring about the ruin of the body politic.

In order, then, that the social pact may not be a vain formulary, it tacitly includes this engagement, which can alone give force to the others — that whoever refuses to obey the general will shall be constrained to do so by the whole body; which means nothing else than that he shall be forced to be free; for such is the condition which, uniting every citizen to his native land, guarantees him from all personal dependence, a condition that ensures the control and working of the political machine, and alone renders legitimate civil engagements, which, without it, would be absurd and tyrannical, and subject to the most enormous abuses.

1. What are the chains Rousseau denounces in his opening statement?
2. What forms the basis of the social contract? What dilemmas face the establishment of the social contract?
3. How does Rousseau personalize liberty?
4. How does Rousseau's description of the relationship between subject and sovereign compare to the Bourbon system of government?

Voltaire

Voltaire (1694–1778), the pen name of François Marie Arouet, was the most famous *philosophe* of the Enlightenment. His works on social customs, history, philosophy, literature, and politics were well-known, and he challenged the rigid societies in France and on the rest of the European continent in an effort to propagate a doctrine of tolerance and social progress. An admirer of the English, Voltaire associated himself with the science of Francis Bacon and Isaac Newton, and with the political philosophy of John Locke. Living most of his lifetime outside of France, Voltaire was a critic of arbitrary justice and what he deemed to be unfair and archaic institutions. In his satire *Candide* (1759), Voltaire challenged both authority and blind optimism as he professed a position of reasonable reform.

 Candide opens with an introduction to the young Candide and his teacher Pangloss. The latter was modelled after the rationalist philosopher Gottfried Wilhelm Leibniz (1646–1716). To Voltaire, Pangloss represents the foolishness of a scientist of unbounded optimism whose theory does not permit him to see the world as it is.

> In the castle of Baron Thunder-ten-tronckh in Westphalia there lived a youth, endowed by Nature with the most gentle character. His face was the expression of his soul. His judgment was quite honest and he was extremely simple-minded; and this was the reason, I think, that he was named Candide. Old servants in the house suspected that he was the son of the Baron's sister and a decent honest gentleman of the neighborhood, whom this young lady would never marry because he could only prove seventy-one quarterings, and the rest of his genealogical tree was lost, owing to the injuries of time. The Baron was one of the most powerful lords in Westphalia, for his castle possessed a door and windows. His Great Hall was even decorated with a piece of tapestry. The dogs in his stable-yards formed a pack of hounds when necessary; his grooms were his huntsmen; the village curate was his Grand Almoner. They all called him "My Lord," and laughed heartily at his stories. The Baroness weighed about three hundred and fifty pounds, was therefore greatly respected, and did the honors of the house with a dignity which rendered her still more respectable. Her daughter Cunegonde, aged seventeen, was rosy-cheeked, fresh, plump and tempting. The Baron's son appeared in every respect worthy of his father. The tutor Pangloss was the oracle of the house, and little Candide followed his lessons with all the candor of his age and character. Pangloss taught metaphysico-theologo-cosmolonigology. . . . My Lord the Baron's castle was the best of castles and his wife the best of all possible Baronesses. "'Tis demonstrated," said he, "that things cannot be otherwise; for, since everything is made for an end, everything is necessarily for the best end. Observe

Source: Voltaire, *Candide and Other Writings*. New York: The Modern Library, 1956, pp. 110–112, 151–152, 186–189.

that noses were made to wear spectacles; and so we have spectacles. Legs were visibly instituted to be breeched, and we have breeches. Stones were formed to be quarried and to build castles; and My Lord has a very noble castle; the greatest Baron in the province should have the best house; and as pigs were made to be eaten, we eat pork all the year round; consequently, those who have asserted that all is well talk nonsense; they ought to have said that all is for the best." Candide listened attentively and believed innocently; for he thought Mademoiselle Cunegonde extremely beautiful, although he was never bold enough to tell her so. He decided that after the happiness of being born Baron of Thunder-ten-tronckh, the second degree of happiness was to be Mademoiselle Cunegonde; the third, to see her every day; and the fourth to listen to Doctor Pangloss, the greatest philosopher of the province and therefore of the whole world. . . . On her way back to the castle [Cunegonde] met Candide and blushed; Candide also blushed. She bade him good-morning in a hesitating voice; Candide replied without knowing what he was saying. Next day, when they left the table after dinner, Cunegonde and Candide found themselves behind a screen; Cunegonde dropped her handkerchief, Candide picked it up; she innocently held his hand; the young man innocently kissed the young lady's hand with remarkable vivacity, tenderness and grace; their lips met, their eyes sparkled, their knees trembled, their hands wandered. Baron Thunder-ten-tronckh passed near the screen, and, observing this cause and effect, expelled Candide from the castle by kicking him in the backside frequently and hard. Cunegonde swooned; when she recovered her senses, the Baroness slapped her in the face; and all was in consternation in the noblest and most agreeable of all possible castles.

B Slavery is attacked in the work, as Candide travels with his servant Cacambo and learns about the world. Voltaire also begins to challenge the optimism of Pangloss.

Our two travelers' first day was quite pleasant. They were encouraged by the idea of possessing more treasures than all Asia, Europe and Africa could collect. Candide in rapture carved the name of Cunegonde on the trees. On the second day two of the sheep stuck in a marsh and were swallowed up with their loads; two other sheep died of fatigue a few days later; then seven or eight died of hunger in a desert; several days afterwards others fell off precipices. Finally, after they had traveled for a hundred days, they had only two sheep left. Candide said to Cacambo: "My friend, you see how perishable are the riches of this world; nothing is steadfast but virtue and the happiness of seeing Mademoiselle Cunegonde again." "I admit it," said Cacambo, "but we still have two sheep with more treasures than the King of Spain will ever have, and in the distance I see a town I suspect is Surinam, which belongs to the Dutch. We are at the end of our troubles and the beginning of our happiness." As they drew near the town they came upon a Negro lying on the ground wearing only half his clothes, that is to say, a pair of blue cotton drawers; this poor man had no left leg and no right hand. "Good heavens!" said Candide to him in Dutch, "what are you doing there, my friend, in that horrible state?" "I am waiting for my master, the famous merchant Monsieur Vanderdendur." "Was it Monsieur Vanderdendur," said Candide, "who treated you in that way?" "Yes, sir," said the Negro, "it is the custom. We are given a pair of cotton drawers twice a year as clothing. When we work in the sugar-mills and the grindstone catches our fingers, they cut off the hand; when we try to run away, they cut off a leg. Both these things happened to me. This is the price paid for the sugar you eat in Europe. But when my mother sold me for ten patagons on the coast of Guinea, she said to me: 'My dear child, give thanks to our fetishes [religious leaders], always worship them, and they will make you happy; you have the honor to be a slave of our lords the white men and thereby you have made the fortune of your father and mother.' Alas! I do not know whether I made their fortune, but, they certainly did not make mine. Dogs, monkeys and parrots are a thousand times less miserable than we are; the Dutch fetishes who converted me tell me that we are all of us, whites and blacks, the children of Adam. I am not a genealogist, but if these preachers tell the truth, we are all second cousins. Now, you will admit that no one could treat his relatives in a more horrible way." "O Pangloss!" cried Candide. "This is an abomination you had not guessed; this is too much, in the end I shall have to renounce optimism." "What is optimism?" said Cacambo. "Alas!" said Candide, "it is the mania of maintaining that everything is well when we are wretched." And he shed tears as he looked at his Negro; and he entered Surinam weeping.

C Candide goes through many hardships and trials as Voltaire attacks the Church, the state, and other institutions. At the end of the work the hero achieves wisdom and is able to instruct his friends, who include Martin, a pessimist, and the ever-optimistic Pangloss.

Martin . . . concluded that man was born to live in the convulsions of distress or in the lethargy of boredom. Candide did not agree, but he asserted nothing. Pangloss confessed that he had always suffered horribly; but, having once maintained that everything was for the best, he had continued to maintain it without believing it. . . .

In the neighborhood there lived a very famous Dervish, who was supposed to be the best philosopher in Turkey; they went to consult him; Pangloss was the spokesman and said; "Master, we have come to beg you to tell us why so strange an animal as man was ever created." "What has it to do with you?" said the Dervish. "Is it your business?" "But, reverend father," said Candide, "there is a horrible amount of evil in the world." "What does it matter," said the Dervish, "whether there is evil or good? When his highness sends a ship to Egypt, does he worry about the comfort or discomfort of the rats in the ship?" "Then what should we do?" said

Pangloss. "Hold your tongue," said the Dervish. "I flattered myself," said Pangloss, "that I should discuss with you effects and causes, this best of all possible worlds, the origin of evil, the nature of the soul and pre-established harmony." At these words the Dervish slammed the door in their faces.

During this conversation the news went round that at Constantinople two viziers and the mufti had been strangled and several of their friends impaled. This catastrophe made a prodigious noise everywhere for several hours. As Pangloss, Candide and Martin were returning to their little farm, they came upon an old man who was taking the air under a bower of orange-trees at his door. Pangloss, who was as curious as he was argumentative, asked him what was the name of the mufti who had just been strangled. "I do not know," replied the old man. "I have never known the name of any mufti or of any vizier. I am entirely ignorant of the occurrence you mention; I presume that in general those who meddle with public affairs sometimes perish miserably and that they deserve it; but I never inquire what is going on in Constantinople; I content myself with sending there for sale the produce of the garden I cultivate." Having spoken thus, he took the strangers into his house. His two daughters and his two sons presented them with several kinds of sherbet which they made themselves, caymac flavored with candied citron peel, oranges, lemons, limes, pineapples, dates, pistachios and Mocha coffee which had not been mixed with the bad coffee of Batavia and the Isles. After which this good Mussulman's two daughters perfumed the beards of Candide, Pangloss and Martin. "You must have a vast and magnificent estate?" said Candide to the Turk. "I have only twenty acres," replied the Turk. "I cultivate them with my children; and work keeps at bay three great evils: boredom, vice and need."

As Candide returned to his farm he reflected deeply on the Turk's remarks. He said to Pangloss and Martin: "That good old man seems to me to have chosen an existence preferable by far to that of the six kings with whom we had the honor to sup." "Exalted rank," said Pangloss, "is very dangerous, according to the testimony of all philosophers; for Eglon, King of the Moabites, was murdered by Ehud; Absalom was hanged by the hair and pierced by three darts; King Nadab, son of Jeroboam, was killed by Baasha; King Elah by Zimri; Ahaziah by Jehu; Athaliah by Jehoiada; the Kings Jehoiakim, Jeconiah and Zedekiah were made slaves. You know in what manner died Croesus, Astyages, Darius, Denys of Syracuse, Pyrrhus, Perseus, Hannibal, Jugurtha, Ariovistus, Caesar, Pompey, Nero, Otho, Vitellius, Domitian, Richard II of England, Edward II, Henry VI, Richard III, Mary Stuart, Charles I, the three Henrys of France, the Emperor Henry IV. You know . . ." "I also know," said Candide, "that we should cultivate our garden." "You are right," said Pangloss, "for, when man was placed in the Garden of Eden, he was placed there *ut operaretur eum*, to dress it and to keep it; which proves that man was not born for idleness." "Let us work without theorizing," said Martin; "'tis the only way to make life endurable."

The whole small fraternity entered into this praiseworthy plan, and each started to make use of his talents. The little farm yielded well. Cunegonde was indeed very ugly, but she became an excellent pastry-cook; Paquette embroidered; the old woman took care of the linen. Even Friar Giroflée performed some service; he was a very good carpenter and even became a man of honor; and Pangloss sometimes said to Candide: "All events are linked up in this best of all possible worlds; for, if you had not been expelled from the noble castle, by hard kicks in your backside for love of Mademoiselle Cunegonde, if you had not been clapped into the Inquisition, if you had not wandered about America on foot, if you had not stuck your sword in the Baron, if you had not lost all your sheep from the land of Eldorado, you would not be eating candied citrons and pistachios here." "That's well said," replied Candide. "but we must cultivate our garden."

1. Locate examples of Voltaire's satire in describing the Baron and his family.

2. What insights about society does the Turkish farmer present to Candide?

3. What philosophical point does Voltaire make when he says: "We must cultivate our garden"?

4. How does Voltaire's view of humanity compare with the philosophy of Rousseau (see pages 92–95)?

Rights and Revolution

In the late eighteenth century, rights and revolution became major concerns as the American and French revolutions led to a reconsideration of the nature of government, the sources of authority, and the basis of sovereignty. Influenced especially by Locke and Rousseau, revolutionaries in the West sought to justify both their challenge to the old authority and the establishment of a new policy. Major documents included the American Declaration of Independence and the French Declaration of the Rights of Man and the Citizen.

 On July 4, 1776, the Second Continental Congress in Philadelphia adopted the Declaration of Independence, justifying the right of revolution in general and giving the reasons why Americans believed they had a right to rebel at that time.

When, in the course of human events, it becomes necessary for one people to dissolve the political bands which have connected them with another, and to assume, among the powers of the earth, the separate and equal station to which the laws of nature and of nature's God entitle them, a decent respect to the opinions of mankind requires that they should declare the causes which impel them to the separation.

Sources: Bernard Bailyn et al., *The Great Republic: A History of the American People*, third edition. Lexington, Massachusetts: D. C. Heath and Company, 1985, appendix, pp. v–vi; John Hall Stewart, *A Documentary Survey of the French Revolution*. New York: The Macmillan Company, 1951, pp. 113–115.

We hold these truths to be self-evident: That all men are created equal; that they are endowed by their Creator with certain unalienable rights; that among these are life, liberty, and the pursuit of happiness; that, to secure these rights, governments are instituted among men, deriving their just powers from the consent of the governed; that whenever any form of government becomes destructive of these ends, it is the right of the people to alter or to abolish it, and to institute new government, laying its foundation on such principles, and organizing its powers in such form, as to them shall seem most likely to effect their safety and happiness. Prudence, indeed, will dictate that governments long established should not be changed for light and transient causes; and accordingly all experience hath shown that mankind are more disposed to suffer, while evils are sufferable, than to right themselves by abolishing the forms to which they are accustomed. But when a long train of abuses and usurpations, pursuing invariably the same object, evinces a design to reduce them under absolute despotism, it is their right, it is their duty, to throw off such government, and to provide new guards for their future security. Such has been the patient sufferance of these colonies; and such is now the necessity which constrains them to alter their former systems of government. The history of the present King of Great Britain is a history of repeated injuries and usurpations, all having in direct object the establishment of an absolute tyranny over these states. To prove this, let facts be submitted to a candid world.

He has refused his assent to laws, the most wholesome and necessary for the public good.

He has forbidden his governors to pass laws of immediate and pressing importance, unless suspended in their operation till his assent should be obtained; and, when so suspended, he has utterly neglected to attend to them.

He has refused to pass other laws for the accommodation of large districts of people, unless those people would relinquish the right of representation in the legislature, a right inestimable to them, and formidable to tyrants only.

He has called together legislative bodies at places unusual, uncomfortable, and distant from the depository of their public records, for the sole purpose of fatiguing them into compliance with his measures.

He has dissolved representative houses repeatedly, for opposing, with manly firmness, his invasions on the rights of the people. . . .

He has kept among us, in times of peace, standing armies, without the consent of our legislatures. . . .

He is at this time transporting large armies of foreign mercenaries to complete the works of death, desolation, and tyranny already begun with circumstances of cruelty and perfidy scarcely paralleled in the most barbarous ages, and totally unworthy the head of a civilized nation.

He has constrained our fellow-citizens, taken captive on the high seas, to bear arms against their country, to become the executioners of their friends and brethren, or to fall themselves by their hands.

He has excited domestic insurrection among us, and has endeavored to bring on the inhabitants of our frontiers the merciless Indian savages, whose known rule of warfare is an undistinguished destruction of all ages, sexes, and conditions.

In every stage of these oppressions we have petitioned for redress in the most humble terms; our repeated petitions have been answered only by repeated injury. A prince, whose character is thus marked by every act which may define a tyrant, is unfit to be the ruler of a free people.

Nor have we been wanting in our attentions to our British brethren. We have warned them, from time to time, of attempts by their legislature to extend an unwarrantable jurisdiction over us. We have reminded them of the circumstances of our emigration and settlement here. We have appealed to their native justice and magnanimity; and we have conjured them, by the ties of our common kindred, to disavow these usurpations, which would inevitably interrupt our connections and correspondence. They, too, have been deaf to the voice of justice and of consanguinity. We must, therefore, acquiesce in the necessity which denounces our separation, and hold them, as we hold the rest of mankind, enemies in war, in peace friends.

We, therefore, the representatives of the United States of America, in General Congress assembled, appealing to the Supreme Judge of the world for the rectitude of our intentions, do, in the name and by the authority of the good people of these colonies, solemnly publish and declare, that these United Colonies are, and of right ought to be, FREE AND INDEPENDENT STATES; that they are absolved from all allegiance to the British crown, and that all political connection between them and the state of Great Britain is, and ought to be, totally dissolved; and that, as free and independent states, they have full power to levy war, conclude peace, contract alliances, establish commerce, and do all other acts and things which independent states may of right do. And for the support of this declaration, with a firm reliance on the protection of Divine Providence, we mutually pledge to each other our lives, our fortunes, and our sacred honor.

JOHN HANCOCK [*President*]
[*and fifty-five others*]

B The French National Assembly adopted the Declaration of the Rights of Man and the Citizen on August 27, 1789. This document, an important and influential statement on rights, was the product of the first constitutional debates in the National Assembly.

The representatives of the French people, organized in National Assembly, considering that ignorance, forgetfulness, or contempt of the rights of man are the sole causes of public misfortunes and of the corruption of governments, have resolved to set forth in a solemn declaration the natural, inalienable, and sacred rights of man, in order that such declaration, continually before all members of the social body, may be a perpetual reminder of their rights and duties; in order that the acts of the legislative power and those of the executive power may constantly be compared with the aim of every political institution and may accordingly be more respected; in order that the demands of the citizens, founded henceforth upon simple and incontestable principles, may always be directed towards the maintenance of the Constitution and the welfare of all.

Accordingly, the National Assembly recognizes and proclaims, in the presence and under the auspices of the Supreme Being, the following rights of man and citizen.

1. Men are born and remain free and equal in rights; social distinctions may be based only upon general usefulness.

2. The aim of every political association is the preservation of the natural and inalienable rights of man; these rights are liberty, property, security, and resistance to oppression.

3. The source of all sovereignty resides essentially in the nation; no group, no individual may exercise authority not emanating expressly therefrom.

4. Liberty consists of the power to do whatever is not injurious to others; thus the enjoyment of the natural rights of every man has for its limits only those that assure other members of society the enjoyment of those same rights; such limits may be determined only by law.

5. The law has the right to forbid only actions which are injurious to society. Whatever is not forbidden by law may not be prevented, and no one may be constrained to do what it does not prescribe.

6. Law is the expression of the general will; all citizens have the right to concur personally, or through their representatives, in its formation; it must be the same for all, whether it protects or punishes. All citizens, being equal before it, are equally admissible to all public offices, positions, and employments, according to their capacity, and without other distinction than that of virtues and talents.

7. No man may be accused, arrested, or detained except in the cases determined by law, and according to the forms prescribed thereby. Whoever solicit, expedite, or execute arbitrary orders, or have them executed, must be punished; but every citizen summoned or apprehended in pursuance of the law must obey immediately; he renders himself culpable by resistance.

8. The law is to establish only penalties that are absolutely and obviously necessary; and no one may be punished except by virtue of a law established and promulgated prior to the offence and legally applied.

9. Since every man is presumed innocent until declared guilty, if arrest be deemed indispensable, all unnecessary severity for securing the person of the accused must be severely repressed by law.

10. No one is to be disquieted because of his opinions, even religious, provided their manifestation does not disturb the public order established by law.

11. Free communication of ideas and opinions is one of the most precious of the rights of man. Consequently, every citizen may speak, write, and print freely, subject to responsibility for the abuse of such liberty in the cases determined by law.

12. The guarantee of the rights of man and citizen necessitates a public force; such a force, therefore, is instituted for the advantage of all and not for the particular benefit of those to whom it is entrusted.

13. For the maintenance of the public force and for the expenses of administration a common tax is indispensable; it must be assessed equally on all citizens in proportion to their means.

14. Citizens have the right to ascertain, by themselves or through their representatives, the necessity of the public tax, to consent to it freely, to supervise its use, and to determine its quota, assessment, payment, and duration.

15. Society has the right to require of every public agent an accounting of his administration.

16. Every society in which the guarantee of rights is not assured or the separation of powers not determined has no constitution at all.

17. Since property is a sacred and inviolable right, no one may be deprived thereof unless a legally established public necessity obviously requires it, and upon condition of a just and previous indemnity.

1. What ideas from the Declaration of Independence reflect Locke and Rousseau's philosophies on government (see pages 46–48 and 92–95)?

2. Compare the similarities and differences between the Declaration of Independence and the Declaration of the Rights of Man and the Citizen. What accounts for the differences?

3. Summarize the articles of the Declaration of the Rights of Man and the Citizen under appropriate titles that reflect the focus of the articles.

4. Review the articles of the Declaration of the Rights of Man and the Citizen and describe the system of government and justice employed by the Bourbon monarchy.

5. Why do you think there is no specific mention of women in these documents?

Mary Wollstonecraft

Mary Wollstonecraft (1759–1797) wrote the first major feminist work of the modern period, *A Vindication of the Rights of Woman* (1792). Wollstonecraft was a supporter of educational equality and an advocate of women's rights. She lived in Paris during much of the French Revolution and was close to many of its leading figures.

A believer in human rights and social progress, Wollstonecraft extended her support of the principles of the Revolution to her own gender, and she argued for a new attitude toward women as part of the belief in progress, equality, and reason during the Enlightenment.

A Wollstonecraft states that women do not cultivate much of their intellectual potential because of prevailing social attitudes.

It is vain to expect virtue from women till they are, in some degree, independent of men; nay, it is vain to expect that strength of natural affection, which would make them good wives and mothers. Whilst they are absolutely dependent on their husbands they will be cunning, mean, and selfish, and the men who can be gratified by the fawning fondness of spaniel-like affection, have not much delicacy, for love is not to be bought, in any sense of the word, its silken wings are instantly shrivelled up when any thing beside a return in kind is sought. Yet whilst wealth enervates men; and women live, as it were, by their personal charms, how can we expect them to discharge those ennobling duties which equally require exertion and self-denial. . . .

To illustrate my opinion, I need only observe, that when a woman is admired for her beauty, and suffers herself to be so far intoxicated by the admiration she receives, as to neglect to discharge the indispensable duty of a mother, she sins against herself by neglecting to cultivate an affection that would equally tend to make her useful and happy. True happiness, I mean all the contentment, and virtuous satisfaction, that can be snatched in this imperfect state, must arise from well regulated affections; and an affection includes a duty. Men are not aware of the misery they cause, and the vicious weakness they cherish, by only inciting women to render themselves pleasing; they do not consider that they thus make natural and artificial duties clash, by sacrificing the comfort and respectability of a woman's life to voluptuous notions of beauty, when in nature they all harmonize. . . .

It is a melancholy truth; yet such is the blessed effect of civilization! the most respectable women are the most oppressed; and, unless they have understandings far superiour to the common run of understandings, taking in both sexes, they must, from being treated like contemptible beings, become contemptible. How many women thus waste life away the prey of discontent, who might have practised as physicians, regulated a farm, managed a shop, and stood erect, supported by their own industry, instead of hanging their heads surcharged with the dew of sensibility, that consumes the beauty to which it at first gave lustre; nay, I doubt whether pity and love are so near akin as poets feign, for I have seldom seen much compassion excited by the helplessness of females, unless they were fair; then, perhaps, pity was the soft handmaid of love, or the harbinger of lust.

Source: Mary Wollstonecraft, *A Vindication of the Rights of Woman*, ed. Carol H. Poston. New York: W. W. Norton & Company, Inc., 1975, pp. 141, 142, 149, 150, 167, 168–169, 192–194.

How much more respectable is the woman who earns her own bread by fulfilling any duty, than the most accomplished beauty! — beauty did I say? — so sensible am I of the beauty of moral loveliness, or the harmonious propriety that attunes the passions of a well-regulated mind, that I blush at making the comparison; yet I sigh to think how few women aim at attaining this respectability by withdrawing from the giddy whirl of pleasure, or the indolent calm that stupifies the good sort of women it sucks in.

Proud of their weakness, however, they must always be protected, guarded from care, and all the rough toils that dignify the mind. — If this be the fiat of fate, if they will make themselves insignificant and contemptible, sweetly to waste 'life away,' let them not expect to be valued when their beauty fades, for it is the fate of the fairest flowers to be admired and pulled to pieces by the careless hand that plucked them. In how many ways do I wish, from the purest benevolence, to impress this truth on my sex; yet I fear that they will not listen to a truth that dear bought experience has brought home to many an agitated bosom, nor willingly resign the privileges of rank and sex for the privileges of humanity, to which those have no claim who do not discharge its duties. . . .

Would men but generously snap our chains, and be content with rational fellowship instead of slavish obedience, they would find us more observant daughters, more affectionate sisters, more faithful wives, more reasonable mothers — in a word, better citizens. We should then love them with true affection, because we should learn to respect ourselves.

B   Equality in education is a major part of Wollstonecraft's reform program.

Let an enlightened nation then try what effect reason would have to bring them back to nature, and their duty; and allowing them to share the advantages of education and government with man, see whether they will become better, as they grow wiser and become free. They cannot be injured by the experiment; for it is not in the power of man to render them more insignificant than they are at present.

To render this practicable, day schools, for particular ages, should be established by government, in which boys and girls might be educated together. . . .

Girls and boys still together? I hear some readers ask: yes. And I should not fear any other consequences than that some early attachment might take place; which, whilst it had the best effect on the moral character of the young people, might not perfectly agree with the views of the parents, for it will be a long time, I fear, before the world will be so far enlightened that parents, only anxious to render their children virtuous, shall allow them to choose companions for life themselves.

Besides, this would be a sure way to promote early marriages, and from early marriages the most salutary physical and moral effects naturally flow.

What a different character does a married citizen assume from the selfish coxcomb, who lives, but for himself, and who is often afraid to marry lest he should not be able to live in a certain style. Great emergencies excepted, which would rarely occur in a society of which equality was the basis, a man can only be prepared to discharge the duties of public life, by the habitual practice of those inferiour ones which form the man.

In this plan of education the constitution of boys would not be ruined by the early debaucheries, which now make men so selfish, or girls rendered weak and vain, by indolence, and frivolous pursuits. But, I presuppose, that such a degree of equality should be established between the sexes as would shut out gallantry and coquetry, yet allow friendship and love to temper the heart for the discharge of higher duties.

These would be schools of morality — and the happiness of man, allowed to flow from the pure springs of duty and affection, what advances might not the human mind make? Society can only be happy and free in proportion as it is virtuous; but the present distinctions, established in society, corrode all private, and blast all public virtue.

C In her conclusion, Wollstonecraft asks for a revolution in the social system and in attitudes toward both sexes.

That women at present are by ignorance rendered foolish or vicious, is, I think, not to be disputed; and, that the most salutary effects tending to improve mankind might be expected from a REVOLUTION in female manners, appears, at least, with a face of probability, to rise out of the observation. For as marriage has been termed the parent of those endearing charities which draw man from the brutal herd, the corrupting intercourse that wealth, idleness, and folly, produce between the sexes, is more universally injurious to morality than all the other vices of mankind collectively considered. To adulterous lust the most sacred duties are sacrificed, because before marriage, men, by a promiscuous intimacy with women, learned to consider love as a selfish gratification — learned to separate it not only from esteem, but from the affection merely built on habit, which mixes a little humanity with it. Justice and friendship are also set at defiance, and that purity of taste is vitiated which would naturally lead a man to relish an artless display of affection rather than affected airs. But that noble simplicity of affection, which dares to appear unadorned, has few attractions for the libertine, though it be the charm, which by cementing the matrimonial tie, secures to the pledges of a warmer passion the necessary parental attention; for children will never be properly educated till friendship subsists between parents. Virtue flies from a house divided against itself — and a whole legion of devils take up their residence there.

The affection of husbands and wives cannot be pure when they have so few sentiments in common, and when so little confidence is established at home, as must be the case when their pursuits are so different. That intimacy from which tenderness should flow, will not, cannot subsist between the vicious.

Contending, therefore, that the sexual distinction which men have so warmly insisted upon, is arbitrary, I have dwelt on an observation, that several sensible men, with whom I have conversed on the subject, allowed to be well founded; and it is simply this, that the little chastity to be found amongst men, and consequent disregard of modesty, tend to degrade both sexes; and further, that the modesty of women, characterized as such, will often be only the artful veil of wantonness instead of being the natural reflection of purity, till modesty be universally respected.

From the tyranny of man, I firmly believe, the greater number of female follies proceed; and the cunning, which I allow makes at present a part of their character, I likewise have repeatedly endeavoured to prove, is produced by oppression. . . .

Let woman share the rights and she will emulate the virtues of man; for she must grow more perfect when emancipated, or justify the authority that chains such a weak being to her duty.

1. According to Wollstonecraft, why have women not progressed in society?

2. How does Wollstonecraft's view of equality in education compare to contemporary views?

3. In the last sentence of this reading Wollstonecraft mentions women being chained. Would Rousseau equate these chains with the ones he discusses in his opening statement (see pages 92–95)?

4. Are Wollstonecraft's observations about the role of women relevant today? Defend your position.

Edmund Burke

Edmund Burke (1729–1797) was the most important critic of the French Revolution. His *Reflections on the Revolution in France* was written in 1790, in response to those in Britain who supported the activities of the Revolution. Burke had supported the American colonists in their revolution because he believed they were agitating for their legitimate rights as British subjects. Now, arguing for the importance of tradition, religion, and established institutions, he claimed that the French had changed so much so fast that chaos and destruction would result. A strong supporter of government under law and in favour of a monarchy restrained by custom and traditional institutions, Burke became the spokesperson for the conservative position in the West.

A Burke views a constitution as an inherited system, and believes in the value of using tradition as a guide in social and political affairs.

You will observe that from Magna Charta to the Declaration of Right it has been the uniform policy of our constitution to claim and assert our liberties as an *entailed inheritance* derived to us from our forefathers, and to be transmitted to our posterity — as an estate specially belonging to the people of this kingdom, without any reference whatever to any other more general or prior right. By this means our constitution preserves a unity in so great a diversity of its parts. We have an inheritable crown, an inheritable peerage, and a House of Commons and a people inheriting privileges, franchises, and liberties from a long line of ancestors.

This policy appears to me to be the result of profound reflection, or rather the happy effect of following nature, which is wisdom without reflection, and above it. A spirit of innovation is generally the result of a selfish temper and confined views. People will not look forward to posterity, who never look backward to their ancestors. Besides, the people of England well know that the idea of inheritance furnishes a sure principle of conservation and a sure principle of transmission, without at all excluding a principle of improvement. It leaves acquisition free, but it secures what it acquires. . . . By a constitutional policy, working after the pattern of nature, we receive, we hold, we transmit our government and our privileges in the same manner in which we enjoy and transmit our property and our lives. The institutions of policy, the goods of fortune, the gifts of providence are handed down to us, and from us, in the same course and order. . . . Thus, by preserving the method of nature in the conduct of the state, in what we improve we are never wholly new; in what we retain we are never wholly obsolete. . . .

We procure reverence to our civil institutions on the principle upon which nature teaches us to revere individual men: on account of their age and on account of those from whom they are descended.

B Rights for Burke are inherited, part of the tradition of a society. Thus, he attacks the concept of natural rights and the idea of universal rules of justice.

If civil society be made for the advantage of man, all the advantages for which it is made become his right. It is an institution of beneficence; and law itself is only beneficence acting by a rule. Men have a right to live by that rule; they have a right to do justice, as between their fellows, whether their fellows are in public function or in ordinary occupation. They have a right to the fruits of their industry and to the means of making their industry fruitful. They have a right to the acquisitions of their parents, to the nourishment and improvement of their offspring, to instruction in life, and to consolation in death. Whatever each man can separately do, without trespassing upon others, he has a right to do for himself; and he has a right to a fair portion of all which society, with all its combinations of skill and force, can do in his favor. In this partnership all men have equal rights, but not to equal things. He that has but five shillings in the partnership

Source: Edmund Burke, *Reflections on the Revolution in France*, ed. Thomas H. D. Mahoney. Indianapolis: The Bobbs-Merrill Company, Inc., 1955, pp. 37–38, 39, 67–69, 97–100, 191–192, 193, 196–197.

has as good a right to it as he that has five hundred pounds has to his larger proportion. But he has not a right to an equal dividend in the product of the joint stock; and as to the share of power, authority, and direction which each individual ought to have in the management of the state, that I must deny to be amongst the direct original rights of man in civil society, for I have in my contemplation the civil social man, and no other. It is a thing to be settled by convention.

If civil society be the offspring of convention, that convention must be its law. That convention must limit and modify all the descriptions of constitution which are formed under it. Every sort of legislative, judicial, or executory power are its creatures. . . . Men cannot enjoy the rights of an uncivil and of a civil state together. That he may obtain justice, he gives up his right of determining what it is in points the most essential to him. That he may secure some liberty, he makes a surrender in trust of the whole of it.

Government is not made in virtue of natural rights, which may and do exist in total independence of it, and exist in much greater clearness and in a much greater degree of abstract perfection; but their abstract perfection is their practical defect. By having a right to everything they want everything. Government is a contrivance of human wisdom to provide for human *wants*. Men have a right that these wants should be provided for by this wisdom. Among these wants is to be reckoned the want, out of civil society, of a sufficient restraint upon their passions. Society requires not only that the passions of individuals should be subjected, but that even in the mass and body, as well as in the individuals, the inclinations of men should frequently be thwarted, their will controlled, and their passions brought into subjection. This can only be done *by a power out of themselves*, and not, in the exercise of its function, subject to that will and to those passions which it is its office to bridle and subdue. In this sense the restraints on men, as well as their liberties, are to be reckoned among their rights. But as the liberties and the restrictions vary with times and circumstances and admit to infinite modifications, they cannot be settled upon any abstract rule; and nothing is so foolish as to discuss them upon that principle. . . .

. . . Thanks to our sullen resistance to innovation, thanks to the cold sluggishness of our national character, we still bear the stamp of our forefathers. We have not (as I conceive) lost the generosity and dignity of thinking of the fourteenth century, nor as yet have we subtilized ourselves into savages. We are not the converts of Rousseau; we are not the disciples of Voltaire. . . . Atheists are not our preachers; madmen are not our lawgivers. We know that *we* have made no discoveries, and we think that no discoveries are to be made, in morality, nor many in the great principles of government, nor in the ideas of liberty, which were understood long before we were born, altogether as well as they will be after the grave has heaped its mold upon our presumption and the silent tomb shall have imposed its law on our pert loquacity. In England we have not yet been completely embowelled of our natural entrails; we still feel within us, and we cherish and cultivate, those inbred sentiments which are the faithful guardians, the active monitors of our duty, the true supporters of all liberal and manly morals. We have not been drawn and trussed, in order that we may be filled, like stuffed birds in a museum, with chaff and rags and paltry blurred shreds of paper about the rights of men. We preserve the whole of our feelings still native and entire, unsophisticated by pedantry and infidelity. We have real hearts of flesh and blood beating in our bosoms. We fear God; we look up with awe to kings, with affection to parliaments, with duty to magistrates, with reverence to priests, and with respect to nobility. . . .

You see, Sir, that in this enlightened age I am bold enough to confess that we are generally men of untaught feelings, that, instead of casting away all our old prejudices, we cherish them to a very considerable degree, and, to take more shame to ourselves, we cherish them because they are prejudices; and the longer they have lasted and the more generally they have prevailed, the more we cherish them. We are afraid to put men to live and trade each on his own private stock of reason, because we suspect that this stock in each man is small, and that the individuals would do better to avail themselves of the general bank and capital of nations and of ages. . . .

Your literary men and your politicians, and so do the whole clan of the enlightened among us, essentially differ in these points. They have no respect for the wisdom of others, but they pay it off by a very full measure of confidence in their own. With them it is a sufficient motive to destroy an old scheme of things because it is an old one. As to the new, they are in no sort of fear with regard to the duration of a building run up in haste, because duration is no object to those who think little or nothing has been done before their time, and who place all their hopes in discovery. They conceive, very systematically, that all things which give perpetuity are mischievous, and therefore they are at inexpiable war with all establishments. They think that government may vary like modes of dress, and with as little ill effect; that there needs no principle of attachment, except a sense of present convenience, to any constitution of the state.

C Burke challenges the validity of the National Assembly of France.

I have taken a view of what has been done by the governing power in France. I have certainly spoken of it with freedom. Those whose principle it is to despise the ancient, permanent sense of mankind and to set up a scheme of society on new principles must naturally expect that such of us who think better of the judgment of the human race than of theirs should consider both them and their devices as men and schemes upon their trial. They must take it for granted that we attend much to their reason, but not at all to their authority. They have not one of the great influencing prejudices of mankind in their favor. They avow their hostility to opinion. Of course, they must expect no support from that influence which, with every other authority, they have deposed from the seat of its jurisdiction.

I can never consider this Assembly as anything else than a voluntary association of men who have availed themselves of circumstances to seize upon the power of the state. They have not the sanction and authority of the character under which they first met. They have assumed another of a very different nature and have completely altered and inverted all the relations in which they originally stood. They do not hold the authority they exercise under any constitutional law of the state. They have departed from the instructions of the people by whom they were sent, which instructions, as the Assembly did not act in virtue of any ancient usage or settled law, were the sole source of their authority....

... This Assembly has hardly a year's prescription. We have their own word for it that they have made a revolution. To make a revolution is a measure which, *prima fronte* [on the face of it], requires an apology. To make a revolution is to subvert the ancient state of our country; and no common reasons are called for to justify so violent a proceeding. The sense of mankind authorizes us to examine into the mode of acquiring new power, and to criticize on the use that is made of it, with less awe and reverence than that which is usually conceded to a settled and recognized authority....

At once to preserve and to reform is quite another thing. When the useful parts of an old establishment are kept, and what is superadded is to be fitted to what is retained, a vigorous mind, steady, persevering attention, various powers of comparison and combination, and the resources of an understanding fruitful in expedients are to be exercised; they are to be exercised in a continued conflict with the combined force of opposite vices, with the obstinacy that rejects all improvement and the levity that is fatigued and disgusted with everything of which it is in possession. But you may object — "A process of this kind is slow. It is not fit for an assembly which glories in performing in a few months the work of ages. Such a mode of reforming, possibly, might take up many years." Without question it might; and it ought. It is one of the excellences of a method in which time is amongst the assistants, that its operation is slow and in some cases almost imperceptible.

1. What benefits does Burke see in tradition and inheritance as the basis of government?

2. How do Burke's views on government differ from those of Rousseau and Voltaire (see pages 92–95 and 96–100)?

3. How does Burke differentiate between reform and revolution?

4. Using hindsight, was Burke accurate in his analysis of the French Revolution? Explain.

Thomas Paine

The first part of Thomas Paine's *Rights of Man* appeared in early 1791, several months after Edmund Burke's *Reflections* was printed. Thus began the modern argument between radical and conservative, which has continued to the present. Paine

(1737–1809) was an Anglo-American whose earlier work *Common Sense* (1776) strongly supported the American rebellion against the British. Now, he wrote to discredit Burke's position on the French Revolution. Paine believed in a political authority that was contractual, as did Burke, but he also supported natural rights and the idea that democratic institutions must be implemented in order to guarantee those rights. The dialogue between Burke and Paine set the tone for the main political debate of the time.

A   Paine immediately attacks many of Burke's premises, including the value of tradition, the nature of change, and the importance of inherited institutions.

> There never did, there never will, and there never can exist a parliament, or any description of men, or any generation of men, in any country, possessed of the right or the power of binding and controlling posterity to the *"end of time,"* or of commanding for ever how the world shall be governed, or who shall govern it; and therefore, all such clauses, acts or declarations, by which the makers of them attempt to do what they have neither the right nor the power to do, nor the power to execute, are in themselves null and void. — Every age and generation must be as free to act for itself, *in all cases*, as the ages and generations which preceded it. The vanity and presumption of governing beyond the grave, is the most ridiculous and insolent of all tyrannies. . . . Every generation is, and must be, competent to all the purposes which its occasions require. It is the living, and not the dead, that are to be accommodated. When man ceases to be, his power and his wants cease with him; and having no longer any participation in the concerns of this world, he has no longer any authority in directing who shall be its governors, or how its government shall be organized, or how administered.
>
> I am not contending for nor against any form of government, nor for nor against any party here or elsewhere. That which a whole nation chooses to do, it has a right to do. Mr. Burke says, No. Where then *does* the right exist? I am contending for the rights of the *living*, and against their being willed away, and controlled and contracted for, by the manuscript assumed authority of the dead; and Mr. Burke is contending for the authority of the dead over the rights and freedom of the living. There was a time when kings disposed of their crowns by will upon their deathbeds, and consigned the people, like beasts of the field, to whatever successor they appointed. This is now so exploded as scarcely to be remembered, and so monstrous as hardly to be believed: But the parliamentary clauses upon which Mr. Burke builds his political church, are of the same nature. . . .
>
> A greater absurdity cannot present itself to the understanding of man, than what Mr. Burke offers to his readers. He tells them, and he tells the

Source: Thomas Paine, *Rights of Man*. Harmondsworth: Penguin Books, 1969, pp. 63–64, 65, 67, 70–71, 72, 73, 90–91, 93–95.

world to come, that a certain body of men, who existed a hundred years ago, made a law; and that there does not now exist in the nation, nor ever will, nor ever can, a power to alter it. Under how many subtleties, or absurdities, has the divine right to govern been imposed on the credulity of mankind! Mr. Burke has discovered a new one, and he has shortened his journey to Rome, by appealing to the power of this infallible parliament of former days; and he produces what it has done, as of divine authority: for that power must certainly be more than human, which no human power to the end of time can alter. . . .

The circumstances of the world are continually changing, and the opinions of men change also; and as government is for the living, and not for the dead, it is the living only that has any right in it. That which may be thought right and found convenient in one age, may be thought wrong and found inconvenient in another. In such cases, Who is to decide, the living, or the dead?

As almost one hundred pages of Mr. Burke's book are employed upon these clauses, it will consequently follow, that if the clauses themselves, so far as they set up an *assumed, usurped* dominion over posterity for ever, are unauthoritative, and in their nature null and void; that all his voluminous inferences and declamation drawn therefrom, or founded thereon, are null and void also: and on this ground I rest the matter.

B Paine claims that Burke opposed the rights of human beings and supported privilege and aristocracy.

When a man reflects on the condition which France was in from the nature of her government, he will see other causes for revolt than those which immediately connect themselves with the person or character of Louis XVI. There were, if I may so express it, a thousand despotisms to be reformed in France, which had grown up under the hereditary despotism of the monarchy, and became so rooted as to be in a great measure independent of it. Between the monarchy, the parliament, and the church, there was a *rivalship* of despotism, besides the feudal despotism operating locally, and the ministerial despotism operating everywhere. But Mr. Burke, by considering the King as the only possible object of a revolt, speaks as if France was a village, in which everything that passed must be known to its commanding officer, and no oppression could be acted but what he could immediately control. Mr. Burke might have been in the Bastille his whole life, as well under Louis XVI as Louis XIV and neither the one nor the other have known that such a man as Mr. Burke existed. The despotic principles of the government were the same in both reigns, though the dispositions of the men were as remote as tyranny and benevolence.

What Mr. Burke considers as a reproach to the French Revolution, (that of bringing it forward under a reign more mild than the preceding ones), is one of its highest honours. The revolutions that have taken place in other European countries, have been excited by personal hatred. The rage was against the man, and he became the victim. But, in the same instance of France, we see a revolution generated in the rational contemplation of the rights of man, and distinguishing from the beginning between persons and principles.

But Mr. Burke appears to have no idea of principles, when he is contemplating governments. "Then years ago" (says he) "I could have felicitated France on her having a government, without inquiring what the nature of that government was, or how it was administered." Is this the language of a rational man? Is it the language of a heart feeling as it ought to feel for the rights and happiness of the human race? On this ground, Mr. Burke must compliment all the governments in the world, while the victims who suffer under them, whether sold into slavery, or tortured out of existence, are wholly forgotten. It is power, and not principles, that Mr. Burke venerates; and under this abominable depravity, he is disqualified to judge between them. — Thus much for his opinion as to the occasions of the French Revolution. . . .

Through the whole of Mr. Burke's book I do not observe that the Bastille is mentioned more than once, and that with a kind of implication as if he were sorry it was pulled down, and wished it were built up again. . . .

From his violence and his grief, his silence on some points, and his excess on others, it is difficult not to believe that Mr. Burke is sorry, extremely sorry, that arbitrary power, the power of the Pope, and the Bastille, are pulled down.

Not one glance of compassion, not one commiserating reflection, that I can find throughout this book, has he bestowed on those who lingered out the most wretched of lives, a life without hope, in the most miserable of prisons. It is painful to behold a man employing his talents to corrupt himself. Nature has been kinder to Mr. Burke than he is to her. He is not affected by the reality of distress touching his heart, but by the showy resemblance of it striking his imagination. He pities the plumage but forgets the dying bird.

C Rights, contract, and constitutional authority are central to Paine's concerns.

Hitherto we have spoken only (and that but in part) of the natural rights of man. We have now to consider the civil rights of man, and to show how the one originates from the other. Man did not enter into society to become *worse* than he was before, nor to have fewer rights than he had before, but to have those rights better secured. His natural rights are the foundation of all his civil rights. . . .

. . . Natural rights are those which appertain to man in right of his existence. Of this kind are all the intellectual rights, or rights of the mind, and also all those rights of acting as an individual for his own comfort and happiness, which are not injurious to the natural rights of others. — Civil rights are those which appertain to man in right of his being a member of society. Every civil right has for its foundation, some natural right pre-existing in the individual, but to the enjoyment of which his individual power is not, in all cases, sufficiently competent. Of this kind are all those which relate to security and protection.

From this short review, it will be easy to distinguish between that class of natural rights which man retains after entering into society, and those which he throws into the common stock as a member of society.

The natural rights which he retains, are all those in which the *power* to execute is as perfect in the individual as the right itself. Among this class, as is before mentioned, are all the intellectual rights, or rights of the mind: consequently, religion is one of those rights. The natural rights which are not retained, are all those in which, though the right is perfect in the individual, the power to execute them is defective. They answer not his purpose. A man, by natural right, has a right to judge in his own cause; and so far as the right of mind is concerned, he never surrenders it: But what availeth it him to judge, if he has not power to redress? He therefore deposits this right in the common stock of society, and takes the arm of society, of which he is a part, in preference and in addition to his own. Society *grants* him nothing. Every man is a proprietor in society, and draws on the capital as a matter of right.

From these premises, two or three certain conclusions will follow.

First, That every civil right grows out of a natural right; or, in other words, is a natural right exchanged.

Secondly, That civil power, properly considered as such, is made up of the aggregate of that class of the natural rights of man, which becomes defective in the individual in point of power, and answers not his purpose; but when collected to a focus, becomes competent to the purpose of every one.

Thirdly, That the power produced from the aggregate of natural rights, imperfect in power in the individual, cannot be applied to invade the natural rights which are retained in the individual, and in which the power to execute is as perfect as the right itself. . . .

Can then Mr. Burke produce the English Constitution? If he cannot, we may fairly conclude, that though it has been so much talked about, no such thing as a constitution exists, or ever did exist, and consequently that the people have yet a constitution to form. . . .

The present National Assembly of France is, strictly speaking, the personal social compact. — The members of it are the delegates of the nation in its *original* character; future assemblies will be the delegates of the nation in its *organized* character. The authority of the present Assembly is different to what the authority of future Assemblies will be. The authority of the present one is to form a constitution: the authority of future Assemblies will be to legislate according to the principles and forms prescribed in that constitution; and if experience should hereafter show that alterations, amendments, or additions, are necessary, the constitution will point out the mode by which such things shall be done, and not leave it to the discretionary power of the future government.

1. Why does Paine reject the necessity of tradition in government?

2. How does Paine define a constitution compared to a government?

3. Do you think that Paine would still defend the French Revolution during the Reign of Terror? Defend your position.

4. What are the major philosophical differences between Burke's (see pages 108–112) and Paine's interpretation of the French Revolution?

The Ottoman Empire Responds to the French Revolution

Under the Treaty of Campo Formio (October 1797), France took possession of some of the Ionian Islands, which had belonged to the Venetian Republic, and of adjacent territory on the coasts of Albania and Greece, which bordered on Ottoman domains. The Russian ambassador to Istanbul warned the Ottoman authorities that the French would make dangerous neighbours. When they received reports of talk in those regions about creating a Greek state, about annexing Crete and, especially, about French preparations for an invasion of Egypt, the Ottomans took these warnings very seriously. Ahmed Atif Efendi (1759?–1819) was instructed to prepare an analysis of the situation and how the Ottoman Empire should react. When the French did eventually land in Egypt in July 1798, the Ottoman government distributed an Arabic document in Egypt, Syria, and Arabia that refuted the doctrines of the French Revolution.

A Atif Efendi opposes the rationalism and secular politics of the revolutionary period. *[handwritten: → as well as the enlightenment in general]*

It is one of the things known to all well informed persons that the conflagration of sedition and wickedness that broke out a few years ago in France, scattering sparks and shooting flames of mischief and tumult in all directions, had been conceived many years previously in the minds of certain accursed heretics, and had been a quiescent evil which they sought an opportunity to awaken. In this way: the known and famous atheists Voltaire and Rousseau, and other materialists like them, had printed and published various works, consisting, God preserve us, of insults and vilification against the pure prophets and great kings, of the removal and abolition of all religion, and of allusions to the sweetness of equality and republicanism, all expressed in easily intelligible words and phrases, in the form of mockery, in the language of the common people. Finding the pleasure of novelty in these writings, most of the people, even youths and

[handwritten left margin: strong religious connections to gov still]
[handwritten right margin: threat to religion and monarchy]

Source: Guy S. Métraux and François Crouzet, *The New Asia: Readings in the History of Mankind.* New York: New American Library, 1965, pp. 48, 49–51.

women, inclined toward them and paid close attention to them so that heresy and wickedness spread like syphilis to the arteries of their brains and corrupted their beliefs. When the Revolution became more intense, none took offense at the closing of churches, the killing and expulsion of monks, and the abolition of religion and doctrine: they set their hearts on equality and freedom, through which they hoped to attain perfect bliss in this world, in accordance with the lying teachings increasingly disseminated among the common people by this pernicious crew, who stirred up sedition and evil because of selfishness or self-interest. It is well known that the ultimate basis of the order and cohesion of every state is a firm grasp of the roots and branches of holy law, religion, and doctrine; that the tranquillity of the land and the control of the subjects cannot be encompassed by political means alone; that the necessity for the fear of God and the regard for retribution in the hearts of God's slaves is one of the unshakably established divine decrees; that in both ancient and modern times every state and people has had its own religion, whether true or false. Nevertheless the leaders of the sedition and evil appearing in France, in a manner without precedent, in order to facilitate the accomplishment of their evil purposes and in utter disregard of the fearsome consequences, have removed the fear of God and the regard for retribution from the common people, made lawful all kinds of abominable deeds, utterly obliterated all shame and decency, and thus prepared the way for the reduction of the people of France to the state of cattle. Nor were they satisfied with this alone, but, finding supporters like themselves in every place, in order to keep other states busy with the protection of their own regimes and thus forestall an attack on themselves, they had their rebellious declaration which they call "The Rights of Man" translated into all languages and published in all parts, and strove to incite the common people of the nations and religions to rebel against the kings to whom they were subject.

B Atif Efendi argues that the Ottoman Empire must prepare to defend its interests against the expansion of French influence.

In view of the foregoing observations, the question under consideration is this: is the Empire subject to the same danger as the other states, or is it not? Though since the beginning of this conflict, the Empire has chosen the path of neutrality, it has not refrained from showing friendship and good will and conducting itself in such a way as virtually to give assistance to the French republic, to such a degree as to occasion repeated protests from the other powers. At the time when France was in grave straits and afflicted by dearth and famine, the Empire permitted the export of copious supplies from the God-guarded realms and their transport to the ports of France, and thus saved them from the pangs of hunger. In recompense, the French Republic and its generals have not refrained from attempting, by word and deed, to subvert the subjects of the Empire. . . . Accordingly, at this time, it is obligatory for the Empire, in order to be forearmed against their threatening evil, to make powerful preparations, neglecting none of the means of defense, and not omitting to make a careful inquiry into all circumstances and activities. . . . For every state must have two kinds of policy. One is the permanent policy, which is taken as the foundation of all its actions and activities; the other is a temporary policy, followed for a period, in accordance with the requirements of the time and circumstances. The permanent policy of the Empire is to prevent any increase in the strength of Russia and Austria, which by virtue of their position are its natural enemies, and to be allied with those states which might be able to break their power and are thus the natural friends of the Empire. But in the present time and circumstances, the policy more conducive to the interests of the Empire is, first, to exert its strength to extinguish this fire of sedition and evil and then, this purpose having been accomplished, to act once more as required by its permanent policy.

two diff goals of the empire

C The French landed at Alexandria, in Egypt, on July 1, 1798. A proclamation was distributed challenging French ideas and goals.

In the Name of God, the Merciful and the Compassionate.

Praise be to God the Lord of the Universe, and blessings and peace on the chief of the Prophets and all his house and companions.

O you who believe in the unity of God, community of Muslims, know that the French nation (may God devastate their dwellings and abase their banners) are rebellious infidels and dissident evildoers; they do not believe in the unity of the Lord of Heaven and Earth, nor in the mission of the intercessor on the Day of Judgment, but have abandoned all religions, and denied the afterworld and its penalties. They do not believe in the day of resurrection, and pretend that only the passage of time destroys us, and that beyond this there is no resurrection and no reckoning, no examination and no retribution, no question and no answer. So that they have pillaged their churches and the adornments of their crucifixes and attacked their priests and monks. They assert that the books which the prophets brought are clear error, and that the Quran, the Torah, and the Gospels are nothing but lies and idle talk; and that those who claimed to be prophets, as Moses, Jesus, Muhammad, and others were not true, and that no prophet or apostle has ever come to the world, but that they lied to ignorant people; that all men are equal in humanity, and alike in being men, none has any superiority or merit over any other, and every one himself disposes of his soul and arranges his own livelihood in this life. And in this vain belief and preposterous opinion they have erected new principles and set laws, and established what Satan whispered to them, and destroyed the bases of religions, and made lawful to themselves forbidden things, and permitted to themselves whatever their passions desire, and have enticed into their iniquity the common people, who are as raving madmen, and sown sedition among religions, and thrown mischief between kings and states. With lying books and

i.e a secular gov

challenging ideology is a cultural death threat

meretricious falsehoods they address themselves to every party and say: "We belong to you, to your religion and to your community," and they make them vain promises, and utter fearful warnings. They are wholly given up to villainy and debauchery, and ride the steed of perfidy and presumption, and dive in the sea of error and impiety and are united under the banner of Satan. . . .

They compelled those who would not obey or follow them so that the other nations of the Franks were thrown into confusion and disorder by their iniquities; the French, baying like dogs and biting like wolves, gathered against these nations and communities, seeking to destroy the foundations of their religions and to plunder their women and their property. Blood flowed like water, and the French gained their object, and ruled over them with injustice and evil. Then their wickedness and evil plots were turned against the community of Muhammad. There has come into our hands through some of our spies the letters written to them by the director of their republic and head of their armies, Bonaparte.

1. What are Atif Efendi's main criticisms of the French Revolution?

2. Why might such criticism appeal to an Islamic audience?

3. How accurate is the description of the French Republic's attitude toward religion?

4. Why would the French Revolution have been seen as a threat to both Islamic and European monarchies?

Toussaint L'Ouverture

By 1793, Toussaint L'Ouverture (1743–1803) became the commander of the slave armies rebelling on the island of Saint Domingue. When France abolished slavery, he abandoned his Spanish allies and changed sides, becoming governor of Saint Domingue shortly thereafter. In 1801 he invaded Hispaniola and abolished slavery there. Napoleon was determined to remove Toussaint and re-impose slavery. A French army invaded Saint Domingue, and Toussaint was imprisoned in France, where he died of consumption. He remains Haiti's national hero.

 In a letter of April 13, 1799, Toussaint wrote about his reasons for joining the French.

The first successes obtained in Europe by the partisans of liberty over the agents of despotism were not slow to ignite the sacred fire of patriotism in the souls of all Frenchmen in St. Domingue. At that time, men's hopes turned to France, whose first steps toward her regeneration promised them a happier future; . . . they wanted to escape from their arbitrary government, but they did not intend the revolution to destroy either the prejudice that

Source: George F. Tyson, Jr., *Toussaint L'Ouverture*. Englewood Cliffs, N. J.: Prentice-Hall, Inc., 1973, pp. 30–31, 37–39, 43, 114.

debased the men of color or the slavery of the blacks, whom they held in dependency by the strongest law. In their opinion, the benefits of the French regeneration were only for them. They proved it by their obstinate refusal to allow the people of color to enjoy their political rights and the slaves to enjoy the liberty that they claimed. Thus, while the whites were erecting another form of government upon the rubble of despotism, the men of color and the blacks united themselves in order to claim their political existence; the resistance of the former having become stronger, it was necessary for the latter to rise up in order to obtain [political recognition] by force of arms. The whites, fearing that this legitimate resistance would bring general liberty to St. Domingue, sought to separate the men of color from the cause of the blacks in accordance with Machiavelli's principle of divide and rule. Renouncing their claims over the men of color, they accepted the April Decree [1792]. As they had anticipated, the men of color, many of whom were slaveholders, had only been using the blacks to gain their own political demands. Fearing the enfranchisement of the blacks, the men of color deserted their comrades in arms, their companions in misfortune, and aligned themselves with the whites to subdue them.

Treacherously abandoned, the blacks fought for some time against the reunited whites and the men of color; but, pressed on all sides, losing hope, they accepted the offers of the Spanish king, who, having at that time declared war on France, offered freedom to those blacks of St. Domingue who would join his armies. Indeed, the silence of pre-Republican France on the long-standing claims for their natural rights made by the most interested, the noblest, the most useful portion of the population of St. Domingue . . . extinguished all glimmer of hope in the hearts of the black slaves and forced them, in spite of themselves, to throw themselves into the arms of a protective power that offered the only benefit for which they would fight. More unfortunate than guilty, they turned their arms against their fatherland . . . .

Such were the crimes of these blacks, which have earned them to this day the insulting titles of brigands, insurgents, rebels under the orders of Jean François. At that time I was one of the leaders of these auxiliary troops, and I can say without fear of contradiction that I owed my elevation in these circumstances only to the confidence that I had inspired in my brothers by the virtues for which I am still honored today.

B On October 28, 1797, Toussaint wrote to the government of France about conditions in Saint Domingue. He defended his actions as supporting the ideals of the French Revolution, liberty and equality.

If, upon the arrival of the Commission, St. Domingue groaned under a military government, this power was not in the hands of the blacks; they were subordinate to it, and they only executed the orders of General Laveaux. These were the blacks who, when France was threatened with the loss of this Colony, employed their arms and their weapons to conserve it, to reconquer the greatest part of its territory that treason had handed over to the Spanish and English. . . . These were the blacks who, with the good citizens of the other two colors, flew to the rescue of General Laveaux . . . and who, by repressing the audacious rebels who wished to destroy the national representation, restored it to its rightful depository.

Such was the conduct of those blacks in whose hands citizen Vienot Vaublanc said the military government of St. Domingue found itself, such are those negroes he accuses of being ignorant and gross; undoubtedly they are, because without education there can only be ignorance and grossness. But must one impute to them the crime of this educational deficiency or, more correctly, accuse those who prevented them by the most atrocious punishments from obtaining it? And are only civilized people capable of distinguishing between good and evil, of having notions of charity and justice? The men of St. Domingue have been deprived of an education; but even so, they no longer remain in a state of nature, and because they haven't arrived at the degree of perfection that education bestows, they do not merit being classed apart from the rest of mankind, being confused with animals. . . .

Undoubtedly, one can reproach the inhabitants of St. Domingue, including the blacks, for many faults, even terrible crimes. But even in France, where the limits of sociability are clearly drawn, doesn't one see its inhabitants, in the struggle between despotism and liberty, going to all the excesses for which the blacks are reproached by their enemies? The fury of the two parties has been equal in St. Domingue; and if the excesses of the blacks in these critical moments haven't exceeded those committed in Europe, must not an impartial judge pronounce in favor of the former? Since it is our enemies themselves who present us as ignorant and gross, aren't we more excusable than those who, unlike us, were not deprived of the advantages of education and civilization? Surrounded by fierce enemies, oft cruel masters; without any other support than the charitable intentions of the friends of freedom in France, of whose existence we were hardly aware; driven to excessive errors by opposing parties who were rapidly destroying each other; knowing, at first, only the laws of the Mother-Country that favored the pretensions of our enemies and, since our liberty, receiving only the semiyearly or yearly instructions of our government, and no assistance, but almost always slanders or diatribes from our old oppressors — how can we not be pardoned some moments of ill-conduct, some gross faults, of which we were the first victims? Why, above all, reflect upon unreproachable men, upon the vast majority of the blacks, the faults of the lesser part, who, in time, had been reclaimed by the attentions of the majority to order and respect for the superior authorities? . . .

If General Rochambeau had reflected philosophically on the course of events, especially those of the human spirit, he would not find it so astonishing that the laws of liberty and equality were not precisely established in an American country whose connection with the Mother Country had been neglected for so long; he would have felt that at a time when

Europeans daily perjured themselves by handing over their quarters to the enemies of their country, prudence dictated that Government entrust its defense to the men of color and blacks whose interests were intimately linked to the triumph of the Republic; he would have felt that the military government then ruling the colony, by giving great power to the district commanders, could have led them astray in the labyrinths of uncertainty resulting from the absence of laws; he would have recalled that Martinique, defended by Europeans, fell prey to the English, whereas, St. Domingue, defended by the blacks and men of color whom Rochambeau accuses, remained constantly faithful to France. More accurately, if he had made the slightest effort to familiarize himself impartially with the law before his pronouncement, he wouldn't have generalized on the intentions of the blacks in respect to some antirepublican whites; he wouldn't have been so certain that they were all vexed and humiliated. I shall not call upon those among the whites who remained faithful to the principles of the Constitution by respecting them regardless of men's color . . . it was natural for the blacks to pay them the tribute of their gratitude; but it is to those who, openly declaring themselves the enemies of the principles of the Constitution, fought against them and whom a change of mind, more or less sincere, has brought back amongst us and reconciled with the country; it is these people whom I call upon to report the truth, to tell whether they weren't welcomed and protected and if, when they professed republican sentiments, they experienced the least vexation. When the proprietors of St. Domingue, when the Europeans who go there, instead of becoming the echoes of citizen Vaublanc by seeking to spread doubt about the liberty of the black people, show the intention of respecting this liberty, they will see growing in the hearts of these men the love and attachment that they have never ceased to hold for the whites in general and their former masters in particular, despite all of those who have tried to re-establish slavery and restore the rule of tyranny in St. Domingue. . . .

Far be it from me to want to excuse the crimes of the revolution in St. Domingue by comparing them to even greater crimes, but citizen Vaublanc, while threatening us in the *Corps Legislatif*, didn't bother to justify the crimes that have afflicted us and which could only be attributed to a small number. . . . However, this former proprietor of slaves couldn't ignore what slavery was like; perhaps he had witnessed the cruelties exercised upon the miserable blacks, victims of their capricious masters, some of whom were kind but the greatest number of whom were true tyrants. And what would Vaublanc say . . . if, having only the same natural rights as us, he was in his turn reduced to slavery? Would he endure without complaint the insults, the miseries, the tortures, the whippings? And if he had the good fortune to recover his liberty, would he listen without shuddering to the howls of those who wished to tear it from him? . . . Certainly not; in the same way he so indecently accuses the black people of the excesses of a few of their members, we would unjustly accuse the entirety of France of the excesses of a small number of partisans of the old system. Less enlightened than citizen Vaublanc, we know, nevertheless, that whatever their color, only one distinction must exist between men, that of good and evil. When blacks, men of color, and whites are under the same laws, they must be equally protected and they must be equally repressed when they deviate from them. Such is my opinion; such are my desires.

C In 1802, while Toussaint was in prison in France, the English Romantic poet William Wordsworth (1770–1850) wrote a sonnet, "To Toussaint L'Ouverture," in which he asks Toussaint to find consolation in his contributions to freedom and in his having achieved a kind of immortality.

> Toussaint, the most unhappy man of men!
> Whether the whistling rustic tends his plough
> Within thy hearing, or thy head be now
> Pillowed in some deep dungeon's earless den;
> Oh, miserable chieftain! where and when
> Wilt thou find patience? Yet die not: do thou
> Wear rather in thy bonds a cheerful brow;
> Though fallen thyself, never to rise again,
> Live and take comfort. Thou hast left behind
> Powers that work for thee: air, earth, and skies.
> There's not a breathing of the common wind
> That will forget thee: thou hast great allies:
> Thy friends are exultations, agonies,
> And love, and man's unconquerable mind.

1. According to Toussaint, how did the whites "divide and rule" men of colour?

2. How does Toussaint attempt to appeal to French Republicans by attacking the stereotype of Blacks?

3. What hope does Toussaint see in the French Revolution for Haiti?

4. According to Wordsworth, what is Toussaint's legacy?

Simón Bolívar

Simón Bolívar (1783–1830) was born into an aristocratic family in Venezuela. He studied in Europe, visited the United States, and was exposed to the era's most advanced ideas. Bolívar imagined an independent Spanish America, and the French invasion of Spain in 1808 gave him the opportunity to try and realize this goal. He participated in the independence struggles that began in 1811, and when he defeated the Spaniards in 1819 he was named President of the new Republic of Gran Colombia. He then turned to Ecuador, Peru, and Bolivia, all of which he dreamed of incorporating into a single nation. The attempt collapsed into civil war. With his dream in ruins, Bolívar died before he could be exiled to Europe.

A Following the failure of his initial attempt to liberate Colombia and Venezuela, Bolívar fled to the British colony of Jamaica. In his "Jamaica Letter" (1815), Bolívar describes the situation of the South American people as he saw it.

> We are a young people. We inhabit a world apart, separated by broad seas. We are young in the ways of almost all the arts and sciences, although, in a certain manner, we are old in the ways of civilized society. I look upon the present state of America as similar to that of Rome after its fall. . . .
>
> Americans today, and perhaps to a greater extent than ever before, who live within the Spanish system occupy a position in society no better than that of serfs destined for labor, or at best they have no more status than that of mere consumers. Yet even this status is surrounded with galling restrictions, such as being forbidden to grow European crops, or to store products which are royal monopolies, or to establish factories of a type the Peninsula itself does not possess. To this add the exclusive trading privileges, even in articles of prime necessity, and the barriers between American provinces, designed to prevent all exchange of trade, traffic, and understanding. In short, do you wish to know what our future held? — simply the cultivation of the fields of indigo, grain, coffee, sugar cane, cacao, and cotton; cattle raising on the broad plains; hunting wild game in the jungles; digging in the earth to mine its gold — but even these limitations could never satisfy the greed of Spain.
>
> So negative was our existence that I can find nothing comparable in any other civilized society, examine as I may the entire history of time and the politics of all nations. Is it not an outrage and a violation of human rights to expect a land so splendidly endowed, so vast, rich, and populous, to remain merely passive?
>
> As I have just explained, we were cut off and, as it were, removed from the world in relation to the science of government and administration of the state. We were never viceroys or governors, save in the rarest of instances; seldom archbishops and bishops; diplomats never; as military men, only subordinates; as nobles, without royal privileges. In brief, we were neither magistrates nor financiers and seldom merchants — all in flagrant contradiction to our institutions.

B After analyzing the situation in each of the Spanish colonies, Bolívar expresses his view of the region's future and the form of government that would suit it best.

> From the foregoing, we can draw these conclusions: The American provinces are fighting for their freedom, and they will ultimately succeed. . . .
>
> It is a grandiose idea to think of consolidating the New World into a single nation, united by pacts into a single bond. It is reasoned that, as these

Sources: Simón Bolívar, *Selected Writings of Bolívar*, trans. Lewis Bertrand. New York: The Colonial Press Inc., 1951, pp. 110–112, 118–119, 176–179, 185–186.

parts have a common origin, language, customs, and religion, they ought to have a single government to permit the newly formed states to unite in a confederation. But this is not possible. Actually, America is separated by climatic differences, geographic diversity, conflicting interests, and dissimilar characteristics. . . .

Among the popular and representative systems, I do not favor the federal system. It is over-perfect, and it demands political virtues and talents far superior to our own. For the same reason I reject a monarchy that is part aristocracy and part democracy, although with such a government England has achieved much fortune and splendor. Since it is not possible for us to select the most perfect and complete form of government, let us avoid falling into demagogic anarchy or monocratic tyranny. These opposite extremes would only wreck us on similar reefs of misfortune and dishonor; hence, we must seek a mean between them. I say: Do not adopt the best system of government, but the one that is most likely to succeed.

C Bolívar's speech, "Message to the Congress of Angostura, February 15, 1819," is considered one of the most important declarations he ever made. The speech led to the Congress electing him President and agreeing to establish a single state, Gran Colombia. Bolívar begins his speech by describing the differences between the people of the former British North American colonies and those of Venezuela.

We are not Europeans; we are not Indians; we are but a mixed species of aborigines and Spaniards. Americans by birth and Europeans by law, we find ourselves engaged in a dual conflict: we are disputing with the natives for titles of ownership, and at the same time we are struggling to maintain ourselves in the country that gave us birth against the opposition of the invaders. Thus our position is most extraordinary and complicated. But there is more. As our role has always been strictly passive and political existence nil, we find that our quest for liberty is now even more difficult of accomplishment; for we, having been placed in a state lower than slavery, had been robbed not only of our freedom but also of the right to exercise an active domestic tyranny. . . . We have been ruled more by deceit than by force, and we have been degraded more by vice than by superstition. Slavery is the daughter of darkness: an ignorant people is a blind instrument of its own destruction. . . . If a people, perverted by their training, succeed in achieving their liberty, they will soon lose it, for it would be of no avail to endeavor to explain to them that happiness consists in the practice of virtue; that the rule of law is more powerful than the rule of tyrants, because, as the laws are more inflexible, every one should submit to their beneficent austerity; that proper morals, and not force, are the bases of law; and that to practice justice is to practice liberty.

Although those people [North Americans], so lacking in many respects, are unique in the history of mankind, it is a marvel, I repeat, that so weak and complicated a government as the federal system has managed to govern them in the difficult and trying circumstances of their past. But, regardless of the effectiveness of this form of government with respect to North America, I must say that it has never for a moment entered my mind to compare the position and character of two states as dissimilar as the English-American and the Spanish-American. Would it not be most difficult to apply to Spain the English system of political, civil, and religious liberty: Hence, it would be even more difficult to adapt to Venezuela the laws of North America.

D Bolívar then explains why he favours the centralized British system of government over the federal system of the United States.

Nothing in our fundamental laws would have to be altered were we to adopt a legislative power similar to that held by the British Parliament. Like the North Americans, we have divided national representation into two chambers: that of Representatives and the Senate. The first is very wisely constituted. . . . If the Senate were hereditary rather than elective, it would, in my opinion, be the basis, the tie, the very soul of our republic. In political storms this body would arrest the thunderbolts of the government and would repel any violent popular reaction. Devoted to the government because of a natural interest in its own preservation, a hereditary senate would always oppose any attempt on the part of the people to infringe upon the jurisdiction and authority of their magistrates. . . . The creation of a hereditary senate would in no way be a violation of political equality. I do not solicit the establishment of a nobility, for as a celebrated republican has said, that would simultaneously destroy equality and liberty. What I propose is an office for which the candidates must prepare themselves, an office that demands great knowledge and the ability to acquire such knowledge. All should not be left to chance and the outcome of elections. . . . The hereditary senate will also serve as a counterweight to both government and people; and as a neutral power it will weaken the mutual attacks of these two eternally rival powers.

1. What dilemmas do Bolívar and his contemporaries face in developing an identity in America?

2. Based on Bolívar's descriptions, how did Spain politically and economically administer its colonies?

3. Why does Bolívar reject federalism as an appropriate form of government in South America?

4. How does Bolívar, a strong republican, support the creation of a hereditary senate?

5. How might Spanish colonial rule have influenced Bolívar's support for a British-style system of government?

Mirza Abu Taleb Khan

Mirza Abu Taleb Khan (1752–1806) was born in Lucknow, India, after his family had emigrated from Persia. He worked as a revenue officer for the East India Company. After incurring some debts and having some family misfortune, he accepted an offer from a British friend to visit England, where he stayed for several years. Abu Taleb Khan was well received by elite British society, who called him "the Persian Prince." Once home, he published an account of his travels. His Persian text was translated into English in 1810, making it one of the first books about the West by a non-Westerner to be published in English. It was translated into French and German four years later. Abu Taleb Khan also wrote poetry, histories, and a treatise on astronomy.

 Abu Taleb Khan contrasts the status and the liberty of women in England with women in Islamic society.

> The English legislators and philosophers have wisely determined, that the best mode of keeping women out of the way of temptation, and their minds from wandering after improper desires, is by giving them sufficient employment; therefore whatever business can be effected without any great exertion of mental abilities or corporeal strength, is assigned to the women. Thus they have all the internal management and care of the house, and washing the clothes. They are also employed to take care of shops, and, by their beauty and eloquence, often attract customers. This I can speak from my own experience; for I scarcely ever passed the pastry-cook's shop at the corner of Newman street in Oxford road, that I did not go in and spend money for the pleasure of talking to a beautiful young woman who kept it. To the men is assigned the business of waiting at table, taking care of the horses and cattle, and management of the garden, farm, etc. This division of labour is attended with much convenience, and prevents confusion.
>
> Besides the above important regulation, the English lawgivers have placed the women under many salutary restraints, which prevent their making an improper use of the liberty they have, of mixing in company, and conversing with men. In the first place, strangers, or persons whose characters are not well known, are seldom introduced to them; secondly the women never visit any bachelor, except he be a near relation; thirdly, no woman of respectability ever walks out (in London), unless attended by her husband, a relation or a confidential servant. They are upon no account allowed to walk out after dark; and they never think of sleeping abroad, even at the house of their father or mother, unless the husband is with them. They therefore have seldom an opportunity of acting improperly.

Source: Mirza Abu Taleb Khan, *Travels of Mirza Abu Taleb Khan in Asia, Africa, and Europe During the Years 1799 to 1803*, trans. Charles Stewart. New Delhi: Sona Publications, 1972, pp. 128–129, 130–131, 148, 168–169, 170–171, 173–179.

The father, mother, and whole family, also consider themselves disgraced by the bad conduct of a daughter or a sister. And as, by the laws of England, a man may beat his wife with a stick which will not endanger the breaking of a limb, or may confine her in a room, the women dare not even give their tongues too much liberty.

If, notwithstanding all these restraints, a woman should be so far lost to all sense of shame as to commit a disgraceful action, she is for ever after shunned by all her relations, acquaintances, and every lady of respectability. Her husband is also authorised by law to take away all her property and ornaments, to debar her from the sight of her children, and even to turn her out of the house; and if proof can be produced of her misconduct, he may obtain a divorce, by which she is entirely separated from him, and loses all her dower, and even her marriage portion. From what has been stated, it is evident that the English women, notwithstanding their apparent liberty, and the politeness and flattery with which they are addressed, are, by the wisdom of their lawgivers, confined in strict bondage; and that, on the contrary, the Mohammedan women, who are prohibited from mixing in society, and are kept concealed behind curtains, but are allowed to walk out in veils, and to go to the baths (in Turkey), and to visit their fathers and mothers and even female acquaintances, and to sleep abroad for several nights together, are much more mistresses of their own conduct and much more liable to fall into the paths of error.

Liberty may be considered as the idol, or tutelary deity, of the English; and I think the common people here enjoy more freedom and equality than in any other well-regulated government in the world.

B Abu Taleb Khan comments on the status of servants and the right of criticism.

In England, no gentleman can punish his servant for any crime (except by turning him away), but must make his complaint before a magistrate. The servants in England receive very high wages, are as well fed, sleep as comfortably in raised beds (not on the floor, as in India), and are as well clothed, as their masters, who, in general, prefer plain clothes for themselves, while their servants are covered with lace; nor are they obliged to run after their masters while they are riding (as our grooms do) . . . .

In their newspapers and daily publications, the common people often take the liberty of abusing their superiors; also, in all public meetings, and even at the play houses, they frequently hiss and reproach any nobleman and gentleman they dislike. Another mode they have of expressing their displeasure is by *caricatures*: in these, they frequently pourtray the Ministers, or any other public characters, in ridiculous situations . . . . In these pictures the Minister is always placed in so ludicrous a point of view, that even when he sees it himself he cannot refrain from laughing.

After all, this equality is more in appearance than in reality; for the difference between the comforts of the rich and of the poor is, in England, much greater than in India. The servants are not at liberty to quit their master without giving proper warning; and, in general, they are as respectful in their behaviour as the slaves of Hindoostan.

C He admires the parliamentary system.

The next persons in rank to the Lords are the Members of the House of Commons. Their number is above three hundred and fifty. Two of them are elected by the inhabitants of every town in the kingdom, to be their agents or representatives in Parliament. They are, in general, men of very superior abilities and considerable property. For seven months in the year they remain in London, and attend five days in the week at the Parliament House. Some of their duties have been before described; but when their attention is not taken up with great political subjects, they employ themselves in considering the internal regulations, and plans for improving the state of the country, and in fact, take cognizance of every thing that is going forward. Even the laws respecting culprits are abrogated or altered by Parliament; for the Christians, contrary to the systems of the Jews and Mohammedans, do not acknowledge to have received any laws respecting *temporal* matters from Heaven, but take upon themselves to make such regulations as the exigencies of the times require.

D In his work, Abu Taleb Khan lists twelve "defects" of the English.

The first and greatest defect I observed in the English, is their want of faith in religion, and their great inclination to philosophy (atheism). The effects of these principles, or rather want of principle, is very conspicuous in the lower orders of people, who are totally devoid of honesty. . . .

The second defect, most conspicuous in the English character, is pride, or insolence. Puffed up with their power and good fortune for the last fifty years, they are not apprehensive of adversity, and take no pains to avert it. . . .

Their third defect is a passion for acquiring money, and their attachment to worldly affairs. . . .

The fourth of their frailties is a desire of ease, and a dislike to exertion: this, however, prevails only in a moderate degree, and bears no proportion to the apathy and indolence of the smokers of opium of Hindoostan and Constantinople . . . .

Their fifth defect is nearly allied to the former, and is termed irritability of temper. This passion often leads them to quarrel with their friends and acquaintances, without any substantial cause. . . .

The sixth defect of the English is their throwing away their time, in sleeping, eating, and dressing; for, besides the necessary ablutions, they every morning shave, and dress their hair; then, to accommodate themselves to the fashion, they put on twenty-five different articles of dress: all this, except shaving, is repeated before dinner, and the whole of these clothes are again to be taken off at night: so that not less than two complete hours can be allowed on this account. One hour is expended at breakfast; three hours at dinner; and the three following hours are devoted to tea, and the company of the ladies. . . .

Their seventh defect is a luxurious manner of living, by which their wants are increased a hundred-fold. Observe their kitchens, filled with various utensils; their rooms, fitted up with costly furniture; their side-boards, covered with plate; their tables, loaded with expensive glass and china; their cellars, stocked with wines from every quarter of the world; their parks, abounding in game of various sorts; and their ponds, stored with fish. All these expences are incurred to pamper their appetites, which, from long indulgence, have gained such absolute sway over them, that a diminution of these luxuries would be considered, by many, as a serious misfortune. . . .

The eighth defect of the English is vanity, and arrogance, respecting their acquirements in science, and a knowledge of foreign languages . . . .

A ninth failing prevalent among the English is selfishness. They frequently endeavour to benefit themselves, without attending to the injury it may do to others . . . .

The tenth vice of this nation is want of chastity; for under this head I not only include the reprehensible conduct of young women running away with their lovers, and others cohabiting with a man before marriage, but the great degree of licentiousness practised by numbers of both sexes in London; evinced by the multiplicity of public-houses and bagnios in every part of the town. I was credibly informed, that in the single parish of Mary-la-bonne, which is only a sixth part of London, there reside sixty thousand courtezans . . . .

The eleventh vice of the English is extravagance, that is, living beyond their incomes by incurring useless expences, and keeping up unnecessary establishments. . . . Much money is also lavished in London, on balls, masquerades, routs etc. Sometimes the sum of £1000 [$2248] is thus expended in one night's entertainment. . . . It also encourages dissipation and profligacy in the lower classes, which tend to the subversion of all order and good government. . . .

Their twelfth defect is a contempt for the customs of other nations, and the preference they give to their own; although theirs, in fact, may be much inferior. . . .

Few of the English have good sense or candour enough to acknowledge the prevalence and growth of these vices, or defects, among them; but, like the smokers of *beng* (hempseed) in Turkey, when told of the virtues of their ancestors, and their own present degeneracy, make themselves ready for battle, and say, "No nation was ever exempt from vices: the people and the governments you describe as possessing such angelic virtues were not a bit better than ourselves; and so long as we are not worse than our neighbours, no danger is to be apprehended." This reasoning is, however, false; for fire still retains its inflammable nature, whether it is summer or winter; and the flame, though for a short time smothered by a heap of fuel thrown on it, breaks out in the sequel with the greatest violence. In like manner, vice will, sooner or later, cause destruction to its possessor.

1. How does Abu Taleb Khan compare the status of women in England with Turkey?

2. How has the status of women evolved in contemporary England and Turkey? Are Abu Taleb Khan's observations relevant today?

3. Locate examples of Abu Taleb Khan's criticism of English society and institutions.

4. Based on Abu Taleb Khan's criticism of English society, what would he expect from Islamic society?

5. Write a defence of British society and institutions in response to Abu Taleb Khan's criticisms.

Industrialization, Liberalism, and Nationalism, 1815–1871

Don't Meddle With It is the title of this 1834 lithograph by Honoré Daumier (1808–1879), one of the foremost political commentators in the nineteenth-century popular press. Here, a monumental heroic printer, in his work-clothes, with fists clenched, defends a plot called "Freedom of the Press." Going forward on the left is the French King Louis-Philippe, brandishing his umbrella as a weapon. The former king, Charles X, who was driven from the French throne in the revolution of 1830, in part for his support of press censorship, is the figure who has fainted on the right. The implication is clear: King Louis-Philippe will also be overthrown if he meddles with press freedom.

William Wordsworth

William Wordsworth (1770–1850) led the Romantic movement in England, which challenged the neo-classical ideal, and attacked the beliefs that serious poetry was about the lives of epic heroes, and that the language of poetry was artificial. Wordsworth asserted that poetry could deal with the feelings of ordinary people, its language could resemble that of everyday life, and the source of literary inspiration was the inner life of the creative poet.

A Wordsworth's "Tintern Abbey" (the full title is "Lines Composed a Few Miles Above Tintern Abbey on Revisiting the Banks of the Wye During a Tour, July 13, 1798") was the last poem printed in *Lyrical Ballads*, which he and Samuel Taylor Coleridge (1772–1834) published in 1798. Here, Wordsworth discusses themes related to nature and memory; the relationship between past, present, and future; and human suffering and the human spirit.

Five years have passed; five summers, with
    the length
Of five long winters! and again I hear
These waters, rolling from their mountain-springs
With a sweet inland murmur. — Once again
Do I behold these steep and lofty cliffs,
Which on a wild secluded scene impress
Thoughts of more deep seclusion; and connect
The landscape with the quiet of the sky.
The day is come when I again repose
Here, under this dark sycamore, and view
These plots of cottage-ground, these orchard-tufts,
Which, at this season, with their unripe fruits,
Among the woods and copses lose themselves,
Nor, with their green and simple hue, disturb
The wild green landscape. Once again I see
These hedge-rows, hardly hedge-rows, little lines
Of sportive wood run wild; these pastoral farms
Green to the very door; and wreathes of smoke
Sent up, in silence, from among the trees,
With some uncertain notice, as might seem,
Of vagrant dwellers in the houseless woods,
Or of some hermit's cave, where by his fire
The hermit sits alone.

Though absent long,
These forms of beauty have not been to me,
As is a landscape to a blind man's eye:

But oft, in lonely rooms, and mid the din
Of towns and cities, I have owed to them,
In hours of weariness, sensations sweet,
Felt in the blood, and felt along the heart,
And passing even into my purer mind
With tranquil restoration: — feelings too
Of unremembered pleasure; such, perhaps,
As may have had no trivial influence
On that best portion of a good man's life;
His little, nameless, unremembered acts
Of kindness and of love. Nor less, I trust,
To them I may have owed another gift,
Of aspect more sublime; that blessed mood,
In which the burthen of the mystery,
In which the heavy and the weary weight
Of all this unintelligible world
Is lighten'd: — that serene and blessed mood,
In which the affections gently lead us on,
Until, the breath of this corporeal frame,
And even the motion of our human blood
Almost suspended, we are laid asleep
In body, and become a living soul:
While with an eye made quiet by the power
Of harmony, and the deep power of joy,
We see into the life of things.

If this
Be but a vain belief, yet, oh! how oft,

Source: William Wordsworth and Samuel Taylor Coleridge, *Lyrical Ballads, 1798,* ed. W. J. B. Owen. Oxford: Oxford University Press, 1969, pp. 111–117.

In darkness, and amid the many shapes
Of joyless day-light; when the fretful stir
Unprofitable, and the fever of the world,
Have hung upon the beatings of my heart,
How oft, in spirit, have I turned to thee
O sylvan Wye! Thou wanderer through
    the woods,
How often has my spirit turned to thee!

And now, with gleams of half-extinguish'd
    thought,
With many recognitions dim and faint,
And somewhat of a sad perplexity,
The picture of the mind revives again:
While here I stand, not only with the sense
Of present pleasure, but with pleasing thoughts
That in this moment there is life and food
For future years. And so I dare to hope
Though changed, no doubt, from what I was,
    when first
I came among these hills; when like a roe
I bounded o'er the mountains, by the sides
Of the deep rivers, and the lonely streams,
Wherever nature led; more like a man
Flying from something that he dreads, than one
Who sought the thing he loved. For nature then
(The coarser pleasures of my boyish days,
And their glad animal movements all gone by,)
To me was all in all. — I cannot paint
What then I was. The sounding cataract
Haunted me like a passion: the tall rock,
The mountain, and the deep and gloomy wood,
Their colours and their forms, were then to me

An appetite: a feeling and a love,
That had no need of a remoter charm,
By thought supplied, or any interest
Unborrowed from the eye. — That time is past,
And all its aching joys are now no more,
And all its dizzy raptures. Not for this
Faint I, nor mourn nor murmur: other gifts
Have followed, for such loss, I would believe,
Abundant recompence. For I have learned
To look on nature, not as in the hour
Of thoughtless youth, but hearing oftentimes
The still, sad music of humanity,
Not harsh nor grating, though of ample power
To chasten and subdue. And I have felt
A presence that disturbs me with the joy
Of elevated thoughts; a sense sublime
Of something far more deeply interfused,
Whose dwelling is the light of setting suns,
And the round ocean, and the living air,
And the blue sky, and in the mind of man,
A motion and a spirit, that impels
All thinking things, all objects of all thought,
And rolls through all things. Therefore am I still
A lover of the meadows and the woods,
And mountains; and of all that we behold
From this green earth; of all the mighty world
Of eye and ear, both what they half-create,
And what perceive; well pleased to recognize
In nature and the language of the sense,
The anchor of my purest thoughts, the nurse,
The guide, the guardian of my heart, and soul
Of all my moral being.
. . . .

1. Considering the social and economic conditions that existed in Britain when this poem was written, why would it have appealed to the general population?

2. How does Wordsworth compare the mood of cities and towns with nature?

3. How does nature provide a calming influence on the writer?

Mary Shelley

Mary Shelley (1797–1851) produced a modern myth with *Frankenstein* (1818), among the first writings of science fiction. *Frankenstein* deals with the relationship between creator and creation, and the idea of the monstrous in all of our lives. Shelley, the daughter of Mary Wollstonecraft, was a young woman when she wrote this gothic tale on a holiday in Italy. She claimed the story grew out of her imagination, in a dream. The tale, subtitled "the modern Prometheus," is about the scientist Dr. Frankenstein, who creates life and is destroyed by his own work.

A In the novel, Frankenstein is the scientist (not the monster, as in many modern film and television versions). In the following passages, he emotionally recounts his horror at his creation of life.

> It was on a dreary night of November, that I beheld the accomplishment of my toils. With an anxiety that almost amounted to agony, I collected the instruments of life around me, that I might infuse a spark of being into the lifeless thing that lay at my feet. It was already one in the morning; the rain pattered dismally against the panes, and my candle was nearly burnt out, when, by the glimmer of the half-extinguished light, I saw the dull yellow eye of the creature open; it breathed hard, and a convulsive motion agitated its limbs.
>
> How can I describe my emotions at this catastrophe, or how delineate the wretch whom with such infinite pains and care I had endeavoured to form? His limbs were in proportion, and I had selected his features as beautiful. Beautiful! — Great God! His yellow skin scarcely covered the work of muscles and arteries beneath; his hair was of a lustrous black, and flowing; his teeth of a pearly whiteness; but these luxuriances only formed a more horrid contrast with his watery eyes, that seemed almost of the same colour as the dun white sockets in which they were set, his shrivelled complexion and straight black lips.
>
> The different accidents of life are not so changeable as the feelings of human nature. I had worked hard for nearly two years, for the sole purpose of infusing life into an inanimate body. For this I had deprived myself of rest and health. I had desired it with an ardour that far exceeded moderation; but now that I had finished, the beauty of the dream vanished, and breathless horror and disgust filled my heart. Unable to endure the aspect of the being I had created, I rushed out of the room, and continued a long time traversing my bed-chamber, unable to compose my mind to sleep. At length lassitude succeeded to the tumult I had before endured; and I threw myself on the bed in my clothes, endeavouring to seek a few moments of forgetfulness. But it was in vain: I slept, indeed, but I was disturbed by the wildest dreams. I thought I saw Elizabeth, in the bloom of health, walking in the streets of Ingolstadt. Delighted and surprised, I embraced her; but as I imprinted the first kiss on her lips, they became livid with the hue of death; her features appeared to change, and I thought that I held the corpse of my dead mother in my arms; a shroud enveloped her form, and I saw the graveworms crawling in the folds of the flannel. I started from my sleep with horror; a cold dew covered my forehead, my teeth chattered, and every limb became convulsed: when, by the dim and yellow light of the moon,

Source: Mary Shelley, *Frankenstein*. Oxford: Oxford University Press, 1969, pp. 57–58, 98–101, 166–167.

as it forced its way through the window shutters, I beheld the wretch — the miserable monster whom I had created. He held up the curtain of the bed; and his eyes, if eyes they may be called, were fixed on me. His jaws opened, and he muttered some inarticulate sounds, while a grin wrinkled his cheeks. He might have spoken, but I did not hear; one hand was stretched out, seemingly to detain me, but I escaped, and rushed down stairs. I took refuge in the courtyard belonging to the house which I inhabited; where I remained during the rest of the night, walking up and down in the greatest agitation, listening attentively, catching and fearing each sound as if it were to announce the approach of the demoniacal corpse to which I had so miserably given life.

Oh! no mortal could support the horror of that countenance. A mummy again endued with animation could not be so hideous as that wretch.

B In the middle of the work, Dr. Frankenstein and the monster meet on Mont Blanc, a favourite place in Romantic literature to depict the sublime. They discuss their relationship, and it is revealed that the monster has deep emotions and feels abandoned by his creator.

I suddenly beheld the figure of a man, at some distance, advancing towards me with superhuman speed. He bounded over the crevices in the ice, among which I had walked with caution; his stature, also, as he approached, seemed to exceed that of man. I was troubled: a mist came over my eyes, and I felt a faintness seize me; but I was quickly restored by the cold gale of the mountains. I perceived, as the shape came nearer (sight tremendous and abhorred?) that it was the wretch whom I had created. I trembled with rage and horror, resolving to wait his approach, and then close with him in mortal combat. He approached; his countenance bespoke bitter anguish, combined with disdain and malignity, while its unearthly ugliness rendered it almost too horrible for human eyes. But I scarcely observed this; rage and hatred had at first deprived me of utterance, and I recovered only to overwhelm him with words expressive of furious detestation and contempt.

'Devil,' I exclaimed, 'do you dare approach me? and do not you fear the fierce vengeance of my arm wreaked on your miserable head? Begone, vile insect! or rather, stay, that I may trample you to dust! and, oh! that I could, with the extinction of your miserable existence, restore those victims whom you have so diabolically murdered!'

'I expected this reception,' said the dæmon. 'All men hate the wretched; how, then, must I be hated, who am miserable beyond all living things! Yet you, my creator, detest and spurn me, thy creature, to whom thou art bound by ties only dissoluble by the annihilation of one of us. You purpose to kill me. How dare you sport thus with life? Do your duty towards me, and I will do mine towards you and the rest of mankind. If you will comply with my conditions, I will leave them and you at peace; but if you refuse, I will glut the maw of death, until it be satiated with the blood of your remaining friends.'

'Abhorred monster! fiend that thou art! the tortures of hell are too mild a vengeance for thy crimes. Wretched devil! you reproach me with your creation; come on, then, that I may extinguish the spark which I so negligently bestowed.'

My rage was without bounds; I sprang on him, impelled by all the feelings which can arm one being against the existence of another.

He easily eluded me, and said —

'Be calm! I entreat you to hear me, before you give vent to your hatred on my devoted head. Have I not suffered enough, that you seek to increase my misery? Life, although it may only be an accumulation of anguish, is dear to me, and I will defend it. Remember, thou hast made me more powerful than thyself; my height is superior to thine; my joints more supple. But I will not be tempted to set myself in opposition to thee. I am thy creature, and I will be even mild and docile to my natural lord and king, if thou wilt also perform thy part, the which thou owest me. Oh, Frankenstein, be not equitable to every other, and trample upon me alone, to whom thy justice, and even thy clemency and affection, is most due. Remember, that I am thy creature; I ought to be thy Adam; but I am rather the fallen angel, whom thou drivest from joy for no misdeed. Every where I see bliss, from which I alone am irrevocably excluded. I was benevolent and good; misery made me a fiend. Make me happy, and I shall again be virtuous.'

'Begone! I will not hear you. There can be no community between you and me; we are enemies. Begone, or let us try our strength in a fight, in which one must fall.'

'How can I move thee? Will no entreaties cause thee to turn a favourable eye upon thy creature, who implores thy goodness and compassion? Believe me, Frankenstein: I was benevolent; my soul glowed with love and humanity: but am I not alone, miserably alone? You, my creator, abhor me; what hope can I gather from your fellow-creatures, who owe me nothing? they spurn and hate me. The desert mountains and dreary glaciers are my refuge. I have wandered here many days; the caves of ice, which I only do not fear, are a dwelling to me, and the only one which man does not grudge. These bleak skies I hail, for they are kinder to me than your fellow-beings. If the multitude of mankind knew of my existence, they would do as you do, and arm themselves for my destruction. Shall I not then hate them who abhor me? I will keep no terms with my enemies. I am miserable, and they shall share my wretchedness. Yet it is in your power to recompense me, and deliver them from an evil which it only remains for you to make so great, that not only you and your family, but thousands of others, shall be swallowed up in the whirlwinds of its rage. Let your compassion be moved, and do not disdain me. Listen to my tale: when you have heard that, abandon or commiserate me, as you shall judge that I deserve. But hear me. The guilty are allowed, by human laws, bloody as they are, to speak in their own defence before they are condemned. Listen to me, Frankenstein. You accuse me of murder; and yet you would, with a satisfied conscience, destroy your own creature. Oh, praise the eternal justice of man! Yet I ask you not to spare me: listen to me; and then, if you can, and if you will, destroy the work of your hands.'

'Why do you call to my remembrance,' I rejoined, 'circumstances, of which I shudder to reflect, that I have been the miserable origin and author? Cursed be the day, abhorred devil, in which you first saw light! Cursed (although I curse myself) be the hands that formed you! You have made me wretched beyond expression. You have left me no power to consider whether I am just to you, or not. Begone! relieve me from the sight of your detested form.'

'Thus I relieve thee, my creator,' he said, and placed his hated hands before my eyes, which I flung from me with violence; 'thus I take from thee a sight which you abhor. Still thou canst listen to me, and grant me thy compassion. By the virtues that I once possessed, I demand this from you. Hear my tale; it is long and strange, and the temperature of this place is not fitting to your fine sensations; come to the hut upon the mountain. The sun is yet high in the heavens; before it descends to hide itself behind yon snowy precipices, and illuminate another world, you will have heard my story, and can decide. On you it rests, whether I quit for ever the neighbourhood of man, and lead a harmless life, or become the scourge of your fellow-creatures, and the author of your own speedy ruin.'

C   Dr. Frankenstein agrees to make a mate for the monster, but then has second thoughts. The two remain inseparably related to one another as a result of this act.

I trembled, and my heart failed within me; when, on looking up, I saw, by the light of the moon, the dæmon at the casement. A ghastly grin wrinkled his lips as he gazed on me, where I sat fulfilling the task which he had allotted to me. Yes, he had followed me in my travels; he had loitered in forests, hid himself in caves, or taken refuge in wide and desert heaths; and he now came to mark my progress, and claim the fulfilment of my promise.

As I looked on him, his countenance expressed the utmost extent of malice and treachery. I thought with a sensation of madness on my promise of creating another like to him, and trembling with passion, tore to pieces the thing on which I was engaged. The wretch saw me destroy the creature on whose future existence he depended for happiness, and, with a howl of devilish despair and revenge, withdrew. . . .

Presently I heard the sound of footsteps along the passage; the door opened, and the wretch whom I dreaded appeared. Shutting the door, he approached me, and said, in a smothered voice —

'You have destroyed the work which you began; what is it that you intend? Do you dare to break your promise? I have endured toil and misery: I left Switzerland with you; I crept along the shores of the Rhine, among its willow islands, and over the summits of its hills. I have dwelt many months in the heaths of England, and among the deserts of Scotland. I have endured incalculable fatigue, and cold, and hunger; do you dare destroy my hopes?'

'Begone! I do break my promise; never will I create another like yourself, equal in deformity and wickedness.'

'Slave, I before reasoned with you, but you have proved yourself unworthy of my condescension. Remember that I have power; you believe yourself miserable, but I can make you so wretched that the light of day will be hateful to you. You are my creator, but I am your master; — obey!'

1. What human qualities does the creature exhibit?

2. Why does Frankenstein abhor his creation?

3. Since technology was employed to animate the creature, how is the last statement by the monster a warning to future generations?

Karl Marx and Friedrich Engels

Karl Marx (1818–1883) and Friedrich Engels (1820–1895) were friends and collaborators who were appalled at the price paid by many human beings to make industrial society work. In the 1840s they began their analysis of capitalism, the middle-class, and contemporary society with a critique of the conditions of working life. This analysis was to have a profound influence on future social thought. In the *Manifesto of the Communist Party* of February 1848, the most influential work in the history of socialism, the two men summarized their position on the idea of historical development, the importance of the economic mode of production, the role of class struggle, and the nature of social and political change.

 Engels, whose father was a wealthy German manufacturer, went to Manchester, England in 1842 to work in one of the branches of his father's business. He stayed until 1844 and in that year wrote *The Condition of the Working Class in England*. In the book he catalogues the horrible conditions of labour during the industrial revolution and places the blame on the system and on the bourgeoisie.

No one can be complacent about a situation which injures and cripples so many workers for the benefit of a single class. It is tragic that so many industrious workers are injured in the factories and are condemned to a lifetime of poverty and hunger. Their middle-class employers must bear the sole responsibility for this disgraceful state of affairs. . . .

One day I walked with one of these middle-class gentlemen into Manchester. I spoke to him about the disgraceful unhealthy slums and drew his attention to the disgusting condition of that part of the town in which

Sources: Friedrich Engels, *The Condition of the Working Class in England*. Oxford: Basil Blackwell, 1971, pp. 188, 312; Robert C. Tucker, ed., *The Marx-Engels Reader*, second edition. New York: W. W. Norton & Company, Inc., 1978, pp. 74, 681–682, 713, 715–716; Karl Marx and Friedrich Engels, *Basic Writings on Politics and Philosophy*, ed. Lewis S. Feuer. New York: Doubleday & Company, Inc., 1959, pp. 6–8, 9–12, 13–17, 20–21, 23, 26, 28, 29, 41, 106, 108–109.

the factory workers lived. I declared that I had never seen so badly built a town in my life. He listened patiently and at the corner of the street at which we parted company he remarked: 'And yet there is a great deal of money made here. Good morning, Sir'. . . .

The middle classes in England have become the slaves of the money they worship. Even the English language is permeated by the one idea that dominates the waking hours of the bourgeoisie. People see 'valued' in terms of hard cash. They say of a man: 'He is worth £10,000', and by that they mean that he possesses that sum. Anyone who has money is 'respectable'. He belongs to 'the better sort of people'. He is said to be 'influential', which means that what he says carried weight in the circles in which he moves. The spirit of petty bargaining permeates the whole language. Everything is expressed in commercial terms or in the categories of the science of economics.

B Marx, in 1844, discussed the concept of the alienation of labour.

What, then, constitutes the alienation of labour?

First, the fact that labour is *external* to the worker, i.e., it does not belong to his essential being; that in his work, therefore, he does not affirm himself but denies himself, does not feel content but unhappy, does not develop freely his physical and mental energy but mortifies his body and ruins his mind. The worker therefore only feels himself outside his work, and in his work feels outside himself. He is at home when he is not working, and when he is working he is not at home. His labour is therefore not voluntary, but coerced; it is *forced labour*. It is therefore not the satisfaction of a need; it is merely a *means* to satisfy needs external to it. Its alien character emerges clearly in the fact that as soon as no physical or other compulsion exists, labour is shunned like the plague. External labour, labour in which man alienates himself, is a labour of self-sacrifice, of mortification. Lastly, the external character of labour for the worker appears in the fact that it is not his own, but someone else's, that it does not belong to him, that in it he belongs, not to himself, but to another. Just as in religion the spontaneous activity of the human imagination, of the human brain and the human heart, operates independently of the individual — that is, operates on him as an alien, divine or diabolical activity — in the same way the worker's activity is not his spontaneous activity. It belongs to another, it is the loss of his self.

C The *Manifesto of the Communist Party* is a powerful polemic based upon an analysis of historical change.

A spectre is haunting Europe — the spectre of communism. All the powers of old Europe have entered into a holy alliance to exorcise this spectre: Pope and Czar, Metternich and Guizot, French radicals and German police spies.

Where is the party in opposition that has not been decried as communistic by its opponents in power? Where the opposition that has not hurled back the branding reproach of communism, against the more advanced opposition parties, as well as against its reactionary adversaries?

Two things result from this fact:

I. Communism is already acknowledged by all European powers to be itself a power.

II. It is high time that communists should openly, in the face of the whole world, publish their views, their aims, their tendencies, and meet this nursery tale of the specter of communism with a Manifesto of the party itself.

To this end, communists of various nationalities have assembled in London, and sketched the following Manifesto, to be published in the English, French, German, Italian, Flemish and Danish languages.

The history of all hitherto existing society is the history of class struggles.

Free man and slave, patrician and plebeian, lord and serf, guild master and journeyman, in a word, oppressor and oppressed, stood in constant opposition to one another, carried on an uninterrupted, now hidden, now open fight, a fight that each time ended, either in a revolutionary re-constitution of society at large, or in the common ruin of the contending classes.

In the earlier epochs of history, we find almost everywhere a complicated arrangement of society into various orders, a manifold gradation of social rank. In ancient Rome we have patricians, knights, plebeians, slaves; in the Middle Ages, feudal lords, vassals, guild masters, journeymen, apprentices, serfs; in almost all of these classes, again, subordinate gradations.

The modern bourgeois society that has sprouted from the ruins of feudal society has not done away with class antagonisms. It has but established new classes, new conditions of oppression, new forms of struggle in place of the old ones.

Our epoch, the epoch of the bourgeoisie, possesses, however, this distinctive feature: it has simplified the class antagonisms. Society as a whole is more and more splitting up into two great hostile camps, into two great classes directly facing each other: bourgeoisie and proletariat.

D The bourgeoisie was the controlling class in industrial society, and Marx and Engels praise it in the *Manifesto* as a historical advance.

We see, therefore, how the modern bourgeoisie is itself the product of a long course of development, of a series of revolutions in the modes of production and of exchange. . . .

. . . The executive of the modern state is but a committee for managing the common affairs of the whole bourgeoisie.

The bourgeoisie, historically, has played a most revolutionary part.

The bourgeoisie, wherever it has got the upper hand, has put an end to all feudal, patriarchal, idyllic relations. . . .

The bourgeoisie has stripped of its halo every occupation hitherto honored and looked up to with reverent awe. It has converted the physician, the lawyer, the priest, the poet, the man of science, into its paid wage laborers.

The bourgeoisie has torn away from the family its sentimental veil, and has reduced the family relation to a mere money relation.

The bourgeoisie . . . has accomplished wonders far surpassing Egyptian pyramids, Roman aqueducts, and Gothic cathedrals; it has conducted expeditions that put in the shade all former exoduses of nations and crusades.

The bourgeoisie cannot exist without constantly revolutionising the instruments of production, and thereby the relations of production, and with them the whole relations of society. . . .

The bourgeoisie has through its exploitation of the world market given a cosmopolitan character to production and consumption in every country. . . .

The bourgeoisie, by the rapid improvement of all instruments of production, by the immensely facilitated means of communication, draws all, even the most barbarian, nations into civilization. . . .

The bourgeoisie has subjected the country to the rule of the towns. It has created enormous cities, has greatly increased the urban population as compared with the rural, and has thus rescued a considerable part of the population from the idiocy of rural life. . . .

The bourgeoisie, during its rule of scarce one hundred years, has created more massive and more colossal productive forces than have all preceding generations together. Subjection of nature's forces to man, machinery, application of chemistry to industry and agriculture, steam navigation, railways, electric telegraphs, clearing of whole continents for cultivation, canalization of rivers, whole populations conjured out of the ground — what earlier century had even a presentiment that such productive forces slumbered in the lap of social labour?

E The two men theorize that the proletariat will develop consciousness, overthrow the bourgeoisie, and establish a new society.

But not only has the bourgeoisie forged the weapons that bring death to itself; it has also called into existence the men who are to wield those weapons — the modern working class — the proletarians.

In proportion as the bourgeoisie, i.e., capital, is developed, in the same proportion is the proletariat, the modern working class, developed — a class of laborers, who live only so long as they find work, and who find work only so long as their labor increases capital. These laborers, who must sell themselves piecemeal, are a commodity, like every other article of commerce, and are consequently exposed to all the vicissitudes of competition, to all the fluctuations of the market. . . .

The proletariat goes through various stages of development. With its birth begins its struggle with the bourgeoisie. At first the contest is carried on by individual laborers, then by the workpeople of a factory, then by the operatives of one trade, in one locality, against the individual bourgeois who directly exploits them. They direct their attacks not against the bourgeois conditions of production, but against the instruments of production themselves; they destroy imported wares that compete with their labor, they smash to pieces machinery, they set factories ablaze, they seek to restore by force the vanished status of the workman of the Middle Ages. . . .

But with the development of industry the proletariat not only increases in number; it becomes concentrated in greater masses, its strength grows, and it feels that strength more. . . . Here and there the contest breaks out into riots.

Now and then the workers are victorious, but only for a time. The real fruit of their battles lies, not in the immediate result, but in the ever-expanding union of the workers. This union is helped on by the improved means of communication that are created by modern industry and that place the workers of different localities in contact with one another. It was just this contact that was needed to centralize the numerous local struggles, all of the same character, into one national struggle between classes. But every class struggle is a political struggle. . . .

This organization of the proletarians into a class, and consequently into a political party, is continually being upset again by the competition between the workers themselves. But it ever rises up again, stronger, firmer, mightier. It compels legislative recognition of particular interests of the workers, by taking advantage of the divisions among the bourgeoisie itself. Thus the ten-hour bill in England was carried. . . .

Finally, in times when the class struggle nears the decisive hour, the process of dissolution going on within the ruling class, in fact within the whole range of society, assumes such a violent, glaring character, that a small section of the ruling class cuts itself adrift, and joins the revolutionary class, the class that holds the future in its hands. Just as, therefore, at an earlier period, a section of the nobility went over to the bourgeoisie, so now a portion of the bourgeoisie goes over to the proletariat, and in particular, a portion of the bourgeois ideologists, who have raised themselves to the level of comprehending theoretically the historical movement as a whole.

Of all the classes that stand face to face with the bourgeoisie today, the proletariat alone is a really revolutionary class. The other classes decay and finally disappear in the face of modern industry; the proletariat is its special and essential product.

F The aims of the communists, then one of the many branches of socialism, are made clear:

The immediate aim of the communists is the same as that of all the other proletarian parties: formation of the proletariat into a class, overthrow of the bourgeois supremacy, conquest of political power by the proletariat. . . .

In this sense, the theory of the communists may be summed up in the single sentence: Abolition of private property. . . .

You are horrified at our intending to do away with private property. But in your existing society, private property is already done away with for nine tenths of the population; its existence for the few is solely due to its non-existence in the hands of those nine tenths. You reproach us, therefore, with intending to do away with a form of property, the necessary condition for whose existence is the non-existence of any property for the immense majority of society....

The communists are further reproached with desiring to abolish countries and nationality.

The workingmen have no country. We cannot take from them what they have not got. Since the proletariat must first of all acquire political supremacy, must rise to be the leading class of the nation, must constitute itself *the* nation, it is, so far, itself national, though not in the bourgeois sense of the word....

[I]n the most advanced countries, the following will be pretty generally applicable:

1. Abolition of property in land and application of all rents of land to public purposes.
2. A heavy progressive or graduated income tax.
3. Abolition of all right of inheritance.
4. Confiscation of the property of all emigrants and rebels.
5. Centralization of credit in the hands of the state, by means of a national bank with state capital and an exclusive monopoly.
6. Centralization of the means of communication and transport in the hands of the state.
7. Extension of factories and instruments of production owned by the state; the bringing into cultivation of wastelands, and the improvement of the soil generally in accordance with a common plan.
8. Equal liability of all to labor. Establishment of industrial armies, especially for agriculture.
9. Combination of agriculture with manufacturing industries; gradual abolition of the distinction between town and country, by a more equable distribution of the population over the country.
10. Free education for all children in public schools. Abolition of children's factory labor in its present form. Combination of education with industrial production, etc.

In place of the old bourgeois society, with its classes and class antagonisms, we shall have an association, in which the free development of each is the condition for the free development of all....

In short, the communists everywhere support every revolutionary movement against the existing social and political order of things.

In all these movements they bring to the front, as the leading question in each, the property question, no matter what its degree of development at the time.

Finally, they labor everywhere for the union and agreement of the democratic parties of all countries.

The communists disdain to conceal their views and aims. They openly declare that their ends can be attained only by the forcible overthrow of all existing social conditions. Let the ruling classes tremble at a communistic revolution. The proletarians have nothing to lose but their chains. They have a world to win.

WORKINGMEN OF ALL COUNTRIES, UNITE!

G At the funeral of his friend in 1883, Engels delivered an address at the graveside, summing up what he believed to have been Marx's accomplishments.

Just as Darwin discovered the law of development of organic nature, so Marx discovered the law of development of human history: the simple fact, hitherto concealed by an overgrowth of ideology, that mankind must first of all eat, drink, have shelter and clothing, before it can pursue politics, science, art, religion, etc.; that therefore the production of the immediate material means of subsistence and consequently the degree of economic development attained by a given people or during a given epoch form the foundation upon which the state institutions, the legal conceptions, art, and even the ideas on religion, of the people concerned have been evolved, and in the light of which they must, therefore, be explained, instead of *vice versa*, as had hitherto been the case.

But that is not all. Marx also discovered the special law of motion governing the present-day capitalist mode of production and the bourgeois society that this mode of production has created. The discovery of surplus value suddenly threw light on the problem, in trying to solve which all previous investigations, of both bourgeois economists and socialist critics, had been groping in the dark. . . .

Marx was before all else a revolutionist. His real mission in life was to contribute, in one way or another, to the overthrow of capitalist society and of the state institutions which it had brought into being, to contribute to the liberation of the modern proletariat, which *he* was the first to make conscious of its own position and its needs, conscious of the conditions of its emancipation. . . .

. . . Marx was the best hated and most calumniated man of his time. Governments, both absolutist and republican, deported him from their territories. Bourgeois, whether conservative or ultra-democratic, vied with one another in heaping slanders upon him. All this he brushed aside as though it were cobweb, ignoring it, answering only when extreme necessity compelled him. And he died beloved, revered and mourned by millions of revolutionary fellow workers — from the mines of Siberia to California, in all parts of Europe and America — and I make bold to say that though he may have had many opponents he had hardly one personal enemy.

His name will endure through the ages, and so also will his work!

Engels published his own summary of Marxian thought, *Socialism: Utopian and Scientific*, in 1880. The work became the most important popular statement of Marx's ideas and vision. At the end of the work, Engels discusses the future and its meaning.

The proletariat seizes political power and turns the means of production into state property.

But, in doing this, it abolishes itself as proletariat, abolishes all class distinctions and class antagonisms, abolishes also the state as state. . . . The state is not "abolished." *It dies out.* . . .

The socialized appropriation of the means of production does away, not only with the present artificial restrictions upon production, but also with the positive waste and devastation of productive forces and products that are at the present time the inevitable concomitants of production, and that reach their height in the crises. Further, it sets free for the community at large a mass of means of production and of products, by doing away with the senseless extravagance of the ruling classes of today and their political representatives. The possibility of securing for every member of society, by means of socialized production, an existence not only fully sufficient materially, and becoming day by day more full, but an existence guaranteeing to all the free development and exercise of their physical and mental faculties — this possibility is now for the first time here, but *it is here.*

With the seizing of the means of production by society, production of commodities is done away with, and, simultaneously, the mastery of the product over the producer. Anarchy in social production is replaced by systematic, definite organization. The struggle for individual existence disappears. Then for the first time man, in a certain sense, is finally marked off from the rest of the animal kingdom, and emerges from mere animal conditions of existence into really human ones. The whole sphere of the conditions of life which environ man, and which have hitherto ruled man, now comes under the dominion and control of man, who for the first time becomes the real, conscious lord of nature, because he has now become master of his own social organization. The laws of his own social action, hitherto standing face to face with man as laws of nature foreign to and dominating him, will then be used with full understanding, and so mastered by him. Man's own social organization, hitherto confronting him as a necessity imposed by nature and history, now becomes the result of his own free action. The extraneous objective forces that have hitherto governed history pass under the control of man himself. Only from that time will man himself, more and more consciously, make his own history —

only from that time will the social causes set in movement by him have, in the main and in a constantly growing measure, the results intended by him. It is the ascent of man from the kingdom of necessity to the kingdom of freedom.

1. What does Engels see as being wrong with English middle-class priorities?

2. Is Marx's description of the alienation of labour a call for a return to cottage industries? Explain.

3. How does Marx justify his interpretation of history as one of class struggles?

4. According to Marx and Engels, how do the economic policies of the bourgeoisie sow the seeds of its own destruction?

5. If communism was meant to improve the conditions of the majority of the people, why did it not succeed in gaining power until the early twentieth century?

6. How would a contemporary evaluation of Marx's significance compare to Engels' pronouncements at Marx's funeral?

7. In order for the state to disappear, how must human nature evolve?

Benjamin Disraeli

As a young politician, Benjamin Disraeli (1804–1881) became one of the leaders of a group of Conservative British Members of Parliament known as Young England. Reformers, they combined a love of tradition with profound concern for the conditions of the new urban working class, a concern that Disraeli expressed in his novels, especially in *Sybil; or The Two Nations* (1845). Disraeli was an important figure in getting the 1867 Reform Act passed, a law which gave the vote to the urban working class. He went on to become Prime Minister, supporting the growth and expansion of the British Empire as well as trying to improve living conditions for the lower class.

A In *Sybil*, Disraeli describes the effect of industry on the traditional countryside.

The situation of the rural town of Marney was one of the most delightful easily to be imagined. In a spreading dale, contiguous to the margin of a clear and lively stream, surrounded by meadows and gardens, and backed by lofty hills, undulating and richly wooded, the traveller on the opposite heights of the dale would often stop to admire the merry prospect that recalled to him the traditional epithet of his country.

Beautiful illusion! For behind that laughing landscape, penury and disease fed upon the vitals of a miserable population.

Source: Benjamin Disraeli, *Sybil; or The Two Nations*, ed. Sheila M. Smith. Oxford: Oxford University Press, 1981, pp. 51–53, 59, 64–66, 114–115.

The contrast between the interior of the town and its external aspect was as striking as it was full of pain. With the exception of the dull high street, which had the usual characteristics of a small agricultural market town, some sombre mansions, a dingy inn, and a petty bourse, Marney mainly consisted of a variety of narrow and crowded lanes formed by cottages built of rubble, or unhewn stones without cement, and, from age or badness of the material, looking as if they could scarcely hold together. The gaping chinks admitted every blast; the leaning chimneys had lost half their original height; the rotten rafters were evidently misplaced; while in many instances the thatch, yawning in some parts to admit the wind and wet, and in all utterly unfit for its original purpose of giving protection from the weather, looked more like the top of a dunghill than a cottage. Before the doors of these dwellings, and often surrounding them, ran open drains full of animal and vegetable refuse, decomposing into disease, or sometimes in their imperfect course filling foul pits or spreading into stagnant pools, while a concentrated solution of every species of dissolving filth was allowed to soak through, and thoroughly impregnate, the walls and ground adjoining.

These wretched tenements seldom consisted of more than two rooms, in one of which the whole family, however numerous, were obliged to sleep, without distinction of age, or sex, or suffering. With the water streaming down the walls, the light distinguished through the roof, with no hearth even in winter, the virtuous mother in the sacred pangs of childbirth gives forth another victim to our thoughtless civilisation; surrounded by three generations whose inevitable presence is more painful than her suffering in that hour of travail; while the father of her coming child, in another corner of the sordid chamber, lies stricken by that typhus which his contaminating dwelling has breathed into his veins, and for whose next prey perhaps destined his new-born child. These swarming walls had neither windows nor doors sufficient to keep out the weather, or admit the sun, or supply the means of ventilation; the humid and putrid roof of thatch exhaling malaria like all other decaying vegetable matter. The dwelling-rooms were neither boarded nor paved; and whether it were that some were situate in low and damp places, occasionally flooded by the river, and usually much below the level of the road; or that the springs, as was often the case, would burst through the mud floor; the ground was at no time better than so much clay, while sometimes you might see little channels cut from the centre under the doorways to carry off the water, the door itself removed from its hinges; a resting-place for infancy in its deluged home. These hovels were in many instances not provided with the commonest conveniences of the rudest police; contiguous to every door might be observed the dung-heap on which every kind of filth was accumulated, for the purpose of being disposed of for manure, so that, when the poor man opened his narrow habitation in the hope of refreshing it with the breeze of summer, he was met with a mixture of gases from reeking dunghills.

B Disraeli's hero, Lord Egremont, reflects on the new England.

Why was England not the same land as in the days of his light-hearted youth? Why were these hard times for the poor? He stood among the ruins that, as the farmer had well observed, had seen many changes: changes of creeds, of dynasties, of laws, of manners. New orders of men had arisen in the country, new sources of wealth had opened, new dispositions of power to which that wealth had necessarily led. His own house, his own order, had established themselves on the ruins of that great body, the emblems of whose ancient magnificence and strength surrounded him. And now his order was in turn menaced. And the People, the millions of Toil on whose unconscious energies during these changeful centuries all rested, what changes had these centuries brought to them? Had their advance in the national scale borne a due relation to that progress of their rulers, which had accumulated in the treasuries of a limited class the riches of the world, and made their possessors boast that they were the first of nations; the most powerful and the most free, the most enlightened, the most moral, and the most religious?

C Egremont is having a conversation with a stranger, when a third voice intervenes and defines the meaning of the novel's subtitle.

'As for community,' said a voice which proceeded neither from Egremont nor the stranger, 'with the monasteries expired the only type that we ever had in England of such an intercourse. There is no community in England; there is aggregation, but aggregation under circumstances which make it rather a dissociating than a uniting principle.'

It was a still voice that uttered these words, yet one of a peculiar character; one of those voices that instantly arrest attention: gentle and yet solemn, earnest yet unimpassioned. With a step as whispering as his tone; the man who had been kneeling by the tomb had unobserved joined his associate and Egremont. He hardly reached the middle height; his form slender, but well-proportioned; his pale countenance, slightly marked with the small-pox, was redeemed from absolute ugliness by a highly intellectual brow, and large dark eyes that indicated deep sensibility and great quickness of apprehension. Though young, he was already a little bald; he was dressed entirely in black; the fairness of his linen, the neatness of his beard, his gloves much worn, yet carefully mended, intimated that his faded garments were the result of necessity rather than of negligence.

'You also lament the dissolution of these bodies,' said Egremont.

'There is so much to lament in the world in which we live,' said the younger of the strangers, 'that I can spare no pang for the past.'

'Yet you approve of the principle of their society; you prefer it, you say, to our existing life.'

'Yes; I prefer association to gregariousness.'

'That is a distinction,' said Egremont, musingly.

'It is a community of purpose that constitutes society,' continued the younger stranger; 'without that, men may be drawn to contiguity, but they still continue virtually isolated.'

'And is that their condition in cities?'

'It is their condition everywhere; but in cities that condition is aggravated. A density of population implies a severer struggle for existence, and a consequent repulsion of elements brought into too close contact. In great cities men are brought together by the desire of gain. They are not in a state of cooperation, but of isolation, as to the making of fortunes; and for all the rest they are careless of neighbours. Christianity teaches us to love our neighbour as ourself; modern society acknowledges no neighbour.'

'Well, we live in strange times,' said Egremont, struck by the observation of his companion, and relieving a perplexed spirit by an ordinary exclamation, which often denotes that the mind is more stirred than it cares to acknowledge, or at the moment is able to express.

'When the infant begins to walk, it also thinks that it lives in strange times,' said his companion.

'Your inference?' asked Egremont.

'That society, still in its infancy, is beginning to feel its way.'

'This is a new reign,' said Egremont, 'perhaps it is a new era.'

'I think so,' said the younger stranger.

'I hope so,' said the elder one.

'Well, society may be in its infancy,' said Egremont, slightly smiling; 'but, say what you like, our Queen reigns over the greatest nation that ever existed.'

'Which nation?' asked the younger stranger, 'for she reigns over two.'

The stranger paused; Egremont was silent, but looked inquiringly.

'Yes,' resumed the younger stranger after a moment's interval. 'Two nations; between whom there is no intercourse and no sympathy; who are as ignorant of each other's habits, thoughts, and feelings, as if they were dwellers in different zones, or inhabitants of different planets; who are formed by a different breeding, are fed by a different food, are ordered by different manners, and are not governed by the same laws.'

'You speak of — ' said Egremont, hesitatingly.

'THE RICH AND THE POOR.'

D A worker at his loom reflects on how the dignity of labour has been completely undermined, from artisan to factory worker.

It was a single chamber of which he was the tenant. In the centre, placed so as to gain the best light which the gloomy situation could afford, was a loom. In two corners of the room were mattresses placed on the floor, a check curtain, hung upon a string, if necessary, concealing them. On one was his sick wife; on the other, three young children: two girls, the eldest about eight years of age; between them their baby brother. An iron kettle was by the hearth, and on the mantelpiece some candles, a few lucifer matches, two tin mugs, a paper of salt, and an iron spoon. In a farther part, close to the wall, was a heavy table or dresser; this was a fixture, as well as the form which was fastened by it.

The man seated himself at his loom; he commenced his daily task.

'Twelve hours of daily labour, at the rate of one penny each hour, and even this labour is mortgaged! How is this to end? Is it rather not ended?' And he looked around him at his mugs, a paper of salt, and an iron spoon. In a farther part, chamber without resources: no food, no fuel, no furniture and four human beings dependent on him, and lying in their wretched beds, because they had no clothes. 'I cannot sell my loom,' he continued, 'at the price of old firewood, and it cost me gold. It is not vice that has brought me to this, nor indolence, nor imprudence. I was born to labour, and I was ready to labour. I loved my loom, and my loom loved me. It gave me a cottage in my native village, surrounded by a garden of whose claims on my solicitude it was not jealous. There was time for both. It gave me for a wife the maiden that I had ever loved; and it gathered my children round my hearth with plenteousness and peace. I was content: I sought no other lot. It is not adversity that makes me look back upon the past with tenderness.

'Then why am I here? Why am I, and six hundred thousand subjects of the Queen, honest, loyal, and industrious, why are we, after manfully struggling for years, and each year sinking lower in the scale, why are we driven from our innocent and happy homes, our country cottages that we loved, first to bide in close towns without comforts and gradually to crouch into cellars, or find a squalid lair like this, without even the common necessaries of existence; first the ordinary conveniences of life, then raiment, and at length food, vanishing from us.

'It is that the Capitalist has found a slave that has supplanted the labour and ingenuity of man. Once he was an artisan: at the best, he now only watches machines; and even that occupation slips from his grasp to the woman and the child. The capitalist flourishes, he amasses immense wealth; we sink, lower and lower; lower than the beasts of burthen; for they are fed better than we are, cared for more. And it is just, for according to the present system they are more precious. And yet they tell us that the interests of Capital and of Labour are identical.

'If a society that has been created by labour suddenly becomes independent of it, that society is bound to maintain the race whose only property is labour, out of the proceeds of that other property, which has not ceased to be productive.

'When the class of the Nobility were supplanted in France, they did not amount in number to one-third of us Hand-loom weavers; yet all Europe went to war to avenge their wrongs, every state subscribed to maintain them in their adversity, and when they were restored to their own country their own land supplied them with an immense indemnity. Who cares for us? Yet we have lost our estates. Who raises a voice for us? Yet we are at least as innocent as the nobility of France. We sink among no sighs except our own. And if they give us sympathy, what then? Sympathy is the solace of the Poor; but for the Rich there is compensation.'

1. How does Disraeli's description of the town reflect the mood and conditions of nineteenth-century England?

2. What observations does Disraeli make concerning the divisions among the classes?

3. How had England become a country of two nations?

4. Compare Disraeli's description of industrial England with Marx and Engels' (see pages 140–148). What are the major similarities regarding the relationship between classes?

Lin Zexu

When the Chinese Qing emperor and his court decided to close down the illegal opium trade, Lin Zexu (1785–1850) was made the Imperial Commissioner with full powers to punish all offenders. Commissioner Lin used strong-arm tactics to deal with foreign traders in Canton (Guangzhou), the only Chinese port where they were allowed. He succeeded in stopping the opium trade for a time. But since China was not prepared to negotiate with the British to relax the restrictions on all trade, Lin's actions eventually led to war. British victory in the Opium War (1839–1842) opened China for Western trade, and began a new era in the relations between East Asia and the West. Commissioner Lin's letter to Queen Victoria (1839) was written during his campaign for the suppression of opium. It exemplifies the traditional Chinese disdain for foreigners and foreign trade, as well as the Qing government's position toward opium at that time.

 Up until this time, the Chinese Empire had a self-image of innate superiority. The Chinese emperor was believed to be the Son of Heaven, the Lord of All Under Heaven and the father-ruler of the only civilized country on earth. All other rulers were thought to be barbarian chieftains who did not know Confucian morality, and only chased after unworthy material profits. Lin begins:

> A communication: magnificently our great emperor soothes and pacifies China and the foreign countries, regarding all with the same kindness. If there is profit, then he shares it with the peoples of the world; if there is harm, then he removes it on behalf of the world. This is because he takes the mind of Heaven and earth as his mind.
>
> The kings of your honorable country by a tradition handed down from generation to generation have always been noted for their politeness and submissiveness. We have read your successive tributary memorials

Source: W. T. de Bary et al., eds., *Sources of Chinese Tradition*, vol. 2. New York: Columbia University Press, 1960, pp. 6–7, 8–9.

saying: "In general our countrymen who go to trade in China have always received His Majesty the Emperor's gracious treatment and equal justice," and so on. Privately we are delighted with the way in which the honorable rulers of your country deeply understand the grand principles and are grateful for the Celestial grace. For this reason the Celestial Court in soothing those from afar has redoubled its polite and kind treatment. The profit from trade has been enjoyed by them continuously for two hundred years. This is the source from which your country has become known for its wealth.

But after a long period of commercial intercourse, there appear among the crowd of barbarians both good persons and bad, unevenly. Consequently there are those who smuggle opium to seduce the Chinese people and so cause the spread of the poison to all provinces. Such persons who only care to profit themselves, and disregard their harm to others, are not tolerated by the laws of Heaven and are unanimously hated by human beings. His Majesty the Emperor, upon hearing of this, is in a towering rage. He has especially sent me, his commissioner, to come to Kwangtung, and together with the governor-general and governor jointly to investigate and settle this matter.

B Lin questions the motives of the British and appeals to moral ends.

We find that your country is sixty or seventy thousand *li* [30 000–35 000 km] from China. Yet there are barbarian ships that strive to come here for trade for the purpose of making a great profit. The wealth of China is used to profit the barbarians. That is to say, the great profit made by barbarians is all taken from the rightful share of China. By what right do they then in return use the poisonous drug to injure the Chinese people? Even though the barbarians may not necessarily intend to do us harm, yet in coveting profit to an extreme, they have no regard for injuring others. Let us ask, where is your conscience? I have heard that the smoking of opium is very strictly forbidden by your country; that is because the harm caused by opium is clearly understood. Since it is not permitted to do harm to your own country, then even less should you let it be passed on to the harm of other countries — how much less to China! Of all that China exports to foreign countries, there is not a single thing which is not beneficial to people; they are of benefit when eaten, or of benefit when used, or of benefit when resold: all are beneficial. Is there a single article from China which has done any harm to foreign countries? Take tea and rhubarb, for example; the foreign countries cannot get along for a single day without them. If China cuts off these benefits with no sympathy for those who are to suffer, then what can the barbarians rely upon to keep themselves alive? Moreover the woolens, camlets, and longells [i.e., textiles] of foreign countries cannot be woven unless they obtain Chinese silk. If China, again, cuts off this beneficial export, what profit can the barbarians expect to make?

As for other foodstuffs, beginning with candy, ginger, cinnamon, and so forth, and articles for use, beginning with silk, satin, chinaware, and so on, all the things that must be had by foreign countries are innumerable. On the other hand, articles coming from the outside to China can only be used as toys. We can take them or get along without them. Since they are not needed by China, what difficulty would there be if we closed the frontier and stopped the trade? Nevertheless our Celestial Court lets tea, silk, and other goods be shipped without limit and circulated everywhere without begrudging it in the slightest. This is for no other reason but to share the benefit with the people of the whole world.

The goods from China carried away by your country not only supply your own consumption and use, but also can be divided up and sold to other countries, producing a triple profit. Even if you do not sell opium, you still have this threefold profit. How can you bear to go further, selling products injurious to others in order to fulfill your insatiable desire?

C Lin informs the British of the new regulations.

Now we have set up regulations governing the Chinese people. He who sells opium shall receive the death penalty and he who smokes it also the death penalty. Now consider this: if the barbarians do not bring opium, then how can the Chinese people resell it, and how can they smoke it? The fact is that the wicked barbarians beguile the Chinese people into a death trap. How then can we grant life only to these barbarians? He who takes the life of even one person still has to atone for it with his own life; yet is the harm done by opium limited to the taking of one life only? Therefore in the new regulations, in regard to those barbarians who bring opium to China, the penalty is fixed at decapitation or strangulation. This is what is called getting rid of a harmful thing on behalf of mankind.

Moreover we have found that in the middle of the second month of this year [April 9] Consul [Superintendent] Elliot of your nation, because the opium prohibition law was very stern and severe, petitioned for an extension of the time limit. He requested a limit of five months for India and its adjacent harbors and related territories, and ten months for England proper, after which they would act in conformity with the new regulations. Now we, the commissioner and others, have memorialized and have received the extraordinary Celestial grace of His Majesty the Emperor, who has redoubled his consideration and compassion. All those who within the period of the coming one year (from England) or six months (from India) bring opium to China by mistake, but who voluntarily confess and completely surrender their opium, shall be exempt from their punishment. After this limit of time, if there are still those who bring opium to China then they will plainly have committed a willful violation and shall at once be executed according to law, with absolutely no clemency or pardon. This may be called the height of kindness and the perfection of justice.

Our Celestial Dynasty rules over and supervises the myriad states, and surely possesses unfathomable spiritual dignity. Yet the Emperor cannot bear to execute people without having first tried to reform them by instruction. Therefore he especially promulgates these fixed regulations. The barbarian merchants of your country, if they wish to do business for a prolonged period, are required to obey our statutes respectfully and to cut off permanently the source of opium. They must by no means try to test the effectiveness of the law with their lives. May you, O King, check your wicked and sift out your vicious people before they come to China, in order to guarantee the peace of your nation, to show further the sincerity of your politeness and submissiveness, and to let the two countries enjoy together the blessings of peace. How fortunate, how fortunate indeed! After receiving this dispatch will you immediately give us a prompt reply regarding the details and circumstances of your cutting off the opium traffic. Be sure not to put this off. The above is what has to be communicated.

1. What moral and economic arguments does Commissioner Lin present to the British government to prohibit opium imports?

2. How do the Chinese attempt to demonstrate their civility in the regulations proclaimed to curb opium imports?

3. How might the British importation of opium reinforce the Chinese impression of foreigners as barbarians?

The Irish Famine

In 1845, a blight devastated the potato crop in Ireland. The potato was the principal food of the Irish population, and the loss of the crop produced a widespread famine. The effects of the potato blight were worsened by the response of the British government. The population, which had been over 8 million in 1841, was reduced to 6.5 million by 1851 due to deaths and emigration, especially to North America. The following documents reflect both the indecision in London and the determination of some British politicians to be guided by their ideological beliefs.

 In 1845, Sir Robert Peel, the British Prime Minister, had correspondence regarding the famine. He supported the repeal of the Corn Laws and protective tariffs, as someone believing in laissez faire and free trade. This resulted in a cabinet memorandum and in opposition within his own Conservative Party. The bill for repeal passed in 1846, though Peel was forced to resign afterwards.

We must consider whether it is possible to apply a remedy to the great evil with which we are threatened. The application of such remedy involves considerations of the utmost magnitude. The remedy is the removal of all impediments to the import of all kinds of human food; that is, the total and absolute repeal for ever of all duties on all articles of subsistence.

You might remit nominally for one year. But who will re-establish the Corn Laws once abrogated, though from a casual and temporary pressure?. . .

I cannot consent to the issue of these instructions, and undertake at the same time to maintain the existing Corn Law.

The instructions contain a proof, not only that the crisis is great, not only that there is the probability of severe suffering from the scarcity of food, but that we are ourselves convinced of it.

I am prepared for one to take the responsibility of suspending the law by an Order in Council, or of calling Parliament at a very early period and advising in a speech from the Throne the suspension of the law.

I conceal from myself none of the difficulties that attend on suspension of the law. It will compel a very early decision on the course to be pursued in anticipation of the period when the suspension would expire. It will compel a deliberate review of the whole subject of agricultural protection.

I firmly believe that it would be better for the country that that review should be undertaken by others. Under ordinary circumstances I should advise that it should be so undertaken, but I look now to the immediate emergency, and to the duties it imposes on a Minister.

I am ready to take the responsibility of meeting that emergency, if the opinions of my colleagues as to the extent of the evil and the nature of the remedy concur with mine.

B Lord John Russell, the new Whig Prime Minister, supported free trade and the merchant class, which meant that large amounts of foodstuffs — butter, eggs, fish, and cattle — were actually exported from Ireland during the famine. He wrote on October 17, 1846:

> I am sorry to see that, in several parts of Ireland, calls are made upon the Government to undertake and perform tasks which are beyond the power and apart from the duties of Government.
>
> For instance, it seems to be expected that we should not only pay at an unusual rate of wages, but that we should maintain in this time of scarcity the usual price of food. A moment's thought will show that this is impossible. A smaller quantity of food is to be divided among the same number of human beings. It must be scarcer, it must be dearer. Any attempt to feed one class of the people of the United Kingdom by the Government would, if successful, starve another part; would feed the producers of potatoes, which had failed, by starving the producers of wheat, barley, and oats, which had not failed.

Sources: Sir Robert Peel, *Sir Robert Peel: From His Private Papers,* ed. Charles Stuart Parker, vol. III. New York: Kraus Reprint Co., 1970, pp. 224, 235; Lord John Russell, "Letter from Lord John Russell to the Duke of Leinster." www.swan.ac.uk/history/teaching/teaching%20resources/An%20Gorta%20Mor/ politicaleconomists/ljrussell.htm (Apr. 14, 2003); *The Times,* "London, Wednesday, October 4, 1848." www.people.virginia.edu/~eas5e/Irish/Winter.html (Feb. 5, 2003).

All that we have undertaken with respect to food, therefore, is to endeavour to create a provision trade, at fair mercantile prices, where no provision trade has hitherto existed, and where, without assistance, none might be willing to undertake a new and unpopular occupation.

But that which is not possible for a Government, is possible by individual and social exertion. Every one who travels through Ireland observes the large stacks of corn, which are the produce of the late harvest. There is nothing to prevent the purchase of grain by proprietors or by committees, and the disposal of these supplies in shops furnished on purpose with flour at a fair price, with a moderate profit.

This has been done, I am assured, in parts of the Highlands of Scotland, where the failure of the potatoes has been as great and as severe a calamity, as it has been in Ireland.

There is no doubt some inconvenience attending even these modes of interference with the market price of food; but the good over-balances the evil. Local committees, or agents of landowners, can ascertain the pressure of distress, measure the wants of a district, and prevent waste or mis-application. Besides, the general effect is to bring men together, and induce them to exert their energy in a social effort directed to one spot; whereas, the interference of the State deadens private energy, prevents forethought, and after super-seding all other exertion, finds itself at last unequal to the gigantic task it has undertaken.

There are other questions, however, extending beyond the exigency of the day, which, it seems to me, demand the attention of the landed proprietors of Ireland much more than that of the Government.

It has been calculated that one-fifth of the cultivated land in Ireland has hitherto produced potatoes. After the present lamentable failure, what course is to be taken? Some men of science deem that the potato can no longer be relied upon as an article of food; others say that time may remove the disease.

The editor of the "Gardeners' Chronicle" states that the explanation of the potato disease, founded on the hypothesis of some unknown miasma, cannot be accepted as satisfactory; but neither can it be rejected, seeing how signally all other explanations have failed.

Seeing, then, that science furnishes us with no means of estimating the effects of the prevalent disease upon the potato plant in future years, it would be impossible for the Government with any propriety to give any advice to the owners and occupiers of land in Ireland. They must form their own conclusions from the facts that are known, and the experience of the present and past years.

It is clear, however, that potatoes cannot be relied upon as they have been hitherto. A cottier [person who rents land to farm] cannot hope to be able to pay a large rent for con-acre [system of letting land for one or more crops], and the farmer cannot hope to obtain the cottier's labour by allowing him land for potatoes, which may probably fail. It is, therefore, a most important question for the people of Ireland, in what manner the deficiency of food is in future to be supplied; the nature of the grain or root which is best adapted for this purpose; the course of husbandry which ought to be followed; the means of procuring seed: all these are important problems to which the attention of the Agricultural Society of Ireland cannot too soon be directed.

One thing is certain; in order to enable Ireland to maintain her population, her agriculture must be greatly improved. Cattle, corn, poultry, pigs, eggs, butter, and salt provisions have been, and will probably continue to be her chief articles of export; but beyond the food exchanged for clothing and colonial products, she will require in future a large supply of food of her own growth or produce, which the labourer should be able to buy with his wages.

In effecting this great change, much good may ultimately be done; but unless all classes co-operate, and meet the infliction of Providence with fortitude and energy, the loss of the potato will only aggravate the woes and sufferings of Ireland.

Such, then, is the great lesson which, by the influence of the higher classes, and of such good patriots as yourself, may be taught to the Irish people. They should be taught to take advantage of the favourable conditions of their soil and surrounding sea; to work patiently for themselves in their own country as they work in London and Liverpool for their employers; to study economy, cleanliness, and the value of time; to aim at improving the condition of themselves and their children.

I would here conclude this letter, which is already too long, but I cannot do so without expressing my conviction that there is every disposition in persons of property in Ireland to meet their difficulties fairly, and submit to any sacrifice which the public good may require.

C The London *Times*, in an editorial on October 4, 1848, blamed Ireland and the Irish for their time of troubles.

Another winter is approaching, and Ireland again appeals to the sympathies and solicitudes of her provident and more fortunate sister. The rebellion has been suppressed, but not the famine. Throughout extensive districts there is as great a failure of the potato as there was two years since, and with a return of the cause we must expect a renewal of the disastrous consequences. There are, it is true, some circumstances now in our favour. The white crops have not been as deficient as in 1846. There is not a European famine, nor is there likely to be. We have also the benefit of our former experience. . . .

As measures of relief are in actual operation, and we have not to construct at the eleventh hour an original machinery for the purpose, there will be no overpowering pressure on official responsibility and public resources. What, then, is the work to be done? In the first place, there are vast accumulations of misery in certain parts, owing partly to the immigration of outcasts, and partly to the secluded nature of the region, and the consequent extraordinary ignorance and inaction of the people. . . . The people there have always been listless, improvident, and wretched, under whatever rulers. Ever since the onward Celtic wave was first stopped by the great Atlantic barrier, these people have remained the same, and their present misfortune is that they are simply what they have always been, and that from want of variety and intermixture they have not participated in the great progress of mankind. When we see a dense population on one of the finest shores of the world, with an inexhaustible ocean before their eyes, yearly allowing immense shoals of fish to pass visibly before their eyes, with scarcely to exact a toll from the passing masses of food, we must either rebuke their perverseness or pity their savage condition. We do pity them, because they have yet to be civilized. In Canada we have Indians in our borders, many of whom we yearly subsidize and maintain. In Ireland we have Celts equally helpless and equally the objects of national compassion. Such cases are only to be met by some form of public alms. Should the local resources be utterly drained, or so severely drawn upon as to paralyze industrial employment, England must make up her mind to some amount of imperial assistance, for the present at least.

But how far can Ireland maintain herself? That is a question which demands an immediate answer. It does not follow because there are districts of intense destitution that Ireland is, on the whole, unequal to the task of supporting her people. Nor is it so in fact. There is great wealth in Ireland. The state of cultivation, the value of the stock, and the produce, the manufactories, the pits, the mines, the edifices, and every other form of fixed wealth, has been immensely developed since the Union. We have given Ireland a commerce. Her ports are prosperous. The alleged decay of her cities is a gross fable. Dublin is a thriving metropolis . . . . A vast amount of British capital has been sunk with more or less profit. Such a country cannot be a pauper. She may have her poor; but it is ridiculous to imagine that she should throw herself altogether upon the alms of an English population, the greater part of whom are as well acquainted with hunger, and far more familiar with toil, than the most unfortunate of our Irish neighbors. . . .

There can, we think, be no doubt that Ireland is able to maintain herself. Indeed, who does doubt it? The very cry of rebellion is that she should keep her own produce at home, a demand which implies much folly and dishonesty, but yet testifies to the general opinion of Irish self-competency. We have therefore only to set the wealth of Ireland against its poverty, and draw the more favoured districts to the material and moral assistance required by the rest. There are two alternatives before us, and only two. Either we must have an Irish system, amply sufficient for Ireland, without this perpetual recurrence to English bounty, or the Imperial system must be applied without any reserve. Either Ireland must distribute fairly over all her resources the burden of her great houses and plague spot of misery, by the operation of a property tax or other comprehensive means, or she must submit to the Imperial taxation as the condition of Imperial relief.

1. What are the Corn Laws and what impact would their repeal have had on the British economy?

2. Why does Lord Russell believe that the government should not provide relief to the Irish?

3. Do Lord Russell's solutions to the dependency on the Irish potato demonstrate a lack of awareness of agricultural policy and conditions in Ireland? Explain.

4. Does the *Times* editorial demonstrate the advantages or disadvantages of British imperialism? Explain.

5. What does the editorial writer fail to recognize when condemning the Irish for not exploiting their vast resources?

6. Can the English be held responsible for the devastating impact of the famine? Defend your position.

Nationalism

Nationalism took many forms in the West in the nineteenth century. It became a way peoples understood their identity, even their destiny, and it was an ideology that legitimized both revolution and reaction. Some, like Giuseppe Mazzini (1805–1872), believed that nationalism and liberalism could work together for the benefit of all humanity, and he devoted his life to the cause of Italian unity. Others, like Friedrich List (1789–1846), used economic nationalism to aid future political unity. And there were those, like the Russian novelist Fyodor Dostoyevsky (1821–1881), whose nationalism was intended to defend his people against the influence of western European models and ideas.

 Mazzini helped to define nationalism for the modern world.

> Since any system of ideas rests upon a definition of terms, let us attempt first of all to determine what we ourselves understand by *nationality*.
>
> The essential characteristics of a nationality are common ideas, common principles and a common purpose. A nation is an association of all those who are brought together by language, by given geographical conditions or by the role assigned them by history, who acknowledge the same principles and who march together to the conquest of a single definite goal under the rule of a uniform body of law.

Sources: Herbert H. Rowen, ed., *From Absolutism to Revolution, 1648–1848*. New York: The Macmillan Company, 1963, pp. 266–267, 269–270, 273–274; Fyodor Dostoyevsky, *A Writer's Diary*, vol. Two, 1877–1881, trans. and annotated by Kenneth Lantz. Evanston, Illinois: Northwestern University Press, 1994, pp. 1372, 1373–1375.

The *life* of a nation consists in harmonious activity (that is, the employment of all individual abilities and energies comprised within the association) towards this single goal.

Where there is no general uniform body of law, we find castes, privileges, inequality and oppression. Where individual energies are stultified or left unorganized, we find inertia, immobility and obstacles in the way of progress. But where men do not acknowledge a common principle and all its consequences, where all do not share a common purpose, we find not a nation but only a crowd, a mass, a congeries which will fall apart in the very first crisis; it is a chance collection of men which chance events will dissolve sooner or later, and which will give way to anarchy.

To us these principles seem so self-evident, so much a part of the very nature of any association of men, that we see no need to prove them. The very history before our eyes teaches that whenever men lack ties of association and common purpose, nationality is just a meaningless word; it also teaches us that whenever a people does not live by the principles which gave it birth, it perishes.

But nationality means more even than this. Nationality also consists in the share of mankind's labors which God assigns to a people. This mission is the task which a people must perform to the end that the Divine Idea shall be realized in this world; it is the work which gives a people its rights as a member of Mankind; it is the baptismal rite which endows a people with its own character and its rank in the brotherhood of nations. . . .

If nationality is to be inviolable for all, friends and foes alike, it must be regarded inside a country as holy, like a religion, and outside a country as a grave mission. It is necessary too that the ideas arising within a country grow steadily, as part of the general law of Humanity which is the source of all nationality. It is necessary that these ideas be shown to other lands in their beauty and purity, free from any alien admixture, from any slavish fears, from any skeptical hesitancy, strong and active, embracing in their evolution every aspect and manifestation of the life of the nation. These ideas, a necessary component in the order of universal destiny, must retain their originality even as they enter harmoniously into mankind's general progress.

The people must be the *basis* of nationality; its logically derived and vigorously applied principles its *means*; the strength of all its *strength*; the improvement of the life of all and the happiness of the greatest possible number its *results*; and the accomplishment of the task assigned to it by God its *goal*.

This is what we mean by nationality.

B List discusses the role of the national economy.

[A]n infinite difference exists in the condition and circumstances of the various nations: we observe among them giants and dwarfs, well-formed bodies and cripples, civilised, half-civilised, and barbarous nations; but in all of them, as in the individual human being, exists the impulse of self-preservation, the striving for improvement which is implanted by nature. It is the task of politics to civilise the barbarous nationalities, to make the small and weak ones great and strong, but above all, to secure to them existence and continuance. It is the task of national economy to accomplish *the economical development of the nation*, and to prepare it for admission into the universal society of the future.

A nation in its normal state possesses one common language and literature, a territory endowed with manifold natural resources, extensive, and with convenient frontiers and a numerous population. Agriculture, manufactures, commerce, and navigation must be all developed in it proportionately; arts and sciences, educational establishments, and universal cultivation must stand in it on an equal footing with material production. Its constitution, laws, and institutions must afford to those who belong to it a high degree of security and liberty, and must promote religion, morality, and prosperity; in a word, must have the well-being of its citizens as their object. It must possess sufficient power on land and at sea to defend its independence and to protect its foreign commerce. It will possess the power of beneficially affecting the civilisation of less advanced nations, and by means of its own surplus population and of their mental and material capital to found colonies and beget new nations.

A large population, and an extensive territory endowed with manifold national resources, are essential requirements of the normal nationality; they are the fundamental conditions of mental cultivation as well as of material development and political power. A nation restricted in the number of its population and in territory, especially if it has a separate language, can only possess a crippled literature, crippled institutions for promoting art and science. A small State can never bring to complete perfection within its territory the various branches of production. In it all protection becomes mere private monopoly. Only through alliances with more powerful nations, by partly sacrificing the advantages of nationality, and by excessive energy, can it maintain with difficulty its independence.

A nation which possesses no coasts, mercantile marine, or naval power, or has not under its dominion and control the mouths of its rivers, is in its foreign commerce dependent on other countries; it can neither establish colonies of its own nor form new nations; all surplus population, mental and material means, which flows from such a nation to uncultivated countries, is lost to its own literature, civilisation and industry, and goes to the benefit of other nationalities.

C Dostoyevsky was a Slavophile, someone who defended Russian culture and its tradition. He sees Russia as suspended between Europe and Asia, and views Asia as the new creative frontier.

Europe is ready to praise us, pat us on the head, but will not acknowledge us as her own, secretly despises us, and openly considers us as people beneath her, as a lower species; and at times we inspire such disgust in them, real disgust, especially when we throw ourselves on them in a brotherly embrace.

But it's hard for us to turn away from our window on Europe; it's a matter of destiny here. Yet Asia might truly serve as an outlet to our future — this I shout out once more! And if, even in part, we could accept this idea and make it our own — oh, then what a root could be made healthy! Asia — our Asiatic Russia — why, this is also our ailing root that must not merely be refreshed but completely restored and reformed! A principle, a new principle, a new view on the matter — this is what we need! . . .

. . . We can't abandon Europe entirely, nor do we need to. It's 'the land of holy miracles,' and that was said by the most ardent Slavophile. Europe is also our mother, just as Russia is; she is our second mother; we have taken much from her, and we will take still more; we don't wish to be ungrateful to her. . . .

"Come now," someone will interrupt, "how can Asia help us become independent? We'll just fall into an Asiatic slumber there and won't become independent!"

"But you see," I continue, "when we turn to Asia, with our new view of her, something of the same sort may happen to us as happened to Europe when America was discovered. For, in truth, Asia for us is that same America which we still have not discovered. With our push toward Asia we will have a renewed upsurge of spirit and strength. Just as soon as we become more independent we'll at once find out what we have to do; but living with Europe for two centuries we've become unaccustomed to any kind of activity and have become windbags and idlers."

"Well, then, how are you going to rouse us up to go to Asia if we are idlers? And who among us is going to rise up first, even if you do prove to everyone, as clearly as twice two is four, that it is there we shall find our happiness?"

"In Europe we were hangers-on and slaves, while in Asia we shall be the masters. In Europe we were Tatars, while in Asia we are the Europeans. Our mission, our civilizing mission in Asia will encourage our spirit and draw us on; the movement needs only to be started. Just build two railways and begin with that — one railway to Siberia, another to Central Asia, and you shall see the results at once." . . .

"Well, you've made a lot of exclamations about science, yet you're pushing us to betray science and enlightenment in asking us to become Asians."

"But we'll need even more science over there!" I exclaim, "since what are we in science now? Merely semieducated dilettantes. But there we'll become real workers; we'll be forced into it by necessity itself the moment an independent, enterprising spirit arises; we'll at once become masters in science as well, not hangers-on as we so often are now. And the most important thing is that we shall understand and accept our civilizing mission in Asia from its very first steps (and this is beyond doubt). Our mission will elevate our spirits; it will help give us dignity and self-awareness —

and these are things we lack altogether now, or at least have in very small quantity. Beyond that, our push to Asia, if it begins, would serve as an outlet for many restless minds, for all who are fraught with anguish, for all who have grown lazy, for all who have grown tired of idleness. Give water an outlet and the scum and stench will vanish. And once people are drawn into work they will be bored no longer; everyone will be reborn. Even some fellow without talent, whose vanity is badly bruised and aching, would find his outlet there, since often an untalented fellow in one place will be reborn as a virtual genius somewhere else. This often happens in the European colonies. And Russia won't be emptied, don't worry: it will begin gradually; first a few will set off, but soon there'll be news of them that will attract others. And yet, this won't even be noticed in the broad ocean of Russia. Free the fly from the molasses; set his wings aright as best you can; still, only a most insignificant portion of the population will go there, so change won't even be noticeable. But over there — there it truly will be noticeable. Every place the 'Russ' settles in Asia will at once become Russian land. A new Russia will be created that will also restore and resurrect the old one in time and will clearly show her the path to follow.

"But for all this to happen we need a new principle and change of direction. And such a thing requires a minimum of disruption and upheaval. Just let people begin to understand (and they will understand) that our outlet is in the Asia of the future; that our riches are there; that our ocean is there."

1. How might nationalists from various countries define the "mission" Mazzini promotes?
2. How could List's description of nationalism justify imperialism?
3. Reflecting on their definitions of a nation, would Mazzini and List consider Canada a nation?
4. How does Dostoyevsky hope to counteract European influences by looking toward Asia?
5. How does Dostoyevsky's promotion of Russian skills reinforce the stereotype of Asians?

Elizabeth Cady Stanton

On July 19 and 20, 1848, a group of women's rights advocates met at Seneca Falls, New York. The Convention, which is considered to have launched the feminist movement in the United States, was organized by Lucretia Mott (1793–1880) and Elizabeth Cady Stanton (1815–1902), both of whom were also active in the movement to abolish slavery. In fact, their commitment to women's rights was strengthened when they and a number of other women were not recognized as official delegates to the World's Anti-Slavery Convention in London in 1840 because of their gender. At the Seneca Falls meeting, Stanton read the Declaration of Sentiments, which was modeled on the American Declaration of Independence.

The Declaration of Sentiments states "that all men and women are created equal," and goes on to explore this new premise.

When, in the course of human events, it becomes necessary for one portion of the family of man to assume among the people of the earth a position different from that which they have hitherto occupied, but one to which the laws of nature and of nature's God entitle them, a decent respect to the opinions of mankind requires that they should declare the causes that impel them to such a course.

We hold these truths to be self-evident: that all men and women are created equal; that they are endowed by their Creator with certain inalienable rights; that among these are life, liberty, and the pursuit of happiness; that to secure these rights governments are instituted, deriving their just powers from the consent of the governed. Whenever any form of government becomes destructive of these ends, it is the right of those who suffer from it to refuse allegiance to it, and to insist upon the institution of a new government, laying its foundation on such principles, and organizing its powers in such form, as to them shall seem most likely to effect their safety and happiness. Prudence, indeed, will dictate that governments long established should not be changed for light and transient causes; and accordingly all experience hath shown that mankind are more disposed to suffer while evils are sufferable, than to right themselves by abolishing the forms to which they are accustomed. But when a long train of abuses and usurpations, pursuing invariably the same object, evinces a design to reduce them under absolute despotism, it is their duty to throw off such government, and to provide new guards for their future security. Such has been the patient sufferance of the women under this government, and such is now the necessity which constrains them to demand the equal station to which they are entitled. The history of mankind is a history of repeated injuries and usurpations on the part of man toward woman, having in direct object the establishment of an absolute tyranny over her. To prove this, let facts be submitted to a candid world.

He has never permitted her to exercise her inalienable right to the elective franchise.

He has compelled her to submit to laws, in the formation of which she had no voice.

He has withheld from her rights which are given to the most ignorant and degraded men — both natives and foreigners.

Having deprived her of this first right of a citizen, the elective franchise, thereby leaving her without representation in the halls of legislation, he has oppressed her on all sides.

He has made her, if married, in the eye of the law, civilly dead. He has taken from her all right in property, even to the wages she earns.

Source: Elizabeth Cady Stanton, *A History of Woman Suffrage*, vol. 1. Rochester: Anthony, 1889, pp. 70–71.

He has made her, morally, an irresponsible being, as she can commit many crimes with impunity, provided they be done in the presence of her husband.

In the covenant of marriage, she is compelled to promise obedience to her husband, he becoming, to all intents and purposes, her master — the law giving him power to deprive her of her liberty, and to administer chastisement.

He has so framed the laws of divorce, as to what shall be the proper causes, and in case of separation, to whom the guardianship of the children shall be given, as to be wholly regardless of the happiness of women — the law, in all cases, going upon a false supposition of the supremacy of man, and giving all power into his hands.

After depriving her of all rights as a married woman, if single, and the owner of property, he has taxed her to support a government which recognizes her only when her property can be made profitable to it.

He has monopolized nearly all the profitable employments, and from those she is permitted to follow, she receives but a scanty remuneration. He closes against her all the avenues to wealth and distinction which he considers most honorable to himself. As a teacher of theology, medicine, or law, she is not known.

He has denied her the facilities for obtaining a thorough education, all colleges being closed against her.

He allows her in Church, as well as State, but a subordinate position, claiming Apostolic authority for her exclusion from the ministry, and with some exceptions, from any public participation in the affairs of the Church.

He has created a false public sentiment by giving to the world a different code of morals for men and women, by which moral delinquencies which exclude women from society, are not only tolerated, but deemed of little account in man.

He has usurped the prerogative of Jehovah himself, claiming it as his right to assign for her a sphere of action, when that belongs to her conscience and to her God.

He has endeavored, in every way that he could, to destroy her confidence in her own powers, to lessen her self-respect and to make her willing to lead a dependent and abject life.

Now, in view of this entire disfranchisement of one-half the people of this country, their social and religious degradation — in view of the unjust laws above mentioned, and because women do feel themselves aggrieved, oppressed, and fraudulently deprived of their most sacred rights, we insist that they have immediate admission to all the rights and privileges which belong to them as citizens of the United States.

In entering upon the great work before us, we anticipate no small amount of misconception, misrepresentation, and ridicule; but we shall use every instrumentality within our power to effect our object. We shall employ agents, circulate tracts, petition the State and National legislatures, and endeavor to enlist the pulpit and the press in our behalf. We hope this Convention will be followed by a series of Conventions embracing every part of the country.

B The Convention then passed twelve resolutions demanding new rights for women.

WHEREAS, The great precept of nature is conceded to be, that "man shall pursue his own true and substantial happiness." Blackstone in his Commentaries remarks, that this law of Nature being coeval with mankind, and dictated by God himself, is of course superior in obligation to any other. It is binding over all the globe, in all countries and at all times; no human laws are of any validity if contrary to this, and such of them as are valid, derive all their force, and all their validity, and all their authority, mediately and immediately, from this original; therefore:

Resolved, That such laws as conflict, in any way with the true and substantial happiness of woman, are contrary to the great precept of nature and of no validity, for this is "superior in obligation to any other."

Resolved, That all laws which prevent woman from occupying such a station in society as her conscience shall dictate, or which place her in a position inferior to that of man, are contrary to the great precept of nature, and therefore of no force or authority.

Resolved, That woman is man's equal — was intended to be so by the Creator, and the highest good of the race demands that she should be recognized as such.

Resolved, That the women of this country ought to be enlightened in regard to the laws under which they live, that they may no longer publish their degradation by declaring themselves satisfied with their present position, nor their ignorance, by asserting that they have all the rights they want.

Resolved, That inasmuch as man, while claiming for himself intellectual superiority, does accord to woman moral superiority, it is pre-eminently his duty to encourage her to speak and teach, as she has an opportunity, in all religious assemblies.

Resolved, That the same amount of virtue, delicacy, and refinement of behavior that is required of woman in the social state, should also be required of man, and the same transgressions should be visited with equal severity on both man and woman.

Resolved, That the objection of indelicacy and impropriety, which is so often brought against woman when she addresses a public audience, comes with a very ill-grace from those who encourage, by their attendance, her appearance on the stage, in the concert, or in feats of the circus.

Resolved, That woman has too long rested satisfied in the circumscribed limits which corrupt customs and a perverted application of the Scriptures have marked out for her, and that it is time she should move in the enlarged sphere which her great Creator has assigned her.

Resolved, That it is the duty of the women of this country to secure to themselves their sacred right to the elective franchise.

Resolved, That the equality of human rights results necessarily from the fact of the identity of the race in capabilities and responsibilities.

Resolved, therefore, That being invested by the creator with the same capabilities, and the same consciousness of responsibility for their exercise, it is demonstrably the right and duty of woman, equally with man, to promote every righteous cause by every righteous means; and especially in regard to the great subjects of morals and religion, it is self-evidently her right to participate with her brother in teaching them, both in private and in public, by writing and by speaking, by any instrumentalities proper to be used, and in any assemblies proper to be held; and this being a self-evident truth growing out of the divinely implanted principles of human nature, any custom or authority adverse to it, whether modern or wearing the hoary sanction of antiquity, is to be regarded as a self-evident falsehood, and at war with mankind.

Resolved, That the speedy success of our cause depends upon the zealous and untiring efforts of both men and women, for the overthrow of the monopoly of the pulpit, and for the securing to women an equal participation with men in the various trades, professions, and commerce.

1. What are the main similarities and differences between this declaration and the Declaration of Independence?

2. According to this declaration, what abuses did women face?

3. How relevant to society today are the abuses and demands listed in the declaration?

European Hegemony, 1871–1914

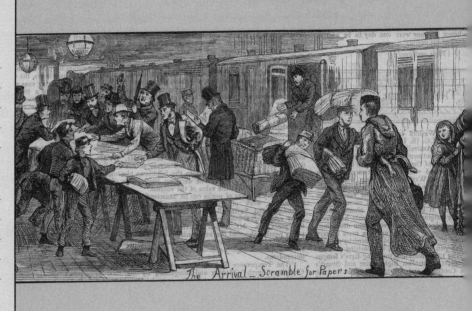

The Arrival — Scramble for Papers

Population growth and migration to urban areas in the West led to the emergence of many large cities, with populations of half a million or more. As the working classes crowded into the central areas of the cities, the middle classes sought more congenial residential surroundings in the suburbs. The spatial expansion of the city was made possible by the creation of new modes of transportation, particularly the commuter train. In this 1875 image, commuters at an English railway station rush to buy mass-circulation newspapers, their main source of news about their region and the world.

John Stuart Mill

John Stuart Mill (1806–1873) was among the greatest liberals of the period. He was also a logician and political economist. Much of his life was spent trying to define and confirm the rights of the individual, without losing sight that we all live in a community and have social responsibilities.

A Mill discusses the issue of personal freedom and social obligations in *On Liberty* (1859).

The object of this Essay is to assert one very simple principle, as entitled to govern absolutely the dealings of society with the individual in the way of compulsion and control, whether the means used be physical force in the form of legal penalties, or the moral coercion of public opinion. That principle is, that the sole end for which mankind are warranted, individually or collectively, in interfering with the liberty of action of any of their number, is self-protection. That the only purpose for which power can be rightfully exercised over any member of a civilised community, against his will, is to prevent harm to others. His own good, either physical or moral, is not a sufficient warrant. He cannot rightfully be compelled to do or forbear because it will be better for him to do so, because it will make him happier, because, in the opinions of others, to do so would be wise, or even right. These are good reasons for remonstrating with him, or reasoning with him, or persuading him, or entreating him, but not for compelling him, or visiting him with any evil in case he do otherwise. To justify that, the conduct from which it is desired to deter him must be calculated to produce evil to some one else. The only part of the conduct of any one, for which he is amenable to society, is that which concerns others. In the part which merely concerns himself, his independence is, of right, absolute. Over himself, over his own body and mind, the individual is sovereign. . . .

. . . This, then, is the appropriate region of human liberty. It comprises, first, the inward domain of consciousness; demanding liberty of conscience in the most comprehensive sense; liberty of thought and feeling; absolute freedom of opinion and sentiment on all subjects, practical or speculative, scientific, moral, or theological. The liberty of expressing and publishing opinions may seem to fall under a different principle, since it belongs to that part of the conduct of an individual which concerns other people; but, being almost of as much importance as the liberty of thought itself, and resting in great part on the same reasons, is practically inseparable from it. Secondly, the principle requires liberty of tastes and pursuits; of framing the plan of our life to suit our own character; of doing as we

Sources: John Stuart Mill, *On Liberty*, ed. David Spitz. New York: W. W. Norton & Company, 1975, pp. 10–11, 13–14; John Stuart Mill, *Considerations on Representative Government*, ed. Currin V. Shields. New York: The Liberal Arts Press, 1958, pp. 103–104, 127–128; John Stuart Mill, *The Subjection of Women*. Cambridge, Massachusetts: The MIT Press, 1970, pp. 21, 22, 79–81, 82.

like, subject to such consequences as may follow: without impediment from our fellow-creatures, so long as what we do does not harm them, even though they should think our conduct foolish, perverse, or wrong. Thirdly, from this liberty of each individual, follows the liberty, within the same limits, of combination among individuals; freedom to unite, for any purpose not involving harm to others: the persons combining being supposed to be of full age, and not forced or deceived.

No society in which these liberties are not, on the whole, respected, is free, whatever may be its form of government; and none is completely free in which they do not exist absolute and unqualified. The only freedom which deserves the name, is that of pursuing our own good in our own way, so long as we do not attempt to deprive others of theirs, or impede their efforts to obtain it. Each is the proper guardian of his own health, whether bodily, or mental and spiritual. Mankind are greater gainers by suffering each other to live as seems good to themselves, than by compelling each to live as seems good to the rest.

B In *Considerations on Representative Government* (1861), Mill discusses democracy in the context of the times.

In a really equal democracy every or any section would be represented, not disproportionately, but proportionately. A majority of the electors would always have a majority of the representatives, but a minority of the electors would always have a minority of the representatives. Man for man they would be as fully represented as the majority. Unless they are, there is not equal government, but a government of inequality and privilege: one part of the people rule over the rest; there is a part whose fair and equal share of influence in the representation is withheld from them, contrary to all just government, but, above all, contrary to the principle of democracy, which professes equality as its very root and foundation. . . .

Such a representative democracy as has now been sketched, representative of all, and not solely of the majority — in which the interests, the opinions, the grades of intellect which are outnumbered would nevertheless be heard, and would have a chance of obtaining by weight of character and strength of argument an influence which would not belong to their numerical force — this democracy, which is alone equal, alone impartial, alone the government of all by all, the only true type of democracy, would be free from the greatest evils of the falsely-called democracies which now prevail . . . . All trust in constitutions is grounded on the assurance they may afford, not that the depositaries of power will not, but that they cannot, misemploy it. Democracy is not the ideally best form of government unless this weak side of it can be strengthened, unless it can be so organized that no class, not even the most numerous, shall be able to reduce all but itself to political insignificance and direct the course of legislation and administration by its exclusive class interest. The problem is to find the means of preventing this abuse, without sacrificing the characteristic advantages of popular government.

C Mill always claimed he was indebted to his wife, Harriet Taylor Mill (1807–1858), for many of his ideas. There is much critical speculation on how deeply Mrs. Mill collaborated with her husband on some of his works, including the essay which became *On Liberty*. Mill's *The Subjection of Women* (1871) is concerned with the emancipation of women, and is a tribute to both Harriet Taylor Mill's influence and Mill's willingness to break from earlier social stereotypes.

> The social subordination of women thus stands out an isolated fact in modern social institutions; a solitary breach of what has become their fundamental law; a single relic of an old world of thought and practice exploded in everything else, but retained in the one thing of most universal interest . . . .
>
> The least that can be demanded is, that the question should not be considered as prejudged by existing fact and existing opinion, but open to discussion on its merits, as a question of justice and expediency: the decision on this, as on any of the other social arrangements of mankind, depending on what an enlightened estimate of tendencies and consequences may show to be most advantageous to humanity in general, without distinction of sex. . . .
>
> What is now called the nature of women is an eminently artificial thing — the result of forced repression in some directions, unnatural stimulation in others. It may be asserted without scruple, that no other class of dependents have had their character so entirely distorted from its natural proportions by their relation with their masters; for, if conquered and slave races have been, in some respects, more forcibly repressed, whatever in them has not been crushed down by an iron heel has generally been let alone, and if left with any liberty of development, it has developed itself according to its own laws; but in the case of women, a hot-house and stove cultivation has always been carried on of some of the capabilities of their nature, for the benefit and pleasure of their masters. . . .
>
> . . . The law of servitude in marriage is a monstrous contradiction to all the principles of the modern world, and to all the experience through which those principles have been slowly and painfully worked out. It is the sole case, now that negro slavery has been abolished, in which a human being in the plentitude of every faculty is delivered up to the tender mercies of another human being, in the hope forsooth that this other will use the power solely for the good of the person subjected to it. Marriage is the only actual bondage known to our law. There remain no legal slaves, except the mistress of every house.
>
> It is not, therefore, on this part of the subject, that the question is likely to be asked, *Cui bono?* We may be told that the evil would outweigh the good, but the reality of the good admits of no dispute. In regard, however, to the larger question, the removal of women's disabilities — their recognition as

the equals of men in all that belongs to citizenship — the opening to them of all honourable employments, and of the training and education which qualifies for those employments — there are many persons for whom it is not enough that the inequality has no just or legitimate defence; they require to be told what express advantage would be obtained by abolishing it.

To which let me first answer, the advantage of having the most universal and pervading of all human relations regulated by justice instead of injustice. The vast amount of this gain to human nature, it is hardly possible, by any explanation or illustration, to place in a stronger light than it is placed by the bare statement, to anyone who attaches a moral meaning to words. All the selfish propensities, the self-worship, the unjust self-preference, which exist among mankind, have their source and root in, and derive their principal nourishment from, the present constitution of the relation between men and women. Think what it is to a boy, to grow up to manhood in the belief that without any merit or any exertion of his own, though he may be the most frivolous and empty or the most ignorant and stolid of mankind, by the mere fact of being born a male he is by right the superior of all and every one of an entire half of the human race: including probably some whose real superiority to himself he has daily or hourly occasion to feel; but even if in his whole conduct he habitually follows a woman's guidance, still, if he is a fool, she thinks that of course she is not, and cannot be, equal in ability and judgment to himself; and if he is not a fool, he does worse — he sees that she is superior to him, and believes that, notwithstanding her superiority, he is entitled to command and she is bound to obey. What must be the effect on his character, of this lesson?. . . [Many] are little aware, when a boy is differently brought up, how early the notion of his inherent superiority to a girl arises in his mind; how it grows with his growth and strengthens with his strength; how it is inoculated by one schoolboy upon another; how early the youth thinks himself superior to his mother, owing her perhaps forbearance, but no real respect; and how sublime and sultan-like a sense of superiority he feels above all, over the woman whom he honours by admitting her to a partnership of his life. Is it imagined that all this does not pervert the whole manner of existence of the man, both as an individual and as a social being? It is an exact parallel to the feeling of a hereditary king that he is excellent above others by being born a king, or a noble by being born a noble. The relation between husband and wife is very like that between lord and vassal, except that the wife is held to more unlimited obedience than the vassal was. . . .

. . . The principle of the modern movement in morals and politics, is that conduct, and conduct alone, entitles to respect: that not what men are, but what they do, constitutes their claim to deference; that, above all, merit, and not birth, is the only rightful claim to power and authority. If no authority, not in its nature temporary, were allowed to one human being over another, society would not be employed in building up propensities with one hand which it has to curb with the other. . . .

The second benefit to be expected from giving to women the free use of their faculties, by leaving them the free choice of their employments, and opening to them the same field of occupation and the same prizes and encouragements as to other human beings, would be that of doubling the mass of mental faculties available for the higher service of humanity.

1. What does Mill identify as the only justification for society interfering with the life of an individual? Do you agree? Defend your position.

2. "Democracy is not the ideally best form of government . . . unless it can be so organized that no class, not even the most numerous, shall be able to reduce all but itself to political insignificance . . . ." What is Mill's primary concern with the dominance of the majority in a democracy?

3. Outline the argument in which Mill equates the treatment of women with legalized slavery.

Charles Darwin

Charles Darwin (1809–1882) was the giant of the natural sciences in the nineteenth century. His work *The Origin of Species by Means of Natural Selection or the Preservation of Favoured Races in the Struggle for Life* (1859), caused an immediate sensation and changed the dialogue on how we think about human nature, nature itself, and biological relations. His concept of evolution, and the supporting material he presented to substantiate it, have shaped research in the biological sciences for over a century.

 In *The Origin of Species* Darwin discusses what he intends to do.

When on board H.M.S. *Beagle*, as naturalist, I was much struck with certain facts in the distribution of the inhabitants of South America, and in the geological relations of the present to the past inhabitants of that continent. These facts seemed to me to throw some light on the origin of species — that mystery of mysteries, as it has been called by one of our greatest philosophers. . . .

In considering the Origin of Species, it is quite conceivable that a naturalist, reflecting on the mutual affinities of organic beings, on their embryological relations, their geographical distribution, geological succession, and other such facts, might come to the conclusion that each species had not been independently created, but had descended, like varieties, from other species. Nevertheless, such a conclusion, even if well founded, would be unsatisfactory, until it could be shown how the innumerable species inhabiting this world have been modified, so as to acquire that perfection of

Sources: Charles Darwin, *The Origin of Species*, ed. J. W. Burrow. Harmondsworth: Penguin Books, 1968, pp. 65, 66–69, 116–117, 119, 169–170, 459–460; Charles Darwin, *The Descent of Man*. New York: Random House, 1936, pp. 909–910, 914–915, 919–920.

structure and coadaptation which most justly excites our admiration. Naturalists continually refer to external conditions, such as climate, food etc., as the only possible cause of variation. In one very limited sense, as we shall hereafter see, this may be true; but it is preposterous to attribute to mere external conditions, the structure, for instance, of the woodpecker, with its feet, tail, beak, and tongue, so admirably adapted to catch insects under the bark of trees. . . .

It is, therefore, of the highest importance to gain a clear insight into the means of modification and coadaptation. At the commencement of my observations it seemed to me probable that a careful study of domesticated animals and of cultivated plants would offer the best chance of making out this obscure problem. Nor have I been disappointed; in this and in all other perplexing cases I have invariably found that our knowledge, imperfect though it be, of variation under domestication, afforded the best and safest clue. . . .

From these considerations, I shall devote the first chapter of this Abstract to Variation under Domestication. We shall thus see that a large amount of hereditary modification is at least possible; and, what is equally or more important, we shall see how great is the power of man in accumulating by his Selection successive slight variations. I will then pass on to the variability of species in a state of nature; but I shall, unfortunately, be compelled to treat this subject far too briefly, as it can be treated properly only by giving long catalogues of facts. We shall, however, be enabled to discuss what circumstances are most favourable to variation. In the next chapter the Struggle for Existence amongst all organic beings throughout the world, which inevitably follows from their high geometrical powers of increase, will be treated of. This is the doctrine of Malthus, applied to the whole animal and vegetable kingdoms. As many more individuals of each species are born than can possibly survive; and as, consequently, there is a frequently recurring struggle for existence, it follows that any being, if it vary however slightly in any manner profitable to itself, under the complex and sometimes varying conditions of life, will have a better chance of surviving, and thus be *naturally selected*. From the strong principle of inheritance, any selected variety will tend to propagate its new and modified form.

This fundamental subject of Natural Selection will be treated at some length in the fourth chapter; and we shall then see how Natural Selection almost inevitably causes much Extinction of the less improved forms of life, and induces what I have called Divergence of Character. . . .

No one ought to feel surprise at much remaining as yet unexplained in regard to the origin of species and varieties, if he makes due allowance for our profound ignorance in regard to the mutual relations of all the beings which live around us. Who can explain why one species ranges widely and is very numerous, and why another allied species has a narrow range and is rare? Yet these relations are of the highest importance, for they determine the present welfare, and, as I believe, the future success and modification of every inhabitant of this world. Still less do we know of the mutual relations of the innumerable inhabitants of the world during the many past geological epochs in its history. Although much remains obscure, and will long remain obscure, I can entertain no doubt, after the most deliberate study and dispassionate judgement of which I am capable, that the view which most naturalists entertain, and which I formerly entertained — namely, that each species has been independently created — is erroneous. I am fully convinced that species are not immutable; but that those belonging to what are called the same genera are lineal descendants of some other and generally extinct species, in the same manner as the acknowledged varieties of any one species are the descendants of that species. Furthermore, I am convinced that Natural Selection has been the main but not exclusive means of modification.

B Darwin's discussion on the struggle for existence is among his most controversial theories.

A struggle for existence inevitably follows from the high rate at which all organic beings tend to increase. Every being, which during its natural lifetime produces several eggs or seeds, must suffer destruction during some period of its life, and during some season or occasional year, otherwise, on the principle of geometrical increase, its numbers would quickly become so inordinately great that no country could support the product. Hence, as more individuals are produced than can possibly survive, there must in every case be a struggle for existence, either one individual with another of the same species, or with the individuals of distinct species, or with the physical conditions of life. . . . Although some species may be now increasing, more or less rapidly, in numbers, all cannot do so, for the world would not hold them. . . .

   In looking at Nature, it is most necessary . . . never to forget that every single organic being around us may be said to be striving to the utmost to increase in numbers; that each lives by a struggle at some period of its life; that heavy destruction inevitably falls either on the young or old, during each generation or at recurrent intervals. Lighten any check, mitigate the destruction ever so little, and the number of the species will almost instantaneously increase to any amount. The face of Nature may be compared to a yielding surface, with ten thousand sharp wedges packed close together and driven inwards by incessant blows, sometimes one wedge being struck, and then another with greater force.

C Natural selection came to be a term used in numerous areas, and unsettled many people in its assumption that nature is not always benign.

[I]f variations useful to any organic being do occur, assuredly individuals thus characterised will have the best chance of being preserved in the struggle for life; and from the strong principle of inheritance they will tend to produce offspring similarly characterised. This principle of preservation, I have called, for the sake of brevity, Natural Selection. Natural selection, on the principle of qualities being inherited at corresponding ages, can modify the egg, seed, or young, as easily as the adult. Amongst many animals, sexual selection will give its aid to ordinary selection, by assuring to the most vigorous and best adapted males the greatest number of offspring. Sexual selection will also give [characteristics] useful to the males alone, in their struggles with other males.

Whether natural selection has really thus acted in nature, in modifying and adapting the various forms of life to their several conditions and stations, must be judged of by the general tenour and balance of evidence given in the following chapters. But we already see how it entails extinction; and how largely extinction has acted in the world's history, geology plainly declares. Natural selection, also, leads to divergence of character; for more living beings can be supported on the same area the more they diverge in structure, habits, and constitution, of which we see proof by looking at the inhabitants of any small spot or at naturalised productions. Therefore during the modification of the descendants of any one species, and during the incessant struggle of all species to increase in numbers, the more diversified these descendants become, the better will be their chance of succeeding in the battle of life. Thus the small differences distinguishing varieties of the same species, will steadily tend to increase till they come to equal the greater differences between species of the same genus, or even of distinct genera.

D Darwin closes *The Origin of Species* with a description of a new kind of garden:

It is interesting to contemplate an entangled bank, clothed with many plants of many kinds, with birds singing on the bushes, with various insects flitting about, and with worms crawling through the damp earth, and to reflect that these elaborately constructed forms, so different from each other, and dependent on each other in so complex a manner, have all been produced by laws acting around us. These laws, taken in the largest sense, being Growth with Reproduction; Inheritance which is almost implied by reproduction; Variability from the indirect and direct action of the external conditions of life, and from use and disuse; a Ratio of Increase so high as to lead to a Struggle for Life, and as a consequence to Natural Selection, entailing Divergence of Character and the Extinction of less-improved forms. Thus, from the war of nature, from famine and death, the most exalted object which we are capable of conceiving, namely, the production of the higher animals, directly follows. There is grandeur in this view of life, with its several powers, having been originally breathed into a few forms or into one; and that, whilst this planet has gone cycling on according to the fixed law of gravity, from so simple a beginning endless forms most beautiful and most wonderful have been, and are being evolved.

E While Darwin tried to steer clear of controversy surrounding theology and social systems, he followed *The Origin of Species* with another massive and important work in 1871, *The Descent of Man*. Here he speculates on human nature.

The main conclusion here arrived at, and now held by many naturalists who are well competent to form a sound judgment is that man is descended from some less highly organised form. The grounds upon which this conclusion rests will never be shaken, for the close similarity between man and the lower animals in embryonic development, as well as in innumerable points of structure and constitution, both of high and of the most trifling importance, — the rudiments which he retains, and the abnormal reversions to which he is occasionally liable, — are facts which cannot be disputed. They have long been known, but until recently they told us nothing with respect to the origin of man. Now when viewed by the light of our knowledge of the whole organic world, their meaning is unmistakable. The great principle of evolution stands up clear and firm, when these groups or facts are considered in connection with others, such as the mutual affinities of the members of the same group, their geographical distribution in past and present times, and their geological succession. It is incredible that all these facts should speak falsely. He who is not content to look, like a savage, at the phenomena of nature as disconnected, cannot any longer believe that man is the work of a separate act of creation. He will be forced to admit that the close resemblance of the embryo of man to that, for instance of a dog — the construction of his skull, limbs and whole frame on the same plan with that of other mammals, independently of the uses to which the parts may be put — the occasional re-appearance of various structures, for instance of several muscles, which man does not normally possess, but which are common to the Quadrumana — and a crowd of analogous facts — all point in the plainest manner to the conclusion that man is the co-descendant with other mammals of a common progenitor. . . .

The belief in God has often been advanced as not only the greatest, but the most complete of all the distinctions between man and the lower animals. It is however impossible, as we have seen, to maintain that this belief is innate or instinctive in man. . . . The idea of a universal and beneficent Creator does not seem to arise in the mind of man, until he has been elevated by long-continued culture. . . .

I am aware that the conclusions arrived at in this work will be denounced by some as highly irreligious; but he who denounces them is bound to shew why it is more irreligious to explain the origin of man as a distinct species by descent from some lower form, through the laws of variation and natural selection, than to explain the birth of the individual through the laws of ordinary reproduction. The birth both of the species and of the individual are equally parts of that grand sequence of events, which our minds refuse to accept as the result of blind chance. The understanding revolts at such a conclusion, whether or not we are able to believe that every slight variation of structure, — the union of each pair in marriage, — the dissemination of each seed, — and other such events, have all been ordained for some special purpose. . . .

The main conclusion arrived at in this work, namely, that man is descended from some lowly organised form, will, I regret to think, be highly distasteful to many. But there can hardly be a doubt that we are descended from barbarians. . . .

Man may be excused for feeling some pride at having risen, though not through his own exertions, to the very summit of the organic scale; and the fact of his having thus risen, instead of having been aboriginally placed there, may give him hope for a still higher destiny in the distant future. But we are not here concerned with hopes or fears, only with the truth as far as our reason permits us to discover it; and I have given the evidence to the best of my ability. We must, however, acknowledge, as it seems to me, that man with all his noble qualities, with sympathy which feels for the most debased, with benevolence which extends not only to other men but to the humblest living creature, with his god-like intellect which has penetrated into the movements and constitution of the solar system — with all these exalted powers — Man still bears in his bodily frame the indelible stamp of his lowly origin.

1. What scientific evidence does Darwin present to support his theory of natural selection?

2. Why would some religious leaders criticize Darwin's theory? How does he respond to their criticisms?

3. Has humanity pursued the higher destiny that Darwin felt was a logical evolutionary step?

Charles Baudelaire

Charles Baudelaire (1821–1867), French poet, art critic, and essayist, was among the first commentators on the modern city and its new and exciting experiences. He recorded the Paris of his time, which was being rebuilt under the leadership of Baron Haussmann (1809–1891). Baudelaire loved the excitement of the city: the crowds, the cafés, the gaslight, and the variety of experience of the new, modern, urban life.

 In Baudelaire's "The Eyes of the Poor," the café is a meeting place to see and be seen, as well as something that dazzles.

Oh, so you wish to know why I hate you today. It will without a doubt be less easy for you to understand, than for me to explain; for you are, I believe, the most extreme example of feminine impermeability that can be encountered.

Source: Charles Baudelaire, "Les yeux des pauvres," *Petits Poèmes en Prose*. Paris: Garnier-Flammarion, 1967, pp. 101–102. Translated by Arthur Haberman.

We had spent a long day together, though it seemed short to me. We had deeply promised one another that all our thoughts would be shared, and that from this moment on our two souls would be but one — an ideal which has nothing original about it, after all. It has been dreamed by everyone, realized by none.

That evening, a bit tired, you wanted to sit at the front of a new café which formed the corner of a new boulevard, one still littered with gravel, though already displaying its incomplete splendours. The café dazzled. The gas itself burned with the joy of a debut, and lit with all its power the blinding white walls, the dazzling expanse of mirrors, the gold of the cornices and moldings, chubby-cheeked pages dragged by dogs on leashes, ribald ladies with falcons perched on their fists, nymphs and goddesses bearing fruits, pastries, and game on their heads, goddesses of youth and beautiful cupbearers holding in their arms tiny jars of syrups of two-coloured obelisks with ices; all of history and all of mythology putting themselves at the service of gluttony.

B However, the lovers encounter another side of the new city, and this causes the personal and the political to intersect.

In front of us, on the street, a kind-looking man of about forty was standing, with a tired face and a gray beard, holding a small boy by the hand and carrying in the other arm a child too weak to walk. He had the role of the nursemaid taking the children for an evening stroll. All were in rags. The three faces were extraordinarily serious, and those six eyes were directed fixedly at the new café with equal admiration, but with shades of difference according to their years.

The eyes of the father said: "How beautiful! How beautiful! One can say that all the gold of the world can be found on these walls." — The eyes of the small boy: "How beautiful! How beautiful! But it is a house where only those who are not like us can enter." As for the eyes of the baby, he was much too fascinated to express anything but a joy both stupid and profound.

Cabaret singers tell us that pleasure uplifts the soul and softens the heart. The song was right that evening, by my lights. Not only was I made tender by this family of eyes, but I felt a bit ashamed of our glasses and decanters, too large for our thirst. I turned my face to yours, dear love, to read *my* thoughts in it; I plunged into your eyes, so beautiful and so strangely soft, into your green eyes, home of impulse and inspired by the moon, when you said to me: "Those people are unbearable with their wide open eyes! Can't you please tell the owner of the café to move them away from here?"

It is so difficult to know one another, my dear angel, and thought cannot be communicated, even between people in love!

1. How does Baudelaire use the bright lights of the city to illustrate class discrepancies?

2. Describe the elements of city life that appeal to Baudelaire.

3. How does Baudelaire criticize his own class for extravagance and callousness?

Adelheid Popp

Adelheid Popp (1869–1939) was the fifteenth child of a working-class family in Vienna. The early death of her father forced Popp to start work at a very young age. She became a member of the Social Democratic Party and founded *Working Women's News*. In the Austrian Republic, which was created following the collapse of the Hapsburg Empire, she became a socialist member of parliament. Her autobiography (1909) describes the hardships faced by many members of the working class, but also the particular problems faced by working women.

A After a long and frustrating search for work around Christmastime, Popp gets a job at a factory that produces sandpaper and emery boards.

> My new workplace was on the third floor of a building that was used exclusively for industrial purposes. Not having known the bustle of a factory, I had never felt so uncomfortable. Everything displeased me — the dirty, sticky work; the unpleasant glass dust; the crowd of people; the crude tone; and the whole way that the girls and even married women behaved. . . .
>
> [The women] often spoke of a Herr Berger, who was the company's traveling representative and was expected back about then. All the women raved about him so I was curious to see the man. . . . Accompanied by the owner's wife, he came into the room where I worked. I didn't like him at all. That afternoon I was called into his office; Herr Berger sent me on a silly errand and made a silly remark about my "beautiful hands". It was already dark when I returned; I had to pass through an empty anteroom that wasn't lighted . . . Herr Berger was in the anteroom when I came in. He took me by the hands and inquired sympathetically about my circumstances. I answered him truthfully and told of our poverty. He spoke a few words, taking pity on me and promising to use his influence to get me higher wages. Of course I was delighted with the prospect opening up to me for I was getting only two and a half gulders [about $1.25] a week, for which I had to work twelve hours a day. . . . Before I even knew what was happening, Herr Berger kissed me. He tried to calm my fright with the words, "It was just a fatherly kiss". He was twenty-six years old and I was fifteen, so fatherliness was out of the question. . . .
>
> The next day I was overwhelmed with reproaches from one of my co-workers, a young blonde girl whom I liked most of all. She reproached me with having taken her place with the traveler . . . he had loved her, she protested through tears and sobs, and now I'd put an end to everything. The other girls joined in too; they called me a hypocrite . . . I was defenceless against their taunts and sneers and longed for the hour when I could go home. It was Saturday, and when I received my wages, I went home with the intention of not returning on Monday.

Source: Alfred Kelly, ed., *The German Worker*. Berkeley: University of California Press, 1987, pp. 123–126, 129–133.

When I spoke of the matter at home, I was severely scolded. It was strange. My mother, who was always so intent on raising me to be a respectable girl, who always gave me instructions and warning not to talk to men ("You should only allow yourself to be kissed by the man you're going to marry", she used to impress upon me) — in this instance my mother was against me. She said I was going too far. A kiss was nothing bad, and if I was getting more wages as a result, then it would be silly to give up my job.

B Popp is unable to make herself return to the factory. She turns to an aunt who works as a maid for a countess, but she refuses to help Popp find work. Finally Popp gets another factory job.

I found work again; I grasped at everything offered me to show my willingness to work, and still I had some hard times. But finally things got better. I was referred to a large factory that stood in the best repute. Three hundred women and about fifty men were employed there. I was put into a large room where sixty women and girls worked. There were twelve tables by the windows and at each table sat four girls. Our job was to sort the merchandise that had been manufactured; other women counted it and a third group branded it with the company's stamp. We worked from 7:00 A.M. to 7:00 P.M. At noon we had a one-hour break and in the afternoon a half hour off. . . . I'd never been paid that well . . . in half a year I was already making five gulders [$2.50] a week; later I got six gulders [$3.00]. . . .

From the women in this factory you can judge how sad and deprived the lot of factory women is. Here were recognizably the best working conditions. In none of the neighbouring factories were wages so high. We were envied everywhere. Parents considered themselves fortunate if they could get their fourteen-year-old daughters positions there when they left school. . . . But even here, in this "paradise", everyone was badly nourished. Those who stayed in the factory during lunch break bought sausage or scraps . . . for a few [cents]. Often they ate buttered bread and cheap fruit. Some drank a glass of beer and sopped bread in it. When we got disgusted by this food, we fetched our lunch from a restaurant. For about five kreuzers [3 cents] we got either soup or vegetables. It was rarely well prepared, and the smell of the fat they used was sickening. We often felt such disgust that we threw the food away, preferring to eat dry bread and console ourselves with the thought of the coffee we'd brought for the afternoon.

C Popp reflects on the solidarity and ingeniousness the women show, and the dangers to which they are exposed.

I saw among my co-workers — the despised factory women — examples of the most extraordinary sacrifices for others. If there was a special emergency in one family, then they chipped in their [pennies] to help. Even though they had worked twelve hours in the factory and many still had an hour's walk home, they mended their own clothes, without ever having been taught how. They took apart their old dresses to fashion new ones from the separate pieces, which they sewed at night and on Sundays.

Nor did they rest during lunch or afternoon breaks. Their sparse meal quickly out of the way, they would knit, crochet, or embroider stockings. And despite their diligence and thrift, every one of them was poor and trembled at the thought of losing her job. They all humbled themselves and put up with the worst injustices from their superiors, lest they lose their good jobs and go hungry.

Many girls had the misfortune of being especially favoured by one of the superiors. Then suddenly he'd change his attitude. She couldn't do anything right anymore; no longer was she promoted; instead of a wage increase, she received reprimands. She was threatened with dismissal, and so the poor girl was harassed until she couldn't stand it any longer and left of her own accord.

Then there would be rumours about some of the ones to whom this happened. People would whisper, she's been seen on certain streets showily dressed or leaning out windows to entice men. She was always condemned and I was outraged. No one considered whether it would have turned out differently if at the outset the girl had abandoned resistance and yielded to her superior.

At the time, I knew nothing of either hidden or open prostitution; I hadn't even heard the word. Later on, when I could better judge cause and effect, I began to think differently of these girls, especially when, in the course of the years I worked in the factory, I got to know a lot of older women of whom it was said that they owed their privileged positions to certain relations with a superior. Or when a woman made a scene with a foreman because he suddenly began to oppress her because he'd gotten tired of her and preferred to have her out of the way so that he might, unhindered, "bless" [a new girl].

1. Besides poor working conditions and low wages, what other challenges did female workers face?

2. How would factory work have a negative physical and psychological impact on the workers?

3. How might these factories with their many workers be breeding grounds for the socialist movement?

The Ottoman Imperial Rescript of Gülhane, 1839

The Imperial Rescript of Gülhane developed out of the reforms of Mahmud II (1808–1839) and was the handiwork of the foremost Ottoman reformer of the period, Grand Vizier Mustafa Resit Pasa (1800–1858). The Rescript was read to an assemblage of Ottoman dignitaries and the European diplomatic community gathered at the imperial gardens of Gülhane, in 1839. The Rescript should not be interpreted as introducing a constitutional monarchy since it offered only self-imposed limitations on the powers of the Sultan who could abolish them at will, but it was nonetheless a milestone in the transformation of the Ottoman state.

A The Rescript opens with an introduction that presents the philosophical grounds for reform.

> All the world knows that in the first days of the Ottoman monarchy, the glorious precepts of the Kuran and the laws of the empire were always honored.
>
> The empire in consequence increased in strength and greatness, and all its subjects, without exception, had risen in the highest degree to ease and prosperity. In the last one hundred and fifty years a succession of accidents and divers causes have arisen which have brought about a disregard for the sacred code of laws and the regulations flowing therefrom, and the former strength and prosperity have changed into weakness and poverty; an empire in fact loses all its stability so soon as it ceases to observe its laws.
>
> These considerations are ever present to our mind, and ever since the day of our advent to the throne the thought of the public weal, of the improvement of the state of the provinces, and of relief to the (subject) peoples, has not ceased to engage it. If, therefore, the geographical position of the Ottoman provinces, the fertility of the soil, the aptitude and intelligence of the inhabitants are considered, the conviction will remain that by striving to find efficacious means, the result, which by the help of God we hope to attain, can be obtained within a few years. Full of confidence, therefore, in the help of the Most High, and certain of the support of our Prophet, we deem it right to seek by new institutions to give to the provinces composing the Ottoman Empire the benefit of a good administration.

B The reforms fall under three categories:

> These institutions must be principally carried out under three heads, which are:
>
> 1. The guarantees insuring to our subjects perfect security for life, honor, and fortune.
> 2. A regular system of assessing and levying taxes.
> 3. An equally regular system for the levying of troops and the duration of their service.
>
> And, in fact, are not life and honor the most precious gifts to mankind? What man however much his character may be against violence, can prevent himself from having recourse to it, and thereby injure the government and

Source: "The Rescript of Gülhane — Gülhane Hatt-1 Hümayunu — 3 November 1839."
www.ata.boun.edu.tr/Department%20Webpages/ATA_517/The%20Edict%20of%20Gulhane,%203%20November%201839.pdf (Apr. 21, 2003)

the country, if his life and honor are endangered? If, on the contrary, he enjoys in that respect perfect security, he will not depart from the ways of loyalty, and all his actions will contribute to the good of the government and of his brothers.

If there is an absence of security as to one's fortune, everyone remains insensible to the voice of the Prince and the country; no one interests himself in the progress of public good, absorbed as he is in his own troubles. If, on the contrary, the citizen keeps possession in all confidence of all his goods, then, full of ardor in his affairs, which he seeks to enlarge in order to increase his comforts, he feels daily growing and bubbling in his heart not only his love for the Prince and country, but also his devotion to his native land.

These feelings become in him the source of the most praiseworthy actions.

As to the regular and fixed assessment of the taxes, it is very important that it be regulated; for the state which is forced to incur many expenses for the defense of its territory cannot obtain the money necessary for its armies and other services except by means of contributions levied on its subjects. Although, thanks be to God, our empire has for some time past been delivered from the scourge of monopolies, falsely considered in times of war as a source of revenue, a fatal custom still exists, although it can only have disastrous consequences; it is that of venal concessions, known under the name of "iltizam".

Under that name the civil and financial administration of a locality is delivered over to the passions of a single man; that is to say, sometimes to the iron grasp of the most violent and avaricious passions, for if that contractor is not a good man, he will only look to his own advantage.

It is therefore necessary that henceforth each member of Ottoman society should be taxed for a quota of a fixed tax according to his fortune and means, and that it should be impossible that anything more could be exacted from him. It is also necessary that special laws should fix and limit the expenses of our land and sea forces.

Although, as we have said, the defense of the country is an important matter, and that it is the duty of all the inhabitants to furnish soldiers for that object, it has become necessary to establish laws to regulate the contingent to be furnished by each locality according to the necessity of the time, and to reduce the term of military service to four or five years. For it is at the same time doing an injustice and giving a mortal blow to agriculture and to industry to take, without consideration to the respective population of the localities, in the one more, in the other less, men that they can furnish; it is also reducing the soldiers to despair and contributing to the depopulation of the country by keeping them all their lives in the service.

In short, without the several laws, the necessity for which has just been described, there can be neither strength, nor riches, nor happiness, nor tranquility for the empire; it must, on the contrary, look for them in the existence of these new laws.

From henceforth, therefore, the cause of every accused person shall be publicly judged, as the divine law requires, after inquiry and examination, and so long as a regular judgement shall not have been pronounced, no one can secretly or publicly put another to death by poison or in any other manner.

No one shall be allowed to attack the honor of any other person whatever.

Each one shall possess his property of every kind, and shall dispose of it in all freedom, without let or hindrance from any person whatever; thus, for example, the innocent heirs of a criminal shall not be deprived of their legal rights, and the property of the criminal shall not be confiscated. These imperial concessions shall extend to all our subjects, of whatever religion or sect they may be; they shall enjoy them without exception. We therefore grant perfect security to the inhabitants of our empire in their lives, their honor, and their fortunes, as they are secured to them by the sacred text of the law.

As for the other points as they must be settled with the assistance of enlightened opinions, our council of justice (increased by new members as shall be found necessary), to whom shall be joined, on certain days which we shall determine, our ministers and the notabilities of the empire, shall assemble in order to frame laws regulating the security of life and fortune and the assessment of the taxes. Each one in those assemblies shall freely express his ideas and give his advice. . . .

As the object of those institutions is solely to revivify religion, government, the nation, and the empire, we engage not to do anything which is contrary thereto.

In testimony of our promise we will, after having deposited these presents in the hall containing the glorious mantle of the prophet, in the presence of all the ulemas and the grandees of the empire, take oath thereto in the name of God, and shall afterwards cause the oath to be taken by the ulemas and the grandees of the empire.

After that, those from among the ulemas or the grandees of the empire, or any other persons whatsoever who shall infringe these institutions, shall undergo, without respect of rank, position, and influence, the punishment corresponding to his crime, after having been well authenticated. A penal code shall be compiled to that effect. . . .

. . . [A] rigorous law shall be passed against the traffic of favoritism and bribery (rüşvet), which the Divine law reprobates, and which is one of the principal causes of the decay of the empire. . . .

. . . May those who shall commit an act contrary to the present regulations be the object of Divine malediction, and be deprived forever of every kind of (protection) happiness.

1. Why does the Sultan see the need for more imperial institutions?

2. How do the Sultan's policies compare to the enlightened despots of the eighteenth century, such as Frederick the Great?

3. How would the reforms benefit the Ottoman Empire?

George Washington Williams

The rule of Belgian King Leopold II (1865–1909) in the Congo was the most brutal and openly exploitative of all the European colonies in Africa. The outrages committed there moved George Washington Williams (1849–1891), an African-American, to write an open letter to Leopold II in 1890. Williams served in the Union army during the US Civil War, in the Mexican army, and in the US cavalry against the Plains Indians. Afterwards, he studied to become a minister, founded an African-American newspaper, became a lawyer, was the first African-American elected to the Ohio legislature, wrote a major history of African-Americans, and became a journalist. In this last capacity he visited the Congo.

A Williams begins by addressing King Leopold in a friendly tone.

> Good and Great Friend,
>   I have the honour to submit for your Majesty's consideration some reflections respecting the Independent State of the Congo, based upon a careful study and inspection of the country and character of the personal Government you have established upon the African Continent. . . .
>   It afforded me great pleasure to avail myself of the opportunity afforded me last year, of visiting your State in Africa; and how thoroughly I have been disenchanted, disappointed and disheartened, it is now my painful duty to make known to your Majesty in plain but respectful language.

B Williams then makes some general observations before proceeding to a list of twelve "specific charges." In this section, he quotes from a letter written by one of Leopold's supporters.

> Your Majesty's title to the territory of the State of Congo is badly clouded, while many of the treaties made with the natives by the "Association Internationale du Congo", of which you were Director and Banker, were tainted by frauds of the grossest character. The world may not be surprised to learn that your flag floats over territory to which your Majesty has no legal or just claim, since other European Powers have doubtful claims to the territory which they occupy upon the African Continent; but all honest people will be shocked to know by what groveling means the fraud was consummated. . . .
>   . . . Thus you assumed the headship of the State of Congo, and at once organized a personal Government. You have named its officers, created its laws, furnished its finances, and every act of the Government has been clothed with the majesty of your authority. . . .
>   I was anxious to see to what extent the natives had "adopted the fostering care" of your Majesty's "benevolent enterprise" (?), and I was doomed

Source: John Hope Franklin, *George Washington Williams: A Biography*. Chicago: University of Chicago Press, 1985, pp. 243–254.

to bitter disappointment. Instead of the natives of the Congo "adopting the fostering care" of your Majesty's Government, they everywhere complain that their land has been taken from them by force; that the Government is cruel and arbitrary, and declare that they neither love nor respect the Government or its flag. Your Majesty's Government has sequestered their land, burned their towns, stolen their property, enslaved their women and children, and committed other crimes too numerous to mention in detail. . . .

There has been, to my absolute knowledge, no "honest and practical effort made to increase their knowledge and secure their welfare". Your Majesty's Government has never spent one franc for educational purposes nor instituted any practical system of industrialism. . . .

From these general observations I wish now to pass to specific charges against your Majesty's Government.

FIRST — Your Majesty's Government is deficient in the moral, military and financial strength necessary to govern a territory of 1,508,000 square miles [3 905 720 km²], 7,251 miles [11 666 km] of navigation and 31,694 square miles [82 087 km²] of lake surface. . . . [S]lave raids, accomplished by the most cruel and murderous agencies, are carried on within the territorial limits of your Majesty's Government which is impotent. . . .

FOURTH — The Courts of your Majesty's Government are abortive, unjust, partial and delinquent. I have personally witnessed and examined their clumsy operations. The laws printed and circulated in Europe "for the protection of the blacks" in the Congo are a dead letter and a fraud. . . .

FIFTH — Your Majesty's Government is excessively cruel to its prisoners, condemning them, for the slightest offences, to the chain gang, the like of which cannot be seen in any other Government in the civilized or uncivilized world. . . .

NINTH — Your Majesty's Government has been and is now guilty of waging unjust and cruel wars against natives, with the hopes of securing slaves and women, to minister to the behests of the officers of your Government. In such slave-hunting raids, one village is armed by the State against the other. . . . I have no adequate terms in which to depict to your Majesty the brutal acts of your soldiers upon raids such as these. . . .

TENTH — Your Majesty's Government is engaged in the slave trade, wholesale and retail. It buys and sells and steals slaves. Your Majesty's Government gives £3 [$6.75] per head for able-bodied slaves for military service. . . . The labour force at the stations of your Majesty's Government in the Upper River is composed of slaves of all ages and both sexes.

C After completing his list of charges, Williams concludes his letter with an emotional appeal.

Against the deceit, fraud, robberies, arson, murders, slave-raiding, and general policy of cruelty of your Majesty's Government to the natives, stands their record of unexampled patience, long-suffering and forgiving spirit, which put the boasted civilization and professed religion of your Majesty's Government in blush. During thirteen years only one white man has lost his life by the hands of the natives, and only two white men have been killed in the Congo. . . .

All the crimes perpetrated in the Congo have been done in *your* name, and *you* must answer at the bar of Public Sentiment for the misgovernment of a people, whose lives and fortunes were entrusted to you by the august Conference of Berlin, 1884–1885. I now appeal to the Powers, which committed the infant State to your Majesty's charge, and to the great States which gave it international being; and whose majestic law you have scorned and trampled upon, to call and create an International Commission to investigate the charges herein preferred in the name of Humanity, Commerce, Constitutional Government and Christian Civilization. . . .

I appeal to the Belgian people and to their Constitutional Government, so proud of its traditions, replete with the song and story of its champions of human liberty, and so jealous of its present position in the sisterhood of European States, — to cleanse itself from the imputation of the crimes with which your Majesty's personal State of Congo is polluted.

I appeal to Anti-Slavery Societies in all parts of Christendom, to Philanthropists, Christians, Statesmen, and to the great mass of people everywhere, to call upon the Governments of Europe, to hasten the close of the tragedy your Majesty's unlimited Monarchy is enacting in the Congo.

I appeal to our Heavenly father, whose service is perfect love, in witness of the purity of my motives and the integrity of my aims, and to history and mankind I appeal for the demonstration and vindication of the truthfulness of the charges I have herein briefly outlined.

And all this upon the word of honour of a gentleman, I subscribe myself your Majesty's humble and obedient servant.

GEO. W. WILLIAMS
Stanley Falls, Central Africa
July 18th, 1890

1. According to Williams, how are Leopold's paternalistic pronouncements contradicted by his administration of the Congo?

2. How could Leopold's policies result in future civil strife?

3. Compare Leopold's colonial administration to other colonial powers at the same time. Should Leopold be condemned? Defend your position.

Indian Home Rule

Indian home rule (emancipation from Britain and its empire) became an important issue in India in the 1890s. Its first leader was Bal Gangadhar Tilak (1856–1920), a language scholar and astronomer, who led the Indian independence movement.

"Swaraj [self-rule] is my birthright, and I shall have it!" he claimed, and later in life he was imprisoned for his activities and beliefs. Mohandas K. Gandhi (1869–1948), Tilak's successor, transformed the Indian National Congress into a mass movement that changed India and the world. India achieved independence in 1947.

A The following is Tilak's 1907 address to the Indian National Congress where he calls for resistance to British rule, including a boycott of British goods.

Two new words have recently come into existence with regard to our politics, and they are *Moderates* and *Extremists*. These words have a specific relation to time, and they, therefore, will change with time. The Extremists of today will be Moderates tomorrow, just as the Moderates of today were Extremists yesterday. When the National Congress was first started and Mr. Dadabhai's views, which now go for Moderates, were given to the public, he was styled an Extremist, so that you will see that the term Extremist is an expression of progress. We are Extremists today and our sons will call themselves Extremists and us Moderates. Every new party begins as Extremists and ends as Moderates. The sphere of practical politics is not unlimited. We cannot say what will or will not happen 1,000 years hence — perhaps during that long period, the whole of the white race will be swept away in another glacial period. We must, therefore, study the present and work out a program to meet the present condition.

It is impossible to go into details within the time at my disposal. One thing is granted, namely, that this government does not suit us. As has been said by an eminent statesman — the government of one country by another can never be a successful, and therefore, a permanent government. There is no difference of opinion about this fundamental proposition between the old and new schools. One fact is that this alien government has ruined the country. In the beginning, all of us were taken by surprise. We were almost dazed. We thought that everything that the rulers did was for our good and that this English government has descended from the clouds to save us . . . not only from foreign invasions but from internecine warfare, or the internal or external invasions, as they call it. . . . We are not armed, and there is no necessity for arms either. We have a stronger weapon, a political weapon, in boycott. We have perceived one fact, that the whole of this administration, which is carried on by a handful of Englishmen, is carried on with our assistance. We are all in subordinate service. This whole government is carried on with our assistance and they try to keep us in ignorance of our power of cooperation between ourselves by which that which is in our own hands at present can be claimed by us and administered by us. The point is to have the entire control in our hands. I want

Sources: William T. de Bary et al., *Sources of Indian Tradition*. New York: Columbia University Press, 1958, pp. 719–723; Alfred J. Andrea and James H. Overfield, *The Human Record: Sources of Global History*, Vol. II. Boston: Houghton Mifflin, 1990, pp. 455–459.

to have the key of my house, and not merely one stranger turned out of it. Self-government is our goal; we want a control over our administrative machinery. We don't want to become clerks and remain [clerks]. At present, we are clerks and willing instruments of our own oppression in the hands of an alien government, and that government is ruling over us not by its innate strength but by keeping us in ignorance and blindness to the perception of this fact. . . . Every Englishman knows that they are a mere handful in this country and it is the business of every one of them to befool you in believing that you are weak and they are strong. This is politics. We have been deceived by such policy so long. What the new party wants you to do is to realize the fact that your future rests entirely in your own hands. If you mean to be free, you can be free; if you do not mean to be free, you will fall and be for ever fallen. So many of you need not like arms; but if you have not the power of active resistance, have you not the power of self-denial and self-abstinence in such a way as not to assist this foreign government to rule over you? This is boycott and this is what is meant when we say, boycott is a political weapon. We shall not give them assistance to collect revenue and keep peace. We shall not assist them in fighting beyond the frontiers or outside India with Indian blood and money. We shall not assist them in carrying on the administration of justice. We shall have our own courts, and when time comes we shall not pay taxes. Can you do that by your united efforts? If you can, you are free from tomorrow. Some gentlemen who spoke this evening referred to half bread as against the whole bread. I say I want the whole bread and that immediately. But if I can not get the whole, don't think that I have no patience.

I will take the half they give me and then try for the remainder. This is the line of thought and action in which you must train yourself. . . . This is the way in which a nation progresses, and this is the lesson you have to learn from the struggle now going on. This is a lesson of progress, a lesson of helping yourself as much as possible, and if you really perceive the force of it, if you are convinced by these arguments, then and then only is it possible for you to effect your salvation from the alien rule under which you labor at this moment.

B Gandhi developed the idea of Satyagraha ("insistence upon spiritual truth"), a form of non-violent non-cooperation. He wrote a pamphlet, *Indian Home Rule* (1909), which explained his ideas of non-resistance and his attitude toward Western civilization. The pamphlet is written in dialogue form, with a reader and an editor, who is Gandhi.

Reader: Now you will have to explain what you mean by civilization. . . .

Editor: Let us first consider what state of things is described by the word "civilization." Its true test lies in the fact that people living in it make bodily welfare the object of life. We will take some examples: The people of Europe today live in better-built houses than they did a hundred years ago. This is considered an emblem of civilization, and this is also a matter to promote bodily happiness. Formerly, they wore skins, and used as their weapons spears. Now, they wear long trousers, and for embellishing their bodies they wear a variety of clothing, and, instead of spears, they carry with them revolvers containing five or more chambers. If people of a certain country, who have hitherto not been in the habit of wearing much clothing, boots, etc., adopt European clothing, they are supposed to have become civilized out of savagery. Formerly, in Europe, people plowed their lands mainly by manual labor. Now, one man can plow a vast tract by means of steam-engines, and can thus amass great wealth. This is called a sign of civilization. Formerly, the fewest men wrote books, that were most valuable. Now, anybody writes and prints anything he likes and poisons people's minds. Formerly, men traveled in wagons; now they fly through the air, in trains at the rate of four hundred and more miles per day. This is considered the height of civilization. It has been stated that, as men progress, they shall be able to travel in airships and reach any part of the world in a few hours. Men will not need the use of their hands and feet. They will press a button, and they will have their clothing by their side. They will press another button, and they will have their newspaper. A third, and a motor-car will be in waiting for them. They will have a variety of delicately dished up food. Everything will be done by machinery. Formerly, when people wanted to fight with one another, they measured between them their bodily strength; now it is possible to take away thousands of lives by one man working behind a gun from a hill. This is civilization. Formerly, men worked in the open air only so much as they liked. Now, thousands of workmen meet together and for the sake of maintenance work in factories or mines. Their condition is worse than that of beasts. They are obliged to work, at the risk of their lives, at most dangerous occupations, for the sake of millionaires. Formerly, men were made slaves under physical compulsion, now they are enslaved by temptation of money and of the luxuries that money can buy. There are now diseases of which people never dreamed before, and an army of doctors is engaged in finding out their cures, and so hospitals have increased. This is a test of civilization. Formerly, special messengers were required and much expense was incurred in order to send letters; today, anyone can abuse his fellow by means of a letter for one penny. True, at the same cost, one can send one's thanks also. Formerly, people had two or three meals consisting of homemade bread and vegetables; now, they require something to eat every two hours, so that they have hardly leisure for anything else. What more need I say? All this you can ascertain from several authoritative books. These are all true tests of civilization. And, if any one speaks to the contrary, know that he is ignorant. This civilization takes note neither of morality nor of religion. . . .

This civilization is irreligion, and it has taken such a hold on the people in Europe that those who are in it appear to be half mad. They lack real physical strength or courage. They keep up their energy by intoxication. They can hardly be happy in solitude. Women, who should be the queens of households, wander in the streets, or they slave away in factories. For the sake of a pittance, half a million women in England alone are laboring under trying circumstances in factories or similar institutions. This awful fact is one of the causes of the daily growing suffragette movement.

This civilization is such that one has only to be patient and it will be self-destroyed.

C   Gandhi discusses his view of the value of Indian civilization.

Reader: You have denounced railways, lawyers and doctors. I can see that you will discard all machinery. What, then, is civilization?

Editor: The answer to that question is not difficult. I believe that the civilization India has evolved is not to be beaten in the world. Nothing can equal the seeds sown by our ancestors. Rome went, Greece shared the same fate, the might of the Pharaohs was broken, Japan has become westernized, of China nothing can be said, but India is still, somehow or other, sound at the foundation. The people of Europe learn their lessons from the writings of the men of Greece or Rome, which exist no longer in their former glory. In trying to learn from them, the Europeans imagine that they will avoid the mistakes of Greece and Rome. Such is their pitiable condition. In the midst of all this, India remains immovable, and that is her glory. It is a charge against India that her people are so uncivilized, ignorant and stolid, that it is not possible to induce them to adopt any changes. It is a charge really against our merit. What we have tested and found true on the anvil of experience, we dare not change. Many thrust their advice upon India, and she remains steady. This is her beauty; it is the sheet-anchor of our hope.

Civilization is that mode of conduct which points out to man the path of duty. Performance of duty and observance of morality are convertible terms. To observe morality is to attain mastery over our mind and our passions. So doing, we know ourselves. The Gujarati equivalent for civilization means "good conduct."

If this definition be correct, then India, as so many writers have shown, has nothing to learn from anybody else, and this is as it should be.

D   Gandhi's ideas of passive resistance have had great influence throughout the world.

Reader: According to what you say, it is plain that instances of the kind of passive resistance are not to be found in history. It is necessary to understand this passive resistance more fully. It will be better, therefore, if you enlarge upon it.

Editor: Passive resistance is a method of securing rights by personal suffering; it is the reverse of resistance by arms. When I refuse to do a thing that is repugnant to my conscience, I use soul-force. For instance, the government of the day has passed a law which is applicable to me: I do not like it, if, by using violence, I force the government to repeal the law, I am employing what may be termed body-force. If I do not obey the law and accept the penalty for its breach, I use soul-force. It involves sacrifice of self.

Everybody admits that sacrifice of self is infinitely superior to sacrifice of others. Moreover, if this kind of force is used in a cause that is unjust only the person using it suffers. He does not make others suffer for his mistakes. Men have before now done many things which were subsequently found to have been wrong. No man can claim to be absolutely in the right, or that a particular thing is wrong, because he thinks so, but it is wrong for him so long as that is his deliberate judgment. It is, therefore, meet that he should not do that which he knows to be wrong, and suffer the consequence whatever it may be. This is the key to the use of soul-force. . . .

Reader: From what you say, I deduce that passive resistance is a splendid weapon of the weak but that, when they are strong, they may take up arms.

Editor: This is gross ignorance. Passive resistance, that is, soul-force, is matchless. It is superior to the force of arms. How, then, can it be considered only a weapon of the weak? Physical-force men are strangers to the courage that is requisite in a passive resister. Do you believe that a coward can ever disobey a law that he dislikes? Extremists are considered to be advocates of brute-force. Why do they, then, talk about obeying laws? I do not blame them. They can say nothing else. When they succeed in driving out the English, and they themselves become governors, they will want you and me to obey their laws. And that is a fitting thing for their constitution. But a passive resister will say he will not obey a law that is against his conscience, even though he may be blown to pieces at the mouth of a cannon.

What do you think? Wherein is courage required — in blowing others to pieces from behind a cannon or with a smiling face to approach a cannon and to be blown to pieces? Who is the true warrior — he who keeps death always as a bosom-friend or he who controls the death of others? Believe me that a man devoid of courage and manhood can never be a passive resister.

This, however, I will admit: that even a man, weak in body, is capable of offering this resistance. One man can offer it just as well as millions. Both men and women can indulge in it. It does not require the training of an army; it needs no Jiu-jitsu. Control over the mind is alone necessary, and, when that is attained, man is free like the king of the forest, and his very glance withers the enemy.

Passive resistance is an all-sided sword; it can be used anyhow; it blesses him who uses it and him against whom it is used. Without drawing a drop of blood, it produces far-reaching results.

1. What is the meaning of Tilak's statement, "The Extremists of today will be Moderates tomorrow . . ."?

2. How does the British system of government manipulate the population and yet still provide opportunity for resistance?

3. What arguments does Gandhi present against the European model of civilization?

4. Why does Gandhi feel India had little to learn from European powers?

5. How does Gandhi use his own Indian civilization to inspire resistance to British rule?

6. How does Gandhi's philosophy of passive resistance challenge human nature's aggressive tendencies?

Fukuzawa Yukichi

Fukuzawa Yukichi (1835–1901) was one of the most outspoken advocates for the Westernization of Japan. He travelled widely in both Europe and the United States and found much that he admired, including what he saw as the relatively equal treatment of women. After returning to Japan, Yukichi founded what would become Keio University, started a newspaper, and wrote numerous books and articles. The following text is part of a long series of editorials, "On Japanese Women," which he wrote for his newspaper, *Jijishimpo*, in 1885.

 Yukichi makes a case for using what he believes to be the Western relationship between men and women as a model.

"Know yourself." This is an old saying in the West, meaning that it is necessary for a person to realize the status he holds in society in order to conduct himself properly. For instance, for a woman of today, it is very important that she realizes her position in relation to men. The main difference between men and women is only in their reproductive organs. In this, too, the difference is only in their structure and function. It is impossible to say which is more important than the other. As for the other parts of the body — ears, eyes, nose, mouth, arms, legs, and their functions, their proportions with other organs, the number of bones and the circulation of the blood — every minor detail of the body is exactly the same in both men and women. The workings of the mind are also the same. There is nothing in men's activities that women cannot do. As civilization advances, the instances of women taking up work increases. Already in America, it

Source: Eiichi Kiyooka, ed. and trans., *Fukuzawa Yukichi on Japanese Women: Selected Works*. Toyko: University of Tokyo Press, 1988, pp. 38–39, 48, 60, 63, 69.

is not rare to see women in the work force of the telegraphic service and other such mechanical work. Some women become medical doctors or secretaries in commercial companies or even officials in the government. And it is said that in certain types of work, women are more efficient than men.

My one regret is that the women of Japan have not been given a chance to try. Or is it that there is no use in trying because our women are incapable? If that is the case, I must declare that Japanese women were not born useless; there is a cause which makes them so, and our first duty is to remove that cause. Whatever forced arguments one may raise, one can never prove that Japanese women alone are incapable while those of the West are capable; human beings are human beings anywhere in the world. When it is proven that differences in customs, of those of Japan from those of the West, are what make our women incapable, we should change our customs and adopt those of the West as quickly as possible so that our women will also become capable of contributing their fair share. Both men and women should now strive for this goal.

B Yukichi supports openness and modernity.

Confucianism characterizes men as *yang* (positive) and women *yin* (negative); that is, men are like the heavens and the sun, and women are like the earth and the moon. In other words, one is high and the other is humble, and there are many men who take this idea as the absolute rule of nature. But this *yin-yang* theory is the fantasy of the Confucianists and has no proof or logic. Its origins go back several thousand years to dark and illiterate ages when men looked around and whenever they thought they recognized pairs of something, one of which seemed to be stronger or more remarkable than the other, they called one *yang* and the other *yin*. For instance, the heavens and the earth looked very much like the ceiling and the floor of a room. One of them was low and trampled on with feet, but the other was high and beyond reach. One was classed *yang* and the other *yin*. The sun and the moon are both round and shining; one is very bright, even hot, while the other is less bright. Therefore, the sun is *yang* and the moon is *yin*. This is the level of the logic behind this theory and we today should regard it as no more than childish nonsense. . . .

In our society, the most humiliating expression for women is that a man's purpose in taking a wife is to ensure his posterity. The tone of this expression resembles "The purpose of buying a rice cooker is to cook rice." This implies that when you do not cook rice, you do not need the cooker, or if you do not care for posterity, you do not need a wife. The true meaning of marriage should be for a husband and a wife to share a house, helping and being helped, enjoying the greatest happiness in life. But here nothing of this rule of nature is mentioned. They simply say that the purpose of marriage is for posterity. This is the starting point of all evils. The wife who bears children is no different from the cooker that boils rice. This implies that a wife is a mere instrument. A cooker unfit for boiling rice will be discarded, and therefore, a wife who does not bear children may be divorced. If a pot can take the place of a cooker, then a concubine may be just as useful as a wife. One big cooker in a kitchen is normal, but there are no objections to having a number of pots besides. One legal wife in the central part of the house and a number of concubines in other quarters is acceptable. These are real situations in which human beings are treated like instruments. . . .

When a husband and wife live together, they support the house with their combined forces, and differences between the two in rank and importance should never be considered. This is too obvious to need any further explanation. And women should not be confined to their homes either; they should be free to go out and make friends among women and men too. Also, their interests should range over things both inside and outside their homes, and they should rejoice over good and grieve over unhappy events and keep both their minds and bodies active. Women should not limit themselves to just carrying half of the burden and responsibility of the house. They need to realize that half of the country belongs to women. They should alter their attitude from the bottom of their hearts and decide that in all matters they will never be behind men. Such ought to be their spirit, but in reality, after being trampled under foot by self-centered men for hundreds of years, women's bodies have weakened and their spirits dampened. Their quick comeback will be difficult. . . .

To know how to coddle one's wife but never to think of respecting her is the normal and very sad way of Japanese men. Even in the so-called good families, this tendency is evident. And even those who call themselves scholars of Western civilization, on this particular point, choose the old Japanese and Chinese ways as more convenient and at times angrily reject the equality of men and women. These men, I believe, are not even monkeys wearing crowns; they are Confucianists who have plated themselves with gold on one side only and turn themselves to show one side or the other side to suit the circumstances. . . .

Therefore, if experience teaches us that the policy of a closed country was disadvantageous even though the opening of trade caused some trouble for a while, then we should know that there is no reason to abandon the present movement for women for fear of minor difficulties, even if it presents some initial worries.

1. How do Yukichi's arguments for female equality differ from nineteenth-century European attitudes?

2. How does Yukichi both criticize the attitude of men and encourage action by women?

3. Were Yukichi's arguments too Western for Japanese society? Did he have the right to attempt to impose Western values? Defend your position.

José Rizal

José Rizal (1861–1896) was a doctor and writer whose novels, mostly written while he lived in Europe, criticized Spain's colonial rule in the Philippines. He advocated greater opportunities and rights for Filipinos within the Spanish colony, not independence from Spain. Even so, Rizal was convicted of sedition when the Katipunan, a secret nationalist organization with which he had no connection, began a revolt for independence in 1896. *My Last Goodbye* was written as Rizal awaited execution.

Farewell my adored Fatherland, region of the beloved sun,
Pearl of the Eastern Sea, our lost Eden!
For you I happily give up my sad, hopeless life,
And if it were more brilliant, fresher, more flowery,
I would also give it for you, I'd give it for your well being.

On the battlefields, fighting deliriously
Others give you their lives without a doubt, without a thought;
The place matters not, cypress, laurel or lily,
Gibbet or open field, in battle or cruel martyrdom,
It's all the same if the Fatherland and their home ask it.

I will die when I see the sky take on its colours
And finally announce the day after the dead night;
If you need colour to tint your dawn,
Spill my blood, scatter it in a good hour
And let it shine with a reflection of your newborn light.

My dreams, when I was barely an adolescent boy,
My dreams, when I was young and full of life,
Were to see you one day, Pearl of the Eastern Sea,
With your black eyes dry, your brow uplifted,
Without a blemish, without wrinkles, without a trace of shame.

Dream of my life, my burning lively desire,
To your health shouts the soul soon to depart!
To your health! How beautiful it is to fall so you may take flight
Die to give you life, die beneath your sky,
And to sleep forever in your enchanted earth.
. . . .

Pray for all those who die without fortune,
For those who suffer unspeakable torments,
For our poor mothers who sigh their bitterness;
For orphans and widows, for prisoners under torture
And pray for yourself, that you may see your final redemption.

Source: José Rizal, "José Rizal: *Mi Ultimo Adios.*" www.vcn.bc.ca/spcw/adioriza.htm (Apr. 21, 2003). Translated by Adrian Shubert.

And when the dark night embraces the cemetery,
And only the dead, alone, keep vigil there
Do not disturb your sleep, nor the mystery
Perhaps you will hear the songs of the zither or psalter,
It is I, beloved Fatherland, I who sing to you.

And when my tomb, forgotten by all,
Has not a cross or stone to mark its place,
Let man plough it, and break it with his spade,
And before my ashes return to nothing,
Return as dust to join your carpet.

Then I will care not about being forgotten,
I shall cross your skies, your space, your valleys
I shall be a clean and vibrant note to your ears,
Aroma, light, colours, whispers, songs and sighs
Constantly repeating the essence of my faith.

Fatherland that I idolize, pain of my pains
Beloved Philippines, hear my final word.
To you I leave everything, my parents, my loves.
I am going where there are neither slaves, nor oppressors,
     nor executioners,
Where faith does not kill, where God alone reigns.

Farewell parents and brothers, fragments of my soul;
Childhood friends, that lost home,
Give thanks that I rest from the restless day.
Farewell sweet stranger, my friend, my joy!
Farewell beloved beings. To die is to rest.

1. Why does Rizal feel that his death is not in vain?

2. How does he encourage his fellow Filipinos to continue the struggle?

3. What nationalist sentiments does Rizal express?

The Independent of Korea

Like China and Japan, Korea had to determine how to respond to Western power. However, Koreans had to deal with the growing competition for influence between China, the traditional power in the region, and the newly opened Japan. This culminated in 1895 with military intervention by both countries, and a clear Japanese victory. Japanese influence over the government in turn produced a backlash. Led by So Chaep'il (1866–1951), who had spent a decade in the United States, a movement for both independence and modernization emerged. Two of the most important features of this movement were a newspaper, *The Independent*, which started publication in April 1896, and the formation of a group of government

officials, the Independence Club, sympathetic to So's program of modernization. So was forced to leave Korea in 1898 and the Independence Club was closed
down shortly afterwards. *The Independent* was purchased by the government and
disappeared at the end of 1899.

A   *The Independent* published an "Inaugural Message" in its first issue, April 7, 1896.

> As we publish the first issue of *The Independent* today, we shall declare to
> everyone in Korea, foreigners and natives alike, what we believe.
>
> We are impartial and nonpartisan and recognize no distinction between
> upper and lower classes; everyone shall be treated equally as a Korean. We
> shall speak only to benefit Korea, and we shall be fair. We shall speak not
> only for the people in Seoul but for everyone throughout the country on
> every subject.
>
> We shall communicate to the people what the government does and
> convey the conditions of the people to the government, thereby benefiting
> both sides who need not feel uncomfortable nor suspicious.
>
> Since we are not publishing the paper for the sake of profit, the price of
> a copy is low. We write in the vernacular (*hangŭl*) to enable men and women
> of all social classes to read; we also insert spaces between the words to make
> reading easier.
>
> We shall be truthful: we shall report on those government officials who
> may misconduct themselves; we shall let the whole nation know about any
> corrupt and self-enriching officials; and we shall investigate and publicize
> any private persons who may violate the law.
>
> We are for His Majesty, the government of Korea, and the Korean people;
> there shall not be any partisan discourse nor words to benefit only one side
> printed in our paper.
>
> We have a page written in English because foreigners are not well
> informed on the Korean situation and, therefore, are liable to be misguided
> in their thoughts by relying solely on biased words. In order to give them
> correct information we shall prepare a section in English.
>
> It will become evident, then, that this newspaper exists only for the
> interests of Korea. Foreigners and Koreans, men and women, people of
> diverse social classes and stations, all will become informed about Korea.
> We will also report from time to time on the situations in foreign lands
> so that those Koreans who cannot travel to foreign countries may learn
> about them.
>
> As today is our first day of publication, we have outlined where we
> stand. We believe that by reading our paper the opinions and wisdom of
> the Korean people will be improved.

Source: Peter H. Lee, ed., *Sourcebook of Korean Civilization*. New York: Columbia University Press,
1996, pp. 388–390, 391–392.

B In April 1897, *The Independent* published Chu Sigyŏng's "Essay on the Korean Language." Chu (1876–1914) was a proponent of a new form of the written languages.

> If the people of our country continue to study only the Chinese classics and neglect new subjects, our nation will remain ignorant and weak, and, before long, the land we have inherited from our forefathers, our homes, our bodies, and those of our descendants will be owned by foreigners. This is shocking and deplorable. How can we afford not to be on our guard?
>
> If we should replace our study of Chinese graphs with a study of such useful subjects as parliament, domestic and foreign affairs, finance, law, the army and navy, navigation, hygiene, economics, craftsmanship, commerce, agriculture, and other pursuits, within ten or more years everyone would become proficient in at least one of these practical occupations. Afterwards, the people would work diligently, each at his own station, and become wealthy. The level of learning would then be advanced, and our nation would become civilized, rich, and strong.
>
> I sincerely pray that all our brethren will realize this and move quickly into practical lines of work. One hour at this time in our country is as valuable as one whole day in another country. Let no one waste precious time learning yet another Chinese graph. The Korean letters that were developed by our great scholars for our use are easy to learn and write, and they should be used in recording everything. Everyone in his youth should take the time to study for practical employment and, by doing his work, should become the foundation, and the pillar, for our national independence. . . .
>
> Our nation's dignified status, based on wealth and strength, and its honor, based on its high level of civilization, shall then be recognized throughout the world.

C The "Essay on Working Only for Korea" was published in May 1897.

> If Korea were to cause Russia and Japan to go to war against each other, we Koreans would be caught in the middle and would perish regardless of who won the war. We mention Koreans causing discontent between the Japanese and the Russians because, to cite an example, our government leaders relied on Japan's protection at the time of the *Kabo* Reforms [1894], discriminated against other nations, and allowed the Japanese to gain too much, thereby alienating other foreigners. It is for this reason that Russia reversed the situation at the next opportunity, and Japanese influence and the pro-Japanese government were overthrown. Lately, it is said that there are those who take the side of Russia; they are no better than those who took Japan's side.
>
> When a person is born Korean and works for the government of Korea, it is only natural that he should favor Korea and maintain close relations with the Koreans. If he should instead favor the Russians, the Japanese, or any other foreigners, turning his back on his own people, the discriminated nations would seek an opportunity to overthrow the Korean government.

When there are frequent changes in the government, it is the people of Korea who suffer. If Korean officials favor Korea and protect their own people, however, there is no cause for any foreign nation to feel resentment, and Korea will grow in strength. The king and the people will be treated with respect throughout the world and will prosper together forever.

This is an easy course to follow, yet a twisted path has been selected instead. There are several parties: a party that puts its faith in Japan, a party that trusts Russia, an American party, a British party, and so on. We have not yet heard of a Korean party. We advise those who wish to work for Korea to be impartial, fair, and friendly to all foreign nations alike so that no jealousy will develop among them. Only the Korean people should receive special favor so that they will work together to defend and aid the nation. Should there be a rebellion, the people of the entire nation will join in defeating the rebels. When there is no longer any foreign party, everyone will belong to a Korean party, and more will be accomplished to strengthen the nation. Whoever loves himself, his family, and his people and is loyal to His Majesty should discard any notion of relying on foreigners. The Korean people may be uneducated, foolish, and uncivilized, but they can be taught, directed, and trusted in preserving the nation. Although foreign institutions and teachings must be actively studied, we should think only of Korea. A little knowledge of a foreign tongue and customs should not lead one to depend on the foreign nation for the work that needs to be done in Korea. Such reliance would surely result in a disaster every time and cause injury to oneself and the nation.

1. How does the "Inaugural Message" reflect the newspaper's name?
2. Why does the writer of the "Essay on the Korean Language" feel education is the key for Korean autonomy?
3. What problems had Korea faced with its many alliances?
4. Why does "Essay on Working Only for Korea" not advocate Korean isolation?

He Xiangning

He Xiangning (1878–1972) was born to a wealthy tea merchant's family in Hong Kong. Like all other young ladies in Chinese society in the nineteenth century, servants attended to her every need, and she never learned to cook. This excerpt, "When I Learned How to Cook," from her memoir published in 1938, tells how she and her husband joined the republican revolutionary movement led by Sun Yat-sen (1866–1925) after they went to Japan to study in 1903. It shows the radical path that she took, in political, social, and gender terms. She remained active politically throughout the 1930s, interested in promoting civil liberty in China. Some of her children remained with the Nationalists, while others became leaders of the Communist Party — not uncommon among political families in twentieth-century China.

By the first decade of the twentieth century, there were thousands of Chinese students in Japan, many wanting to learn how an Asian society could succeed in modernizing into a great power in a short period of time. Unusual in Chinese society, He Xiangning was one of several dozen women among the students. She and her husband, along with many others, became involved in movements for political reform in China.

In our China — especially several decades ago — any young woman who was well loved by her parents and enjoyed the comforts of a well-to-do home knew practically nothing about cooking, because that was done by servants. Naturally, I was no exception. My parents regarded me as a precious treasure, so since our family circumstances were good, in our household I never had anything to do with the kitchen. And when I married Mr. Liao [Chung-k'ai], the preparation of all food and meals was done entirely by the servants. When I went to study in Japan, however, in response to a unique responsibility demanded of me, I voluntarily gave up my status as a proper young lady and learned how to cook from a hired Japanese maid. As I think back on these events, I realized that my reflections and memories are well worth commemorating.

When Mr. Sun Yat-sen made his second trip to Japan, the relationships among China, Japan, and Russia were tense. Consequently, the Japanese police surveillance of the Chinese overseas students was very strict and repressive. For some time, the Japanese authorities had already been paying close attention to the voice of revolution that Mr. Sun was raising in those years. . . . The first time Mr. Sun had come to Japan, Mr. Liao and I had talked with him two or three times. We had then expressed our wish to participate in the revolution, and he had treated us as comrades. . . . Mr. Sun was planning to organize a revolutionary group, and that the hotel was not convenient for a number of reasons — especially because there was no suitable place to hold meetings. I understood and had no doubt at all that this was for advancing the revolution. But the greatest difficulty that I perceived would be that of meals. Since I, myself, could not cook, how would we manage without a maid? . . . But then I thought to myself: since I do not know how to cook, I should learn, at once, from my servant. Who could object to a lady learning menial work, if it were for the revolution? . . .

. . . The first important task was to learn how to cook, to prepare simple meals. Ordinarily I simply ate whatever was put in front of me, never even asking what the servants had prepared. Now it was different. I watched carefully as my servant washed the rice, put it in the pot, added water, and started the fire. I paid close attention to the amount of rice, the proportions of water, how big to make the fire, and how long to cook the rice. As for cooking meats and vegetables, the Japanese method was much easier, and after watching a few times I had learned it. In less than two days I felt that

Source: Li Yu-ning, ed., *Chinese Women Through Chinese Eyes*. Armonk, New York: M. E. Sharpe, 1992, pp. 135–139, 141–143.

I had grasped it. The servant did not understand why I suddenly took so much interest in cooking. How was she to know that I was intent on learning her skills so that I could then dismiss her?

B He Xiangning describes her routine as well as her involvement in Sun Yat-sen's revolutionary political movement.

After moving into the Kanda *kashiya* [a Japanese rental house], on the one hand, I had to attend classes; on the other, I had to manage the daily livelihood myself. I felt rather pressed and harried. Formerly, as a young lady at my father's side, there were people to take care of me. When I married Mr. Liao, I still had two of my maids to accompany me. Suddenly, however, I was leading a double life of student and maidservant, to which I was not accustomed. Ordinarily, I had been concerned only with my own studies, leaving all the other menial and miscellaneous tasks to the maid. Now it was really something! Getting up every morning, I first had to straighten the bedding and even had to fetch my own wash water. Returning after class, I would buy food, make the fire — at that time Tokyo did not yet have gas — boil some rice, and cook a meal. I was busy all the time. After eating, I still had to wash dishes and clean up. In those days, there was no electricity in Japan either, so I had to go through all the mess and bother of lighting kerosene lamps — cleaning and filling them with kerosene. Washing clothes was especially inconvenient. Getting water was a nuisance, too, even though Chung-shih got several buckets of water for me every day. Sometimes I used it all up and had to run down the street to the well and get water myself. I had one belief, however: that the hardships I was enduring were for China's revolution. As I thought about that, whatever the misery or discomfort, I endured it happily and untiringly. . . .

Mr. Sun often came with Li Chung-shih to my *kashiya* to plan for organizing the T'ung Meng Hui. I joined the T'ung Meng Hui very early — what number on the list I do not remember. The procedure for joining required two sponsors. My entry in the register included only the signature of Chung-shih. Later, when Mr. Sun saw it, he signed his own signature. At that time, I was the only female member of the T'ung Meng Hui, and since I joined very early, Mr. Sun called me "Obasan" [grandmother in Japanese]. Later, all the comrades followed suit.

C He Xiangning reflects on her experience and on women in Chinese society.

Thinking back to when I began to learn to cook brings with it associations of a number of past events concerning Mr. Sun's organization of the T'ung Meng Hui in Tokyo at that time. In truth, I dare not assert that my *kashiya* in Kanda was the fermenting ground of the T'ung Meng Hui. But if one were to say that in those days I was a loyal maidservant to the T'ung Meng Hui, perhaps there would be some who would nod their heads in agreement.

At that time in Tokyo, working and meeting together with us were comrades from many provinces of China. Whoever came to my *kashiya* I treated alike, as a member of the family, as a brother. However, since I could not speak Mandarin (the common dialect), I was unable to communicate (except with my Cantonese friends), because our speech was mutually unintelligible. Even when we would have liked to have a long talk, it was impossible. Last year in Nanking, Chang Chi (P'u-ch'üan) and Chü Cheng (Chüeh-sheng) came to see me. P'u-ch'üan said to me, "We have been old friends for over thirty years. During that [early] time in Japan, since we could not understand each other's dialects, although we met often, we said little to each other. Also, because you had natural, unbound feet, whenever we spoke of you, whether to your face or behind you back, we called you Big Feet Ho. Even when you were right there and we called you this, you did not understand." What he said was touching and interesting. Everyone laughed heartily. It was true; among the female overseas students at that time, I was the only one with unbound feet. Two or three years later, I met the heroine Ch'iu Chin, whose feet were still bound.

Time certainly does pass quickly. These events took place thirty-five years ago. In my own life, at my parents' side, I was a young lady; in society, I was able to be a worker. In my home, I could cook and manage all the miscellaneous details of preparing the meals; emerging from the kitchen, I moved into political activities. I have dined on rare delicacies, but I have also been accustomed to coarse, bland fare. I can spend months in quiet, peaceful leisure; but I do not fear difficulty and hardship. I really do not know how wives and young ladies raised in the comfort of luxurious ease and extravagant indulgence can become human beings. And those who have done nothing for the nation but have profited and become wealthy from the revolution must surely be despised by others. Now the nation is in difficulty, and natural disaster strikes. Those who can work should offer their services, and those with money should offer their money. Otherwise, if one schemes only to enrich his own family and clan and to fatten his relatives, he will be criticized by thousands of people, and his luck will not last long.

As for the problem of most women, I believe it should be approached this way: Women themselves should learn a skill to make a living, practice discomfort and hardship, and become involved in the affairs of the nation and society, rather than turn over their own lives to the management of others. And how should the nation treat women? Based on the principle of equality between men and women, it should ensure equal education for men and women alike, and should fully nurture and develop the capabilities of women for social activity and for all kinds of professions. To shut women up rigidly in the kitchen or keep them in the house was already wrong several decades ago. I was an obvious example. There was no uprising of the Chinese revolution in which women did not participate. Nevertheless, even today we still cannot receive truly equal treatment. This is totally irrational — unspeakable. I hope that those who participate in future national assemblies to make the constitution will, in no way, ever again disregard the rights of all women — that they will make detailed stipulations for the full equality of men and women. At this juncture, when we are rescuing the nation from a life-or-death crisis, we must not continue to allow half of all our people to remain paralyzed.

1. Why does having a servant contradict the revolutionary dogma of Sun Yat-sen?
2. How does He's description of her attempt to balance different roles reflect the changes taking place in some Asian nations?
3. What is the significance of He not having bound feet?
4. Why might equality for women seem a more difficult concept to accept in China than in other nations?

Friedrich Nietzsche

Rejecting both traditional religion and modern science as the bases of truth and meaning, Friedrich Nietzsche (1844–1900) demanded that philosophy in the West open itself to different ideas. He emphasized myth, art, and individual will as he abandoned much of the inherited philosophical conventions from the ancient world and the Judeo-Christian tradition. Nietzsche found contemporary morality to be limiting to human potential. He praised the superior individual, disliked democracy and nationalism, and challenged the validity of the Christian conception of the deity. His work, a sometimes startling probe into all that was human, introduced much that became characteristic of the twentieth century.

A Nietzsche writes about entering a new era at the end of the nineteenth century, one of uncertainty and creativity. He discusses the "death of God," the sense that human beings no longer have a belief system that is external to their intelligence, will, and desire.

The Madman. Have you not heard of that madman who lit a lantern in the bright morning hours, ran to the market place, and cried incessantly, "I seek God! I seek God!" As many of those who do not believe in God were standing around just then, he provoked much laughter. Why, did he get lost? said one. Did he lose his way like a child? said another. Or is he hiding? Is he afraid of us? Has he gone on a voyage? or emigrated? Thus they yelled and laughed. The madman jumped into their midst and pierced them with his glances.

"Whither is God" he cried. "I shall tell you. *We have killed him* — you and I. All of us are his murderers. But how have we done this? How were

Sources: Walter Kaufmann, ed. and trans., *The Portable Nietzsche.* New York: Penguin Books, 1976, pp. 95–96; Friedrich Nietzsche, *Beyond Good and Evil.* Chicago: Henry Regnery Company, 1955, pp. 4–5, 47–49.

we able to drink up the sea? Who gave us the sponge to wipe away the entire horizon? What did we do when we unchained this earth from its sun? Whither is it moving now? Whither are we moving now? Away from all suns? Are we not plunging continually? Backward, sideward, forward, in all directions? Is there any up or down left? Are we not straying as through an infinite nothing? Do we not feel the breath of empty space? Has it not become colder? Is not night and more night coming on all the while? Must not lanterns be lit in the morning? Do we not hear anything yet of the noise of the gravediggers who are burying God? Do we not smell anything yet of God's decomposition? Gods too decompose. God is dead. God remains dead. And we have killed him. How shall we, the murderers of all murderers, comfort ourselves? What was holiest and most powerful of all that the world has yet owned has bled to death under our knives. Who will wipe this blood off us? What water is there for us to clean ourselves? What festivals of atonement, what sacred games shall we have to invent? Is not the greatness of this deed too great for us? Must not we ourselves become gods simply to seem worthy of it? There has never been a greater deed; and whoever will be born after us — for the sake of this deed he will be part of a higher history than all history hitherto."

Here the madman fell silent and looked again at his listeners; and they too were silent and stared at him in astonishment. At last he threw his lantern on the ground, and it broke and went out. "I come too early," he said then; "my time has not come yet. This tremendous event is still on its way, still wandering — it has not yet reached the ears of man. Lightning and thunder require time, the light of the stars requires time, deeds require time even after they are done, before they can be seen and heard. This deed is still more distant from them than the most distant stars — *and yet they have done it themselves.*"

It has been related further that on that same day the madman entered divers churches and there sang his *requiem aeternam deo.* Led out and called to account, he is said to have replied each time, "What are these churches now if they are not the tombs and sepulchers of God?"

B In *Beyond Good and Evil* (1885), Nietzsche turns around the usual conceptions of truth and falsehood, philosophy and dogma.

The falseness of a given judgment does not constitute an objection against it, so far as we are concerned. It is perhaps in this respect that our new language sounds strangest. The real question is how far a judgment furthers and maintains life, preserves a given type, possibly cultivates and trains a given type. We are, in fact, fundamentally inclined to maintain that the falsest judgments are the most indispensable to us, that man cannot live without accepting the logical fictions as valid, without measuring reality against the purely invented world of the absolute, the immutable, without constantly falsifying the world by means of numeration. That getting along without false judgments would amount to getting along without life, negating life. To admit untruth as a necessary condition of life: this implies, to be sure, a perilous resistance against customary value-feelings. A philosophy that risks it nonetheless, if it did nothing else, would by this alone have taken its stand beyond good and evil. . . .

One must test oneself to see if one is meant for independence and for command. And one must do it at the right time. Never avoid your tests, though they may be the most dangerous game you can play, and in the end are merely tests at which you are the only witness and the sole judge. . . .

Will they be new friends of "truth," these coming philosophers? Most probably, for all philosophers thus far have loved their truths. But surely they will not be dogmatists. It must run counter to their pride and their taste that their truth should be a truth for everyman, this having been the secret wish and ultimate motive of all dogmatic striving. "My judgment is *my* judgment, to which hardly anyone else has a right," is what the philosopher of the future will say. One must get rid of the bad taste of wishing to agree with many others. "Good" is no longer good in the mouth of my neighbor. And how could there be a "common good"! The expression contradicts itself: what can be common cannot have much value. In the end it must be as it always was: great things remain for the great; abysses for the deep; delicacies and tremors for the subtle; and, all in all, all things rare for the rare!

1. How has humanity killed God? Is this an end of religion?
2. How has judgment changed in Nietzsche's philosophy?
3. Why does Nietzsche object to the "common good"?
4. What relevance, if any, does Nietzsche's philosophy have for contemporary society?

Sigmund Freud

Sigmund Freud (1856–1939) was the individual in the twentieth century who most changed our understanding of the human personality. Freud, a medical doctor, decided that the cause of some of the physical illnesses of his patients was grounded in their mental life. He became a controversial figure at the end of the nineteenth century as he began an exploration of the inner life of human beings, which opened up questions of neuroses, psychoses, and sexuality. He introduced such terms as ego, id, super-ego, repression, and sublimation into the clinical and common languages. Freud argued that each human being had a deep inner life, which needed to be understood if we were ever to comprehend the nature of humanity. He explored areas that had been thought unimportant or had been ignored, and he coined a new terminology about the human personality that changed the way we talk and think about ourselves. No serious thinker since Freud's time could ignore the issues raised by his fertile and original mind.

In 1900, Freud published *The Interpretation of Dreams*. In it, he discusses his belief that dreams have meaning in the lives of both children and adults.

[D]reams which can only be understood as fulfilments of wishes and which bear their meaning upon their faces without disguise are to be found under the most frequent and various conditions. They are mostly short and simple dreams, which afford a pleasant contrast to the confused and exuberant compositions that have in the main attracted the attention of the authorities. Nevertheless, it will repay us to pause for a moment over these simple dreams. We may expect to find the very simplest forms of dreams in *children*, since there can be no doubt that their psychical productions are less complicated than those of adults. . . .

I do not myself know what animals dream of. But a proverb, to which my attention was drawn by one of my students, does claim to know. 'What,' asks the proverb, 'do geese dream of?' And it replies: 'Of maize.' The whole theory that dreams are wish-fulfilments is contained in these two phrases.

It will be seen that we might have arrived at our theory of the hidden meaning of dreams most rapidly merely by following linguistic usage. It is true that common language sometimes speaks of dreams with contempt. . . . But, on the whole, ordinary usage treats dreams above all as the blessed fulfillers of wishes. If ever we find our expectation surpassed by the event, we exclaim in our delight: 'I should never have imagined such a thing even in my wildest dreams.'

. . . If we restrict ourselves to the minimum of new knowledge which has been established with certainty, we can still say this of dreams: they have proved that *what is suppressed continues to exist in normal people as well as abnormal, and remains capable of psychical functioning*. Dreams themselves are among the manifestations of this suppressed material; this is so theoretically in every case, and it can be observed empirically in a great number of cases at least, and precisely in cases which exhibit most clearly the striking peculiarities of dream-life. In waking life the suppressed material in the mind is prevented from finding expression and is cut off from internal perception owing to the fact that the contradictions present in it are eliminated — one side being disposed of in favour of the other; but during the night, under the sway of an impetus towards the construction of compromises, this suppressed material finds methods and means of forcing its way into consciousness. . . .

The interpretation of dreams is the royal road to a knowledge of the unconscious activities of the mind.

Sources: Sigmund Freud, *The Interpretation of Dreams*, trans. James Strachey. New York: Avon Books, 1965, pp. 160, 165–166, 647; Sigmund Freud, *The Origin and Development of Psychoanalysis*. Chicago: Henry Regnery Company, 1965, pp. 21–24, 27–28, 42–43; Sigmund Freud, *Civilization and Its Discontents*. New York: W. W. Norton & Company, 1961, pp. 48–50, 108–109.

By analysing dreams we can take a step forward in our understanding of the composition of that most marvellous and most mysterious of all instruments. Only a small step, no doubt; but a beginning.

B Freud gave several lectures at Clark University in the United States in 1910, explaining his new ideas. These lectures have been collected in *The Origin and Development of Psychoanalysis*. In them, Freud describes the beginnings of the technique of psychoanalysis.

> It is on [the] idea of *resistance* that I based my theory of the psychic processes of hystericals. It had been found that in order to cure the patient it was necessary that this force should be overcome. . . . I called this hypothetical process "repression" (*Verdrangung*), and considered that it was proved by the undeniable existence of resistance.
>
> But now the question arose: what were those forces, and what were the conditions of this repression?. . . In all those experiences, it had happened that a wish had been aroused, which was in sharp opposition to the other desires of the individual, and was not capable of being reconciled with the ethical, æsthetic and personal pretensions of the patient's personality. There had been a short conflict, and the end of this inner struggle was the repression of the idea which presented itself to consciousness as the bearer of this irreconcilable wish. This was, then, repressed from consciousness and forgotten. The incompatibility of the idea in question with the "ego" of the patient was the motive of the repression, the ethical and other pretensions of the individual were the repressing forces. The presence of the incompatible wish, or the duration of the conflict, had given rise to a high degree of mental pain; this pain was avoided by the repression. This latter process is evidently in such a case a device for the protection of the personality.
>
> I will not multiply examples, but will give you the history of a single one of my cases, in which the conditions and the utility of the repression process stand out clearly enough. Of course for my purpose I must abridge the history of the case and omit many valuable theoretical considerations. It is that of a young girl, who was deeply attached to her father, who had died a short time before, and in whose care she had shared. . . . When her older sister married, the girl grew to feel a peculiar sympathy for her new brother-in-law, which easily passed with her for family tenderness. This sister soon fell ill and died, while the patient and her mother were away. The absent ones were hastily recalled, without being told fully of the painful situation. As the girl stood by the bedside of her dead sister, for one short moment there surged up in her mind an idea, which might be framed in these words: "Now he is free and can marry me." We may be sure that this idea, which betrayed to her consciousness her intense love for her brother-in-law, of which she had not been conscious, was the next moment consigned to repression by her revolted feelings. The girl fell ill with severe hysterical symptoms, and, when I came to treat the case, it appeared that she

had entirely forgotten that scene at her sister's bedside and the unnatural, egoistic desire which had arisen in her. She remembered it during the treatment, reproduced the pathogenic moment with every sign of intense emotional excitement, and was cured by this treatment. . . .

. . . [W]e come to the conclusion, from working with hysterical patients and other neurotics, that they have not fully succeeded in repressing the idea to which the incompatible wish is attached. They have, indeed, driven it out of consciousness and out of memory, and apparently saved themselves a great amount of psychic pain, *but in the unconscious the suppressed wish still exists*, only waiting for its chance to become active, and finally succeeds in sending into consciousness, instead of the repressed idea, a disguised and unrecognizable surrogate-creation (*Ersatzbildung*), to which the same painful sensations associate themselves that the patient thought he was rid of through his repression. This surrogate of the suppressed idea — the symptom — is secure against further attacks from the defenses of the ego, and instead of a short conflict there originates now a permanent suffering. . . . If this repressed material is once more made part of the conscious mental functions — a process which supposes the overcoming of considerable resistance — the psychic conflict which then arises, the same which the patient wished to avoid, is made capable of a happier termination, under the guidance of the physician, than is offered by repression. . . .

. . . I may now pass to that group of everyday mental phenomena whose study has become a technical help for psychoanalysis.

These are the bungling of acts (*Fehlhandlungen*) among normal men as well as among neurotics, to which no significance is ordinarily attached; the forgetting of things which one is supposed to know and at other times really does know (for example the temporary forgetting of proper names); mistakes in speaking (*Versprechen*), which occur so frequently; analogous mistakes in writing (*Verschreiben*) and in reading (*Verlesen*), the automatic execution of purposive acts in wrong situations (*Vergreifen*) and the loss or breaking of objects, etc. These are trifles, for which no one has ever sought a psychological determination, which have passed unchallenged as chance experiences, as consequences of absent-mindedness, inattention and similar conditions. Here, too, are included the acts and gestures executed without being noticed by the subject, to say nothing of the fact that he attaches no psychic importance to them; as playing and trifling with objects, humming melodies, handling one's person and clothing and the like.

These little things, the bungling of acts, like the symptomatic and chance acts . . . are not so entirely without meaning as is generally supposed by a sort of tacit agreement. They have a meaning, generally easy and sure to interpret from the situation in which they occur, and it can be demonstrated that they either express impulses and purposes which are repressed, hidden if possible from the consciousness of the individual, or that they spring from exactly the same sort of repressed wishes and complexes which we have learned to know already as the creators of symptoms and dreams.

It follows that they deserve the rank of symptoms, and their observation, like that of dreams, can lead to the discovery of the hidden complexes of the psychic life. With their help one will usually betray the most intimate of his secrets. If these occur so easily and commonly among people in health, with whom repression has on the whole succeeded fairly well, this is due to their insignificance and their inconspicuous nature. But they can lay claim to high theoretic value, for they prove the existence of repression and surrogate creations even under the conditions of health.

C One of Freud's last major works was *Civilization and Its Discontents* (1930). Here he reflects on the nature of civilization and its fragility.

Perhaps we may begin by explaining that the element of civilization enters on the scene with the first attempt to regulate these social relationships. If the attempt were not made, the relationships would be subject to the arbitrary will of the individual: that is to say, the physically stronger man would decide them in the sense of his own interests and instinctual impulses. Nothing would be changed in this if this stronger man should in his turn meet someone even stronger than he. Human life in common is only made possible when a majority comes together which is stronger than any separate individual and which remains united against all separate individuals. The power of this community is then set up as 'right' in opposition to the power of the individual, which is condemned as 'brute force'. This replacement of the power of the individual by the power of a community constitutes the decisive step of civilization. The essence of it lies in the fact that the members of the community restrict themselves in their possibilities of satisfaction, whereas the individual knew no such restrictions. The first requisite of civilization, therefore, is that of justice — that is, the assurance that a law once made will not be broken in favour of an individual. This implies nothing as to the ethical value of such a law. The further course of cultural development seems to tend towards making the law no longer an expression of the will of a small community — a caste or a stratum of the population or a racial group — which, in its turn, behaves like a violent individual towards other, and perhaps more numerous, collections of people. The final outcome should be a rule of law to which all — except those who are not capable of entering a community — have contributed by a sacrifice of their instincts, and which leaves no one — again with the same exception — at the mercy of brute force.

The liberty of the individual is no gift of civilization. It was greatest before there was any civilization, though then, it is true, it had for the most part no value, since the individual was scarcely in a position to defend it. The development of civilization imposes restrictions on it, and justice demands that no one shall escape those restrictions. What makes itself felt in a human community as a desire for freedom may be their revolt against some existing injustice, and so may prove favourable to a further development of civilization; it may remain compatible with civilization. But it may also spring from the remains of their original personality, which is still untamed by civilization and may thus become the basis in them of hostility to civilization. The urge for freedom, therefore, is directed against particular forms and demands of civilization or against civilization altogether. . . . A good part of the struggles of mankind centre round the single task of finding an expedient accommodation — one, that is, that will bring happiness — between this claim of the individual and the cultural claims of the group; and one of the problems that touches the fate of humanity is whether such an accommodation can be reached by means of some particular form of civilization or whether this conflict is irreconcilable.

D According to Freud, civilization takes both effort and restraint, and is itself a source of much anxiety and unhappiness.

[W]e are very often obliged, for therapeutic purposes, to oppose the super-ego, and we endeavour to lower its demands. Exactly the same objections can be made against the ethical demands of the cultural super-ego. It, too, does not trouble itself enough about the facts of the mental constitution of human beings. It issues a command and does not ask whether it is possible for people to obey it. On the contrary, it assumes that a man's ego is psychologically capable of anything that is required of it, that his ego has unlimited mastery over his id. This is a mistake; and even in what are known as normal people the id cannot be controlled beyond certain limits. If more is demanded of a man, a revolt will be produced in him or a neurosis, or he will be made unhappy. The commandment, 'Love thy neighbour as thyself', is the strongest defence against human aggressiveness and an excellent example of the unpsychological proceedings of the cultural super-ego. The commandment is impossible to fulfil; such an enormous inflation of love can only lower its value, not get rid of the difficulty. Civilization pays no attention to all this; it merely admonishes us that the harder it is to obey the precept the more meritorious it is to do so. But anyone who follows such a precept in present-day civilization only puts himself at a disadvantage vis-à-vis the person who disregards it. What a potent obstacle to civilization aggressiveness must be, if the defence against it can cause as much unhappiness as aggressiveness itself!

1. Why does Freud believe dreams are important in the study of the human psyche?

2. Cite examples where Freud attempts to substantiate his theory through scientific means.

3. According to Freud, how does an individual's environment come into play as a possible cause of repression?

4. According to Freud, what are the positive and negative elements of civilization in relation to individuals?

5. Why does Freud downplay the influence of morality and religion?

Albert Einstein

Albert Einstein (1879–1955) is widely regarded as the most important scientific thinker since Newton. His concepts and ideas have transformed the way we see the world. Einstein made many contributions to thermodynamics, mechanics, and quantum theory, but he is best known for introducing the theory of relativity in 1905. In using the idea of relativity as a means of dealing with all physical phenomena, he changed the fundamental principles by which we understand the physical universe. Instead of space and time, the speed of light became the new "absolute." Einstein was always aware that his work had enormous implications in the field of epistemology, the theory of knowledge. He recognized that he and his scientific colleagues were changing our perception of how we understand and relate to the world.

A In "Autobiographical Notes" (1949), Einstein discusses how we think and the nature of concepts and propositions.

> What, precisely, is "thinking"? When, at the reception of sense-impressions, memory-pictures emerge, this is not yet "thinking." And when such pictures form series, each member of which calls forth another, this too is not yet "thinking." When, however, a certain picture turns up in many such series, then — precisely through such return — it becomes an ordering element for such series, in that it connects series which in themselves are unconnected. Such an element becomes an instrument, a concept. I think that the transition from free association or "dreaming" to thinking is characterized by the more or less dominating rôle which the "concept" plays in it. It is by no means necessary that a concept must be connected with a sensorily cognizable and reproducible sign (word); but when this is the case thinking becomes by means of that fact communicable.
>
> With what right — the reader will ask — does this man operate so carelessly and primitively with ideas in such a problematic realm without making even the least effort to prove anything? My defense: all our thinking is of this nature of a free play with concepts; the justification for this play lies in the measure of survey over the experience of the senses which we are able to achieve with its aid. The concept of "truth" can not yet be applied to such a structure; to my thinking this concept can come in question only when a far-reaching agreement (*convention*) concerning the elements and rules of the game is already at hand.
>
> For me it is not dubious that our thinking goes on for the most part without use of signs (words) and beyond that to a considerable degree unconsciously. For how, otherwise, should it happen that sometimes we "wonder" quite spontaneously about some experience? This "wondering"

Source: Paul Arthur Schilpp, ed., *Albert Einstein: Philosopher-Scientist*. New York: Tudor Publishing Company, 1951, pp. 7, 9, 11, 13, 19, 21, 25, 31, 33.

seems to occur when an experience comes into conflict with a world of concepts which is already sufficiently fixed in us. Whenever such a conflict is experienced hard and intensively it reacts back upon our thought world in a decisive way. The development of this thought world is in a certain sense a continuous flight from "wonder.". . .

Now that I have allowed myself to be carried away sufficiently to interrupt my scantily begun obituary, I shall not hesitate to state here in a few sentences my epistemological credo, although in what precedes something has already incidentally been said about this. This credo actually evolved only much later and very slowly and does not correspond with the point of view I held in younger years.

I see on the one side the totality of sense-experiences, and, on the other, the totality of the concepts and propositions which are laid down in books. The relations between the concepts and propositions among themselves and each other are of a logical nature, and the business of logical thinking is strictly limited to the achievement of the connection between concepts and propositions among each other according to firmly laid down rules, which are the concern of logic. The concepts and propositions get "meaning," viz., "content," only through their connection with sense-experiences. The connection of the latter with the former is purely intuitive, not itself of a logical nature. The degree of certainty with which this connection, viz., intuitive combination, can be undertaken, and nothing else, differentiates empty phantasy from scientific "truth." The system of concepts is a creation of man together with the rules of syntax, which constitute the structure of the conceptual systems. . . .

A proposition is correct if, within a logical system, it is deduced according to the accepted logical rules. A system has truth-content according to the certainty and completeness of its co-ordination-possibility to the totality of experience. A correct proposition borrows its "truth" from the truth-content of the system to which it belongs.

B Einstein believed that Newton's laws were insufficient. They were not the final foundation of physics.

Now to the field of physics as it presented itself at that time. In spite of all the fruitfulness in particulars, dogmatic rigidity prevailed in matters of principles: In the beginning (if there was such a thing) God created Newton's laws of motion together with the necessary masses and forces. This is all; everything beyond this follows from the development of appropriate mathematical methods by means of deduction.

We must not be surprised, therefore, that, so to speak, all physicists of the last century saw in classical mechanics a firm and final foundation for all physics, yes, indeed, for all natural science. . . .

Before I enter upon a critique of mechanics as the foundation of physics, something of a broadly general nature will first have to be said concerning the points of view according to which it is possible to criticize physical theories at all. The first point of view is obvious: the theory must not contradict empirical facts. . . .

The factor which finally succeeded, after long hesitation, to bring the physicists slowly around to give up the faith in the possibility that all of physics could be founded upon Newton's mechanics, was the electrodynamics of Faraday and Maxwell. . . .

. . . Newton, forgive me; you found the only way which, in your age, was just about possible for a man of highest thought — and creative power. The concepts, which you created, are even today still guiding our thinking in physics, although we now know that they will have to be replaced by others farther removed from the sphere of immediate experience, if we aim at a profounder understanding of relationships.

1. What is the relationship between concepts and sense experiences as outlined by Einstein?

2. Does Einstein's acknowledgment of God indicate that he felt science and religion could co-exist? Defend your position.

3. Why does Einstein believe that physics has advanced from Newton's initial theory?

4. How could Einstein's desire for further pursuit of scientific knowledge result in negative consequences in the twentieth century?

The Weakening of Europe, 1914–1945

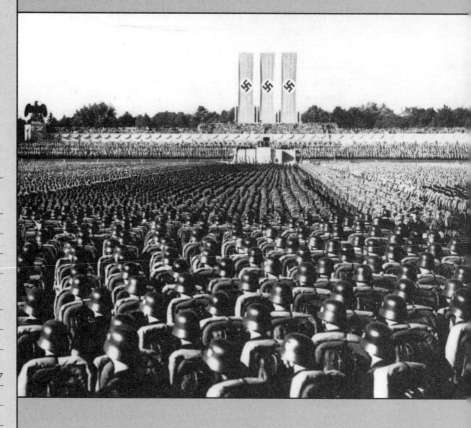

The inter-war period saw the rise of modern dictatorship in the West. At a Nazi rally in 1936, uniformed members of the Nazi Party join in a celebration of their doctrine and their leader. They are organized in a powerful, orderly mass, a body that negates individual identity in favour of belonging to a movement which has cult-like qualities. Now, a single powerful force awaits the presence of the Führer, the leader who embodies the movement and gives it meaning and direction. Nazi symbols abound and the monumental Fascist view of life is celebrated.

Literature of World War I

The novel that came to be the definitive statement on the horrors of the war and the dehumanizing experience of battle was Erich Maria Remarque's *All Quiet on the Western Front* (1929). Remarque (1898–1970) was a German soldier who appealed to humanitarian ideals. He left Germany in 1932, in protest against the rise of the Nazis. The book was later banned during the Nazi period. Another work, Ernst Junger's *The Storm of Steel* (1921), also portrayed war as dreadful, but Junger (1895–1998) found it to be a time of testing and associated the war with a higher national cause.

A   In *All Quiet on the Western Front*, the main character, Paul Baumer, narrates.

> It is strange to think that at home in the drawer of my writing table there lies the beginning of a play called "Saul" and a bundle of poems. Many an evening I have worked over them — we all did something of the kind — but that has become so unreal to me I cannot comprehend it any more. Our early life is cut off from the moment we came here, and that without our lifting a hand. We often try to look back on it and to find an explanation, but never quite succeed. For us young men of twenty everything is extraordinarily vague, for Kropp, Müller, Leer, and me, for all of us whom Kantorek calls the "Iron Youth." All the older men are linked up with their previous life. They have wives, children, occupations, and interests, they have a background which is so strong that the war cannot obliterate it. We young men of twenty, however, have only our parents, and some, perhaps, a girl — that is not much, for at our age the influence of parents is at its weakest and girls have not yet got a hold over us. Besides this there was little else — some enthusiasm, a few hobbies, and our school. Beyond this our life did not extend. And of this nothing remains.
>
> Kantorek would say that we stood on the threshold of life. And so it would seem. We had as yet taken no root. The war swept us away. For the others, the older men, it is but an interruption. They are able to think beyond it. We, however, have been gripped by it and do not know what the end may be. We know only that in some strange and melancholy way we have become a waste land. All the same, we are not often sad.
>
> Though Müller would be delighted to have Kemmerich's boots, he is really quite as sympathetic as another who could not bear to think of such a thing for grief. He merely sees things clearly. Were Kemmerich able to make any use of the boots, then Müller would rather go barefoot over barbed wire than scheme how to get hold of them. But as it is the boots are quite inappropriate to Kemmerich's circumstances, whereas Müller can make

Sources: Erich Maria Remarque, *All Quiet on the Western Front*, trans. A. W. Wheen. London: G. P. Putnam's Sons, 1929, pp. 27–29, 142–146, 148–149, 150, 317–319; Ernst Junger, *The Storm of Steel: From the Diary of a German Storm-Troop Officer on the Western Front*. London: Chatto & Windus, 1929, pp. 316–317, 318–319.

good use of them. Kemmerich will die; it is immaterial who gets them. Why, then, should Müller not succeed to them? He has more right than a hospital orderly. When Kemmerich is dead it will be too late. Therefore Müller is already on the watch.

We have lost all sense of other considerations, because they are artificial. Only the facts are real and important for us. And good boots are scarce. . . .

One morning two butterflies play in front of our trench. They are brimstone-butterflies, with red spots on their yellow wings. What can they be looking for here? There is not a plant nor a flower for miles. They settle on the teeth of a skull. The birds too are just as carefree, they have long since accustomed themselves to the war. Every morning larks ascend from No Man's Land. A year ago we watched them nesting; the young ones grew up too.

We have a spell from the rats in the trench. They are in No Man's Land — we know what for. They grow fat; when we see one we have a crack at it. At night we hear again the rolling behind the enemy lines. All day we have only the normal shelling, so that we are able to repair the trenches. There is always plenty of amusement, the airmen see to that. There are countless fights for us to watch every day.

Battle planes don't trouble us, but the observation planes we hate like the plague; they put the artillery on to us. A few minutes after they appear, shrapnel and high-explosives begin to drop on us. We lose eleven men in one day that way, and five of them stretcher-bearers. Two are so smashed that Tjaden remarks you could scrape them off the wall of the trench with a spoon and bury them in a mess-tin. Another has the lower part of his body and his legs torn off. Dead, his chest leans against the side of the trench, his face is lemon-yellow, in his beard still burns a cigarette. It glows until it dies out on his lips.

We put the dead in a large shell-hole. So far there are three layers, one on top of the other.

Suddenly the shelling begins to pound again. Soon we are sitting up once more with the rigid tenseness of blank anticipation.

Attack, counter-attack, charge, repulse — these are words, but what things they signify! We have lost a good many men, mostly recruits. Reinforcements have again been sent up to our sector. They are one of the new regiments, composed almost entirely of young fellows just called up. They have had hardly any training, and are sent into the field with only a theoretical knowledge. They do know what a hand-grenade is, it is true, but they have very little idea of cover, and what is most important of all, have no eye for it. A fold in the ground has to be quite eighteen inches high before they can see it.

Although we need reinforcement, the recruits give us almost more trouble than they are worth. They are helpless in this grim fighting area, they fall like flies. Modern trench-warfare demands knowledge and experience; a man must have a feeling for the contours of the ground, an ear for the sound and character of the shells, must be able to decide beforehand where they will drop, how they will burst, and how to shelter from them.

The young recruits of course know none of these things. They get killed simply because they can hardly tell shrapnel from high explosive, they are mown down because they are listening anxiously to the roar of the big coal-boxes falling far in the rear, and miss the light, piping whistle of the low spreading little daisy-cutters. They flock together like sheep instead of scattering, and even the wounded are shot down like hares by the airmen.

Their pale turnip faces, their pitiful clenched hands, the fine courage of these poor devils, the desperate charges and attacks made by the poor brave wretches, who are so terrified that they dare not cry out loudly, but with battered chests, with torn bellies, arms and legs only whimper softly for their mothers and cease as soon as one looks at them.

Their sharp, downy, dead faces have the awful expressionlessness of dead children.

It brings a lump into the throat to see how they go over, and run and fall. A man would like to spank them, they are so stupid, and to take them by the arm and lead them away from here where they have no business to be. They wear grey coats and trousers and boots, but for most of them the uniform is far too big, it hangs on their limbs, their shoulders are too narrow, their bodies too slight; no uniform was ever made to these childish measurements.

Between five and ten recruits fall to every old hand.

A surprise gas-attack carries off a lot of them. They have not yet learned what to do. We found one dug-out full of them, with blue heads and black lips. Some of them in a shell hole took their masks off too soon; they did not know that the gas lies longest in the hollows; when they saw others on top without masks they pulled theirs off too and swallowed enough to scorch their lungs. Their condition is hopeless, they choke to death with haemorrhages and suffocation.

B Baumer wonders when it will end.

How long has it been? Weeks — months — years? Only days. We see time pass in the colourless faces of the dying, we cram food into us, we run, we throw, we shoot, we kill, we lie about, we are feeble and spent, and nothing supports us but the knowledge that there are still feebler, still more spent, still more helpless ones there who, with staring eyes, look upon us as gods that escape death many times.

In the few hours of rest we teach them. "There, see that waggle-top? That's a mortar coming. Keep down, it will go clean over. But if it comes this way, then run for it. You can run from a mortar."

We sharpen their ears to the malicious, hardly audible buzz of the smaller shells that are not so easily distinguishable. They must pick them out from the general din by their insect-like hum — we explain to them that these are far more dangerous than the big ones that can be heard long beforehand.

We show them how to take cover from aircraft, how to simulate a dead man when one is overrun in an attack, how to time hand-grenades so that they explode half a second before hitting the ground; we teach them to fling themselves into holes as quick as lightning before the shells with instantaneous fuses; we show them how to clean up a trench with a handful of bombs; we explain the difference between the fuse-length of the enemy bombs and our own; we put them wise to the sound of gas shells; — show them all the tricks that can save them from death.

They listen, they are docile — but when it begins again, in their excitement they do everything wrong. . . .

We see men living with their skulls blown open; we see soldiers run with their two feet cut off, they stagger on their splintered stumps into the next shell-hole; a lance-corporal crawls a mile and a half on his hands dragging his smashed knee after him; another goes to the dressing station and over his clasped hands bulge his intestines; we see men without mouths, without jaws, without faces; we find one man who has held the artery of his arm in his teeth for two hours in order not to bleed to death. The sun goes down, night comes, the shells whine, life is at an end.

Still the little piece of convulsed earth in which we lie is held. We have yielded no more than a few hundred yards of it as a prize to the enemy. But on every yard there lies a dead man.

 Baumer has some final reflections in the autumn of 1918. He dies just before the armistice.

It is autumn. There are not many of the old hands left. I am the last of the seven fellows from our class.

Everyone talks of peace and armistice. All wait. If it again proves an illusion, then they will break up; hope is high, it cannot be taken away again without an upheaval. If there is not peace, then there will be revolution.

I have fourteen days rest, because I have swallowed a bit of gas; in the little garden I sit the whole day long in the sun. The armistice is coming soon, I believe it now too. Then we will go home.

Here my thoughts stop and will not go any farther. All that meets me, all that floods over me are but feelings — greed of life, love of home, yearning of the blood, intoxication of deliverance. But no aims.

Had we returned home in 1916, out of the suffering and the strength of our experiences we might have unleashed a storm. Now if we go back we will be weary, broken, burnt out, rootless, and without hope. We will not be able to find our way any more.

And men will not understand us — for the generation that grew up before us, though it has passed these years with us here, already had a home and a calling; now it will return to its old occupations, and the war will be forgotten — and the generation that has grown up after us will be strange to us and push us aside. We will be superfluous even to ourselves, we will grow older, a few will adapt themselves, some others will merely submit, and most will be bewildered; — the years will pass by and in the end we shall fall into ruin.

But perhaps all this that I think is mere melancholy and dismay, which will fly away as the dust, when I stand once again beneath the poplars and listen to the rustling of their leaves. It cannot be that it has gone, the yearning that made our blood unquiet, the unknown, the perplexing, the oncoming things, the thousand faces of the future, the melodies from dreams and from books, the whispers and divinations of women, it cannot be that this has vanished in bombardment, in despair, in brothels.

Here the trees show gay and golden, the berries of the rowan stand red among the leaves, country roads run white out to the sky line, and the canteens hum like beehives with rumours of peace.

I stand up.

I am very quiet. Let the months and years come, they can take nothing from me, they can take nothing more. I am so alone, and so without hope that I can confront them without fear. The life that has borne me through these years is still in my hands and my eyes. Whether I have subdued it, I know not. But so long as it is there it will seek its own way out, heedless of the will that is within me.

D In *The Storm of Steel*, Junger's hero survives, and his thoughts about the meaning of the war are very different from those of Baumer.

Now I looked back: four years of development in the midst of a generation predestined to death, spent in caves, smoke-filled trenches, and shell-illumined wastes; years enlivened only by the pleasures of a mercenary, and nights of guard after guard in an endless perspective; in short, a monotonous calendar full of hardships and privation, divided by the red-letter days of battles. And almost without any thought of mine, the idea of the Fatherland had been distilled from all these afflictions in a clearer and brighter essence. That was the final winnings in a game on which so often all had been staked: the nation was no longer for me an empty thought veiled in symbols; and how could it have been otherwise when I had seen so many die for its sake, and been schooled myself to stake my life for its credit every minute, day and night, without a thought? And so, strange as it may sound, I learned from this very four years' schooling in force and in all the fantastic extravagance of material warfare that life has no depth of meaning except when it is pledged for an ideal, and that there are ideals in comparison with which the life of an individual and even of a people has no weight. And though the aim for which I fought as an individual, as an atom in the whole body of the army, was not to be achieved, though material force cast us, apparently, to the earth, yet we learned once and for all to stand for a cause and if necessary to fall as befitted men.

Hardened as scarcely another generation ever was in fire and flame, we could go into life as though from the anvil; into friendship, love, politics, professions, into all that destiny had in store. It is not every generation that is so favoured.

And if it be objected that we belong to a time of crude force our answer is: We stood with our feet in mud and blood, yet our faces were turned to things of exalted worth. And not one of that countless number who fell in our attacks fell for nothing. Each one fulfilled his own resolve. . . .

To-day we cannot understand the martyrs who threw themselves into the arena in a transport that lifted them even before their deaths beyond humanity, beyond every phase of pain and fear. Their faith no longer exercises a compelling force. When once it is no longer possible to understand how a man gives his life for his country — and the time will come — then all is over with that faith also, and the idea of the Fatherland is dead; and then, perhaps, we shall be envied, as we envy the saints their inward and irresistible strength. For all these great and solemn ideas bloom from a feeling that dwells in the blood and that cannot be forced. In the cold light of reason everything alike is a matter of expedience and sinks to the paltry and mean. It was our luck to live in the invisible rays of a feeling that filled the heart, and of this inestimable treasure we can never be deprived. . . .

In spite of this it was not long before we were in excellent form for another winter campaign. This was deferred for a while; and we soon had to take part in other battles than we ever dreamed.

Now these too are over, and already we see once more in the dim light of the future the tumult of fresh ones. We — by this I mean those of the youth of this land who are capable of enthusiasm for an ideal — will not shrink from them. We stand in the memory of the dead who are holy to us, and we believe ourselves entrusted with the true and spiritual welfare of our people. We stand for what will be and for what has been. Though force without and barbarity within conglomerate in sombre clouds, yet so long as the blade of a sword will strike a spark in the night may it be said: Germany lives and Germany shall never go under!

1. How does war affect the innocence and idealism of youth?

2. Even though Baumer is a young man, how does his description of the new recruits indicate that he is a veteran of a life-and-death struggle?

3. Why could the description of the impact of trench warfare have been written by any participant of the war?

4. What long-term impact will the war have on Baumer's generation?

5. How does the interpretation of the war's repercussions as described in *The Storm of Steel* compare to Baumer's description in *All Quiet on the Western Front*?

6. Why would Adolf Hitler ban *All Quiet on the Western Front* and approve *The Storm of Steel*?

José Ortega y Gasset

The Spanish philosopher José Ortega y Gasset (1883–1955) was deeply concerned with the problems of liberalism and democracy in the twentieth century. Ortega y Gasset believed that mass society was opposed to traditional culture and civilization, and that Fascism and communism were reflections of the rise of the masses to power. To some his concerns were too traditional and elitist for the problems of the inter-war period. Yet in his writings, Ortega y Gasset defended the humanist tradition of the West, while pointing out some of its paradoxes and contradictions. His essay, *The Revolt of the Masses* (1930), was one of the first important probes into the dilemmas of mass society and culture.

A Ortega y Gasset claims that a major new feature of the twentieth century is the rise to power of the masses.

There is one fact which, whether for good or ill, is of utmost importance in the public life of Europe at the present moment. This fact is the accession of the masses to complete social power. As the masses, by definition, neither should nor can direct their own personal existence, and still less rule society in general, this fact means that actually Europe is suffering from the greatest crisis that can afflict peoples, nations, and civilisation. Such a crisis has occurred more than once in history. Its characteristics and its consequences are well known. So also is its name. It is called the rebellion of the masses. In order to understand this formidable fact, it is important from the start to avoid giving to the words "rebellion," "masses," and "social power" a meaning exclusively or primarily political. Public life is not solely political, but equally, and even primarily, intellectual, moral, economic, religious; it comprises all our collective habits, including our fashions both of dress and of amusement. . . .

Strictly speaking, the mass, as a psychological fact, can be defined without waiting for individuals to appear in mass formation. In the presence of one individual we can decide whether he is "mass" or not. The mass is all that which sets no value on itself — good or ill — based on specific grounds, but which feels itself "just like everybody," and nevertheless is not concerned about it; is, in fact, quite happy to feel itself as one with everybody else. Imagine a humble-minded man who, having tried to estimate his own worth on specific grounds — asking himself if he has any talent for this or that, if he excels in any direction — realises that he possesses no quality of excellence. Such a man will feel that he is mediocre and commonplace, ill-gifted, but will not feel himself "mass."

When one speaks of "select minorities" it is usual for the evil-minded to twist the sense of this expression, pretending to be unaware that the

Source: José Ortega y Gasset, *The Revolt of the Masses.* New York: W. W. Norton & Company, 1957, pp. 11, 14–17, 18, 49–51, 91–92, 94.

select man is not the petulant person who thinks himself superior to the rest, but the man who demands more of himself than the rest, even though he may not fulfil in his person those higher exigencies. For there is no doubt that the most radical division that it is possible to make of humanity is that which splits it into two classes of creatures: those who make great demands on themselves, piling up difficulties and duties; and those who demand nothing special of themselves, but for whom to live is to be every moment what they already are, without imposing on themselves any effort towards perfection; mere buoys that float on the waves. This reminds me that orthodox Buddhism is composed of two distinct religions: one, more rigorous and difficult, the other easier and more trivial: the Mahayana — "great vehicle" or "great path" — and the Hinayana — "lesser vehicle" or "lesser path." The decisive matter is whether we attach our life to one or the other vehicle, to a maximum or a minimum of demands upon ourselves.

The division of society into masses and select minorities is, then, not a division into social classes, but into classes of men, and cannot coincide with the hierarchic separation of "upper" and "lower" classes. It is, of course, plain that in these "upper" classes, when and as long as they really are so, there is much more likelihood of finding men who adopt the "great vehicle," whereas the "lower" classes normally comprise individuals of minus quality. But, strictly speaking, within both these social classes, there are to be found mass and genuine minority. As we shall see, a characteristic of our times is the predominance, even in groups traditionally selective, of the mass and the vulgar. Thus, in the intellectual life, which of its essence requires and presupposes qualification, one can note the progressive triumph of the pseudo-intellectual, unqualified, unqualifiable, and, by their very mental texture, disqualified. Similarly, in the surviving groups of the "nobility," male and female. On the other hand, it is not rare to find to-day amongst working men, who before might be taken as the best example of what we are calling "mass," nobly disciplined minds.

There exist, then, in society, operations, activities, and functions of the most diverse order, which are of their very nature special, and which consequently cannot be properly carried out without special gifts. For example: certain pleasures of an artistic and refined character, or again the functions of government and of political judgment in public affairs. Previously these special activities were exercised by qualified minorities, or at least by those who claimed such qualification. The mass asserted no right to intervene in them; they realised that if they wished to intervene they would necessarily have to acquire those special qualities and cease being mere mass. They recognised their place in a healthy dynamic social system.

If we now revert to the facts indicated at the start, they will appear clearly as the heralds of a changed attitude in the mass. They all indicate that the mass has decided to advance to the foreground of social life, to occupy the places, to use the instruments and to enjoy the pleasures hitherto reserved to the few. It is evident, for example, that the places were never intended for the multitude, for their dimensions are too limited, and the crowd is continuously overflowing; thus manifesting to our eyes and in the clearest manner the new phenomenon: the mass, without ceasing to be mass, is supplanting the minorities. . . .

. . . *The characteristic of the hour is that the commonplace mind, knowing itself to be commonplace, has the assurance to proclaim the rights of the commonplace and to impose them wherever it will.* As they say in the United States: "to be different is to be indecent." The mass crushes beneath it everything that is different, everything that is excellent, individual, qualified and select. Anybody who is not like everybody, who does not think like everybody, runs the risk of being eliminated. And it is clear, of course, that this "everybody" is not "everybody." "Everybody" was normally the complex unity of the mass and the divergent, specialised minorities. Nowadays, "everybody" is the mass alone. Here we have the formidable fact of our times, described without any concealment of the brutality of its features.

B For Ortega y Gasset, the new population growth has important consequences.

The key to this analysis is found when, returning to the starting-point of this essay, we ask ourselves: "Whence have come all these multitudes which nowadays fill to overflowing the stage of history?". . .

The fact is this: from the time European history begins in the VIth Century up to the year 1800 — that is, through the course of twelve centuries — Europe does not succeed in reaching a total population greater than 180 million inhabitants. Now, from 1800 to 1914 — little more than a century — the population of Europe mounts from 180 to 460 millions! I take it that the contrast between these figures leaves no doubt as to the prolific qualities of the last century. In three generations it produces a gigantic mass of humanity which, launched like a torrent over the historic area, has inundated it. This fact, I repeat, should suffice to make us realise the triumph of the masses and all that is implied and announced by it. Furthermore, it should be added as the most concrete item to that rising of the level of existence which I have already indicated. . . .

But although this fact . . . is not as well known as it should be, the confused idea of a considerable population increase in Europe was widespread enough to render unnecessary insistence on it. In the figures cited, then, it is not the increase of population which interests me, but the fact that by the contrast with the previous figures the dizzy rapidity of the increase is brought into relief. This is the point of importance for us at the moment. For that rapidity means that heap after heap of human beings have been dumped on to the historic scene at such an accelerated rate, that it has been difficult to saturate them with traditional culture. And in fact, the average type of European at present possesses a soul, healthier and stronger it is true than those of the last century, but much more simple. Hence, at times he leaves the impression of a primitive man suddenly risen in the midst of a very old civilisation. In the schools, which were such a source of pride to the last century, it has been impossible to do more than instruct the masses in the technique of modern life; it has been found impossible to educate them. They have been given tools for an intenser form of existence, but no feeling for their great historic duties; they have been hurriedly inoculated with the pride and power of modern instruments, but not with their spirit. Hence they will have nothing to do with their spirit, and the new generations are getting ready to take over command of the world as if the world were a paradise without trace of former footsteps, without traditional and highly complex problems.

C Ortega y Gasset fears the growth of a new kind of primitivism in the modern era.

Advanced civilisation is one and the same thing as arduous problems. Hence, the greater the progress, the greater danger it is in. Life gets gradually better, but evidently also gradually more complicated. Of course, as problems become more complex, the means of solving them also become more perfect. But each new generation must master these perfected means. Amongst them — to come to the concrete — there is one most plainly attached to the advance of a civilisation, namely, that it have a great deal of the past at its back, a great deal of experience; in a word: history. Historical knowledge is a technique of the first order to preserve and continue a civilisation already advanced. Not that it affords positive solutions to the new aspect of vital conditions — life is always different from what it was — but that it prevents us committing the ingenuous mistakes of other times. But if, in addition to being old and, therefore, beginning to find life difficult, you have lost the memory of the past, and do not profit by experience, then everything turns to disadvantage. Well, it is my belief that this is the situation of Europe. The most "cultured" people to-day are suffering from incredible ignorance of history. I maintain that at the present day, European leaders know much less history than their fellows of the XVIIIth, even of the XVIIth Century. That historical knowledge of the governing minorities — governing *sensu lato* — made possible the prodigious advance of the XIXth Century. Their policy was thought out — by the XVIIIth Century — precisely in order to avoid the errors of previous politics, thought out in view of those errors and embraced in its substance the whole extent of experience. But the XIXth Century already began to lose "historic culture," although during the century the specialists gave it notable advance as a science. To this neglect is due in great part its peculiar errors, which to-day press upon us. In the last third of the century there began — though hidden from sight — that involution, that retrogression towards barbarism, that is, towards the ingenuousness and primitivism of the man who has no past, or who has forgotten it.

Hence, Bolshevism and Fascism, the two "new" attempts in politics that are being made in Europe and on its borders, are two clear examples of essential retrogression. Not so much by the positive content of their doctrine, which, taken in isolation, naturally has its partial truth — what is there in the universe which has not some particle of truth? — as on account of the *anti*-historic, anachronistic way in which they handle the rational elements which the doctrine contains. Typical movements of mass-men, directed, as all such are, by men who are mediocrities, improvised, devoid of a long memory and a "historic conscience," they behave from the start as if they already belonged to the past, as if, though occurring at the present hour, they were really fauna of a past age. . . .

Both Bolshevism and Fascism are two false dawns; they do not bring the morning of a new day, but of some archaic day, spent over and over again: they are mere primitivism. And such will all movements be which fall into the stupidity of starting a boxing-match with some portion or other of the past, instead of proceeding to digest it. No doubt an advance must be made on the liberalism of the XIXth Century. But this is precisely what cannot be done by any movement such as Fascism, which declares itself anti-liberal. Because it was that fact — the being anti-liberal or non-liberal — which constituted man previous to liberalism. And as the latter triumphed over its opposite, it will either repeat its victory time and again, or else everything — liberalism and anti-liberalism — will be annihilated in the destruction of Europe. There is an inexorable chronology of life. In it liberalism is posterior to anti-liberalism, or what comes to the same, is more vital than it, just as the gun is more of a weapon than the lance.

1. What danger does the author see in the growing predominance of the masses in European society?

2. Is Ortega y Gasset accurate in claiming that history "prevents us committing the ingenuous mistakes of other times"? Defend your position.

3. Defend or refute Ortega y Gasset's assertion that Bolshevism and Fascism are primitive movements.

Fascism

Fascism grew in doctrine and practice in the inter-war period. It glorified power, authority, the nation, and the leader. In Italy, Benito Mussolini (1883–1945) founded the Fascist movement. He said that the Fascist "conceives of life as duty and struggle and conquest," and that the state required "authority, direction and order." Above all, he claimed, Fascism was a "collective" idea. All people had value only insofar as they worked for the state and enhanced its power.

A José Antonio Primo de Rivera (1903–1936) was the son of General Miguel Primo de Rivera, who ruled Spain as a military dictator between 1923 and 1930. José Antonio was one of the founders of Spain's principal Fascist party, the Falange Española, and quickly became its leader. The following excerpt comes from his speech at the Party's founding congress. The speech presents a number of the crucial elements of European Fascism, especially hyper-nationalism and the systematic use of violence as a political weapon. Fascists always opposed both liberalism and democracy.

[T]he liberal state [has] divested itself of its role as resolute executor of the nation's destiny to become a mere spectator of the electoral contest. For the liberal state it was important only that a certain number of gentlemen presided over polling stations, that elections started at eight and finished at four, that no ballot-boxes were smashed — though to be smashed is every ballot-box's noblest fate. Afterwards, all that remained for the state to do was to accept calmly whatever emerged from the poll as though that was not its concern. That is to say, the liberal rulers had no faith even in their own mission; they did not believe that they were installed for the fulfilment of an entirely respectable duty, but that anyone who disagreed and set about taking the state by assault, using fair means or foul, had just as much right to say so and to make the attempt as the keepers of the state had to defend it.

Hence the democratic system which is, first and foremost, a system most ruinous and wasteful of energy. A man with a talent for the lofty function of government — perhaps the noblest of all human functions — would find himself obliged to devote 80, even 90 or 95, per cent of his energies to substantiating formalistic demands, to electioneering, to snoozing on the benches of the Cortes [parliament], to fawning on the voters and withstanding their impertinence because it was from the voters he derived power, to putting up with humiliations and the taunts of those who, precisely because of the almost divine function of government, were destined to obey him. And if after all that he had a few hours to spare at dawn or a few minutes snatched from uneasy slumber, this scanty minimum was all the man with a gift for government could devote to serious reflection on the essential functions of statecraft.

There ensued the ruin of a people's spiritual unity, for since the system demanded that a majority be obtained, anyone intent on capturing the system had to make certain he garnered a majority of the votes — if need be by stealing them from the other parties. To this end he had to slander the other parties without hesitation, to bombard them with the vilest insults, to resort to deliberate lies, to waste not a single ploy of falsehood and vilification. Thus it came about that although fraternity was one of the axioms the liberal state exhibited on its façade, there has never been a situation of collective life wherein men, reviled and hostile to each other, felt less like brothers than in the distasteful turmoil of the liberal state.

Sources: José Antonio Primo de Rivera, *Selected Writings*, trans. Gudie Lawaetz. London: Jonathan Cape, 1972, pp. 50, 51, 54–55, 58; Adolf Hitler, *Mein Kampf*. New York: Reynal & Hitchcock, 1939, pp. 392, 396–397, 412, 416–417, 448–449, 231–234, 238, 239.

Ultimately, the liberal state gave us economic slavery, for it says to the workers, with tragic irony: 'You are free to work as you like; nobody can force you to accept any particular conditions; but remember, being rich, we offer you whatever conditions we please; as free citizens, you are by no means obliged to agree to them; being poor citizens, though, if you will not agree to the conditions we impose, you will die of hunger in the midst of the utmost liberal dignity.' And that is why in the countries where splendid parliaments and exquisite democratic institutions have emerged, you would find that you had only to wander a few hundred yards from the luxurious neighbourhoods to come upon noisome slums where workers and their families lived in cramped conditions at an almost subhuman level of decorum. And you would find agricultural labourers toiling on the land from dawn to dusk with their backs scorched, who — thanks to the laissez-faire liberal economy — earned throughout an entire year some seventy or eighty day-wages of three pesetas.

B Primo de Rivera emphasizes nationalism — the nation as the important group and the source of identity.

The nation is an absolute whole harbouring all individuals and classes; the nation cannot be the domain of the strongest class or of the best organized party. The nation is a transcendental synthesis, an indivisible synthesis with a finality of its own; and what we want is to see the movement of this day, and the state it will create, being the effective, the authoritarian, tool of what is an indisputable whole: that permanent, irrevocable unit we call fatherland and nation. . . .

Let us now state what are the priorities of our total conception of the nation and of the state at the fatherland's service. . . .

The disappearance of political parties. No one has ever been born a member of a political party. But we are all born members of a family; all of us are residents of a borough; all of us toil in the exercise of our trade. Well, if these are our natural categories, if the family, the municipality and the corporation are the pillars of our real existence, why do we need such an intermediary and pernicious apparatus as that of the political parties which, in order to unite us in artificial units, begin by disrupting the unity of our authentic context?

We want less liberal verbiage and more respect of man's profoundest freedom. For the freedom of man is only respected when he is considered, as we consider him, the embodiment of eternal values . . . . Only when man is considered thus can it be said that his freedom is truly respected, and even more so if this freedom is given, as we would wish it to be, a framework of authority, hierarchy and order.

We want everyone to feel part of a dignified and comprehensive community: that is to say, the spheres of action are many and various — some will contribute their manual work; others, works of the spirit; some, accomplishments of morality and refinement. But let me make one thing quite clear: in a community such as we envisage there must be no spongers and no drones.

We want no panegyrics on individual rights that can never be honoured in the homes of the starving, but we do want every man, every member of the body politic, to be by rights entitled to a means of earning by his labour a living that is humane, adequate and fair.

We want the spirit of religion, the keystone of our history's finest arches, to enjoy the respect and protection it merits; which does not mean that the state should meddle in matters beyond its proper concern, or share — as it has done, perhaps not entirely for reasons related to true religious conviction — what are solely its own responsibilities.

C In Germany, the Führer (Leader) of the Fascists was Adolf Hitler (1889–1945), the head of the Nazi Party and the Chancellor of Germany from 1933 to 1945. Hitler wrote *Mein Kampf* from 1923 to 1925. The work candidly presents his views on race and power, the same views that he put into practice when in authority.

Just as little as Nature desires a mating between weaker individuals and stronger ones, far less she desires the mixing of a higher race with a lower one, as in this case her entire work of higher breeding, which has perhaps taken hundreds of thousands of years, would tumble at one blow.

Historical experience offers countless proofs of this. It shows with terrible clarity that with any mixing of the blood of the Aryan with lower races the result was the end of the culture-bearer. North America, the population of which consists for the greatest part of Germanic elements — which mix only very little with the lower, colored races — displays a humanity and a culture different from those of Central and South America, where chiefly the Romanic immigrants have sometimes mixed with the aborigines on a large scale. By this example alone one may clearly and distinctly recognize the influence of the race mixture. The Germanic of the North American continent, who has remained pure and less intermixed, has become the master of that continent, he will remain so until he, too, falls victim to the shame of blood-mixing.

The result of any crossing, in brief, is always the following:

(a) Lowering of the standard of the higher race,

(b) Physical and mental regression, and, with it, the beginning of a slowly but steadily progressive lingering illness.

To bring about such a development means nothing less than sinning against the will of the Eternal Creator. . . .

Everything that today we admire on this earth — science and art, technique and inventions — is only the creative product of a few peoples and perhaps originally of *one* race. On them now depends also the existence of this entire culture. If they perish, then the beauty of this earth sinks into the grave with them. . . .

All great cultures of the past perished only because the originally creative race died off through blood-poisoning.

The ultimate cause of such a decline was always the forgetting that all culture depends on men and not the reverse; that means, that in order to save a certain culture the man who created it has to be saved. But the preservation is bound to the brazen law of necessity and of the right of the victory of the best and the strongest in this world.

He who wants to live should fight, therefore, and he who does not want to battle in this world of eternal struggle does not deserve to be alive. . . .

. . . What we see before us of human culture today, the results of art, science, and techniques, is almost exclusively the creative product of the Aryan. . . .

The Jew forms the strongest contrast to the Aryan. . . .

If the Jews were alone in this world, they would suffocate as much in dirt and filth, as they would carry on a detestable struggle to cheat and to ruin each other, although the complete lack of the will to sacrifice, expressed in their cowardice, would also in this instance make the fight a comedy.

Thus it is fundamentally wrong to conclude, merely from the fact of their standing together in a fight, or, more rightly expressed, in their exploiting their fellow human beings, that the Jews have a certain idealistic will to sacrifice themselves.

Here, too, the Jew is led by nothing but pure egoism on the part of the individual. . . .

For this reason, however, the Jewish people, with all its apparent intellectual qualities, is nevertheless without any true culture, especially without a culture of its own. For the sham culture which the Jew possesses today is the property of other peoples, and is mostly spoiled in his hands.

When judging Jewry in its attitude towards the question of human culture, one has to keep before one's eye as an essential characteristic that there never has been and consequently that today also there is no Jewish art; that above all the two queens of all arts, architecture and music, owe nothing original to Jewry. What he achieves in the field of art is either bowdlerization or intellectual theft. With this, the Jew lacks those qualities which distinguish creatively and, with it, culturally blessed races.

But how far the Jew takes over foreign culture, only imitating, or rather destroying, it, may be seen from the fact that he is found most frequently in that art which also appears directed least of all towards invention of its own, the art of acting. But here, too, he is really only the 'juggler,' or rather the ape; for here, too, he lacks the ultimate touch of real greatness; here, too, he is not the ingenious creator, but the outward imitator, whereby all the turns and tricks he applies cannot deceive us concerning the inner lack of life of his creative ability. . . .

For hours the black-haired Jew-boy, diabolic joy in his face, waits in ambush for the unsuspecting girl whom he defiles with his blood and thus robs her from her people. With the aid of all means he tries to ruin the racial foundations of the people to be enslaved. Exactly as he himself systematically demoralizes women and girls, he is not scared from pulling down the barriers of blood and race for others on a large scale. It was and is the Jews who bring the negro to the Rhine, always with the same concealed thought and the clear goal of destroying, by the bastardization which would necessarily set in, the white race which they hate, to throw it down from its cultural and political height and in turn to rise personally to the position of master.

For a racially pure people, conscious of its blood, can never be enslaved by the Jew. It will forever only be the master of bastards in this world.

Thus he systematically tries to lower the racial level by a permanent poisoning of the individual.

In the political sphere, however, he begins to replace the idea of democracy by that of the dictatorship of the proletariat.

In the organized mass of Marxism he has found the weapon which makes him now dispense with democracy and which allows him, instead, to enslave and to 'rule' the people dictatorially with the brutal fist.

D Hitler was a master at propaganda. His contempt for most people led him to believe that they should be manipulated on behalf of Nazi goals.

The task of propaganda lies not in a scientific training of the individual, but rather in directing the masses towards certain facts, events, necessities, etc., the purpose being to move their importance into the masses' field of vision.

The art now is exclusively to attack this so skilfully that a general conviction of the reality of a fact, of the necessity of an event, that something that is necessary is also right, etc., is created. But as it is not and cannot be science in itself, as its task consists of catching the masses' attention, just like that of the poster, and not in teaching one who is already scientifically experienced or is striving towards education and knowledge, its effect has always to be directed more and more towards the feeling, and only to a certain extent to so-called reason.

All propaganda has to be popular and has to adapt its spiritual level to the perception of the least intelligent of those towards whom it intends to direct itself. Therefore its spiritual level has to be screwed the lower, the greater the mass of people which one wants to attract. But if the problem involved, like the propaganda for carrying on a war, is to include an entire people in its field of action, the caution in avoiding too high spiritual assumptions cannot be too great.

The more modest, then, its scientific ballast is, and the more it exclusively considers the feelings of the masses, the more striking will be its success. This, however, is the best proof whether a particular piece of propaganda is right or wrong, and not the successful satisfaction of a few scholars or 'aesthetic' languishing monkeys.

This is just the art of propaganda that it, understanding the great masses' world of ideas and feelings, finds, by a correct psychological form, the way to the attention, and further to the heart, of the great masses. That our super-clever heads never understand this proves only their mental inertia or their conceit.

But if one understands the necessity of the attitude of the attracting skill of propaganda towards the great masses, the following rule then results:

It is wrong to wish to give propaganda the versatility of perhaps scientific teaching.

The great masses' receptive ability is only very limited, their understanding is small, but their forgetfulness is great. As a consequence of these facts, all effective propaganda has to limit itself only to a very few points and to use them like slogans until even the very last man is able to imagine what is intended by such a word. As soon as one sacrifices this basic principle and tries to become versatile, the effect will fritter away, as the masses are neither able to digest the material offered nor to retain it. Thus the result is weakened and finally eliminated. . . .

Nevertheless, all geniality in the makeup of propaganda will not lead to success unless a fundamental principle is considered with continually sharp attention; it has to confine itself to little and to repeat this eternally. Here, too, persistency, as in so many other things in this world, is the first and the most important condition for success.

In the field of propaganda particularly one must never be guided by aesthetics or *blasé* persons . . . .

Now the purpose of propaganda is not continually to produce interesting changes for a few *blasé* little masters, but to convince; that means, to convince the masses. The masses, however, with their inertia, always need a certain time before they are ready even to notice a thing, and they will lend their memories only to the thousandfold repetition . . . .

A change must never alter the content of what is being brought forth by propaganda, but in the end it always has to say the same. Thus the slogan has to be illuminated from various sides, but the end of every reflection has always and again to be the slogan itself. Only thus can and will propaganda have uniform and complete effect.

1. How can elections in a liberal state divide rather than unite a nation?

2. How can Primo de Rivera claim that the nation cannot be the domain of an organized party, yet demand Fascist control?

3. What elements of the Spanish Falange philosophy are similar to socialism?

4. How does Hitler attempt to make his analysis of "blood mixing" appear scientifically based?

5. What is Hitler's attitude toward the masses in his description of propaganda? Is he accurate in his assumptions?

6. What evidence exists in *Mein Kampf* to foreshadow the racist policies of the future Third Reich?

Lev Kopelev

Lev Kopelev (1912–1997) was raised in a middle-class Ukrainian Jewish family. He became an ardent communist in the Soviet Union — as he described it, a "true believer." He participated in the forced collectivization of agriculture, which was part of the Stalinist plan. In the Soviet Union from 1929 to 1933, many small peasant holdings were consolidated into large units, often in spite of peasant opposition. The class of kulaks, independent peasants with their own land, was liquidated. Kopelev later renounced Stalinism and adopted humanist values. He served in the army in World War II, and ended up in a labour camp near the end of the war, charged with the crime of "bourgeois humanitarianism" for trying to treat the enemy in a humane manner. His continued protests against state terror and in favour of human rights resulted in his exile from the Soviet Union in 1980.

A In *The Education of a True Believer*, Kopelev recalls his enthusiastic participation in the collectivization procedures.

> The grain front! Stalin said the struggle for grain was the struggle for socialism. I was convinced that we were warriors on an invisible front, fighting against kulak sabotage for the grain which was needed by the country, by the five-year plan. Above all, for the grain, but also for the souls of these peasants who were mired in unconscientiousness, in ignorance, who succumbed to enemy agitation, who did not understand the great truth of communism. . . .
>
> The highest measure of coercion on the hard-core holdouts was "undisputed confiscation."
>
> A team consisting of several young kolkhozniks [collective farmers] and members of the village soviet, led as a rule by Vashchenko himself, would search the hut, barn, yard, and take away all the stores of seed, lead away the cow, the horse, the pigs.
>
> In some cases they would be merciful and leave some potatoes, peas, corn for feeding the family. But the stricter ones would make a clean sweep. They would take not only the food and livestock, but also "all valuables and surpluses of clothing," including icons in their frames, samovars, painted carpets and even metal kitchen utensils which might be silver. And any money they found stashed away. . . .
>
> It was excruciating to see and hear all this. And even worse to take part in it. No, it was worse to be present without taking part than when you tried to persuade someone, to explain something. . . . And I persuaded myself, explained to myself. I mustn't give in to debilitating pity. We were realizing historical necessity. We were performing our revolutionary duty. We were obtaining grain for the socialist fatherland. For the five-year plan.

Sources: Lev Kopelev, *The Education of a True Believer*, trans. Gary Kern. New York: Harper & Row, 1980, pp. 226, 234–235, 248, 249–251; Lev Kopelev, *No Jail for Thought*, trans. Anthony Austin. London: Secker & Warburg, 1977, pp. 11–13.

Our only worry was to make sure that there were no "gratuitous" cruelties, that no overeager . . . activist used his fists on a woman lying across her trunk and saying, "I won't give it up!" And to make sure that the confiscated goods were accurately described, in two copies. Because the condition of such confiscation was this: hand over the grain and we'll return everything we took.

Some sort of rationalistic fanaticism overcame my doubts, my pangs of conscience and simple feelings of sympathy, pity and shame, but this fanaticism was nourished not only by speculative newspaper and literary sources. More convincing than these were people who in my eyes embodied, personified our truth and our justice, people who confirmed with their lives that it was necessary to clench your teeth, clench your heart and carry out everything the party and the Soviet power ordered.

B Kopelev reflects on how this kind of behaviour toward others could have occurred.

How could all this have happened?

Who was guilty of the famine which destroyed millions of lives?

How could I have participated in it?. . .

We were raised as the fanatical adepts of a new creed, the only true *religion* of scientific socialism. The party became our church militant, bequeathing to all mankind eternal salvation, eternal peace and the bliss of an earthly paradise. It victoriously surmounted all other churches, schisms and heresies. The works of Marx, Engels and Lenin were accepted as holy writ, and Stalin was the infallible high priest.

Factories, mines, blast furnaces, locomotives, tractors, workbenches, turbines were transformed into objects of a cult, the sacramental objects blessed from on high. "Technology solves everything!" Men genuflected to these objects in poetry, prose, painting, film, music. . . .

Many things then began to be called a struggle. In the workshop they struggled for the plan, for the reduction of wastage, against absenteeism. In the school they struggled against laziness, retardation, lack of social conscience. The janitors struggled for clean sidewalks. Everyone struggled — physicians, literati, ditchdiggers, accountants. . . .

We deliriously sang out the refrain of the "Budyenny March," one of the most popular songs in those years: "And all our life is but a struggle!"

For what, against whom and how exactly we should struggle at any given moment was determined by the party, its leaders. Stalin was the most perspicacious, the most wise (at that time they hadn't yet started calling him "great" and "brilliant"). He said: "The struggle for grain is the struggle for socialism." And we believed him unconditionally. And later we believed that unconditional collectivization was unavoidable if we were to overcome the capriciousness and uncertainty of the market and the backwardness of individual farming, to guarantee a steady supply of grain, milk and meat to the cities. And also if we were to reeducate millions of peasants, those petty landowners and hence potential bourgeoisie, potential kulaks, to transform them into laborers with a social conscience, to liberate them from "the idiocy of country life," from ignorance and prejudice, and to accustom them to culture, to all the boons of socialism.

C In his memoir *No Jail for Thought*, Kopelev raises major questions about the nature of good and evil in the modern world.

Many years would pass before I began to see that my wavering between unresolvable contradictions — a 'greater' or 'lesser' evil, 'objective' or 'subjective' truth — was a reflection of the central contradiction of our whole life, the heart of the dilemma that had shaped the destinies of several of our generations. For did not thousands of our Old Bolsheviks — the very men who had acquitted themselves so heroically on the barricades, in the Czarist prison camps, on the front lines of the Civil War — debase themselves ten or fifteen years later by lying and toadying and glorifying the 'Great Leader' and betraying their friends and bespattering themselves with false confessions? And not entirely out of fear or selfish calculation — and some for neither of these reasons to any degree — but because they believed that it was necessary for the main cause: the security of the Soviet state and the struggle against Fascism. And in spite of everything they saw and experienced in 1930, 1933, 1937 and 1939, in spite of the famines, in spite of . . . Terror and the pact with Hitler and the carving up of Poland, my own contemporaries volunteered for the Finnish campaign, fought bravely in the Great Patriotic War of 1941–45 and put up sacrificial resistance in the German death camps. . . .

With the rest of my generation I firmly believed that the ends justified the means. Our great goal was the universal triumph of Communism, and for the sake of that goal everything was permissible — to lie, to steal, to destroy hundreds of thousands and even millions of people, all those who were hindering our work or could hinder it, everyone who stood in the way. And to hesitate or doubt about all this was to give in to 'intellectual squeamishness' and 'stupid liberalism,' the attributes of people who 'could not see the forest for the trees.'

That was how I had reasoned, and everyone like me, even when I did have my doubts, when I believed what Trotsky and Bukharin were saying, when I saw what 'total collectivization' meant — how they 'kulakized' and 'dekulakized,' how mercilessly they stripped the peasants in the winter of 1932–33. I took part in this myself, scouring the countryside, searching for hidden grain, testing the earth with an iron rod for loose spots that might lead to buried grain. With the others, I emptied out the old folks' storage chests, stopping my ears to the children's crying and the women's wails. For I was convinced that I was accomplishing the great and necessary transformation of the countryside; that in the days to come the people who lived there would be better off for it; that their distress and suffering were a result of their own ignorance or the machinations of the class enemy; that those who sent me — and I myself — knew better than the peasants how they should live, what they should sow and when they should plow.

In the terrible spring of 1933 I saw people dying from hunger. I saw women and children with distended bellies, turning blue, still breathing but with vacant, lifeless eyes. And corpses — corpses in ragged sheepskin coats and cheap felt boots; corpses in peasant huts, in the melting snow of old Vologda, under the bridges of Kharkov. . . . I saw all this and did not go out of my mind or commit suicide. Nor did I curse those who had sent me to take away the peasants' grain in the winter, and in the spring to persuade the barely walking, skeleton-thin or sickly-swollen people to go into the fields in order to 'fulfill the Bolshevik sowing plan in shock-worker style.'

Nor did I lose my faith. As before, I believed because I wanted to believe. Thus from time immemorial men have believed when possessed by a desire to serve powers and values above and beyond humanity: gods, emperors, states; ideals of virtue, freedom, nation, race, class, party. . . .

Any single-minded attempt to realize these ideals exacts its toll of human sacrifice. In the name of the noblest visions promising eternal happiness to their descendants, such men bring merciless ruin on their contemporaries. Bestowing paradise on the dead, they maim and destroy the living. They become unprincipled liars and unrelenting executioners, all the while seeing themselves as virtuous and honorable militants — convinced that if they are forced into villainy, it is for the sake of future good, and that if they have to lie, it is in the name of eternal truths. . . .

That was how we thought and acted — we, the fanatical disciples of the all-saving ideals of Communism. When we saw the base and cruel acts that were committed in the name of our exalted notions of good, and when we ourselves took part in those actions, what we feared most was to lose our heads, fall into doubt or heresy and forfeit our unbounded faith.

I was appalled by what I saw in the 1930s and was overcome by depression. But I would still my doubts the way I had learned to: 'we made a mistake,' 'we went too far,' 'we didn't take into consideration,' 'the logic of the class struggle,' 'objective historical need,' 'using barbaric means to combat barbarism'. . . .

Good and evil, humanity and inhumanity — these seemed empty abstractions. I did not trouble myself with why 'humanity' should be abstract but 'historical necessity' and 'class consciousness' should be concrete. The concepts of conscience, honor, humaneness we dismissed as idealistic prejudices, 'intellectual' or 'bourgeois,' and, hence, perverse.

It was only later, much later, that I began to see things more clearly. Yet in the final months of the war I had already begun to sense a change in me, like some unavoidable oncoming threat. I had already begun to wonder, and had decided that what we lacked was a set of absolute moral norms. Relativist morality — whatever helps us is good, whatever helps the enemy is bad, the creed we proselytized under the name of the 'materialist dialectic' — would debase us in the end, and would debase the cause of Socialism, raising a species of immoral craftsmen of death. Today they apply themselves to killing enemies, real or imaginary; tomorrow they will turn just as willingly against their own.

1. How does the author justify his actions of confiscating property?

2. Marx described religion as the "opiate of the masses." According to Kopelev, how does communism try to replace religion?

3. Why did some find it necessary to ignore morality during the events of the 1930s?

4. Are Kopelev's comments concerning the lack of morality necessary to achieve primary political goals relevant today?

Poetry of the Inter-War Period

In the period after World War I, poets, like visual artists, experimented with new forms and attempted to deal with the alienation and anger of a civilization that saw itself as being in crisis and spiritually empty. Often, the poets used new and different language as a means to both signal their dislocation from tradition and try to get at the core of the feeling of their time.

 In "The Second Coming" (1921), William Butler Yeats (1865–1939) expresses what many believed after World War I: a harsh, dark, iron age had arrived, the beginnings of a new, less hopeful time.

> Turning and turning in the widening gyre
> The falcon cannot hear the falconer;
> Things fall apart; the center cannot hold;
> Mere anarchy is loosed upon the world,
> The blood-dimmed tide is loosed, and everywhere
> The ceremony of innocence is drowned;
> The best lack all conviction, while the worst
> Are full of passionate intensity.
>
> Surely some revelation is at hand;
> Surely the Second Coming is at hand.
> The Second Coming! Hardly are those words out
> When a vast image out of *Spiritus Mundi*
> Troubles my sight; somewhere in sands of the desert
> A shape with lion body and the head of a man,

Sources: M. H. Abrams et al., *The Norton Anthology of English Literature*, Volume II, revised. New York: W. W. Norton & Company Inc., 1968, pp. 1582–1583, 1894–1896; Anna Akhmatova, *Poems*, trans. Lyn Coffin. New York: W. W. Norton & Company, Inc., 1983, pp. 58–59.

A gaze blank and pitiless as the sun,
Is moving its slow thighs, while all about it
Reel shadows of the indignant desert birds.
The darkness drops again; but now I know
That twenty centuries of stony sleep
Were vexed to nightmare by a rocking cradle,
And what rough beast, its hour come round at last,
Slouches towards Bethlehem to be born?

B W. H. Auden (1907–1973), in "Spain 1937," writes about the experience of the Spanish Civil War. That conflict was viewed by many in Europe and the West as a testing time for democracy against the rising tide of Fascism.

Yesterday all the past.
. . . .

Yesterday the assessment of insurance by cards,
The divination of water; yesterday the invention
    Of cart wheels and clocks, the taming of
Horses; yesterday the bustling world of the navigators.

Yesterday the abolition of fairies and giants;
The fortress like a motionless eagle eyeing the valley,
    The chapel built in the forest;
Yesterday the carving of angels and of frightening gargoyles.

The trial of heretics among the columns of stone;
Yesterday the theological feuds in the taverns
    And the miraculous cure at the fountain;
Yesterday the Sabbath of Witches. But today the struggle.

Yesterday the installation of dynamos and turbines;
The construction of railways in the colonial desert;
    Yesterday the classic lecture
On the origin of Mankind. But today the struggle.

Yesterday the belief in the absolute value of Greek;
The fall of the curtain upon the death of a hero;
    Yesterday the prayer to the sunset,
And the adoration of madmen. But today the struggle.
. . . .

"What's your proposal? To build the Just City? I will.
I agree. Or is it the suicide pact, the romantic
    Death? Very well, I accept, for
I am your choice, your decision: yes, I am Spain."
. . . .

Tomorrow, perhaps, the future: the research on fatigue
And the movements of packers; the gradual exploring of all the
  Octaves of radiation;
Tomorrow the enlarging of consciousness by diet and breathing.

Tomorrow the rediscovery of romantic love;
The photographing of ravens; all the fun under
  Liberty's masterful shadow;
Tomorrow the hour of the pageant-master and the musician.

Tomorrow, for the young, the poets exploding like bombs,
The walks by the lake, the winter of perfect communion;
  Tomorrow the bicycle races
Through the suburbs on summer evenings: but today the struggle.

Today the inevitable increase in the chances of death;
The conscious acceptance of guilt in the fact of murder;
  Today the expending of powers
On the flat ephemeral pamphlet and the boring meeting.

Today the makeshift consolations; the shared cigarette;
The cards in the candle-lit barn and the scraping concert,
  The masculine jokes; today the
Fumbled and unsatisfactory embrace before hurting.

The stars are dead; the animals will not look:
We are left alone with our day, and the time is short and
  History to the defeated
May say Alas but cannot help or pardon.

C The poem "In 1940" by Anna Akhmatova (1889–1966) records the mood at the
beginning of World War II.

1.

When they bury an epoch,
No psalms are read while the coffin settles,
The grave will be adorned with a rock,
With bristly thistles and nettles.
Only the gravediggers dig and fill,
Working with zest. Business to do!
And it's so still, my God, so still,
You can hear time passing by you.

And later, like a corpse, it will rise
Ride the river in spring like a leaf, —
But the son doesn't recognize
His mother, the grandson turns away in grief,

Bowed heads do not embarrass,
Like a pendulum goes the moon.

Well, this is the sort of silent tune
That plays in fallen Paris.

2. To LONDONERS

The twenty-fourth drama by William
    Shakespeare
Time is writing with a careless hand.
Since we partake of the feast of fear,
We'd rather read Hamlet, Caesar, Lear,
By the river of lead where today we stand,

Or carry Juliet, sweet as a kiss,
To her grave, with songs and torches to lead,
Or tremble in darkness as in an abyss
With a hired killer Macbeth will need, —
Only . . . not this, not this, not this,
This we don't have the strength to read!

Not as a swallow, reed, or star,
Not as a bell to ring or chime,
Not as the water in a spring,
Not as a maple, branch or beam —
I won't alarm those who are living,
I won't appear in anyone's dream,
Unappeased and unforgiving.

5.

I warn you, that's the way things are:
This is my final lifetime.

1. What is the traditional interpretation of the Second Coming? How does Yeats' message compare to the traditional interpretation?

2. How accurate is Auden's description of Spain before and during the civil war?

3. According to Akhmatova, how have the French and British reacted to the war? Quote specific lines to support your answer.

Virginia Woolf

Virginia Woolf (1882–1941) was one of the most inventive and influential authors of the twentieth century. Her work was often experimental, attempting to portray how we lived and understood the world. Her insights into the form of the novel and the content of our lives have informed many artists. In 1928, Woolf gave two papers to the female students at Cambridge University, which then became the long essay, *A Room of One's Own*.

A Women need independence to become writers and artists, claims Woolf. They need freedom and time. She starts this passage with a quotation from Sir Arthur Quiller-Couch (1863–1944).

'The poor poet has not in these days, nor has had for two hundred years, a dog's chance . . . a poor child in England has little more hope than had the son of an Athenian slave to be emancipated into that intellectual freedom of which great writings are born.' That is it. Intellectual freedom depends upon material things. Poetry depends upon intellectual freedom. And women have always been poor, not for two hundred years merely, but from the beginning of time. Women have had less intellectual freedom than the sons of Athenian slaves. Women, then, have not had a dog's chance of writing poetry. That is why I have laid so much stress on money and a room of one's own. However, thanks to the toils of those obscure women in the past, of whom I wish we knew more, thanks, curiously enough to two wars, the Crimean which let Florence Nightingale out of her drawing-room,

Source: Virginia Woolf, *A Room of One's Own*. London: Grafton, 1977, pp. 116–117, 119, 52–55.

and the European War which opened the doors to the average woman some sixty years later, these evils are in the way to be bettered. Otherwise you would not be here tonight . . . .

. . . [W]hen I ask you to earn money and have a room of your own, I am asking you to live in the presence of reality, an invigorating life, it would appear, whether one can impart it or not.

B Woolf, in a famous passage, imagines what would have happened to a sister of William Shakespeare.

I could not help thinking, as I looked at the works of Shakespeare on the shelf, that . . . it would have been impossible, completely and entirely, for any woman to have written the plays of Shakespeare in the age of Shakespeare. Let me imagine, since facts are so hard to come by, what would have happened had Shakespeare had a wonderfully gifted sister, called Judith, let us say. Shakespeare himself went, very probably, — his mother was an heiress — to the grammar school, where he may have learnt Latin — Ovid, Virgil and Horace — and the elements of grammar and logic. He was, it is well known, a wild boy who poached rabbits, perhaps shot a deer, and had, rather sooner than he should have done, to marry a woman in the neighbourhood, who bore him a child rather quicker than was right. That escapade sent him to seek his fortune in London. He had, it seemed, a taste for the theatre; he began by holding horses at the stage door. Very soon he got work in the theatre, became a successful actor, and lived at the hub of the universe, meeting everybody, knowing everybody, practising his art on the boards, exercising his wits in the streets, and even getting access to the palace of the queen. Meanwhile his extraordinarily gifted sister, let us suppose, remained at home. She was as adventurous, as imaginative, as agog to see the world as he was. But she was not sent to school. She had no chance of learning grammar and logic, let alone of reading Horace and Virgil. She picked up a book now and then, one of her brother's perhaps, and read a few pages. But then her parents came in and told her to mend the stockings or mind the stew and not moon about with books and papers. They would have spoken sharply but kindly, for they were substantial people who knew the conditions of life for a woman and loved their daughter — indeed, more likely than not she was the apple of her father's eye. Perhaps she scribbled some pages up in an apple loft on the sly, but was careful to hide them or set fire to them. Soon, however, before she was out of her teens, she was to be betrothed to the son of a neighbouring wool-stapler. She cried out that marriage was hateful to her, and for that she was severely beaten by her father. Then he ceased to scold her. He begged her instead not to hurt him, not to shame him in this matter of her marriage. He would give her a chain of beads or a fine petticoat, he said; and there were tears in his eyes. How could she disobey him? How could she break his heart?

The force of her own gift alone drove her to it. She made up a small parcel of her belongings, let herself down by a rope one summer's night and took the road to London. She was not seventeen. The birds that sang in the hedge were not more musical than she was. She had the quickest fancy, a gift like her brother's, for the tune of words. Like him, she had a taste for the theatre. She stood at the stage door; she wanted to act, she said. Men laughed in her face. The manager — a fat, loose-lipped man — guffawed. He bellowed something about poodles dancing and women acting — no woman, he said, could possibly be an actress. He hinted — you can imagine what. She could get no training in her craft. Could she even seek her dinner in a tavern or roam the streets at midnight? Yet her genius was for fiction and lusted to feed abundantly upon the lives of men and women and the study of their ways. At last — for she was very young, oddly like Shakespeare the poet in her face, with the same grey eyes and rounded brows — at last Nick Greene the actor-manager took pity on her; she found herself with child by that gentleman and so — who shall measure the heat and violence of the poet's heart when caught and tangled in a woman's body? — killed herself one winter's night and lies buried at some cross-roads where the omnibuses now stop . . . .

That, more or less, is how the story would run, I think, if a woman in Shakespeare's day had had Shakespeare's genius. . . . [I]t is unthinkable that any woman in Shakespeare's day should have had Shakespeare's genius. For genius like Shakespeare's is not born among labouring, uneducated, servile people. It was not born in England among the Saxons and the Britons. It is not born to-day among the working classes. How, then, could it have been born among women whose work began . . . almost before they were out of the nursery, who were forced to it by their parents and held to it by all the power of law and custom? Yet genius of a sort must have existed among women as it must have existed among the working classes. Now and again an Emily Brontë or a Robert Burns blazes out and proves its presence. But certainly it never got itself on to paper. When, however, one reads of a witch being ducked, of a woman possessed by devils, of a wise woman selling herbs, or even of a very remarkable man who had a mother, then I think we are on the track of a lost novelist, a suppressed poet, of some mute and inglorious Jane Austen, some Emily Brontë who dashed her brains out on the moor or mopped and mowed about the highways crazed with the torture that her gift had put her to. Indeed, I would venture to guess that Anon, who wrote so many poems without signing them, was often a woman. It was a woman Edward Fitzgerald, I think, suggested who made the ballads and the folk-songs, crooning them to her children, beguiling her spinning with them, or the length of the winter's night.

This may be true or it may be false — who can say? — but what is true in it, so it seemed to me, reviewing the story of Shakespeare's sister as I had made it, is that any woman born with a great gift in the sixteenth century would certainly have gone crazed, shot herself, or ended her days in some lonely cottage outside the village, half witch, half wizard, feared and mocked at.

1. According to Woolf, why is it impossible to imagine a woman having written the plays of Shakespeare during the age of Shakespeare?

2. What is the importance of a "room of one's own"?

3. Would Betty Friedan (see pages 289–291) compliment Woolf for her insights into the oppression faced by women or criticize her for not being more extreme in promoting women's rights? Examine Friedan's selection and provide supporting quotations or ideas.

The Young Turks

The Young Turks were a group of officers in the Ottoman armed forces who sought to reform the Empire along Western lines as well as to give it a more Turkish nationalist orientation. In July 1908, a military revolt forced Sultan Abdulhammid II to institute a constitutional government. The goals of the Young Turks were set out in their 1908 proclamation.

well some of them

specifically turkish people

1. The basis for the Constitution will be respect for the predominance of the national will. One of the consequences of this principle will be to require without delay the responsibility of the minister before the Chamber, and, consequently, to consider the minister as having resigned, when he does not have a majority of the votes of the Chamber.

2. Provided that the number of senators does not exceed one-third the number of deputies, the Senate will be named as follows: one-third by the Sultan and two-thirds by the nation, and the term of senators will be of limited duration. *→ still constitutional monarchy*

3. It will be demanded that all Ottoman subjects having completed their twentieth year, regardless of whether they possess property or fortune, shall have the right to vote. Those who have lost their civil rights will naturally be deprived of this right.

indv. rights

4. It will be demanded that the right freely to constitute political groups be inserted in a precise fashion in the constitutional charter . . . .

7. The Turkish tongue will remain the official state language. Official correspondence and discussion will take place in Turkish.

growth of turkish nationalism

9. Every citizen will enjoy complete liberty and equality, regardless of nationality or religion, and be submitted to the same obligations. All Ottomans, being equal before the law as regards rights and duties relative to the State, are eligible for government posts, according to their *nationalist* "duties"

Source: "The Young Turks: Proclamation for the Ottoman Empire, 1908." www.fordham.edu/halsall/mod/1908youngturk.html (Dec. 21, 2002)

→ but not protected under it.

individual capacity and their education. Non-Muslims will be equally liable to the military law.   *→ will it be?*

10. The free exercise of the religious privileges which have been accorded to different nationalities will remain intact.

11. The reorganization and distribution of the State forces, on land as well as on sea, will be undertaken in accordance with the political and geographical situation of the country, taking into account the integrity of the other European powers.

14. Provided that the property rights of landholders are not infringed upon (for such rights must be respected and must remain intact, according to law), it will be proposed that peasants be permitted to acquire land, and they will be accorded means to borrow money at a moderate rate.   *attempt to elevate social classes*

16. Education will be free. Every Ottoman citizen, within the limits of the prescriptions of the Constitution, may operate a private school in accordance with the special laws.

17. All schools will operate under the surveillance of the state. In order to obtain for Ottoman citizens an education of a homogenous and uniform character, the official schools will be open, their instruction will be free, and all nationalities will be admitted. Instruction in Turkish will be obligatory in public schools. In official schools, public instruction will be free. Secondary and higher education will be given in the public and official schools indicated above; it will use the Turkish tongue. Schools of commerce, agriculture, and industry will be opened with the goal of developing the resources of the country.

18. Steps shall also be taken for the formation of roads and railways and canals to increase the facilities of communication and increase the sources of the wealth of the country. Everything that can impede commerce or agriculture shall be abolished.   *helpful for economic growth + industrialism*

1. Locate examples in this proclamation that indicate socialist and liberal political influences.

2. How does this proclamation compare to the laws of Sulayman the Magnificent?

3. Why would this proclamation be viewed as a threat to the Sultan?

4. Describe the Young Turks' vision of Turkey.

Western Policy Toward the Muslim World

Western policy toward the Muslim world during and after World War I exhibited a fear of potential Islamic solidarity as a device of anti-colonial resistance in the Middle East and South Asia. Many possible actions were reflected upon. One, advocated by Sir Arthur Hirtzel, a British diplomat, was to militarily crush the Ottoman state in the war so that British colonial rule in Asia and Africa could be sustained. Another, articulated by the Italian Count Carlo Sforza (1873–1952), was to recognize that victory over the Muslim people by force was ill-conceived; it could not work, and it would not create stability in the area.

A Hirtzel's memo was written on May 25, 1916, in the midst of World War I.

> The pan-Islamic danger is a real and permanent one. All the parties to the present war have to face it, except Germany. We cannot get rid of it altogether. But we have the opportunity now (if, in conjunction with Russia, we press the war to its natural conclusion) of immensely diminishing it by reducing to impotence the only existing organised Government that can further the pan-Islamic idea; and when we see the progress which that idea has made in India, under Turkish influence, in the last 10 years, does not common prudence require that we should do so? To leave a Moslem State that will count among the Governments of the world is simply to create a focus of which Germany (who will have nothing to lose) will fan the flame when it suits her — and we, in India and Africa, shall be the principal sufferers.
>
> These considerations seem to point to this conclusion: For Great Britain the war with Turkey can never be a side issue. It is, of course, obvious that by defeating Turkey we have not defeated Germany, whereas if we succeed in defeating Germany, the collapse of Turkey's military power follows automatically. What is less obvious is why this will not suffice for our purpose. Great Britain is an Asiatic and a Moslem power, and what makes the war with Turkey rather a separate war than a mere episode in a world war, is the fact that we are waging it against another Moslem Power with the rest of the Moslem world for spectators. . . . With all these people we shall have to deal after the war, and to live with them on terms of moral supremacy. We shall have to govern India itself — where, besides the Moslem problem, the fact has to be reckoned with that the educated Hindus, though they have thrown in their lot with us, are not averse to seeing British pride humbled, and humbled by an Asiatic Power — and to convince the peoples of India that a handful of white men can still control them, a task which will not have been rendered easier by indiscriminate eulogy of the exploits of the Indian troops in France. In the regions adjoining India, where for a variety of reasons the military prestige of Great Britain had suffered serious eclipse in the 10 years preceding the war, we shall have to rehabilitate it. To restore order on the frontier and maintain tolerable relations with Afghanistan; to conduct the business of everyday life in Persia; to keep order in the Gulf and control those Arab chiefs with whom we already have relations, and to

Sources: C. J. Lowe and M. L. Dockrill, *The Mirage of Power: British Foreign Policy 1902–22*, volume three: the documents. London: Routledge & Kegan Paul, 1972, pp. 536–537; Count Carlo Sforza, *Diplomatic Europe Since the Treaty of Versailles*. New Haven: Yale University Press, 1928, pp. 52–53.

whose number the very important Amir of Nejd has recently been added; and finally, if it should so turn out, to develop the resources of Mesopotamia: in all of which regions the Islamic self-consciousness will have been intensified. The Arabian policy of His Majesty's Government, so far from diminishing the difficulty of these tasks, will add to it, unless Turkey has been decisively defeated — and defeated by us, not merely by Russians or French. For while the Arabs are content to use us now for their own ends, it is certain that if and when those ends are attained their attitude will always be less antagonistic towards the Moslem Turk, whatever their grievances against him in the past, than towards the Christian; and if the former is believed to be the better soldier they will play him off against us to their heart's content. Indeed, the policy of fanning the Arab nationalist spirit to a flame is . . . a two-edged weapon of a very dangerous description — innocuous only if the Turk is beaten in the field, but otherwise likely eventually to result in acute antagonism between the Arabs and ourselves.

B Sforza, in 1928, reflected upon developments and believed in a different policy from that of the British.

Some days after the armistice, England, France, and Italy decided to entrust the guarding of their interests in Turkey to three High Commissioners. The Englishman was Admiral Calthorpe . . . the French, Admiral Amet . . . the Italian, myself.

In reality, at that moment of the apparent destruction of all Turkish authority, and pending the negotiations of the Big Four in Paris, our task was rather that of governors. We had at our orders the squadrons in the Bosphorus and the military contingents on shore. We organized an administration, a guardianship of order, and the revival of the Allies' banking, educational, religious, and other institutions which had been destroyed or closed during the years of war. The three High Commissioners held their meetings once a week in their respective embassies by turns, each time under the presidency of the master of the house. The Serbian, Greek, Rumanian, and other representatives, following each other to Constantinople, presented themselves before us as before a Supreme Local Council and our administration was carried on without too much national rivalry; our harmony and loyalty were constant. At first my two colleagues were inclined to think that I was too lenient in my dealings with the Turks; that I showed, perhaps, a little too much regard for the conquered Sultan; that, personally, I was too cordial toward the former grand viziers and other personages of the Empire, who little by little came out of their hiding places; that I did not sufficiently ignore the Sublime Porte. I am sure that during the first weeks of that winter (1918–1919) the two admirals, in the bottom of their hearts, must have put down this weakness of mine to my unfortunate quality of civilian. But they were men full of good sense. Little by little they felt that I was guided by very serious reasons: the conviction that Turkey was far from dead, that she was only temporarily down and that, if we pulled the rope too tight, she would escape from our hands; we might remain masters of Constantinople, but we should be masters of a wonderful empty house; the active forces of Turkey would retire deeper into Asia, out of our reach, and that, once there, they would turn against us.

1. Why does Hirtzel feel it is essential to defeat Turkey?
2. What warning does Hirtzel issue regarding the exploitation of Islamic nationalism as a tool against the Turks?
3. Why does Sforza believe that Turkey will never be completely defeated?
4. What potential problems do these selections present concerning the relationship between the Islamic and European cultures?

Peng Pai

In the 1920s, Peng Pai (1896–1929), a Chinese communist leader, was a pioneer in organizing peasant associations to fight for their rights against the exploitative land-lords (who habitually charged half the harvest as rent) and the warlords (generals with private armies) who divided up China after the fall of the imperial dynasty. Peng came from a wealthy landlord family, and had studied in Japan, where he converted to communism. This excerpt recalls his experience of learning to communicate with and to organize the peasants after he returned to his home district of Hai-feng on the south coast of China. After some initial fumbling he had a good deal of success from 1921 to 1923. He was later chased out of Hai-feng by the local warlord.

A Peng discusses the beginnings of the peasant movement.

In May, 1921, I was the Head of the Education Bureau of Hai-feng county. Still dreaming of realizing social revolution through education, I called for all the students in the county, most of whom were children of the wealthy, to celebrate the "May First" Labor Day at the county seat. That was an event unprecedented in the history of Hai-feng. Not one single worker or peasant participated in the celebration. The pupils of the First Elementary School paraded the streets, holding red banners with "Join the Reds" [communists] written on them. It was truly childish. The gentry class of Hai-feng thought that we were now going to practice property-sharing and wife-sharing, and they started numerous rumors, attacking us before [the Governor] Ch'en Chiung-ming. As a result, I was discharged from my duties, and, one after another, all the progressive teachers and school principals I had appointed also lost their positions.

Source: Patricia Ebrey, *Chinese Civilization: A Sourcebook*, 2nd ed. New York: Free Press, 1993, pp. 269–270, 271, 272, 273, 274, 275, 276.

At that time we were fighting a confusing battle with Ch'en Chiung-ming's hometown paper, the *Lu An Daily*. Along with . . . others I published a few issues of *Red Heart Weekly* as the mouthpiece of the workers and peasants. In fact, not a single worker on the streets or peasant on the farm was behind our journal or even had a hint of what we were doing. One day when I returned home, my little sister tried to prevent me from entering the house. She said, "I don't know why, but Mother is crying and says she is going to kill you." First I thought she was joking, but when I went into the family hall, I saw that indeed my mother was weeping.

It turned out my seventh younger brother had gotten hold of a "Letter to Peasants" which we published in the *Red Heart Weekly* and read the essay aloud. When my mother happened to hear it, tears flowed down her cheeks. Finally she burst out into loud wails, crying, "Our ancestors must have failed to accumulate virtue, for here we have a prodigal son. Your grandfather worked hard for what we have to-day. If you carry on like this, our family will certainly be ruined!" I tried my best to console her, and she finally calmed down.

At that time it occurred to me that if the peasants could read this essay, they would be very happy, perhaps as happy as my wailing mother was upset. Besides, I was confident that peasants could be organized. Consequently, I abandoned the senseless war of words with the *Lu An Daily* and took up practical action in the farm villages. At the time, all my local friends were against it. They said, "Peasants are extremely disorderly. You won't be able to organize them. Plus, they are ignorant and resistant to campaigns of any kind. You'll just be wasting your energy."

My family could be considered a large landowner. Every year we would collect about 1000 piculs [60 kg] of grain and had over 1500 peasants under our control. Since my family had less than thirty members altogether, each member had fifty peasants as slaves. Consequently, when they heard that I wanted to start a peasant movement, my relatives all hated me with a passion (except for my third elder brother and fifth younger brother). My oldest brother would have liked to kill me, as would all the others in our lineage and village. The only thing I could do was ignore them.

On a certain day in May, I started my own campaign for the peasant movement. The first place I went to was a village in Red Mountain. I was dressed in a white Western-style student suit and wore a white hat. A peasant about thirty years of age was mixing manure in front of the village. When he saw me coming, he said, "Sir, how are you? Are you here to collect taxes? We are not putting on a play here."

"No, I'm not here to collect taxes for plays," I replied. "I'm here to be your friend. I know you have hardships, and I would like to talk with you."

To which the peasant said, "Yup, hardships are our destiny. So long now. We don't have the leisure to talk with you. Excuse me." And he hurried away. . . .

That evening, two things suddenly occurred to me. First, my language was too formal and refined; much of it was lost on the peasants. I would have to translate the jargon into everyday language. Second, my appearance, physique, and clothing were all different from the peasants'. They had long been oppressed and cheated by those who looked different, and naturally suspected that I was an enemy. Also, my appearance indicated my class, and thereby alienated the peasants. I decided, therefore, to wear simpler things. I also came up with a new plan. The next day, instead of going to the villages, I would go to the crossroads where I would meet more peasants.

The next day, I went to a main road in front of Lung-shan Temple. This road was the principal artery for traffic . . . . Every day, countless peasants passed by and rested in front of the Temple. I took this opportunity to talk to them, explaining the reasons for their hardships and the remedies, pointing out to them the evidence of landlords' oppression and discussing the necessity for the peasants to unite. At first I was talking to only a few people, but as the listeners increased, I began giving speeches. The peasants were, however, only half credulous. On that day, four or five peasants actually talked to me, and a dozen or more listened. It was a great achievement.

B Peng decides to organize as a way of uniting the peasant population.

After that day, I spent two weeks at intersections, talking to the peasants who passed by or giving speeches. Those who talked to me increased to a dozen or so, and my audience now consisted of thirty or forty, a major step forward. One day, as I walked into town, I noticed something rather peculiar about how people in the stores looked at me. Then, many relatives started to come to see me, bringing food with them, and asking about my "illness." I was really puzzled. Later, a servant told me, "You'd better just stay home and rest from now on." I asked him why, and he replied, "The people out there all say you've gone mad. You ought to rest and take care of yourself." I almost died of laughter. I later discovered that it was a rumor started by the gentry, but many peasants in the villages also believed that I was insane. They seemed to be afraid of me and tried to avoid me. Nevertheless, I continued my campaign in front of Lung-shan Temple. . . .

"Let's start a Peasants' Union now," suggested Li Lao-ssu. "If more people join us, that's great; but even if no one joins, we'll keep it going. How does that sound?"

"Great idea," I said. "Tomorrow I'll go with two of you to the villages, and at night we'll make a public speech." They all thought that was a good plan, and it was decided that Chang Ma-an and Lin P'ei should go with me the next morning.

We continued our discussion for a long time. After the meeting, I wrote "Victory is in sight."

The next morning, after breakfast, my peasant friends Chang and Lin came to get me, and we went to the villages around Red Mountain. Because of their introduction, the villagers felt close to me and talked to me sincerely.

I asked them to come to the lecture that night, and they responded enthusiastically. When evening came, they had tables, chairs, and lights all prepared for me. I had an audience of sixty to seventy. Children were in front, men behind them, and women in the rear. I talked about the causes of the hardships peasants endured, the facts of landlords' exploitation, and the ways to peasants' liberation. I used the question-and-answer format, and the peasants approved of what I said. I also came to know that they could understand me. I concluded my speech by saying that the next time I would play a phonograph and give a magic show. I promised to let them know in advance. . . .

. . . News got around, and many peasants learned that the brothers of the Union were loyal to each other and were able to help each other. We also used . . . propaganda: "We have no power if we are not united. We will be taken advantage of if we have no power. To have power, join the Peasants' Union immediately." And membership gradually increased.

Not long afterwards, we found that some peasants would try to get others' land to till, and landlords would increase rent and change tenants. So the Union drew up some regulations to prevent such incidents. Briefly, these regulations were:

1. Unless permission is given by the member and by the Union, no one may encroach on a member's rented land.

2. Unless the member relinquishes his lease and the Union gives its permission, no one may rent the land already rented to a member of the Union. Violators are subject to severe punishment.

3. In case a landlord takes back his land from a member by means of increasing the rent, and as a result a member's livelihood is in danger, he may ask for help from the Union, which will either persuade nearby members to allow him to till part of their land, or will introduce him to another trade.

After the regulations were publicized, there was no longer any competition for land among our members, and the landlords also were afraid to raise the rent of members of the Union. At times, non-members would fight for the land already rented by our members, but under the advice of the Union's representatives, they would usually quickly return the land to the members. Once, a landlord became annoyed and refused to lease his land to the original tenant (i.e., a member of our Union). We then announced a boycott, and the landlord, fearing that his land would lie fallow, was forced to lease the land back to the member. This was another victory for us.

C The Hai-feng Central Union comes into being.

The procedure for joining the Union was as follows. The applicant had to appear in person at the Union Headquarters and pay a membership fee of twenty cents.... Then they would receive a briefing and a membership card ....

A "Funeral Expenses Co-op" was formed by the Union. Any member of the Union could join the co-op, and we reached a total of around 150 members. The rule was that for any member who died or who lost a parent, every other member would donate two cents for funeral expenses....

A medical dispensary was also established. It was located on the main street of Hai-feng. The doctor in charge was an enthusiast of the Peasants' Movement and a trained Western-style physician. Any member of the Peasants' Union who needed medicine could present his membership card and get a 50 percent discount. Non-members could also get medicine, but at the full price. All members were entitled to the free clinic operated by the doctor, whose wife also delivered babies for no charge....

On the first day of January, 1923, the Hai-feng Central Union was established. The total membership had reached 20,000. And the population within the Union's jurisdiction was 100,000, a quarter of the population of the entire county....

At this time the Hai-feng Central Union reached its peak of activities. The county Magistrate of the time, Weng Kuai-ch'ing, who was Ch'en Chiung-ming's most trusted man, disapproved of the Union, but he dared not ban it, and we were allowed more freedom to develop our programs. Also, the Union had by now acquired considerable power. The slogans we used for the peasants were:

1. Reduce rent.
2. Abolish the "three lease rules."
3. Abolish presents to landlords (chickens, ducks, rice, or money).
4. Don't give bribes to the police.

The slogans we used for outsiders were:

1. Improve agriculture.
2. Increase peasants' knowledge.
3. Perform charitable deeds....

Soon it was the Chinese New Year of 1923. Dragon dancers and music troupes from all the villages came to celebrate, and the Union organized a New Year's Festival for all peasants in Hai-feng....

On that day, we issued 2000 new membership cards, and received over 400 dollars in dues. It was the highest point in the history of the Union. After that, around 100 new members would join each day, and we could hardly keep up with the work. Every day about 300 peasant friends would come to the Union for information, for conversation, and to sign up as members. We were extremely busy.

But we also caught the attention of the landlords, who said, "We didn't think they would succeed. We thought all that talk was nonsense. But now, it actually has happened!"

1. What misconceptions did some Chinese have of communist theory?

2. Why was it a mistake for Peng to approach the peasants in a Western suit?

3. How does Peng adapt his pronouncements and actions in order to gain peasant support?

4. How does Peng take communist ideals and put them into practice?

Aimé Césaire

Born in the French Caribbean colony of Martinique, Aimé Césaire (1913–   ) went to study in Paris in 1931 and remained there until 1939. In Paris he encountered black students and writers from other French colonies, among them the Senegalese Léopold Senghor (1906–2001). Out of this encounter came the influential cultural concept of Negritude (Blackness). After 1939, Césaire lived in Martinique, where he was a leading political and cultural figure.

 In a 1967 interview with the Haitian writer René Depestre (1926–   ), Césaire looked back on the creation of the Negritude movement and how it was only in Europe that people of African descent were able to develop an African consciousness.

It was simply that in Paris at that time there were a few dozen Negroes of diverse origins. There were Africans, like Senghor, Guianans, Haitians, North Americans, Antilleans, etc. . . . We had come from different parts of the world. It was our first meeting. We were discovering ourselves. This was very important. . . . [The concept of Negritude] was somewhat of a collective creation. I used the term first, that's true. But it's possible we talked about it in our group. It was really a resistance to the politics of assimilation. Until that time, until my generation . . . [the French] had followed the politics of assimilation unrestrainedly. We didn't know what Africa was. Europeans despised everything about Africa, and in France people spoke of a civilized world and a barbarian world. The barbarian world was Africa, and the civilized world was Europe. Therefore the best thing one could do with an African was to assimilate him: the ideal was to turn him into a Frenchman with black skin. . . .

. . . Our struggle was a struggle against alienation. That struggle gave birth to Negritude. Because Antilleans were ashamed of being Negroes, they

Sources: Aimé Césaire, *Discourse on Colonialism*, trans. Joan Pinkham. New York: Monthly Review Press, 2000, pp. 88–92; Aimé Césaire, *Return To My Native Land*. Paris: Présence Africaine, 1968, pp. 47–49, 81–83.

searched for all sorts of euphemisms for Negro: they would say a man of color, a dark-complexioned man, and other idiocies like that. That's when we adopted the word *nègre*, as a term of defiance. It was a defiant name. To some extent it was a reaction of enraged youth. Since there was shame about the word *nègre*, we chose the word *nègre*. . . .

I would like to say that everyone has his own Negritude. . . . But if someone asks me what my conception of Negritude is, I answer that above all it is a concrete rather than an abstract coming to consciousness. What I have been telling you about — the atmosphere in which we lived, an atmosphere of assimilation in which Negro people were ashamed of themselves — has great importance. We lived in an atmosphere of rejection, and we developed an inferiority complex. I have always thought that the black man was searching for his identity. And it has seemed to me that if what we want is to establish this identity, then we must have a concrete consciousness of what we are — that is, of the first fact of our lives: that we are black; that we were black and have a history, a history that contains certain cultural elements of great value . . . . At the time we began to write, people could write a history of world civilization without devoting a single chapter to Africa, as if Africa had made no contributions to the world.

B Césaire states that African achievement is not limited to the past. Africans still have a contribution to make to world civilization; their values are also universal ones.

Therefore we affirmed that we were Negroes and that we were proud of it, and that we thought that Africa was not some sort of blank page in the history of humanity; in sum, we asserted that our Negro heritage was worthy of respect, and that this heritage was not relegated to the past, that its values were values that could still make an important contribution to the world.

Universalizing, living values that had not been exhausted. The field was not dried up: it could still bear fruit if we made the effort to irrigate it with our sweat and plant new seeds. So this was the situation: there were things to tell the world. We were not dazzled by European civilization. We bore the imprint of European civilization but we thought that Africa could make a contribution to Europe. It was also an affirmation of our solidarity. That's the way it was: I have always recognized that what was happening to my brothers in Algeria and the United States had its repercussions in me. I understood that I could not be indifferent to what was happening in Haiti or Africa. Then, in a way, we slowly came to the idea of a sort of black civilization spread throughout the world. And I have come to the realization that there was a "Negro situation" that existed in different geographical areas, that Africa was also my country. There was the African continent, the Antilles, Haiti; there were Martinicans and Brazilian Negroes, etc. That's what Negritude meant to me.

C In 1939, Césaire published his book-length poem, *Return To My Native Land*. This was the first creative writing from the African Caribbean to achieve international acclaim. The following excerpt describes the creation of the African diaspora (the dispersion of African peoples around the globe).

> Mine, these few thousand death-bearers who circle in the gourd of
> an isle, and mine, too, the archipelago bent like the anxious desire
> for self-negation as if with maternal concern for the most frail
> slenderness separating the two Americas; and the womb which spills
> towards Europe the good liquor of the Gulf Streams, and one of the
> two incandescent slopes between which the Equator funambulates
> towards Africa. And my unfenced island, its bold flesh upright at
> the stern of this Polynesia; and right before it, Guadeloupe slit in
> two at the dorsal line, and quite as miserable as ourselves; Haiti,
> where Negritude stood up for the first time and swore by its
> humanity; and the droll little tail of Florida where a Negro is being
> lynched, and Africa caterpillaring gigantically up to the Spanish foot
> of Europe, its nakedness where death cuts a wide swath.
>
> And I told myself of Bordeaux and Nantes and Liverpool and
> New York and San Francisco, not a bit of this earth not smudged
> by my fingerprint,
>
> and my calcaneum dug into the backs of the skyscrapers
> and my dirt in the glory of jewels!
>
> Who can boast of having more than I?
> Virginia. Tennessee. Georgia. Alabama.
> Monstrous putrefaction of ineffective revolts,
>
> swamps of rotten blood
> trumpets absurdly stoppered
> red, blood-red lands of one blood
> . . . .
>
> And this country cried for centuries that we were stupid brutes;
> that the pulsations of humanity stopped before the doors of the
> slave compound; that we are a walking dunghill, hideously promising
> sweet sugar-canes and silky cotton, and they branded us with red-hot
> irons and we slept in our excrement and they sold us on the market
> for less than an ell of English cloth and the salted meat from Ireland
> was cheaper than we, and this country was calm, tranquil, and was
> convinced that it acted in accordance with the will of God.
>
> We the vomit of slavers
> we the venery of the Calebars
> what ? that we should stuff our ears ?
> We, made dead drunk with the ship's rolling,

with jeers, with the sea-fog inhaled !
Forgive us, whirlpool our accomplice !

1. What forms the basis for the concept of Negritude?

2. How did Negritude become a global concept not restricted to a geographical base?

3. What long-term impact did the African diaspora have on Blacks throughout the world?

Anne Frank

Anne Frank (1929–1945) was a Jewish girl born in Germany. Her family left the country in 1933, after the Nazis came to power, and settled in Amsterdam, Holland. Germany invaded Holland in 1940 and then occupied the country throughout World War II. During the occupation, the Germans began a systematic persecution of Jews in Holland: first there were anti-Jewish decrees; then in 1942, Jews were being shipped to camps in Germany. The Frank family went into hiding during this time, helped by business associates. Frank and her family were confined for two years to rooms at the top and back of a warehouse until, on August 4, 1944, their hiding place was discovered. While in hiding, Frank, aged thirteen to fifteen, kept a diary that recorded her life, feelings, and growth. It has become a testament to the ability of the human spirit to survive and even flourish in the midst of hatred, persecution, and an enforced solitary life. Frank was sent to Auschwitz in 1944 by the Nazis and then to Bergen-Belsen, where she died in March 1945.

 In 1942 and 1943, Frank recorded what she learned about the fate of fellow Jews.

> I've only got dismal and depressing news for you today. Our many Jewish friends are being taken away by the dozen. These people are treated by the Gestapo without a shred of decency, being loaded into cattle trucks and sent to Westerbork, the big Jewish camp in Drente. Westerbork sounds terrible: only one washing cubicle for a hundred people and not nearly enough lavatories. There are no separate accommodations. Men, women, and children all sleep together. One hears of frightful immorality because of this: and a lot of the women, and even girls, who stay there any length of time are expecting babies.
>
> It is impossible to escape; most of the people in the camp are branded as inmates by their shaven heads and many also by their Jewish appearance.
>
> If it is as bad as this in Holland whatever will it be like in the distant and barbarous regions they are sent to? We assume that most of them are murdered. The English radio speaks of their being gassed.
>
> Perhaps that is the quickest way to die. I feel terribly upset. I couldn't tear myself away while Miep told these dreadful stories; and she herself

Source: Anne Frank, *Anne Frank: The Diary of a Young Girl*, trans. B. M. Mooyaart-Doubleday. New York: Pocket Books, 1953, pp. 34–35, 57, 71, 200–202, 216, 236–237.

was equally wound up for that matter. Just recently for instance, a poor old crippled Jewess was sitting on her doorstep; she had been told to wait there by the Gestapo, who had gone to fetch a car to take her away. The poor old thing was terrified by the guns that were shooting at English planes overhead, and by the glaring beams of the searchlights. But Miep did not dare take her in; no one would undergo such a risk. The Germans strike without the slightest mercy. Elli too is very quiet: her boy friend has got to go to Germany. She is afraid that the airmen who fly over her home will drop their bombs, often weighing a million kilos, on Dirk's head. Jokes such as "he's not likely to get a million" and "it only takes one bomb" are in rather bad taste. Dirk is certainly not the only one who has to go: train-loads of boys leave daily. If they stop at a small station en route, sometimes some of them manage to get out unnoticed and escape; perhaps a few manage it. This, however, is not the end of my bad news. Have you ever heard of hostages? That's the latest thing in penalties for sabotage. Can you imagine anything so dreadful?

Prominent citizens, innocent people — are thrown into prison to await their fate. . . .

Everything has upset me again this morning, so I wasn't able to fin-ish a single thing properly.

It is terrible outside. Day and night more of those poor miserable people are being dragged off, with nothing but a rucksack and a little money. On the way they are deprived even of these possessions. Families are torn apart, the men, women, and children all being separated. Children coming home from school find that their parents have disappeared. Women return from shopping to find their homes shut up and their families gone.

The Dutch people are anxious too, their sons are being sent to Germany. Everyone is afraid.

And every night hundreds of planes fly over Holland and go to German towns, where the earth is so plowed up by their bombs, and every hour hundreds and thousands of people are killed in Russia and Africa. No one is able to keep out of it, the whole globe is waging war and although it is going better for the Allies, the end is not yet in sight.

And as for us, we are fortunate. Yes, we are luckier than millions of people. It is quiet and safe here, and we are, so to speak, living on capital. We are even so selfish as to talk about "after the war," brighten up at the thought of having new clothes and new shoes, whereas we really ought to save every penny, to help other people, and save what is left from the wreckage after the war. . . .

If I just think of how we live here, I usually come to the conclusion that it is a paradise compared with how other Jews who are not in hiding must be living. Even so, later on, when everything is normal again, I shall be amazed to think that we, who were so spick and span at home, should have sunk to such a low level.

B In May 1944, Frank wrote of her growing sense of self.

> As you can easily imagine we often ask ourselves here despairingly: "What, oh, what is the use of the war? Why can't people live peacefully together? Why all this destruction?"
>
> The question is very understandable, but no one has found a satisfactory answer to it so far. Yes, why do they make still more gigantic planes, still heavier bombs and, at the same time, prefabricated houses for reconstruction? Why should millions be spent daily on the war and yet there's not a penny available for medical services, artists, or for poor people?
>
> Why do some people have to starve, while there are surpluses rotting in other parts of the world? Oh, why are people so crazy?
>
> I don't believe that the big men, the politicians and the capitalists alone, are guilty of the war. Oh no, the little man is just as guilty, otherwise the peoples of the world would have risen in revolt long ago! There's in people simply an urge to destroy, an urge to kill, to murder and rage, and until all mankind, without exception, undergoes a great change, wars will be waged, everything that has been built up, cultivated, and grown will be destroyed and disfigured, after which mankind will have to begin all over again.
>
> I have often been downcast, but never in despair; I regard our hiding as a dangerous adventure, romantic and interesting at the same time. In my diary I treat all the privations as amusing. I have made up my mind now to lead a different life from other girls and, later on, different from ordinary housewives. My start has been so very full of interest, and that is the sole reason why I have to laugh at the humorous side of the most dangerous moments.
>
> I am young and I possess many buried qualities; I am young and strong and am living a great adventure; I am still in the midst of it and can't grumble the whole day long. I have been given a lot, a happy nature, a great deal of cheerfulness and strength. Every day I feel that I am developing inwardly, that the liberation is drawing nearer and how beautiful nature is, how good the people are about me, how interesting this adventure is! Why, then, should I be in despair?

C Frank is determined to keep her sense of life's worth.

> The world has turned topsy-turvy, respectable people are being sent off to concentration camps, prisons, and lonely cells, and the dregs that remain govern young and old, rich and poor. One person walks into the trap through the black market, a second through helping the Jews or other people who've had to go "underground" . . . .
>
> We're going to be hungry, but anything is better than being discovered. . . .
>
> . . . "For in its innermost depths youth is lonelier than old age." I read this saying in some book and I've always remembered it, and found it to be true. Is it true then that grownups have a more difficult time here than

we do? No. I know it isn't. Older people have formed their opinions about everything, and don't waver before they act. It's twice as hard for us young ones to hold our ground, and maintain our opinions, in a time when all ideals are being shattered and destroyed, when people are showing their worst side, and do not know whether to believe in truth and right and God.

Anyone who claims that the older ones have a more difficult time here certainly doesn't realize to what extent our problems weigh down on us, problems for which we are probably much too young, but which thrust themselves upon us continually, until, after a long time, we think we've found a solution, but the solution doesn't seem able to resist the facts which reduce it to nothing again. That's the difficulty in these times: ideals, dreams, and cherished hopes rise within us, only to meet the horrible truth and be shattered.

It's really a wonder that I haven't dropped all my ideals, because they seem so absurd and impossible to carry out. Yet I keep them, because in spite of everything I still believe that people are really good at heart. I simply can't build up my hopes on a foundation consisting of confusion, misery, and death. I see the world gradually being turned into a wilderness, I hear the ever approaching thunder, which will destroy us too, I can feel the sufferings of millions and yet, if I look up into the heavens, I think that it will all come right, that this cruelty too will end, and that peace and tranquillity will return again.

In the meantime, I must uphold my ideals, for perhaps the time will come when I shall be able to carry them out.

1. Describe the reaction Frank and her family might have had upon hearing the news of Jewish persecution.

2. According to Frank, what aspects of human nature cause wars? Do you agree with her assertion? Defend your position.

3. Considering all the literature that has come out of the Holocaust, why is Anne Frank's diary still considered a classic?

Wifredo Lam (1902–1982) was a Cuban artist of mixed Afro-Cuban and Chinese background. He spent the 1920s and 1930s in Madrid and then Paris, where he worked with Pablo Picasso (1881–1973) and other leading figures of Western art. Lam sought to overcome the West's sense of artistic superiority, declaring that "my painting is an act of decolonization." His work also looked forward to the increasing contacts and exchanges among cultures that would characterize the second half of the twentieth century. In this drawing (c. 1943), Lam comments on the connectedness of cultures and the human experience: a woman with European features looks into a mirror to find her gaze returned by an African mask.

Albert Camus

Existentialism, a philosophy with roots in the nineteenth century, became prominent after World War II. For existentialists, human beings have consciousness and will, but there is no absolute truth to which we can cling for certainty. Rather, we live in a world sometimes described as absurd and full of despair, one in which there is no fixed human nature. We are free to act, however, and through our acts we take responsibility for our ethics and our nature. Existentialists believe that humans create their own nature, and through choice we decide about our relationship to others and to an objective, uncaring universe. The reflections of Albert Camus (1913–1960) about the human condition touched many who were seeking some philosophical grounding after the events of the first half of the twentieth century.

A During World War II, Camus wrote his "Letters to a German Friend," reflections on why he believed it necessary to fight in the French resistance against the Nazis. He called it "a document emerging from the struggle against violence."

> For a long time we both thought that this world had no ultimate meaning and that consequently we were cheated. I still think so in a way. But I came to different conclusions from the ones you used to talk about, which for so many years now, you have been trying to introduce into history. I tell myself now that if I had really followed your reasoning, I ought to approve what you are doing. And this is so serious that I must stop and consider it, during this summer night so full of promises for us and of threats for you.
>
> You never believed in the meaning of this world, and you therefore deduced the idea that everything was equivalent and that good and evil could be defined according to one's wishes. You supposed that in the absence of any human or divine code the only values were those of the animal world — in other words, violence and cunning. Hence you concluded that man was negligible and that his soul could be killed, that in the maddest of histories the only pursuit for the individual was the adventure of power and his only morality, the realism of conquests. And, to tell the truth, I, believing I thought as you did, saw no valid argument to answer you except a fierce love of justice which, after all, seemed to me as unreasonable as the most sudden passion.
>
> Where lay the difference? Simply that you readily accepted despair and I never yielded to it. Simply that you saw the injustice of our condition to the point of being willing to add to it, whereas it seemed to me that man must exalt justice in order to fight against injustice, create happiness in order to protest against the universe of unhappiness. Because you turned your despair into intoxication, because you freed yourself from it by making a principle of it, you were willing to destroy man's works and to fight him in

Sources: Albert Camus, *Resistance, Rebellion, and Death*. New York: The Modern Library, 1963, pp. 20–23; Albert Camus, *The Myth of Sisyphus and Other Essays*. New York: Alfred A. Knopf, 1955, pp. 119–123.

order to add to his basic misery. Meanwhile, refusing to accept that despair and that tortured world, I merely wanted men to rediscover their solidarity in order to wage war against their revolting fate.

As you see, from the same principle we derived quite different codes, because along the way you gave up the lucid view and considered it more convenient (you would have said a matter of indifference) for another to do your thinking for you and for millions of Germans. Because you were tired of fighting heaven, you relaxed in that exhausting adventure in which you had to mutilate souls and destroy the world. In short, you chose injustice and sided with the gods. Your logic was merely apparent.

I, on the contrary, chose justice in order to remain faithful to the world. I continue to believe that this world has no ultimate meaning. But I know that something in it has a meaning and that is man, because he is the only creature to insist on having one. This world has at least the truth of man, and our task is to provide its justifications against fate itself. And it has no justification but man; hence he must be saved if we want to save the idea we have of life. With your scornful smile you will ask me: what do you mean by saving man? And with all my being I shout to you that I mean not mutilating him and yet giving a chance to the justice that man alone can conceive.

This is why we are fighting. This is why we first had to follow you on a path we didn't want and why at the end of that path we met defeat. For your despair constituted your strength. The moment despair is alone, pure, sure of itself, pitiless in its consequences, it has a merciless power. That is what crushed us while we were hesitating with our eyes still fixed on happy images. We thought that happiness was the greatest of conquests, a victory over the fate imposed upon us. Even in defeat this longing did not leave us.

But you did what was necessary, and we went down in history. And for five years it was no longer possible to enjoy the call of birds in the cool of the evening. We were forced to despair. We were cut off from the world because to each moment of the world clung a whole mass of mortal images. For five years the earth has not seen a single morning without death agonies, a single evening without prisons, a single noon without slaughters. Yes, we had to follow you. But our difficult achievement consisted in following you into war without forgetting happiness. And despite the clamors and the violence, we tried to preserve in our hearts the memory of a happy sea, of a remembered hill, the smile of a beloved face. For that matter, this was our best weapon, the one we shall never put away. For as soon as we lost it we should be as dead as you are. But we know now that the weapons of happiness cannot be forged without considerable time and too much blood.

We had to enter into your philosophy and be willing to resemble you somewhat. You chose a vague heroism, because it is the only value left in a world that has lost its meaning. And, having chosen it for yourself, you chose it for everybody else and for us. We were forced to imitate you in order not to die. But we became aware then that our superiority over you consisted in our having a direction. Now that all that is about to end, we can tell you what we have learned — that heroism isn't much and that happiness is more difficult.

At present everything must be obvious to you; you know that we are enemies. You are the man of injustice, and there is nothing in the world that my heart loathes so much. But now I know the reasons for what was once merely a passion. I am fighting you because your logic is as criminal as your heart. And in the horror you have lavished upon us for four years, your reason plays as large a part as your instinct. This is why my condemnation will be sweeping; you are already dead as far as I am concerned. But at the very moment when I am judging your horrible behavior, I shall remember that you and we started out from the same solitude, that you and we, with all Europe, are caught in the same tragedy of the intelligence. And, despite yourselves, I shall still apply to you the name of man. In order to keep faith with ourselves, we are obliged to respect in you what you do not respect in others.

B Camus' essay "The Myth of Sisyphus" (1940) was for many a summary of the problems posed by the existentialists. Camus later said: "Although 'The Myth of Sisyphus' poses mortal problems, it sums itself up for me as a lucid invitation to live and to create, in the very midst of the desert."

The gods had condemned Sisyphus to ceaselessly rolling a rock to the top of a mountain, whence the stone would fall back of its own weight. They had thought with some reason that there is no more dreadful punishment than futile and hopeless labor.

If one believes Homer, Sisyphus was the wisest and most prudent of mortals. According to another tradition, however, he was disposed to practice the profession of highwayman. I see no contradiction in this. Opinions differ as to the reasons why he became the futile laborer of the underworld. To begin with, he is accused of a certain levity in regard to the gods. He stole their secrets. . . .

It is said also that Sisyphus, being near to death, rashly wanted to test his wife's love. He ordered her to cast his unburied body into the middle of the public square. Sisyphus woke up in the underworld. And there, annoyed by an obedience so contrary to human love, he obtained from Pluto permission to return to earth in order to chastise his wife. But when he had seen again the face of this world, enjoyed water and sun, warm stones and the sea, he no longer wanted to go back to the infernal darkness. Recalls, signs of anger, warnings were of no avail. Many years more he lived facing the curve of the gulf, the sparkling sea, and the smiles of earth. A decree of the gods was necessary. Mercury came and seized the impudent man by the collar and, snatching him from his joys, led him forcibly back to the underworld, where his rock was ready for him.

You have already grasped that Sisyphus is the absurd hero. He *is*, as much through his passions as through his torture. His scorn of the gods, his hatred of death, and his passion for life won him that unspeakable penalty in which the whole being is exerted toward accomplishing nothing. This is the price that must be paid for the passions of this earth. Nothing is told us about Sisyphus in the underworld. Myths are made for the imagination to breathe life into them. As for this myth, one sees merely the whole effort of a body straining to raise the huge stone, to roll it and push it up a slope a hundred times over; one sees the face screwed up, the cheek tight against the stone, the shoulder bracing the clay-covered mass, the foot wedging it, the fresh start with arms outstretched, the wholly human security of two earth-clotted hands. At the very end of his long effort measured by skyless space and time without depth, the purpose is achieved. Then Sisyphus watches the stone rush down in a few moments toward that lower world whence he will have to push it up again toward the summit. He goes back down to the plain.

It is during that return, that pause, that Sisyphus interests me. A face that toils so close to stones is already stone itself! I see that man going back down with a heavy yet measured step toward the torment of which he will never know the end. That hour like a breathing-space which returns as surely as his suffering, that is the hour of consciousness. At each of those moments when he leaves the heights and gradually sinks toward the lairs of the gods, he is superior to his fate. He is stronger than his rock.

If this myth is tragic, that is because its hero is conscious. . . .

If the descent is thus sometimes performed in sorrow, it can also take place in joy. This word is not too much. . . .

. . . Happiness and the absurd are two sons of the same earth. They are inseparable. . . . "I conclude that all is well," says Œdipus, and that remark is sacred. It echoes in the wild and limited universe of man. It teaches that all is not, has not been, exhausted. It drives out of this world a god who had come into it with dissatisfaction and a preference for futile sufferings. It makes of fate a human matter, which must be settled among men.

All Sisyphus' silent joy is contained therein. His fate belongs to him. His rock is his thing. Likewise, the absurd man, when he contemplates his torment, silences all the idols. . . . The absurd man says yes and his effort will henceforth be unceasing. If there is a personal fate, there is no higher destiny, or at least there is but one which he concludes is inevitable and despicable. For the rest, he knows himself to be the master of his days. At that subtle moment when man glances backward over his life, Sisyphus returning toward his rock, in that slight pivoting he contemplates that series of unrelated actions which becomes his fate, created by him, combined under his memory's eye and soon sealed by his death. Thus, convinced of the wholly human origin of all that is human, a blind man eager to see who knows that the night has no end, he is still on the go. The rock is still rolling.

I leave Sisyphus at the foot of the mountain! One always finds one's burden again. But Sisyphus teaches the higher fidelity that negates the gods and raises rocks. He too concludes that all is well. This universe henceforth without a master seems to him neither sterile nor futile. Each atom of that stone, each mineral flake of that night-filled mountain, in itself forms a world. The struggle itself toward the heights is enough to fill a man's heart. One must imagine Sisyphus happy.

1. How does Camus explain the German victory over France in 1940?

2. How does Camus justify his membership in the French Resistance?

3. How does Sisyphus' never-ending struggle become a quest for happiness?

George Orwell

The novel *1984* by George Orwell (1903–1950), published in 1949, challenged totalitarianism and asked readers to reflect on the nature of freedom and the human condition. In the last two decades of his life, Orwell was a democratic socialist and wrote criticism of all systems, including Fascism and Bolshevism, which limited freedom and supported tyranny.

 1984 has an appendix, "The Principles of Newspeak," in which Orwell makes a penetrating analysis of the role of language in shaping our world and our political understanding. The world of Oceania in 1984 is a dystopia, and seeks complete control over the lives of its inhabitants.

> The purpose of Newspeak was not only to provide a medium of expression for the world view and mental habits proper to the devotees of Ingsoc, but to make all other modes of thought impossible. It was intended that when Newspeak had been adopted once and for all and Oldspeak forgotten, a heretical thought — that is, a thought diverging from the principles of Ingsoc — should be literally unthinkable, at least so far as thought is dependent on words. Its vocabulary was so constructed as to give exact and often very subtle expression to every meaning that a Party member could properly wish to express, while excluding all other meanings and also the possibility of arriving at them by indirect methods. This was done partly by the invention of new words, but chiefly by eliminating undesirable words and by stripping such words as remained of unorthodox meanings, and so far as possible of all secondary meanings whatever. To give a single example. The word *free* still existed in Newspeak, but it could only be used in such statements as 'This dog is free from lice' or 'This field is free from weeds'.

Source: George Orwell, *1984*. Harmondsworth, England: Penguin Books, 1949, pp. 312–319, 322–323, 325.

It could not be used in its old sense of 'politically free' or 'intellectually free', since political and intellectual freedom no longer existed even as concepts, and were therefore of necessity nameless. Quite apart from the suppression of definitely heretical words, reduction of vocabulary was regarded as an end in itself, and no word that could be dispensed with was allowed to survive. Newspeak was designed not to extend but to *diminish* the range of thought, and this purpose was indirectly assisted by cutting the choice of words down to a minimum.

B Three separate vocabularies exist. The A vocabulary is to be used for ordinary life.

The A vocabulary. The A vocabulary consisted of the words needed for the business of everyday life — for such things as eating, drinking, working, putting on one's clothes, going up and down stairs, riding in vehicles, gardening, cooking, and the like. It was composed almost entirely of words that we already possess — words like *hit, run, dog, tree, sugar, house, field* — but in comparison with the present-day English vocabulary their number was extremely small, while their meanings were far more rigidly defined. All ambiguities and shades of meaning had been purged out of them. So far as it could be achieved, a Newspeak word of this class was simply a staccato sound expressing *one* clearly understood concept. It would have been quite impossible to use the A vocabulary for literary purposes or for political or philosophical discussion. It was intended only to express simple, purposive thoughts, usually involving concrete objects or physical actions. . . .

[A]ny word — this again applied in principle to every word in the language — could be negatived by adding the affix *un-*, or could be strengthened by the affix *plus-*, or, for still greater emphasis, *doubleplus-*. Thus, for example, *uncold* meant 'warm', while *pluscold* and *doublepluscold* meant, respectively, 'very cold' and 'superlatively cold'. It was also possible, as in present-day English, to modify the meanings of almost any word by prepositional affixes such as *ante-, post-, up-, down-*, etc. By such methods it was found possible to bring about an enormous diminution of vocabulary. Given, for instance, the word *good*, there was no need for such a word as *bad*, since the required meaning was equally well — indeed, better — expressed by *ungood*. All that was necessary, in any case where two words formed a natural pair of opposites, was to decide which of them to suppress. *Dark*, for example, could be replaced by *unlight*, or *light* by *undark*, according to preference.

C The B vocabulary erases the distinction between language and propaganda. Language is to be used as a form of persuasion and control.

The B vocabulary. The B vocabulary consisted of words which had been deliberately constructed for political purposes: words, that is to say, which not only had in every case a political implication, but were intended to impose a desirable mental attitude upon the person using them. . . .

The B words were in all cases compound words. They consisted of two or more words, or portions of words, welded together in an easily pronounceable form. The resulting amalgam was always a noun-verb, and inflected according to the ordinary rules. To take a single example: the word *goodthink*, meaning, very roughly, 'orthodoxy', or, if one chose to regard it as a verb, 'to think in an orthodox manner'. This inflected as follows: noun-verb, *goodthink*; past tense and past participle, *goodthinked*; present participle, *goodthinking*; adjective, *goodthinkful*; adverb, *goodthinkwise*; verbal noun, *goodthinker.* . . .

. . . But the special function of certain Newspeak words, of which *oldthink* was one, was not so much to express meanings as to destroy them. These words, necessarily few in number, had had their meanings extended until they contained within themselves whole batteries of words which, as they were sufficiently covered by a single comprehensive term, could now be scrapped and forgotten. The greatest difficulty facing the compilers of the Newspeak Dictionary was not to invent new words, but, having invented them, to make sure what they meant: to make sure, that is to say, what ranges of words they cancelled by their existence.

As we have already seen in the case of the word *free*, words which had once borne a heretical meaning were sometimes retained for the sake of convenience, but only with the undesirable meanings purged out of them. Countless other words such as *honour*, *justice*, *morality*, *internationalism*, *democracy*, *science* and *religion* had simply ceased to exist. A few blanket words covered them, and, in covering them, abolished them. All words grouping themselves round the concepts of liberty and equality, for instance, were contained in the single word *crimethink*, while all words grouping themselves round the concepts of objectivity and rationalism were contained in the single word *oldthink*. Greater precision would have been dangerous. . . . In somewhat the same way, the Party member knew what constituted right conduct, and in exceedingly vague, generalised terms he knew what kinds of departure from it were possible. His sexual life, for example, was entirely regulated by the two Newspeak words *sexcrime* (sexual immorality) and *goodsex* (chastity). *Sexcrime* covered all sexual misdeeds whatever. It covered fornication, adultery, homosexuality and other perversions, and, in addition, normal intercourse practised for its own sake. There was no need to enumerate them separately, since they were all equally culpable, and, in principle, all punishable by death. In the C vocabulary, which consisted of scientific and technical words, it might be necessary to give specialised names to certain sexual aberrations, but the ordinary citizen had no need of them. He knew what was meant by *goodsex* — that is to say, normal intercourse between man and wife, for the sole purpose of begetting children, and without physical pleasure on the part of the woman: all else was *sexcrime*. In Newspeak it was seldom possible to follow a heretical thought further than the perception that it *was* heretical: beyond that point the necessary words were non-existent. . . .

... Relative to our own, the Newspeak vocabulary was tiny, and new ways of reducing it were constantly being devised. Newspeak, indeed, differed from almost all other languages in that its vocabulary grew smaller instead of larger every year. Each reduction was a gain, since the smaller the area of choice, the smaller the temptation to take thought. Ultimately it was hoped to make articulate speech issue from the larynx without involving the higher brain centres at all. This aim was frankly admitted in the Newspeak word *duckspeak*, meaning 'to quack like a duck'. Like various other words in the B vocabulary, *duckspeak* was ambivalent in meaning. Provided that the opinions which were quacked out were orthodox ones, it implied nothing but praise, and when the *Times* referred to one of the orators of the Party as a *doubleplusgood duckspeaker* it was paying a warm and valued compliment.

D Now, everything is to be translated into Newspeak.

From the foregoing account it will be seen that in Newspeak the expression of unorthodox opinions, above a very low level, was well-nigh impossible. It was of course possible to utter heresies of a very crude kind, a species of blasphemy. It would have been possible, for example, to say *Big Brother is ungood*. But this statement, which to an orthodox ear merely conveyed a self-evident absurdity, could not have been sustained by reasoned argument, because the necessary words were not available. Ideas inimical to Ingsoc could only be entertained in a vague wordless form, and could only be named in very broad terms which lumped together and condemned whole groups of heresies without defining them in doing so. One could, in fact, only use Newspeak for unorthodox purposes by illegitimately translating some of the words back into Oldspeak. For example, *All mans are equal* was a possible Newspeak sentence, but only in the same sense in which *All men are redhaired* is a possible Oldspeak sentence. It did not contain a grammatical error, but it expressed a palpable untruth — i.e. that all men are of equal size, weight or strength. The concept of political equality no longer existed, and this secondary meaning had accordingly been purged out of the word *equal*. ...

A good deal of the literature of the past was, indeed, already being transformed in this way. Considerations of prestige made it desirable to preserve the memory of certain historical figures, while at the same time bringing their achievements into line with the philosophy of Ingsoc. Various writers, such as Shakespeare, Milton, Swift, Byron, Dickens and some others were therefore in process of translation: when the task had been completed, their original writings, with all else that survived of the literature of the past, would be destroyed.

1. What type of citizens do the leaders who developed Newspeak hope to create?

2. How could limiting vocabulary also limit mental and intellectual activity?

3. Locate contemporary examples of language being manipulated to lessen its impact or change its meaning (for example, collateral damage = civilian deaths).

Bandung Declaration

In 1955, in Bandung, Indonesia, a conference was held by many of the newly independent African and Asian countries. The conference sought to establish an independent group of non-aligned states opposed to colonialism and imperialism by either of the two major Cold War blocs, led by the United States and the Soviet Union. The conference issued a declaration based on human rights and a further communiqué stressing the need for economic development for this group of countries.

A The Bandung Declaration begins with a clear statement of principles, based upon the Charter of the United Nations.

> The Afro-Asiatic Conference takes note of the fact of the existence of colonialism in many places of Asia and Africa, in the different forms in which it exists, not only obstructing cultural cooperation, but also the development of national cultures. Certain colonial powers have refused their colonial subjects elementary rights in educational and cultural matters, they have obstructed the development of their personality as well as cultural collaboration with other African and Asian peoples. This is especially true for Tunisia, Algeria, and Morocco, where the fundamental right of these peoples to study their native language and their culture has been suppressed. Similar discrimination has been practiced against Africans and peoples of colour in certain parts of the African continent.
>
> The Conference condemns any such challenge to the fundamental rights of man . . . as a form of cultural oppression.
>
> The Conference declares full approval of the fundamental principles of the Rights of man, as they are defined in the Charter of the United Nations Organization . . . and entirely supports the principle of the rights of peoples and of nations to arrange their own affairs as defined in the Charter. . . .
>
> The Conference, after having discussed the problems of peoples dependent upon colonialism and the consequences of the submission of peoples to the domination and exploitation of foreigners, is agreed:
> – We declare that colonialism in all its forms is an evil which should speedily be ended.
> – We affirm that the submission of peoples to the yoke of foreigners and to foreign exploitation constitutes a violation of the fundamental rights of man, is contrary to the Charter of the United Nations, and is an obstacle to the establishment of world peace.
> – We affirm our support for the cause of the liberty and independence of such peoples.

Source: "Décolonisation: Déclaration de Bandung." http://hypo.ge-dip.etat-ge.ch/www/cliotexte/html/conference.bandung.html (May 1, 2003) Translated by Arthur Haberman.

B The declaration addresses two major areas of colonialism at the time, North Africa and Indonesia.

> In the face of the troubled situation in North Africa and the persistent refusal to give these peoples their right of self-determination, the Conference agrees to support the right of the peoples of Algeria, Tunisia, and Morocco to self-determination and to independence; we demand that the French government negotiate a peaceful resolution of this matter without delay.
>
> The conference, in conformity with the position it has taken on the abolition of colonialism, supports the Indonesian interpretation of the clause of agreement with Dutch-Indonesia relating to the West. It urges the government of the Netherlands to open negotiations as soon as possible in order to complete the obligations stated above; it expresses the deepest hope that the United Nations assist the interested parties to find a peaceful solution to their differences.

1. How has the colonialism of the 1950s evolved beyond its initial economic exploitation?

2. Why would France and the Netherlands, both members of the United Nations, maintain oppressive colonial administrations?

3. Identify contemporary examples of different colonial systems.

Muhammad Ali Jinnah

Muhammad Ali Jinnah (1876–1948) is considered the founder of Pakistan. Jinnah trained as a lawyer in England. He returned to India in 1896 and soon established himself as one of the best-known lawyers in the subcontinent. He became involved in politics early in the twentieth century, joining the Indian National Congress and working as secretary. Although he joined the Muslim League in 1913, Jinnah continued to advocate a single independent state for Hindus and Muslims. During the 1930s, however, he became increasingly disenchanted with the Indian National Congress and eventually became the leader of the movement for a separate Muslim state.

A In March 1940, Jinnah delivered his presidential address to the Muslim League. At this meeting, the Muslim League adopted the policy of a separate state for Muslims.

> [The British] concept of party government functioning on political planes has become the ideal with them as the best form of government for every country, and . . . has led them into a serious blunder. . . . We find that the most leading statesmen of Great Britain, saturated with these notions, have in their pronouncements seriously asserted and expressed a hope that the passage of time will harmonize the inconsistent elements of India.

Source: Jamil-ud-Din Ahmad, ed., *Some Recent Speeches and Writings of Mr. Jinnah.* Lahore: Ashraf, 1946–1947, pp. 835–838.

A leading journal like the London *Times*, commenting on the Government of India Act of 1935, wrote: "Undoubtedly the differences between the Hindus and Muslims are not of religion in the strict sense of the word but also of law and culture, that they may be said, indeed, to represent two entirely distinct and separate civilizations. However, in the course of time, the superstition will die out and India will be molded into a single nation." So, according to the London *Times*, the only difficulties are superstitions. These fundamental and deep-rooted differences, spiritual, economic, cultural, social, and political, have been euphemized as mere "superstitions." But surely it is a flagrant disregard of the past history of the subcontinent of India as well as the fundamental Islamic conception of society vis-à-vis that of Hinduism to characterize them as mere "superstitions." Notwithstanding a thousand years of close contact, nationalities, which are as divergent today as ever, cannot at any time be expected to transform themselves into one nation merely by means of subjecting them to a democratic constitution and holding them forcibly together by unnatural and artificial methods of British parliamentary statute. What the unitary government of India for one hundred fifty years had failed to achieve cannot be realized by the imposition of a central federal government. It is inconceivable that the fiat or the writ of a government so constituted can ever command a willing and loyal obedience throughout the subcontinent by various nationalities except by means of armed force behind it.

The problem in India is not of an intercommunal character but manifestly of an international one, and it must be treated as such. So long as this basic and fundamental truth is not realized, any constitution that may be built will result in disaster and will prove destructive and harmful not only to the Mussalmans but to the British and Hindus also. If the British government are really in earnest and sincere to secure [the] peace and happiness of the people of this subcontinent, the only course open to us all is to allow the major nations separate homelands by dividing India into "autonomous national states." There is no reason why these states should be antagonistic to each other. . . . It will lead more towards natural good will by international pacts between them, and they can live in complete harmony with their neighbors. This will lead further to a friendly settlement all the more easily with regard to minorities by reciprocal arrangements and adjustments between Muslim India and Hindu India, which will far more adequately and effectively safeguard the rights and interests of Muslims and various other minorities.

B Jinnah argues that Islam and Hinduism are different ways of living, "two different civilizations."

It is extremely difficult to appreciate why our Hindu friends fail to understand the real nature of Islam and Hinduism. They are not religions in the strict sense of the word, but are, in fact, different and distinct social orders, and it is a dream that the Hindus and Muslims can ever evolve a common nationality, and this misconception of one Indian nation has gone far beyond the limits and is the cause of most of your troubles and will lead India to destruction if we fail to revise our notions in time. The Hindus and Muslims belong to two different religious philosophies, social customs, literatures. They neither intermarry nor interdine together and, indeed, they belong to two different civilizations which are based mainly on conflicting ideas and conceptions. Their aspects on life and of life are different. It is quite clear that Hindus and Mussalmans derive their inspiration from different sources of history. They have different epics, different heroes, and different episodes. Very often the hero of one is a foe of the other and, likewise, their victories and defeats overlap. To yoke together two such nations under a single state, one as a numerical minority and the other as a majority, must lead to growing discontent and final destruction of any fabric that may be so built up for the government of such a state.

. . . The present artificial unity of India dates back only to the British conquest and is maintained by the British bayonet, but termination of the British regime, which is implicit in the recent declaration of His Majesty's government, will be the herald of the entire break-up with worse disaster than has ever taken place during the last one thousand years under Muslims. Surely that is not the legacy which Britain would bequeath to India after one hundred fifty years of her rule, nor would Hindu and Muslim India risk such a sure catastrophe.

C Jinnah asserts the necessity for a Muslim state.

Muslim India cannot accept any constitution which must necessarily result in a Hindu majority government. Hindus and Muslims brought together under a democratic system forced upon the minorities can only mean Hindu rāj [rule]. Democracy of the kind with which the Congress High Command is enamored would mean the complete destruction of what is most precious in Islam. . . .

Mussalmans are not a minority as it is commonly known and understood. One has only got to look round. Even today, according to the British map of India, four out of eleven provinces, where the Muslims dominate more or less, are functioning notwithstanding the decision of the Hindu Congress High Command to noncooperate and prepare for civil disobedience. Mussalmans are a nation according to any definition of a nation, and they must have their homelands, their territory, and their state. We wish to live in peace and harmony with our neighbors as a free and independent people. We wish our people to develop to the fullest our spiritual, cultural, economic, social, and political life in a way that we think best and in consonance with our own ideals and according to the genius of our people. Honesty demands and the vital interests of millions of our people impose a sacred duty upon us to find an honorable and peaceful solution, which would be just and fair to all. But at the same time we cannot be moved or diverted from our purpose and objective by threats or intimidations. We must be prepared to face all difficulties and consequences, make all the sacrifices that may be required of us to achieve the goal we have set in front of us.

1. Why does Jinnah reject the British parliamentary system for the Indian subcontinent?

2. Evaluate Jinnah's claim that Islam and Hinduism are two different civilizations.

3. Jinnah had a vision of two peaceful nations residing in the subcontinent. Has this been achieved? Explain.

Sayyid Qutb

Sayyid Qutb (1906–1966) was an Egyptian and a highly respected Islamist thinker. He spent the years 1954 to 1964 in jail in Egypt for having been a member of a radical organization, Muslim Brotherhood, which was accused of being involved in a failed assassination attempt on the head of state, Gamal Abdel Nasser (1956–1970). Released in 1964, he was again arrested in 1965 and hanged a year later. Qutb's work, *Milestones* (1964), has had great influence in the Islamic world, especially among fundamentalist groups.

A Qutb argues that there is a crisis in the modern world and that Islam can provide the leadership for a new era.

> Mankind today is on the brink of a precipice, not because of the danger of complete annihilation which is hanging over its head — this being just a symptom and not the real disease — but because humanity is devoid of those vital values which are necessary not only for its healthy development but also for its real progress. Even the Western world realises that Western civilization is unable to present any healthy values for the guidance of mankind. It knows that it does not possess anything which will satisfy its own conscience and justify its existence.
>
> Democracy in the West has become infertile to such an extent that it is borrowing from the systems of the Eastern bloc, especially in the economic system, under the name of socialism. It is the same with the Eastern bloc. . . .
>
> It is essential for mankind to have new leadership!
>
> The leadership of mankind by Western man is now on the decline, not because Western culture has become poor materially or because its economic and military power has become weak. The period of the Western system has come to an end primarily because it is deprived of those life-giving values which enabled it to be the leader of mankind.

Source: Sayyid Qutb, "Milestones." www.youngmuslims.ca/online_library/books/milestones/Introduction.asp (May 12, 2003)

It is necessary for the new leadership to preserve and develop the material fruits of the creative genius of Europe, and also to provide mankind with such high ideals and values as have so far remained undiscovered by mankind, and which will also acquaint humanity with a way of life which is harmonious with human nature, which is positive and constructive, and which is practicable.

Islam is the only System which possesses these values and this way of life. . . .

At this crucial and bewildering juncture, the turn of Islam and the Muslim community has arrived — the turn of Islam, which does not prohibit material inventions. Indeed, it counts it as an obligation on man from the very beginning of time, when God deputed him as His representative on earth, and regards it under certain conditions as worship of God and one of the purposes of man's creation.

B Qutb suggests that the Islamic community needs a state and material progress to complement its spiritual growth.

Islam cannot fulfill its role except by taking concrete form in a society, rather, in a nation; for man does not listen, especially in this age, to an abstract theory which is not seen materialized in a living society. From this point of view, we can say that the Muslim community has been extinct for a few centuries, for this Muslim community does not denote the name of a land in which Islam resides, nor is it a people whose forefathers lived under the Islamic system at some earlier time. It is the name of a group of people whose manners, ideas and concepts, rules and regulations, values and criteria, are all derived from the Islamic source. The Muslim community with these characteristics vanished at the moment the laws of God became suspended on earth.

If Islam is again to play the role of the leader of mankind, then it is necessary that the Muslim community be restored to its original form.

It is necessary to revive that Muslim community which is buried under the debris of the man-made traditions of several generations, and which is crushed under the weight of those false laws and customs which are not even remotely related to the Islamic teachings, and which, in spite of all this, calls itself the 'world of Islam.'

I am aware that between the attempt at 'revival' and the attainment of 'leadership' there is a great distance, as the Muslim community has long ago vanished from existence and from observation, and the leadership of mankind has long since passed to other ideologies and other nations, other concepts and other systems. This was the era during which Europe's genius created its marvellous works in science, culture, law and material production, due to which mankind has progressed to great heights of creativity and material comfort. It is not easy to find fault with the inventors of such marvellous things, especially since what we call the 'world of Islam' is completely devoid of all this beauty.

But in spite of all this, it is necessary to revive Islam. The distance between the revival of Islam and the attainment of world leadership may be vast, and there may be great difficulties on the way; but the first step must be taken for the revival of Islam. . . .

The Muslim community today is neither capable of nor required to present before mankind great genius in material inventions, which will make the world bow its head before its supremacy and thus re-establish once more its world leadership. Europe's creative mind is far ahead in this area, and at least for a few centuries to come we cannot expect to compete with Europe and attain supremacy over it in these fields.

Hence we must have some other quality, that quality which modern civilization does not possess. . . .

To attain the leadership of mankind, we must have something to offer besides material progress, and this other quality can only be a faith and a way of life which on the one hand conserves the benefits of modern science and technology, and on the other fulfills the basic human needs on the same level of excellence as technology has fulfilled them in the sphere of material comfort. And then this faith and way of life must take concrete form in a human society — in other words, in a Muslim society.

C Qutb supports the revivalist movement in Muslim states.

If we look at the sources and foundations of modern ways of living, it becomes clear that the whole world is steeped in Jahiliyyah, [Ignorance of the Divine guidance] and all the marvellous material comforts and high-level inventions do not diminish this ignorance. This Jahiliyyah is based on rebellion against God's sovereignty on earth. It transfers to man one of the greatest attributes of God, namely sovereignty, and makes some men lords over others. It is now not in that simple and primitive form of the ancient Jahiliyyah, but takes the form of claiming that the right to create values, to legislate rules of collective behavior, and to choose any way of life rests with men, without regard to what God has prescribed. The result of this rebellion against the authority of God is the oppression of His creatures. Thus the humiliation of the common man under the communist systems and the exploitation of individuals and nations due to greed for wealth and imperialism under the capitalist systems are but a corollary of rebellion against God's authority and the denial of the dignity of man given to him by God.

In this respect, Islam's way of life is unique, for in systems other than Islam, some people worship others in some form or another. Only in the Islamic way of life do all men become free from the servitude of some men to others and devote themselves to the worship of God alone, deriving guidance from Him alone, and bowing before Him alone.

This is where the roads separate, and this is that new concept which we possess and can present to mankind — this and the way of life which this concept organizes for all the practical aspects of man's life. This is that vital message of which mankind does not know. It is not a product of Western invention nor of European genius, whether eastern or western.

Without doubt, we possess this new thing which is perfect to the highest degree, a thing which mankind does not know about and is not capable of 'producing'.

But as we have stated before, the beauty of this new system cannot be appreciated unless it takes a concrete form. Hence it is essential that a community arrange its affairs according to it and show it to the world. In order to bring this about, we need to initiate the movement of Islamic revival in some Muslim country. Only such a revivalist movement will eventually attain to the status of world leadership, whether the distance is near or far. How is it possible to start the task of reviving Islam?

It is necessary that there should be a vanguard which sets out with this determination and then keeps walking on the path, marching through the vast ocean of Jahiliyyah which has encompassed the entire world. . . .

It is necessary that this vanguard should know the landmarks and the milestones of the road toward this goal so that they may recognize the starting place, the nature, the responsibilities and the ultimate purpose of this long journey. . . .

The milestones will necessarily be determined by the light of the first source of this faith — the Holy Qur'an — and from its basic teachings, and from the concept which it created in the minds of the first group of Muslims, those whom God raised to fulfill His will, those who once changed the course of human history in the direction ordained by God.

I have written "Milestones" for this vanguard, which I consider to be a waiting reality about to be materialized.

1. According to Qutb, how have Marxism and Western democracy forfeited their leading roles in the global community?

2. How does Islam fill the leadership gap posed by the decline of other ideologies?

3. Why must Islam be revived in the form of a Muslim community?

4. Employ Qutb's description of an Islamic state to evaluate various contemporary Islamic states.

Steve Biko

The South African nationalist leader Steve Biko (1946–1977) died while being held in detention by the security police of his country. Biko had led the black consciousness movement in South Africa and had been banned from public life because of his ideas. His death further galvanized the black movement. In 1973, Biko's essay, "Black Consciousness and the Quest for a True Humanity," was published in Great Britain.

A Biko attacks the teaching of history from the perspective of the colonists, the oppressors.

> As one black writer says, colonialism is never satisfied with having the native in its grip but, by some strange logic, it must turn to his past and disfigure and distort it. Hence the history of the black man in this country [South Africa] is most disappointing to read. It is presented merely as a long succession of defeats. The Xhosas were thieves who went to war for stolen property; the Boers never provoked the Xhosas but merely went on "punitive expeditions" to teach the thieves a lesson. Heroes like Makana who were essentially revolutionaries are painted as superstitious trouble-makers who lied to the people about bullets turning into water. Great nation-builders like Shaka are cruel tyrants who frequently attacked smaller tribes for no reason but for some sadistic purpose. Not only is there no objectivity in the history taught us but there is frequently an appalling misrepresentation of facts that sicken even the uninformed student.
>
> Thus a lot of attention has to be paid to our history if we as blacks want to aid each other in our coming into consciousness. We have to rewrite our history and produce in it the heroes that formed the core of our resistance to the white invaders. More has to be revealed, and stress has to be laid on the successful nation-building attempts of men such as Shaka, Moshoeshoe and Hintsa. These areas call for intense research to provide some sorely-needed missing links. We would be too naive to expect our conquerors to write unbiased histories about us but we have to destroy the myth that our history starts in 1652, the year Van Riebeeck landed at the Cape.
>
> . . . Ours is a true man-centred society whose sacred tradition is that of sharing. We must reject, as we have been doing, the individualistic cold approach to life that is the cornerstone of the Anglo-Boer culture. We must seek to restore to the black man the great importance we used to give to human relations, the high regard for people and their property and for life in general; to reduce the triumph of technology over man and the materialistic element that is slowly creeping into our society.

B Biko attempts to articulate a black culture.

> These are essential features of our black culture to which we must cling. Black culture above all implies freedom on our part to innovate without recourse to white values. . . .
>
> Being part of an exploitative society in which we are often the direct objects of exploitation, we need to evolve a strategy towards our economic situation. We are aware that the blacks are still colonised even within the borders of South Africa. Their cheap labour has helped to make South Africa what it is today. Our money from the townships takes a one-way journey

Source: Steve Biko, *I Write What I Like*. New York: Harper and Row, 1978, pp. 95–98.

to white shops and white banks, and all we do in our lives is pay the white man either with labour or in coin. Capitalistic exploitative tendencies, coupled with the overt arrogance of white racism, have conspired against us. Thus in South Africa now it is very expensive to be poor. It is the poor people who stay furthest from town and therefore have to spend more money on transport to come and work for white people; it is the poor people who use uneconomic and inconvenient fuel like paraffin and coal because of the refusal of the white man to install electricity in black areas; it is the poor people who are governed by many ill-defined restrictive laws and therefore have to spend money on fines for "technical" offences; it is the poor people who have no hospitals and are therefore exposed to exorbitant charges by private doctors; it is the poor people who use untarred roads, have to walk long distances, and therefore experience the greatest wear and tear on commodities like shoes; it is the poor people who have to pay for their children's books while whites get them free. It does not need to be said that it is the black people who are poor.

We therefore need to take another look at how best to use our economic power, little as it may seem to be. We must seriously examine the possibilities of establishing business co-operatives whose interests will be ploughed back into community development programmes. We should think along such lines as the "buy black" campaign once suggested in Johannesburg and establish our own banks for the benefit of the community. Organisational development amongst blacks has only been low because we have allowed it to be. Now that we know we are on our own, it is an absolute duty for us to fulfil these needs.

C Biko seeks a "true humanity" to attack the evil of racism.

The last step in Black Consciousness is to broaden the base of our operation. One of the basic tenets of Black Consciousness is totality of involvement. This means that all blacks must sit as one big unit, and no fragmentation and distraction from the mainstream of events be allowed. . . . We are oppressed not as individuals, not as Zulus, Xhosas, Vendas or Indians. We are oppressed because we are black. We must use that very concept to unite ourselves and to respond as a cohesive group. We must cling to each other with a tenacity that will shock the perpetrators of evil.

Our preparedness to take upon ourselves the cudgels of the struggle will see us through. We must remove from our vocabulary completely the concept of fear. Truth must ultimately triumph over evil, and the white man has always nourished his greed on this basic fear that shows itself in the black community. Special Branch agents will not turn the lie into truth, and one must ignore them. In a true bid for change we have to take off our coats, be prepared to lose our comfort and security, our jobs and positions of prestige, and our families, for just as it is true that "leadership and security are basically incompatible", a struggle without casualties is no struggle.

We must realise that prophetic cry of black students: "Black man, you are on your own!"

Some will charge that we are racist but these people are using exactly the values we reject. We do not have the power to subjugate anyone. We are merely responding to provocation in the most realistic possible way. Racism does not only imply exclusion of one race by another — it always presupposes that the exclusion is for the purposes of subjugation. Blacks have had enough experience as objects of racism not to wish to turn the tables. While it may be relevant now to talk about black in relation to white, we must not make this our preoccupation, for it can be a negative exercise. As we proceed further towards the achievement of our goals let us talk more about ourselves and our struggle and less about whites.

We have set out on a quest for true humanity, and somewhere on the distant horizon we can see the glittering prize. Let us march forth with courage and determination, drawing strength from our common plight and our brotherhood. In time we shall be in a position to bestow upon South Africa the greatest gift possible — a more human face.

1. How does Biko confirm that history is more than a series of dates?
2. What steps need to be taken to improve economic conditions for black South Africans?
3. According to Biko, why would black South Africans who experienced racism never employ it?
4. Has Biko's claim of black South Africa providing a more human face been fulfilled? Explain.

Martin Luther King, Jr.

Human rights remained in the foreground of issues that concerned the West. Many movements in the world stressed the importance of ending inequalities based upon race, origin, class, sex, or age. These movements often translated into social action, as groups rallied to pressure governments. The leading figure in the US civil rights movement for Blacks was Martin Luther King, Jr. (1929–1968). A clergyman, King used the tactic of non-violent civil disobedience to push for equality. In 1963, King was arrested in Birmingham, Alabama. He wrote "Letter from Birmingham Jail" as a reply to his critics and as a justification of his actions.

 King discusses the reasons for the non-violent demonstration for equality.

I cannot sit idly by in Atlanta and not be concerned about what happens in Birmingham. Injustice anywhere is a threat to justice everywhere. We are caught in an inescapable network of mutuality, tied in a single garment of destiny. Whatever affects one directly, affects all indirectly. Never again can we afford to live with the narrow, provincial "outside agitator" idea.

Source: Martin Luther King, Jr., *Why We Can't Wait*. New York: Harper and Row, 1964, pp. 78–87.

Anyone who lives inside the United States can never be considered an outsider anywhere within its bounds.

You deplore the demonstrations taking place in Birmingham. But your statement, I am sorry to say, fails to express a similar concern for the conditions that brought about the demonstrations. I am sure that none of you would want to rest content with the superficial kind of social analysis that deals merely with effects and does not grapple with underlying causes. It is unfortunate that demonstrations are taking place in Birmingham, but it is even more unfortunate that the city's white power structure left the Negro community with no alternative.

In any nonviolent campaign there are four basic steps: collection of the facts to determine whether injustices exist; negotiation; self-purification; and direct action. We have gone through all these steps in Birmingham. There can be no gainsaying the fact that racial injustice engulfs this community. Birmingham is probably the most thoroughly segregated city in the United States. Its ugly record of brutality is widely known. Negroes have experienced grossly unjust treatment in the courts. There have been more unsolved bombings of Negro homes and churches in Birmingham than in any other city in the nation. These are the hard, brutal facts of the case. On the basis of these conditions, Negro leaders sought to negotiate with the city fathers. But the latter consistently refused to engage in good-faith negotiation.

Then, last September, came the opportunity to talk with leaders of Birmingham's economic community. In the course of the negotiations, certain promises were made by the merchants — for example, to remove the stores' humiliating racial signs. . . . As the weeks and months went by, we realized that we were the victims of a broken promise. A few signs, briefly removed, returned; the others remained.

As in so many past experiences, our hopes had been blasted, and the shadow of deep disappointment settled upon us. We had no alternative except to prepare for direct action, whereby we would present our very bodies as a means of laying our case before the conscience of the local and the national community. Mindful of the difficulties involved, we decided to undertake a process of self-purification. We began a series of workshops on nonviolence, and we repeatedly asked ourselves: "Are you able to accept blows without retaliating?" "Are you able to endure the ordeal of jail?" We decided to schedule our direct-action program for the Easter season, realizing that except for Christmas, this is the main shopping period of the year. Knowing that a strong economic-withdrawal program would be the by-product of direct action, we felt that this would be the best time to bring pressure to bear on the merchants for the needed change.

B King suggests that direct action has a purpose.

You may well ask: "Why direct action? Why sit-ins, marches and so forth? Isn't negotiation a better path?" You are quite right in calling for negotiation.

Indeed, this is the very purpose of direct action. Nonviolent direct action seeks to create such a crisis and foster such a tension that a community which has constantly refused to negotiate is forced to confront the issue. It seeks so to dramatize the issue that it can no longer be ignored. . . . Just as Socrates felt that it was necessary to create a tension in the mind so that individuals could rise from the bondage of myths and half-truths to the unfettered realm of creative analysis and objective appraisal, so must we see the need for nonviolent gadflies to create the kind of tension in society that will help men rise from the dark depths of prejudice and racism to the majestic heights of understanding and brotherhood.

The purpose of our direct-action program is to create a situation so crisis-packed that it will inevitably open the door to negotiation. I therefore concur with you in your call for negotiation. Too long has our beloved Southland been bogged down in a tragic effort to live in monologue rather than dialogue.

One of the basic points in your statement is that the action that I and my associates have taken in Birmingham is untimely. Some have asked: "Why didn't you give the new city administration time to act?" The only answer that I can give to this query is that the new Birmingham administration must be prodded about as much as the outgoing one, before it will act. . . . My friends, I must say to you that we have not made a single gain in civil rights without determined legal and nonviolent pressure. Lamentably, it is an historical fact that privileged groups seldom give up their privileges voluntarily. Individuals may see the moral light and voluntarily give up their unjust posture; but, as Reinhold Niebuhr has reminded us, groups tend to be more immoral than individuals.

We know through painful experience that freedom is never voluntarily given by the oppressor; it must be demanded by the oppressed. Frankly, I have yet to engage in a direct-action campaign that was "well timed" in the view of those who have not suffered unduly from the disease of segregation. For years now I have heard the word "Wait!" It rings in the ear of every Negro with piercing familiarity. This "Wait" has almost always meant "Never." We must come to see, with one of our distinguished jurists, that "justice too long delayed is justice denied."

We have waited for more than 340 years for our constitutional and God-given rights. The nations of Asia and Africa are moving with jetlike speed toward gaining political independence, but we still creep at horse-and-buggy pace toward gaining a cup of coffee at a lunch counter. Perhaps it is easy for those who have never felt the stinging darts of segregation to say, "Wait." But when you have seen vicious mobs lynch your mothers and fathers at will and drown your sisters and brothers at whim; when you have seen hate-filled policemen curse, kick and even kill your black brothers and sisters; when you see the vast majority of your twenty million Negro brothers smothering in an airtight cage of poverty in the midst of an affluent society; when you suddenly find your tongue twisted and your speech stammering as you seek to explain to your six-year-old daughter why she can't go to the public amusement park that has just been advertised on television, and see tears welling up in her eyes when she is told that Funtown is closed to colored children, and see ominous clouds of inferiority beginning to form in her little mental sky, and see her beginning to distort her personality by developing an unconscious bitterness toward white people; when you have to concoct an answer for a five-year-old son who is asking: "Daddy, why do white people treat colored people so mean?"; when you take a cross-country drive and find it necessary to sleep night after night in the uncomfortable corners of your automobile because no motel will accept you; when you are humiliated day in and day out by nagging signs reading "white" and "colored"; when your first name becomes "nigger," your middle name becomes "boy" (however old you are) and your last name becomes "John," and your wife and mother are never given the respected title "Mrs."; when you are harried by day and haunted by night by the fact that you are a Negro, living constantly at tiptoe stance, never quite knowing what to expect next, and are plagued with inner fears and outer resentments; when you are forever fighting a degenerating sense of "nobodiness" — then you will understand why we find it difficult to wait. There comes a time when the cup of endurance runs over, and men are no longer willing to be plunged into the abyss of despair. I hope, sirs, you can understand our legitimate and unavoidable impatience.

C King defends his civil disobedience by appealing to justice and natural law.

You express a great deal of anxiety over our willingness to break laws. This is certainly a legitimate concern. Since we so diligently urge people to obey the Supreme Court's decision of 1954 outlawing segregation in the public schools, at first glance it may seem rather paradoxical for us consciously to break laws. One may well ask: "How can you advocate breaking some laws and obeying others?" The answer lies in the fact that there are two types of laws: just and unjust. I would be the first to advocate obeying just laws. One has not only a legal but a moral responsibility to obey just laws. Conversely, one has a moral responsibility to disobey unjust laws. I would agree with St. Augustine that "an unjust law is no law at all."

Now, what is the difference between the two? How does one determine whether a law is just or unjust? A just law is a man-made code that squares with the moral law or the law of God. An unjust law is a code that is out of harmony with the moral law. To put it in terms of St. Thomas Aquinas: An unjust law is a human law that is not rooted in eternal law and natural law. Any law that uplifts human personality is just. Any law that degrades human personality is unjust. All segregation statutes are unjust because segregation distorts the soul and damages the personality. It gives the segregator a false sense of superiority and the segregated a false sense of inferiority. . . . Hence segregation is not only politically, economically and sociologically unsound, it is morally wrong and sinful. . . . Thus it is that I can urge men to obey the 1954 decision of the Supreme Court, for it is morally right; and I can urge them to disobey segregation ordinances, for they are morally wrong. . . .

. . . A law is unjust if it is inflicted on a minority that, as a result of being denied the right to vote, had no part in enacting or devising the law. Who can say that the legislature of Alabama which set up that state's segregation laws was democratically elected? Throughout Alabama all sorts of devious methods are used to prevent Negroes from becoming registered voters, and there are some counties in which, even though Negroes constitute a majority of the population, not a single Negro is registered. Can any law enacted under such circumstances be considered democratically structured? . . .

I hope you are able to see the distinction I am trying to point out. In no sense do I advocate evading or defying the law, as would the rabid segregationist. That would lead to anarchy. One who breaks an unjust law must do so openly, lovingly, and with a willingness to accept the penalty. I submit that an individual who breaks a law that conscience tells him is unjust, and who willingly accepts the penalty of imprisonment in order to arouse the conscience of the community over its injustice, is in reality expressing the highest respect for law.

Of course, there is nothing new about this kind of civil disobedience. It was evidenced sublimely in the refusal of Shadrach, Meshach and Abednego to obey the laws of Nebuchadnezzar, on the ground that a higher moral law was at stake. It was practiced superbly by the early Christians, who were willing to face hungry lions and the excruciating pain of chopping blocks rather than submit to certain unjust laws of the Roman Empire. To a degree, academic freedom is a reality today because Socrates practiced civil disobedience. In our own nation, the Boston Tea Party represented a massive act of civil disobedience.

We should never forget that everything Adolf Hitler did in Germany was "legal" and everything the Hungarian freedom fighters did in Hungary was "illegal." It was "illegal" to aid and comfort a Jew in Hitler's Germany. Even so, I am sure that, had I lived in Germany at the time, I would have aided and comforted my Jewish brothers. If today I lived in a Communist country where certain principles dear to the Christian faith are suppressed, I would openly advocate disobeying that country's antireligious laws.

1. Compare the strategies for black rights proposed by King and Biko (see pages 278–281). Account for the similarities and differences.

2. Why did some black leaders reject non-violence in the fight for black rights?

3. What challenges do people face when trying to distinguish between just and unjust laws?

4. How is racism morally and psychologically damaging?

Thich Nhat Hanh

Thich Nhat Hanh (1926–) is a prime example of the "engaged Buddhism" that emerged in twentieth-century Vietnam, combining traditional elements of Buddhism (Zen and Pure Land schools) and Confucianism with modern social concerns. This religion is committed to the promotion of peace and justice. Nhat Hanh had received a modern education in Vietnamese, Chinese, and French before he entered a monastery at the age of sixteen. He received training in Zen meditation as a novice, and continued with advanced education in Buddhist as well as Western philosophy and social sciences. During the 1950s and 1960s, Nhat Hanh founded a training school for young volunteers to work with the victims of war and help rebuild their communities. The organization continued to grow despite lack of support from the government or the Buddhist church hierarchy.

A In the 1960s, Nhat Hanh was invited to teach Buddhism for two years at Columbia University and Princeton University in the United States. Later, he was invited by US friends for another short visit, to speak out for peace and against US involvement in the Vietnamese civil war. In 1967, Martin Luther King, Jr. nominated Nhat Hanh for the Nobel Peace prize. For his peace advocacy in the United States, Nhat Hanh was condemned as a communist spy by the government in South Vietnam, and was not allowed to return home. Following is an excerpt from his 1966 speech in Washington, D. C.

> Just this morning the U.S. Consulate in Hue was destroyed by angry Vietnamese youths. In the past four days five Vietnamese have immolated themselves by fire, some of them leaving behind messages explaining that their actions were in protest against U.S. policy in South Vietnam. During my short visit to your country I have been repeatedly asked why the Vietnamese people seem to have become so strongly anti-American.
>
> I wish, first of all, to assure you that I am not anti-American. Indeed, it is precisely because I do have a great respect and admiration for America that I have undertaken this long voyage to your country, a voyage which entails great personal risk for me upon my return to South Vietnam. Yet I assume this risk willingly because I have faith that if the American public can begin to understand something of what the Vietnamese people feel about what is happening in our country, much of the unnecessary tragedy and misery being endured by both our peoples might be eliminated.
>
> The demonstrations, the self-immolations, and the protests which we are witnessing in Vietnam are dramatic reflections of the frustrations which the Vietnamese people feel at being so effectively excluded from participation in the determination of their country's future. Eighty years of French domination over Vietnam were ended by a long and bloody

Source: Thich Nhat Hanh, *Vietnam, Lotus in a Sea of Fire*. New York: Hill and Wang, 1967, pp. 109–111, 113–114.

struggle, waged and won by the Vietnamese people against overwhelming odds. During the twelve years since independence most Vietnamese have remained without a voice in the nation's destiny, and this at a time when the nation is being subjected to a destructive force far surpassing anything ever before seen in our country. If anti-Americanism seems to be emerging as a focus for some of the recent protests, it is because the Vietnamese people recognize that it is really only the awesome U.S. power which enables the Saigon governments to rule without a popular mandate and to follow policies contrary to the aspirations of the Vietnamese people. This is not the independence for which the Vietnamese people fought so valiantly.

The war in Vietnam today pits brother against brother, the Viet Cong against the supporters of the Saigon government. Both sides claim to represent the Vietnamese people, but in reality neither side does. The most effective Viet Cong propaganda says that the Saigon governments are mere puppets of the U.S., corrupt lackeys of the imperialists. Every escalation of the war, every new contingent of U.S. troops confirms these charges and wins new recruits to the Viet Cong, for the overwhelming majority of the Vietnamese people now thirst desperately for peace and oppose any further expansion of the war. They see clearly that the present policy of constant escalation only puts peace ever further into the future and merely guarantees an even greater destruction of Vietnamese society. There are now more than 300,000 Americans in my country, most of them knowing and caring little about our customs and practices and many of them involved in destroying Vietnamese people and property. This creates friction which generously feeds the anti-American propaganda, and the fact that the war kills far more innocent peasants than it does Viet Cong is a tragic reality of life in the Vietnamese countryside. Those who escape death by bombings must often abandon their destroyed villages and seek shelter in refugee camps where life is even more miserable than it was in the villages. In general, these people do not blame the Viet Cong for their plight. It is the men in the planes, who drop death and destruction from the skies, who appear to them to be their enemies. How can they see it otherwise?

The United States chooses to support those elements in Vietnam which appear to be most devoted to the U.S.'s wishes for Vietnam's future. But these elements have never been viewed by the Vietnamese people as their spokesmen. Diem was not, nor were Diem's successors. Thus, it has been the U.S.'s antipathy to popular government in South Vietnam, together with its hope for an ultimate military solution, which has not only contradicted the deepest aspirations of the Vietnamese people, but actually undermined the very objective for which we believe Americans to be fighting in Vietnam. To us, America's first objective is to have an anti-Communist, or at least a non-Communist, Vietnam, whereas the Vietnamese people's objective is to have peace. They dislike communism, but they dislike war even more, especially after twenty years of fighting and bitterness which has rotted the very fabric of Vietnamese life. Equally important, we now see clearly that continuance of the war is more likely to spread communism in Vietnam than to contain it. The new social class of military officers and *commerçants* which has been created as a direct result of the U.S. involvement, a class of sycophants who support the war for crass economic reasons, are not the people to whom Washington should listen if it sincerely wishes to hear the voice of South Vietnam. The Vietnamese people reject with scorn this corrupt and self-seeking class which cares neither for Vietnam nor for the great ideals of America, but thinks only of its own interests.

B Nhat Hanh suggests a solution. When peace talks began in Paris between US and North Vietnamese diplomats, Nhat Hanh led a Vietnamese Buddhist peace delegation to present their point of view to the world. For such activities, he was branded by North Vietnam as a CIA spy, and was not permitted to return home after the North had won the civil war. He has been living in exile since 1968.

Since coming to the United States I have been asked repeatedly to outline concrete proposals for ending the strife in Vietnam. Although I am not a politician and cannot therefore suggest every detail of a satisfactory settlement, the general direction which such a solution must take is quite clear to me and to many of the Vietnamese people. It does not involve the U.S. in any negotiations with Hanoi, Peking, or the NLF. To the Vietnamese people such talks, if necessary, are the proper province of Vietnamese officials rather than of Washington.

My solution would be along the following lines.

1. A clear statement by the U.S. of its desire to help the Vietnamese people to have a government truly responsive to Vietnamese aspirations, and concrete U.S. actions to implement this statement, such as a refusal to support one group in preference to another.
2. A cessation of the bombing, north and south.
3. Limitation of all military operations by U.S. and South Vietnamese forces to defensive actions; in effect, a cease-fire if the Viet Cong respond in kind.
4. A convincing demonstration of the U.S. intention to withdraw its forces from Vietnam over a specified period of months, with withdrawal actually beginning to take place as a sign of sincerity.
5. A generous effort to help rebuild the country from the destruction which has been wreaked upon Vietnam, such aid to be completely free of ideological and political strings and therefore not viewed as an affront to Vietnamese independence.

Such a program if implemented with sufficient vigor to convince the now understandably skeptical Vietnamese people of its sincerity offers the best hope for uniting them in a constructive effort and for restoring stability to South Vietnam.

The plan is not perfect, for the question remains of how the U.S. can be sure that the South Vietnamese government and the Viet Cong would co-operate in such a venture. Insofar as the South Vietnamese government is concerned, the past statements of Premier Ky have clearly indicated his unwillingness to seek a peaceful end to the war. In fact, it has been the contradiction between the aggressive words of Saigon and the peaceful statements of Washington which has so discredited the so-called U.S. peace offensive of last winter. The withdrawal of the U.S. support for Ky may thus be a necessary precondition for implementation of such a plan.

It is obviously not possible to predict the response of the Viet Cong to such a program but the installation of a popular government in South Vietnam, plus a cease-fire and the beginnings of an American withdrawal, would so undercut the Viet Cong's position that it is likely to have no alternative but to co-operate.

Finally, if some may question why I ask the U.S. to take the first step, it is because the U.S. is militarily the strongest nation in the world. No one can accuse it of cowardice if it chooses to seek peace. To be a genuine leader requires moral strength as well as big guns. America's history suggests that she has the potential to provide the world this leadership.

1. Has US involvement done more harm than good for the people of Vietnam? Explain.

2. How does Nhat Hanh appeal to the US ideals of popular democracy?

3. How might the governments of South and North Vietnam react to Nhat Hanh's proposed solution?

4. Why has South Vietnamese nationalism been oppressed by various governments?

Feminism

Feminism has become one of the most important ideas spreading social change in the West. It not only discussed and fostered women's rights, but also developed new concepts concerning the role of women in society and culture. All feminists stressed the importance of challenging inherited sexual stereotypes. Feminism became a mass movement in the 1960s as women agitated for political and social reform throughout the world.

 Betty Friedan (1921–) wrote *The Feminine Mystique* (1963) in order to discuss US society and its values. The book calls for new attitudes and perceptions about women, and clarifies what Friedan terms "the problem with no name."

The feminine mystique says that the highest value and the only commitment for women is the fulfillment of their own femininity. It says that the great mistake of Western culture, through most of its history, has been the undervaluation of this femininity. It says this femininity is so mysterious and intuitive and close to the creation and origin of life that man-made science may never be able to understand it. But however special and different, it is in no way inferior to the nature of man; it may even in certain respects be superior. The mistake, says the mystique, the root of women's troubles in the past is that women envied men, women tried to be like men, instead of accepting their own nature, which can find fulfillment only in sexual passivity, male domination, and nurturing maternal love. . . .

Fulfillment as a woman had only one definition for American women after 1949 — the housewife-mother. As swiftly as in a dream, the image of the American woman as a changing, growing individual in a changing world was shattered. Her solo flight to find her own identity was forgotten in the rush for the security of togetherness. Her limitless world shrunk to the cozy walls of home. . . .

"Easy enough to say," the woman inside the housewife's trap remarks, "but what can I do, alone in the house, with the children yelling and the laundry to sort and no grandmother to babysit?" It is easier to live through someone else than to become complete yourself. The freedom to lead and plan your own life is frightening if you have never faced it before. It is frightening when a woman finally realizes that there is no answer to the question "who am I" except the voice inside herself. . . .

To face the problem is not to solve it. . . . "What do I want to do?". . . Once she begins to see through the delusions of the feminine mystique — and realizes that neither her husband nor her children, nor the things in her house, nor sex, nor being like all the other women, can give her a self — she often finds the solution much easier than she anticipated. . . .

It also is time to stop giving lip service to the idea that there are no battles left to be fought for women in America, that women's rights have already been won. It is ridiculous to tell girls to keep quiet when they enter a new field; or an old one, so the men will not notice they are there. In almost every professional field, in business and in the arts and sciences, women are still treated as second-class citizens. It would be a great service to tell girls who plan to work in society to expect this subtle, uncomfortable discrimination — tell them not to be quiet, and hope it will go away, but fight it. A girl should not expect special privileges because of her sex, but neither should she "adjust" to prejudice and discrimination.

She must learn to compete then, not as a woman, but as a human being. . . .

. . . It took, and still takes, extraordinary strength of purpose for women to pursue their own life plans when society does not expect it of them. However, unlike the trapped housewives whose problems multiply with the

Sources: Betty Friedan, *The Feminine Mystique*. New York: Dell Publishing Company, Inc., 1963, pp. 37, 38, 326, 360–361, 362, 363, 364; Barbara A. Crow, ed., *Radical Feminism: A Documentary Reader*. New York: New York University Press, 2000, pp. 454, 456–457, 458–459.

years, these women solved their problems and moved on. They resisted the mass persuasions and manipulations, and did not give up their own, often painful, values for the comforts of conformity.... And they know quite surely now who they are.

... No woman in America today who starts her search for identity can be sure where it will take her. No woman starts that search today without struggle, conflict, and taking her courage in her hands. But the women I met, who were moving on that unknown road, did not regret the pains, the efforts, the risks....

... When their mothers' fulfillment makes girls sure they want to be women, they will not have to "beat themselves down" to be feminine; they can stretch and stretch until their own efforts will tell them who they are. They will not need the regard of boy or man to feel alive. And when women do not need to live through their husbands and children, men will not fear the love and strength of women, nor need another's weakness to prove their own masculinity. They can finally see each other as they are. And this may be the next step in human evolution.

Who knows what women can be when they are finally free to become themselves? Who knows what women's intelligence will contribute when it can be nourished without denying love? Who knows of the possibilities of love when men and women share not only children, home, and garden, not only the fulfillment of their biological roles, but the responsibilities and passions of the work that creates the human future and the full human knowledge of who they are? It has barely begun, the search of women for themselves. But the time is at hand when the voices of the feminine mystique can no longer drown out the inner voice that is driving women on to become complete.

B Toni Morrison (1931–), a winner of the Nobel Prize in Literature, wrote "What the Black Woman Thinks about Women's Lib" (1971). She looks at the new feminism from the point of view of black culture.

What do black women feel about Women's Lib? Distrust. It is white, therefore suspect. In spite of the fact that liberating movements in the black world have been catalysts for white feminism, too many movements and organizations have made deliberate overtures to enroll blacks and have ended up by rolling them. They don't want to be used again to help somebody gain power — a power that is carefully kept out of their hands. They look at white women and see them as the enemy — for they know that racism is not confined to white men, and that there are more white women than men in this country, and that 53 per cent of the population sustained an eloquent silence during times of greatest stress.....

There are strong similarities in the way black and white men treat women, and strong similarities in the way women of both races react. But the relationship is different in a very special way.

For years in this country there was no one for black men to vent their rage on except black women. And for years black women accepted that rage — even regarded that acceptance as their unpleasant duty. But in doing so, they frequently kicked back, and they seem never to have become the "true slave" that white women see in their own history. True, the black woman did the housework, the drudgery; true, she reared the children, often alone, but she did all of that while occupying a place on the job market, a place her mate could not get or which his pride would not let him accept. And she had nothing to fall back on: not maleness, not whiteness, not ladyhood, not anything. And out of the profound desolation of her reality she may very well have invented herself. . . .

So she combined being a responsible person with being a female — and as a person she felt free to confront not only the world at large (the rent man, the doctor and the rest of the marketplace) but her man as well. She fought him and nagged him — but knew that you don't fight what you don't respect. (If you don't respect your man, you manipulate him, the way some parents treat children and the way white women treat their men — if they can get away with it or if they do not acquiesce entirely). And even so, the black man was calling most of the shots — in the home or out of it. The black woman's "bad" relationships with him were often the result of his inability to deal with a competent and complete personality and her refusal to be anything less than that. The saving of the relationship lay in her unwillingness to feel free when her man was not free.

In a way black women have known something of the freedom white women are now beginning to crave. But oddly, freedom is only sweet when it is won. When it is forced, it is called responsibility. The black woman's needs shrank to the level of her responsibility; her man's expanded in proportion to the obstacles that prevented him from assuming his. White women, on the other hand, have had too little responsibility, white men too much. It's a wonder the sexes of either race even speak to each other. . . .

Black women have been able to envy white women (their looks, their easy life, the attention they seem to get from their men); they could fear them (for the economic control they have had over black women's lives) and even love them (as mammies and domestic workers can); but black women have found it impossible to respect white women. . . .

White women were ignorant of the facts of life — perhaps by choice, perhaps with the assistance of men, but ignorant anyway. They were totally dependent on marriage or male support (emotionally or economically). They confronted their sexuality with furtiveness, complete abandon or repression. Those who could afford it, gave over the management of the house and the rearing of children to others. . . . The one great disservice black women are guilty of (albeit not by choice) is that they are the means by which white women can escape the responsibilities of womanhood and remain children all the way to the grave. . . .

This feeling of superiority contributes to the reluctance of black women to embrace Women's Lib. That and the very important fact that black men are formidably opposed to their involvement in it — and for the most part the women understand their fears. . . .

There is also a contention among some black women that Women's Lib is nothing more than an attempt on the part of whites to become black without the responsibilities of being black. Certainly some of the demands of liberationists seem to rack up as our thing: common-law marriage (shacking); children out of wedlock which is even fashionable if you are not a member of the Jet Set (if you are poor and black it is still a crime); families without men; right to work; sexual freedom, and an assumption that a woman is equal to a man. . . .

The winds are changing, and when they blow, new things move. The liberation movement has moved from shrieks to shape. It is focusing itself, becoming a hard-headed power base. . . . [We] see, perhaps, something real: women talking about human rights rather than sexual rights — something other than a family quarrel, and the air is shivery with possibilities.

1. What obstacles do women face to achieve equality?

2. In what ways does gender equality benefit society?

3. Do you think that Friedan would be satisfied with the gains women have made over the last forty years? Explain.

4. Why does Morrison see women's liberation as insensitive to black women's issues?

5. Why might some black males fear female equality? Why might some white males?

6. Why does Morrison view women's liberation as a superficial movement?

Beijing Declaration

In 1975, Mexico City played host to the First United Nations' World Conference on Women. At that meeting, the UN declared 1976–1985 the "Decade for Women." Subsequent World Conferences took place in Copenhagen (1980) and Nairobi (1985). The Nairobi Conference approved the "Forward Looking Strategies," a framework for action at national, regional, and international levels to promote greater equality and opportunities for women. The Fourth World Conference met in Beijing in September 1995. It was the largest conference in the history of the United Nations, and produced the "Beijing Declaration and Platform for Action."

 The declaration opens with a statement of principles.

> 1. We, the Governments participating in the Fourth World Conference on Women,

Source: "Fourth World Conference on Women: Beijing Declaration." www.un.org/womenwatch/daw/beijing/platform/declar.htm (May 2, 2003)

2. Gathered here in Beijing in September 1995, the year of the fiftieth anniversary of the founding of the United Nations,

3. Determined to advance the goals of equality, development and peace for all women everywhere in the interest of all humanity,

4. Acknowledging the voices of all women everywhere and taking note of the diversity of women and their roles and circumstances, honouring the women who paved the way and inspired by the hope present in the world's youth,

5. Recognize that the status of women has advanced in some important respects in the past decade but that progress has been uneven, inequalities between women and men have persisted and major obstacles remain, with serious consequences for the well-being of all people,

6. Also recognize that this situation is exacerbated by the increasing poverty that is affecting the lives of the majority of the world's people, in particular women and children, with origins in both the national and international domains,

7. Dedicate ourselves unreservedly to addressing these constraints and obstacles and thus enhancing further the advancement and empowerment of women all over the world, and agree that this requires urgent action in the spirit of determination, hope, cooperation and solidarity, now and to carry us forward into the next century.

We reaffirm our commitment to:

8. The equal rights and inherent human dignity of women and men and other purposes and principles enshrined in the Charter of the United Nations, to the Universal Declaration of Human Rights and other international human rights instruments. . . .

9. Ensure the full implementation of the human rights of women and of the girl child as an inalienable, integral and indivisible part of all human rights and fundamental freedoms;

10. Build on consensus and progress made at previous United Nations conferences and summits. . . .

11. Achieve the full and effective implementation of the Nairobi Forward-looking Strategies for the Advancement of Women;

12. The empowerment and advancement of women, including the right to freedom of thought, conscience, religion and belief, thus contributing to the moral, ethical, spiritual and intellectual needs of women and men, individually or in community with others and thereby guaranteeing them the possibility of realizing their full potential in society and shaping their lives in accordance with their own aspirations.

We are convinced that:

13. Women's empowerment and their full participation on the basis of equality in all spheres of society, including participation in the decision-making process and access to power, are fundamental for the achievement of equality, development and peace;

14. Women's rights are human rights;

15. Equal rights, opportunities and access to resources, equal sharing of responsibilities for the family by men and women, and a harmonious partnership between them are critical to their well-being and that of their families as well as to the consolidation of democracy;

16. Eradication of poverty based on sustained economic growth, social development, environmental protection and social justice requires the involvement of women in economic and social development, equal opportunities and the full and equal participation of women and men as agents and beneficiaries of people-centred sustainable development;

17. The explicit recognition and reaffirmation of the right of all women to control all aspects of their health, in particular their own fertility, is basic to their empowerment;

18. Local, national, regional and global peace is attainable and is inextricably linked with the advancement of women, who are a fundamental force for leadership, conflict resolution and the promotion of lasting peace at all levels;

19. It is essential to design, implement and monitor, with the full participation of women, effective, efficient and mutually reinforcing gender-sensitive policies and programmes, including development policies and programmes, at all levels that will foster the empowerment and advancement of women;

20. The participation and contribution of all actors of civil society, particularly women's groups and networks and other non-governmental organizations and community-based organizations . . . are important to the effective implementation and follow-up of the Platform for Action;

21. The implementation of the Platform for Action requires commitment from Governments and the international community. By making national and international commitments for action, including those made at the Conference, Governments and the international community recognize the need to take priority action for the empowerment and advancement of women.

B The declaration's goals and actions follow.

We are determined to:

22. Intensify efforts and actions to achieve the goals of the Nairobi Forward-looking Strategies for the Advancement of Women by the end of this century;

23. Ensure the full enjoyment by women and the girl child of all human rights and fundamental freedoms and take effective action against violations of these rights and freedoms;

24. Take all necessary measures to eliminate all forms of discrimination against women and the girl child and remove all obstacles to gender equality and the advancement and empowerment of women;

25. Encourage men to participate fully in all actions towards equality;

26. Promote women's economic independence, including employment, and eradicate the persistent and increasing burden of poverty on women by addressing the structural causes of poverty through changes in economic structures, ensuring equal access for all women, including those in rural areas, as vital development agents, to productive resources, opportunities and public services;

27. Promote people-centred sustainable development, including sustained economic growth, through the provision of basic education, life-long education, literacy and training, and primary health care for girls and women;

28. Take positive steps to ensure peace for the advancement of women and, recognizing the leading role that women have played in the peace movement, work actively towards general and complete disarmament under strict and effective international control. . . .

29. Prevent and eliminate all forms of violence against women and girls;

30. Ensure equal access to and equal treatment of women and men in education and health care and enhance women's sexual and reproductive health as well as education;

31. Promote and protect all human rights of women and girls;

32. Intensify efforts to ensure equal enjoyment of all human rights and fundamental freedoms for all women and girls who face multiple barriers to their empowerment and advancement because of such factors as their race, age, language, ethnicity, culture, religion, or disability, or because they are indigenous people;

33. Ensure respect for international law, including humanitarian law, in order to protect women and girls in particular;

34. Develop the fullest potential of girls and women of all ages, ensure their full and equal participation in building a better world for all and enhance their role in the development process.

We are determined to:

35. Ensure women's equal access to economic resources, including land, credit, science and technology, vocational training, information, communication and markets, as a means to further the advancement and empowerment of women and girls, including through the enhancement of their capacities to enjoy the benefits of equal access to these resources . . . by means of international cooperation;

36. Ensure the success of the Platform for Action, which will require a strong commitment on the part of Governments, international organizations and institutions at all levels. . . . Equitable social development that recognizes empowering the poor, particularly women living in poverty, to utilize environmental resources sustainably is a necessary foundation for sustainable development. We also recognize that broad-based and sustained economic growth in the context of sustainable development is necessary to sustain social development and social justice. . . .

37. Ensure also the success of the Platform for Action in countries with economies in transition, which will require continued international cooperation and assistance;

38. We hereby adopt and commit ourselves as Governments to implement the following Platform for Action, ensuring that a gender perspective is reflected in all our policies and programmes. We urge the United Nations system, regional and international financial institutions, other relevant regional and international institutions and all women and men, as well as non-governmental organizations, with full respect for their autonomy, and all sectors of civil society, in cooperation with Governments, to fully commit themselves and contribute to the implementation of this Platform for Action.

1. Considering its human rights record at the time, how could the Chinese government justify its support for this declaration?
2. How do these articles reflect feminist goals?
3. What opposition could arise in response to this declaration?

Gustavo Gutiérrez

Gustavo Gutiérrez (1928–) was one of the leaders of the critical self-examination that was undertaken by many Christian theologians after World War II. Without losing touch with their fundamental beliefs, many Christians attempted to cope with war, racism, and the Holocaust, to embrace some of the ideas of modern philosophy in a theological context, and to reassert the importance of the religion's mission to aid the poor and suffering. Gutiérrez was a leader of liberation theology, generated by people in the developing world. His major work is *The Power of the Poor in History* (1979).

A Gutiérrez reflects on the relationship between God and the poor, and about justice.

It is not enough, however, to say that God reveals himself in history, and that therefore the faith of Israel fleshes out a historical framework. One must keep in mind that the God of the Bible is a God who not only governs history, but who orientates it in the direction of establishment of justice and right. He is more than a provident God. He is a God who takes sides with the poor and liberates them from slavery and oppression. . . .

This is the meaning of Yahweh's interventions in history. The purpose of his activity is not to demonstrate his power, but to liberate, and make justice reign:

Father of orphans, defender of widows,
such is God in his holy dwelling;
God gives the lonely a permanent home,
makes prisoners happy by setting them free,
but rebels must live in an arid land [Ps. 68:5–6].

This is Yahweh. His might is at the service of justice. His power is expressed in the defense of the rights of the poor (see Ps. 146:7–9). The real theophany, or revelation of God, is in the liberation of the person who is poor. . . .

Knowledge of God is love of God. In the language of the Bible, "to know" is not something purely intellectual. To know means to love. Sin is the absence of the knowledge of Yahweh, and it is on this that the people will be judged: "Sons of Israel, listen to the word of Yahweh, for Yahweh indicts the inhabitants of the country" (Hos. 4:1).

To know God as liberator *is* to liberate, *is* to do justice. For the Bible, the root of behavior that can be called "just" is in the historical fact that constitutes a resumé of its faith: God delivered us from Egypt:. . . .

To deal with a poor man or woman as Yahweh dealt with his people — this is what it is to be just: "He who looks down on his neighbor sins, blessed is he who takes pity on the poor" (Prov. 14:21; cf. Exod. 22:20-23). . . .

Our relationship with God is expressed in our relationship with the poor. . . .

Thus the reciprocal relationship between God and the poor person is the very heart of biblical faith.

B Like others, Gutiérrez insists that history be revisited from the perspective of the poor.

The locus of our encounter with the Father of Jesus Christ is the concrete history of men and women. And in Jesus Christ we proclaim to all men and women that Father's love. We have called this history one of conflict.

Source: Gustavo Gutiérrez, *The Power of the Poor in History.* Maryknoll, New York: Orbis Books, 1983, pp. 7, 8, 20–22.

But there is more to it than that. We have also to insist that history — where God reveals himself, and where we proclaim him — must be reread from the viewpoint of the poor, from a point of departure among "the condemned of the earth."

The history of humanity, as someone has said, has been "written with a white hand." History has been written from the viewpoint of the dominating sectors. We have a clear example of this in the history of Latin America and Peru. The perspective of history's vanquished is something else again. But history's winners have sought to wipe out their victims' memory of the struggles, so as to be able to snatch from them one of their sources of energy and will in history: a source of rebellion.

As it has been lived in history, Christianity has largely been, and still is, closely linked with one culture (Western), one ethnic strain (white), and one class (the dominant). Its history, too, has been written from a white, occidental, bourgeois bias.

We must recover the memory of the "scourged Christs of America," as Bartolomé de las Casas called the Indians of our continent. This memory never really died. It lives on in cultural and religious expressions, it lives on in resistance to ecclesiastical apparatus. It is a memory of the Christ who is present in every starving, thirsting, imprisoned, or humiliated human being, in the despised minorities, in the exploited classes (see Matt. 25:31–45). It is the memory of a Christ who not only "freed us, he meant us to remain free" (Gal. 5:1).

C Gutiérrez calls for action, for the poor to make their own history.

But *rereading* history means *remaking* history. It means repairing it from the bottom up. And so it will be a subversive history. History must be turned upside-down from the bottom, not from the top. What is criminal is not to be *sub*versive, struggling against the capitalist system, but to continue being "*super*versive" — bolstering and supporting the prevailing domination. It is in this subversive history that we can have a new faith experience, a new spirituality — a new proclamation of the gospel.

The gospel read from the viewpoint of the poor, the exploited classes, and their militant struggles for liberation, convokes a church of the people. It calls for a church to be gathered from among the poor, the marginalized. It calls for the kind of church that is indicated in Jesus' predilection for those whom the great ones of this world despise and humiliate (see Matt. 22:1–10; Luke 14:16–24). In a word, it calls together a church that will be marked by the faithful response of the poor to the call of Jesus Christ. It will spring from the people, this church. And the people will snatch the gospel out of the hands of their dominators, never more to permit it to be utilized for the justification of a situation contrary to the will of the God who liberates. . . .

This reincorporation of God will come about only when the poor of the earth effectuate a "social appropriation of the gospel" — when they dispossess those who consider it their private property. The gospel tells us that the sign of the arrival of the kingdom of God is that the poor have the gospel proclaimed to them. The poor are those who believe and hope in Christ. That is to say the poor are the Christians. Strictly speaking, the Christians are, or should be, the poor who receive the gospel — those in solidarity with the interests, aspirations, and combats of the oppressed and repressed of the world today.

Evangelization, the proclamation of the gospel, will be genuinely liberating when the poor themselves become its messengers. That is when we shall see the preaching of the gospel become a stumbling block and a scandal. For then we shall have a gospel that is no longer "presentable" in society. It will not sound nice and it will not smell good. The Lord who scarcely looks like a human at all (cf. the songs of the Servant of Yahweh in Isaiah) will speak to us then, and only at the sound of his voice will we recognize him as our liberator. That voice will convoke the *ek-klesia*, the assembly of those "called apart," in a new and different way.

Long has the church been built *from within*, in function of Christendom and its extension and preservation in the world — "ecclesiocentrism." A more recent perspective has led some to think of the church *from without*, from the world, from a world that does not believe, a world that often is hostile. . . .

Today we understand even better. We are called to build the church *from below*, from the poor up, from the exploited classes, the marginalized ethnic groups, the despised cultures. This is what we call the project of a popular church, a church that, under the influence of the Spirit, arises from within the masses.

1. How does God's exclusive association with the poor, as described by Gutiérrez, limit the Christian message of salvation and love?

2. How can the message of God be truly relevant to the marginalized members of society?

3. Why would Pope John Paul II reject liberation theology?

Zafer Şenocak

Zafer Şenocak was born in Turkey in 1961. When he was eight, his parents moved to Germany, where he has lived ever since. A well-known intellectual, Şenocak's articles have been published in Germany's leading newspapers. An English-language edition of some of his articles, *Atlas of a Tropical Germany*, was published in 2000.

A Şenocak identifies a fundamental change in European thinking after the end of the Cold War.

After the end of the Cold War and the disappearance of the common enemy, the perspective that determined perceptions also changed. Never has Rudyard Kipling's pronouncement that "East is East, and West is West, and never the two shall meet" been more accurate than now. Instead of engaging in ideological dispute with the Other, he is simply disregarded. Regard is reserved for one's own. Who are we? This question is given precedence over "Who am I?". . . . The confusion and disorientation that the individual observes in modern societies give rise to calls for principles of order that are at once new and old: nation, religion, and gender.

An idea is making the rounds: identity. It is an idea born of lack. Because what do we see when we look at ourselves? It is no longer ourselves that we see. Our self-image turns out to be a fiction. The white man's empire no longer exists anywhere. The metropoles of Western civilization, like London and Paris, which for centuries provided the whites with an illusion of homogeneity (we are by ourselves) and superiority (we are different and better), and to which the others looked with a melancholy gaze, are fallen bastions. The idea of a global civilization, dominated by the West, is not working out as planned. Westernization did not mean the simple disappearance of the other cultures. . . .

As a result of the movements of migration, the non-Western today extends as far as London, Paris, or Berlin. It is just as little authentic and unspoiled as the Western. Nevertheless, the longing for authenticity is alive in it too. Origins are often nostalgically distorted. Thus ghettos come into being, in which the marginal continues to exist, and center and periphery confront one another unreconciled. They demonize the Other in themselves and themselves in the Other. . . . This world is threatening to anyone who wants to draw a line between himself and the Other. Because everywhere he expects to encounter the different, the Other, he also finds his own world. Wherever his gaze is directed at his own, it also discovers the Other. The gaze at one's own is disturbed. What consequences does that have for a time in which perception is, in the first instance, determined by a perspective on one's own? Resentment, bewilderment, disorientation, aggression? Is there a fortress into which one can withdraw, where the Other, even if not far away, is at least not noticeable?

B Şenocak reflects on the idea of Western civilization.

Western civilization has undoubtedly created values that it puts into practice more efficiently than other civilizations. Democracy, human rights, freedom of opinion, freedom of worship, freedom of movement, and the right to own property are among them. Yet these values have to be defended not only against external enemies, the Others, but also internally against oneself. The entire Second World War was such an internal defense. It is a tragic mistake to believe that the victory over fascism in 1945 meant its disappearance from the intellectual map of European civilization. . . .

Source: Zafer Şenocak, *Atlas of a Tropical Germany.* Lincoln: University of Nebraska Press, 2000, pp. 84–88, 91–92, 98.

In fact, since the 1980s, at least, Europe has been arming itself for a civilizing battle against strangers. . . . Next to Bolshevism, a second enemy had been sighted. For the third time in history, after the Arab and Turkish military invasions, Islam was again [seen as] threatening Europe's borders. Now it was Arabs and Turks once more, not with armies but with hosts of guest workers. What at first appeared to be a harmless economic phenomenon soon developed into a momentous social phenomenon. The so-called guest workers violated the rules of hospitality, settled down, improved their economic status and became immigrants. . . .

It appears to me that the real clash of civilizations is being prepared in Europe. . . . All the values that seem to be threatened by a confusing pluralist and multicultural society play an important part in this protest: national, religious, and gendered identity.

C Şenocak then discusses the situation of Turks in Germany.

Recently it has become fashionable to organize meetings between Germans and Turks. Germans and Turks live together in Germany. Now they are also supposed to form an intercultural study group. The very fact that such meetings between representatives of two population groups, who have been living together in the same country for more than thirty years, have to be organized . . . is somewhat absurd. If a Turk meets a German on the street, they are at liberty to talk about the weather. But what possibilities are open to interlocutors sitting around a table, in a conversation between Germans and Turks, if they represent "the German" and "the Turk"? . . .

. . . Where does one stand as a German Turk within a German-Turkish dialogue? In the middle, perhaps? Or maybe even off to the side? If one presumes that identities exist in fixed, unbroken ways, then from the vantage point of a German Turk, the German-Turkish encounter becomes a nightmarish phantasm. The question — who and what is a German or a Turk — stands stubbornly and unasked in the room. To make things easier, one leaves it untouched. But then, who is talking, and with whom? . . .

As long as political, sociological, psychological, and biological components are discussed in the debate on migration, but the culture of the Other, in all its diversity, remains unknown, the migrant can appear only as uprooted. . . . The situation in the countries that are the goal of emigration makes clear, however, that it is not uprooting that is taking place but a transformation of cultural identities. This transformation cannot be grasped without knowledge of the cultural backgrounds of those affected. It is obvious that in countries like Germany, where the cultural background of the immigrants is largely unknown, crude ideas, traditional fears, and projections are spreading that cannot be outweighed by a purely political debate, by expressions of concern and solidarity. It is then only a question of time before the latent violence takes on warlike forms.

The Turks in Germany, of my and future generations, can contribute something to ensuring that . . . a war in and about civilization will not take place. . . . Some may consider disunity to be a mark of instability. But for someone at home in the metropoles of Europe, which are all torn cities, being torn is a condition that, for the sake of all our futures, has to be accommodated and lived.

Germany long ago became part of us German Turks. Now a question is being posed that we cannot answer alone. Are we also a part of Germany?

1. Why does Şenocak feel Kipling's quotation is appropriate in describing post-Cold War Europe?

2. How does Islam come to be seen in Europe as a threat?

3. Why might violence occur in a united Germany?

Amartya Sen

Amartya Sen (1933–) was born in India. He is an economist who has held positions at Harvard University and Cambridge University. In 1998, Sen was awarded the Nobel Prize in Economics for his contributions to welfare economics. His best-known works are *On Economic Inequality* (1973) and *Poverty And Famines* (1981).

A Sen begins his article, "Democracy as a Universal Value," with a discussion of the importance of democracy and its premises.

[A]mong the great variety of developments that have occurred in the twentieth century, I did not, ultimately, have any difficulty in choosing one as the preeminent development of the period: the rise of democracy. This is not to deny that other occurrences have also been important, but I would argue that in the distant future, when people look back at what happened in this century, they will find it difficult not to accord primacy to the emergence of democracy as the preeminently acceptable form of governance. . . .

Throughout the nineteenth century, theorists of democracy found it quite natural to discuss whether one country or another was "fit for democracy." This thinking changed only in the twentieth century, with the recognition that the question itself was wrong: A country does not have to be deemed fit *for* democracy; rather, it has to become fit *through* democracy. This is indeed a momentous change, extending the potential reach of democracy to cover billions of people, with their varying histories and cultures and disparate levels of affluence. . . .

What exactly is democracy? We must not identify democracy with majority rule. Democracy has complex demands, which certainly include

Source: Amartya Sen, "Democracy as a Universal Value." http://muse.jhu.edu/demo/jod/10.3sen.html (June 3, 2003)

voting and respect for election results, but it also requires the protection of liberties and freedoms, respect for legal entitlements, and the guaranteeing of free discussion and uncensored distribution of news and fair comment. Even elections can be deeply defective if they occur without the different sides getting an adequate opportunity to present their respective cases, or without the electorate enjoying the freedom to obtain news and to consider the views of the competing protagonists. Democracy is a demanding system, and not just a mechanical condition (like majority rule) taken in isolation.

Viewed in this light, the merits of democracy and its claim as a universal value can be related to certain distinct virtues that go with its unfettered practice. Indeed, we can distinguish three different ways in which democracy enriches the lives of the citizens. First, political freedom is a part of human freedom in general, and exercising civil and political rights is a crucial part of good lives of individuals as social beings. Political and social participation has *intrinsic value* for human life and well-being. To be prevented from participation in the political life of the community is a major deprivation.

Second . . . democracy has an important *instrumental value* in enhancing the hearing that people get in expressing and supporting their claims to political attention (including claims of economic needs). Third — and this is a point to be explored further — the practice of democracy gives citizens an opportunity to learn from one another, and helps society to form its values and priorities. Even the idea of "needs," including the understanding of "economic needs," requires public discussion and exchange of information, views, and analyses. In this sense, democracy has *constructive* importance, in addition to its intrinsic value for the lives of the citizens and its instrumental importance in political decisions. The claims of democracy as a universal value have to take note of this diversity of considerations . . . .

If the above analysis is correct, then democracy's claim to be valuable does not rest on just one particular merit. There is a plurality of virtues here, including, first, the *intrinsic* importance of political participation and freedom in human life; second, the *instrumental* importance of political incentives in keeping governments responsible and accountable; and third, the *constructive* role of democracy in the formation of values and in the understanding of needs, rights, and duties. In the light of this diagnosis, we may now address the motivating question of this essay, namely the case for seeing democracy as a universal value.

B Sen then examines and challenges the claims that something called "Asian values" exists and that democracy is not a universal value.

There is also another argument in defense of an allegedly fundamental regional contrast, one related not to economic circumstances but to cultural differences. Perhaps the most famous of these claims relates to what have been called "Asian values." It has been claimed that Asians traditionally value discipline, not political freedom, and thus the attitude to democracy must inevitably be much more skeptical in these countries. . . .

It is very hard to find any real basis for this intellectual claim in the history of Asian cultures, especially if we look at the classical traditions of India, the Middle East, Iran, and other parts of Asia. For example, one of the earliest and most emphatic statements advocating the tolerance of pluralism and the duty of the state to protect minorities can be found in the inscriptions of the Indian emperor Ashoka in the third century B.C.

Asia is, of course, a very large area, containing 60 percent of the world's population, and generalizations about such a vast set of peoples is not easy. Sometimes the advocates of "Asian values" have tended to look primarily at East Asia as the region of particular applicability. The general thesis of a contrast between the West and Asia often concentrates on the lands to the east of Thailand, even though there is also a more ambitious claim that the rest of Asia is rather "similar." . . .

Even East Asia itself, however, is remarkably diverse, with many variations to be found not only among Japan, China, Korea, and other countries of the region, but also *within* each country. Confucius is the standard author quoted in interpreting Asian values, but he is not the only intellectual influence in these countries (in Japan, China, and Korea for example, there are very old and very widespread Buddhist traditions, powerful for over a millennium and a half, and there are also other influences, including a considerable Christian presence). There is no homogeneous worship of order over freedom in any of these cultures . . . .

The monolithic interpretation of Asian values as hostile to democracy and political rights does not bear critical scrutiny . . . .

It is not hard, of course, to find authoritarian writings within the Asian traditions. But neither is it hard to find them in Western classics: One has only to reflect on the writings of Plato or Aquinas to see that devotion to discipline is not a special Asian taste. To dismiss the plausibility of democracy as a universal value because of the presence of some Asian writings on discipline and order would be similar to rejecting the plausibility of democracy as a natural form of government in Europe or America today on the basis of the writings of Plato or Aquinas (not to mention the substantial medieval literature in support of the Inquisitions).

Due to the experience of contemporary political battles, especially in the Middle East, Islam is often portrayed as fundamentally intolerant of and hostile to individual freedom. But the presence of diversity and variety *within* a tradition applies very much to Islam as well. In India, Akbar and most of the other Moghul emperors (with the notable exception of Aurangzeb) provide good examples of both the theory and practice of political and religious tolerance. The Turkish emperors were often more tolerant than their European contemporaries. Abundant examples can also be found among rulers in Cairo and Baghdad. Indeed, in the twelfth century, the great Jewish scholar Maimonides had to run away from an intolerant

Europe (where he was born), and from its persecution of Jews, to the security of a tolerant and urbane Cairo and the patronage of Sultan Saladin.

Diversity is a feature of most cultures in the world. Western civilization is no exception. The practice of democracy that has won out in the *modern* West is largely a result of a consensus that has emerged since the Enlightenment and the Industrial Revolution, and particularly in the last century or so. To read in this a historical commitment of the West — over the millennia — to democracy, and then to contrast it with non-Western traditions (treating each as monolithic) would be a great mistake . . . .

For every attempt by an Asian government spokesman to contrast alleged "Asian values" with alleged Western ones, there is, it seems, an attempt by a Western intellectual to make a similar contrast from the other side. But even though every Asian pull may be matched by a Western push, the two together do not really manage to dent democracy's claim to be a universal value.

I have tried to cover a number of issues related to the claim that democracy is a universal value. The value of democracy includes its *intrinsic importance* in human life, its *instrumental role* in generating political incentives, and its *constructive function* in the formation of values (and in understanding the force and feasibility of claims of needs, rights, and duties). These merits are not regional in character. Nor is the advocacy of discipline or order. Heterogeneity of values seems to characterize most, perhaps all, major cultures. The cultural argument does not foreclose, nor indeed deeply constrain, the choices we can make today.

Those choices have to be made here and now, taking note of the functional roles of democracy, on which the case for democracy in the contemporary world depends. I have argued that this case is indeed strong and not regionally contingent. The force of the claim that democracy is a universal value lies, ultimately, in that strength. That is where the debate belongs. It cannot be disposed of by imagined cultural taboos or assumed civilizational predispositions imposed by our various pasts.

1. What benefits does Sen ascribe to democracy?

2. What evidence does Sen present to dispel the impression of Asia as a monolithic continent with one set of values and beliefs?

3. Are democratic values innate to humanity or do they require modifications to human attitudes and behaviour?

Credits

Every reasonable effort has been made to trace ownership of copyrighted material. Information that would enable the publisher to correct any reference or credit in future editions would be appreciated.

Photo Credits

1 Afro-Portuguese ivory saltcellar, 11-1.48 (MM033204). Copyright © The British Museum; **49** *The Virgin Mary* signed by Manohar, ca 1590–1595. Ink on paper (7.5 x 5.3 cm, miniature only), Collection Frits Lugt, 1974-T.67, Institut Neerlandais, Paris; **91** *Hungry Women of Paris Marching to Versailles, October 1789*. Picture Collection, The Branch Libraries, the New York Public Library, Astor, Lenox and Tilden Foundations; **133** *Don't Meddle With It* by Honoré Daumier. Iris and B. Gerald Cantor Center for Visual Arts, Stanford University/Museum of Fine Arts, Boston; **170** *Scramble for Newspapers at a Railway Station in England, 1875*. Picture Collection, The Branch Libraries, the New York Public Library, Astor, Lenox and Tilden Foundations; **218** AP/Wide World Photos (APA4839646); **262** *Untitled (Helena Lam Looking in a Mirror Seeing a Horse)* (ca. 1943), ink on paper 19 x 18.4 cm. Copyright © Estate of Wifredo Lam/SODRAC (Montreal) 2003/Collection of the Lowe Art Museum, University of Miami. Bequest of Lydia Cabrera, 91.0295.10.

Text Credits

x "Questions from a Worker Who Reads" by Bertolt Brecht (trans. by Michael Hamburger) from *Poems 1913–1956* by Bertolt Brecht (trans. by John Willett and Ralph Manheim). By permission of Methuen Publishing Limited; **2–4** "Women in the Renaissance" from *The Book of the City of Ladies* by Christine de Pisan, translated by Earl Jeffrey Richards. Copyright © 1982, 1998 by Persea Books, Inc. Reprinted by permission of Persea Books, Inc., (New York); **5–8** from *Concerning the Study of Literature* by Leonardo Bruni in *Main Currents of Western Thought*, 4th edition, Franklin Le Van Baumer, ed. Reprinted with the permission of Cambridge University Press; **10–15** from *The Prince: A Norton Critical Edition*, 2nd edition by Niccolò Machiavelli, translated by Robert M. Adams. Copyright © 1992, 1977 by W. W. Norton & Company, Inc. Used by permission of W. W. Norton & Company, Inc.; **15–19** from *Utopia: A Norton Critical Edition*, 2nd edition by Thomas More, translated by Robert M. Adams. Copyright © 1992, 1975 by W. W. Norton & Company, Inc. Used by permission of W. W. Norton & Company, Inc.; **32–33** from *The Age of the Reformation* by Roland H. Bainton (Princeton, N. J.: D. Van Nostrand Company, 1956). Reprinted with permission of the Estate of Roland H. Bainton; **33–36** Reprinted from *Luther's Works*, Vol. 46 edited by Robert C. Schultz. Copyright © 1967 Fortress Press. Used by permission of Augsburg Fortress; **37–38** from *Discoveries and Opinions of Galileo* by Galileo Galilei, translated by Stillman Drake. Copyright © 1957 by Stillman Drake. Used by permission of Doubleday, a division of Random House, Inc.; **38–39** from *Sir Issac Newton's Mathematical Principles of Natural Philosophy and His System of the World, Book III: The System of the World*. Tr. Andrew Motte, rev. by Floriann Cajori. Copyright © 1934, 1962 The Regents of the University of California. Reprinted with permission of the University of California Press; **39–43** from *Discourse On Method and the Meditations* by René Descartes. Tr. F. E. Sutcliffe (Harmondsworth: Penguin Classics, 1968). Copyright © 1968 F. E. Sutcliffe. Reproduced by permission of Penguin Books Ltd.; **46–48** from *Locke's Two Treatises of Government*, 2nd edition. Ed. Peter Laslett. Copyright © 1960 Cambridge University Press; **54–57** from *The Broken Spears* by Miguel Leon-Portilla. Copyright © 1962, 1990 by Miguel Leon-Portilla. Expanded and Updated Edition © 1992 by Miguel Leon-Portilla. Reprinted with permission of Beacon Press, Boston; **63–66** from *China in the Sixteenth Century* by Matthew Ricci, translated by Louis J. Gallagher S. J. Copyright © 1942, 1953, and renewed 1970 by Louis Gallagher, S. J. Used by permission of Random House, Inc.: **68–70** from "A Micmac Responds to the French ca. 1677" from *New Relations of Gaspesia, with the Customs and Religion of the Gaspesian Indians* by Chrestien LeClerq, translated by William F. Ganong (Toronto: Champlain Society, 1910). Reprinted with permission; **76–79** from *Turkish Embassy Letters* by Lady Mary Wortley Montagu, edited by Malcolm Jack (London: William Pickering,1993); **79–81** Reprinted with permission from the Harriet Tubman Resource Centre on the African Diaspora, Toronto, York University; **92–95** Reprinted and edited with the permission of Pocket Books, a Division of Simon & Schuster Adult Publishing Group, from *The Social Contact and Discourse on the*

Index of Authors